American Society for Public Administration

Series in Public Administration and Public Policy

STRATEGIC COLLABORATION IN PUBLIC AND NONPROFIT ADMINISTRATION

A Practice-Based Approach to Solving Shared Problems

DOROTHY NORRIS-TIRRELL
JOY A. CLAY

CRC Press
Taylor & Francis Group
Boca Raton London New York

CRC Press is an imprint of the
Taylor & Francis Group, an **Informa** business

CRC Press
Taylor & Francis Group
6000 Broken Sound Parkway NW, Suite 300
Boca Raton, FL 33487-2742

© 2010 by Taylor and Francis Group, LLC
CRC Press is an imprint of Taylor & Francis Group, an Informa business

No claim to original U.S. Government works

Printed in the United States of America on acid-free paper
10 9 8 7 6 5 4 3 2 1

International Standard Book Number: 978-1-4200-8875-5 (Hardback)

Library of Congress Cataloging-in-Publication Data

Norris-Tirrell, Dorothy.
   Strategic collaboration in public and nonprofit administration : a practice-based approach to solving shared problems / Dorothy Norris-Tirrell, Joy A. Clay.
      p. cm. -- (American Society for Public Administration book series on public
      administration & public policy)
   Includes bibliographical references and index.
   ISBN 978-1-4200-8875-5 (hardcover : alk. paper)
   1. Local government--United States. 2. Strategic planning--United States. 3. Problem solving--United States. 4. Public-private sector cooperation--United States. 5. Nonprofit organizations--United States--Management. I. Clay, Joy A. II. Title. III. Series.

JS331.N67 2010
361.6068--dc22
                                       2009053435

Visit the Taylor & Francis Web site at
http://www.taylorandfrancis.com

and the CRC Press Web site at
http://www.crcpress.com

Contents

List of Tables

List of Figures

Preface

Market disruptions, terrorism, climate change, and health pandemics lead the growing list of challenges faced by today's leaders. These issues, along with countless others that do not make the daily news, demand the attention of civic leaders, elected officials, and public and nonprofit administrators at local, state, national and international levels, and require novel thinking and collaborative action to find workable solutions.

Public and nonprofit administrators all too often stumble into collaboration without a strategic orientation. For example, a governor or mayor forms an inter-agency collaboration on infant mortality, sustainability, workforce development, or the "current topic of the day" to make innovative recommendations; however, conveners fail to proactively establish a strategic agenda around the collaboration. Thus, the group remains in their comfortable discipline or agency silos and produces limited results. Another example occurs when a major foundation issues a Request for Proposals (RFP) requiring community collaboration. The RFP process brings an eclectic assortment of agencies and groups to the table, all vying for their part of the funding, but without a strategic interest in working together. Unquestionably, collaboration is a useful tool, but one that we argue needs to be used with more intentionality, as public and nonprofit administrators wrestle with skillfully engaging in and facilitating collaborative structures, processes, and outcomes. Although the research literature on collaboration has expanded greatly in the last two decades, a gap remains in the linkage of collaboration theory to effective practice. This book offers essential advice to practitioners to foster shared understanding, creative answers, and transformational results through strategic collaborative action. It provides real-world examples and presents a framework for engaging in collaboration in a way that stretches our current thinking and advances public service practice.

Purpose of the Book

This book is for practicing public and nonprofit administrators who face the everyday challenges of collaboration, students and academics in public administration and policy programs, funders, and policymakers who are seeking to understand the promises and realities of strategic collaborative practice. It provides guidance on how to collaborate more effectively, with less frustration, and with better results. Presented in practitioner-oriented style, the tools, practice tips, and principles strengthen public service practice and draw from both the latest theoretical research and real-world experience.

The need for this book emerged from our many experiences working with local government and community organizations in academic roles and during prior years of public service management (Joy as a Veterans Administration administrator and Dorothy as a nonprofit administrator). Through this experience, we recognized an ever-growing list of obstacles to effective collaboration including

- Too much emphasis on the status quo and protecting turf by participants
- Processes that bring everyone to the table but then reinforce the silos that further solidify their resistance to new ideas
- Recruiting the same participants for every collaborative effort when professionals and volunteers can only actively and effectively engage in a limited number
- Processes that start over again collecting the same data, setting the same goals, and taking us back where we started, while expending countless hours "collaborating"
- Decision making driven by the quest for funding, displacing the collaboration's focus and agreed upon expectations
- Confused sense of authority, delegation, and consensus that all too often results in questions of ownership, frustration, and paralysis

We set out to articulate an approach – Strategic Collaboration – that would take advantage of windows of opportunity for real problem solving; bring multi-disciplinary participants to the table to engage more systematically in planning, analysis, decision making, and implementation; break down barriers to change; and ultimately, lay the foundation for new thinking and acting. To do this, we incorporated what we know from organization and collaboration management research and our experience to create a fresh approach to collaboration practice that highlights:

- Collaboration Life Cycle Model
- Metric for determining why and when to collaborate (Collaboration Readiness)
- Set of principles that distinguish Strategic Collaboration Practice
- Overall Framework of Strategic Collaboration

With an applied emphasis, the book uses scenarios, real-world cases, tables, figures, tools, and a checklist to highlight key points. The appendix includes supplemental resources (such as collaboration operating guidelines, a meeting checklist, and a summary collaboration literature review to help public and nonprofit managers successfully convene, administer, and lead collaborations.

Learning from Cases

The case studies in Chapters 5 through 13 convey real-world lessons for effective and strategic practice of collaboration, including how to think through the decision to collaborate, structuring an effective collaboration, attending to collaborative process, and accountability through defined outcomes. To assure the focus on collaborative practice, each case study emphasizes the perspectives of both researchers and practitioners.

Chapter 5: Attending to the Forgotten: The Elderly, Collaborative Practice, Evacuation

The impact of Hurricane Katrina on the Gulf Coast region clearly demonstrated serious flaws in emergency management processes. This case describes how key agencies and stakeholders were brought together to identify needed resources for responsibly evacuating seniors and illustrates the importance of having an issue "champion."

Chapter 6: Running Out of Classrooms! Solving School Overcrowding through Collaborative School Planning

As long as real estate development and school planning are separate processes, the matching of students with school capacity remains problematic. This case study of Palm Beach County, Florida, describes how a community overcame this challenge through sustained catalytic leadership, third party brokerage, and building trust.

Chapter 7: Moving beyond Hierarchies: Creating Effective Collaboration Networks for West Nile Virus Biosurveillance

The potential swift spread of contagions due to an increasingly interconnected world requires coordination across jurisdictional as well as professional lines. This case describes the State of Oregon's successful effort to foster collaboration and information sharing in a new way to assure effective detection, control, and prevention.

Chapter 8: Information Stewardship and Collaboration: Advancing Evidence-Based Public Policy Decision-Making

Integrating and sharing information across multiple government and community agencies present a significant public administration challenge. This case study describes how a university–community partnership in Memphis, Tennessee, tried to overcome data sharing barriers to broaden accessibility and further technological innovation.

Chapter 9: Choices and Challenges: Sustaining a Rural Health Network when Funding Vanishes

Nonprofit organizations working in rural communities face unique challenges in building and sustaining social service networks. This case about a service network in Kentucky describes these challenges and how they were exacerbated when the funding from the federal grant ended unexpectedly.

Chapter 10: Collaboration, Citizen Participation, and Environmental Protection in the Marine Oil Trade of Alaska

In the aftermath of the *Exxon Valdez* disaster, a citizens' advisory council was created to promote collaboration between the oil industry and the local Alaskan community affected by marine oil trade. This case examines the role of citizen participation in collaborative policy efforts and strategies for policy analysis and multilateral collaborations.

Chapter 11: Paving the Way for Public Transportation: Transportation in Texas through Public Collaboration

To address traffic congestion and air pollution, local government officials, community stakeholders, and citizens need to work together to achieve more environmentally friendly public transportation services. This case describes how a nonprofit's public participation approach achieved mixed results in Denton County, Texas.

Chapter 12: Cape Fear Healthy Carolinians: Taking Risks, Crossing Boundaries

A history of failed attempts to build a sustainable collaboration tests collaboration practice. This case describes a public health network developed in Brunswick and New Hanover Counties, North Carolina, and their strategies for bringing the appropriate mix of stakeholders to the table as well as keeping them committed and focused.

Chapter 13: Building a Community-Higher Education Collaboration to Meet the Needs of the Local Nonprofit Sector

Balancing community expectations and academic standards is a tension that resonates in university–community collaborations. This case describes the various roles played by a collaboration entrepreneur, the primacy of a shared understanding of goals, operations and measurement, and the importance of stakeholder management.

This book offers Strategic Collaboration as a valuable approach for public and nonprofit managers to enable and facilitate positive change. By bringing individuals and organizations out of their silos to think in new ways at the collaboration table, genuine changes in our communities, societies, and nations are possible. We hope that readers will gain insightful and usable information for making a difference in our world and for advancing public service practice.

Dorothy Norris-Tirrell
Joy A. Clay

Acknowledgments

This book is the fruit of our experience and research as public administration practitioners and scholars. We gratefully acknowledge the many organizations and groups that, over several decades, served as a laboratory for our learning about collaboration. We also appreciate the reactions from our master's of public administration (M.P.A.) students over the years as we were working through and developing our thoughts. Feedback from the blind reviewers of our book proposal helped clarify our ideas and provided useful recommendations for us to pursue.

We would like to particularly thank Dr. Evan Berman, editor-in-chief of the ASPA Book Series in Public Administration & Public Policy (Taylor & Francis), senior editor of *Public Performance & Management Review,* and J. William Fulbright Distinguished Scholar at the National Chengchi University. His encouragement, insights, feedback, and support were invaluable throughout the iterative editing process as we advanced and polished the manuscript.

Also, we would like to thank Susan Schmidt, our colleague and friend, for sharing her talents with the figures and tables in this book. Finally, we would be remiss if we did not thank our families for their encouragement, patience, and understanding.

The case chapters in this volume were originally presented at either the 2007 regional Southeastern Conference of Public Administration (SECOPA) or the 2008 national conference of the American Society of Public Administration (ASPA). Each case selected for inclusion in the book highlights both the challenge and potential of effective strategic collaboration practice. We thank our case chapter contributors for their time, effort, and support as well as their tolerance of our suggestions. The editing process with our case authors helped to bring strategic collaboration practice alive as we worked to refine the case narratives and analysis and attend to the interests and concerns of collaborative practitioners. We consider ourselves very fortunate to have worked with such committed researchers and professionals.

A follow-up workshop on collaboration, including many of the case authors, at the 2009 national ASPA conference generated lively and productive exchange among the panelists and with our audience. Clearly, public administration professionals and researchers are deeply interested in improving the practice of collaboration. Strategic collaboration is no panacea for today's problems. However, when adopted systematically and purposefully, the resulting public and nonprofit administration practice will be more effective and have positive consequences for our communities.

About the Authors

Dorothy Norris-Tirrell is the director and an associate professor in the Division of Public and Nonprofit Administration for the School of Urban Affairs and Public Policy at the University of Memphis. Her research and engaged scholarship focus are on governance, strategic planning, evaluation, and board development for nonprofit organizations, university–community partnerships, and cross-sector collaborative processes in a variety of policy settings including community resilience and immigration. Dr. Norris-Tirrell has extensive experience as a nonprofit agency manager, board member, consultant, and volunteer.

Joy A. Clay is a professor of public administration and associate dean for interdisciplinary studies in the College of Arts and Sciences at the University of Memphis. Her research and engaged scholarship focus on administrative theory, performance, evaluation and public health (especially maternal health), and collaborative dynamics. Dr. Clay worked for the Veterans Administration in Washington, D.C., as a management and program analyst for 13 years prior to becoming an academic. She also has extensive experience in the nonprofit sector as a board member and volunteer.

Contributors

Thomas J. Barth is a professor of public administration in the Department of Public and International Affairs at the University of North Carolina–Wilmington. He has 18 years of experience teaching, conducting research, and consulting in the areas of organizational development, human resource management, strategic planning, and public ethics. Prior to his academic career, Dr. Barth served for 10 years in the federal government as a program analyst in the Department of Health and Human Services and the U.S. Environmental Protection Agency.

G. Brian Burke is a senior program associate with the Center for Technology in Government (CTG). He manages projects at CTG involving academic, government, and private-sector partners including a National Science Foundation funded project to model the social and technical processes of intergovernmental information sharing. Prior to CTG, he worked for AT&T Government Solutions in the Office of the Secretary of Defense's Program Analysis and Evaluation Division and served as an officer in the U.S. Air Force.

George J. Busenberg is an associate professor at Soka University of America. His research focuses on environmental management and policy. Major topics in his research include collaboration, citizen participation, policy theory, and processes of policy change.

Esteban Dalehite holds a Ph.D. in Public Affairs from Indiana University Bloomington, and is director of Strategic and Project Management, Tax Administration Service, Mexico. His research interests include international taxation, state and local public finance, education finance, economic development incentives, and performance measurement.

Elizabeth J. Demski is the director of grant development in the Office of Research Services and Sponsored Programs at the University of North Carolina–Wilmington (UNCW). In her grant development role, she has extensive involvement in public outreach activities in the southeastern North Carolina Region, including positions as chair of the Violence Prevention Committee of the Cape Fear Healthy Carolinians and advisor to the Blue Ribbon Commission on Youth Violence. Prior to her work at UNCW, Demski served as a regional engagement specialist in the Division of Public Service for the University of Massachusetts–Amherst.

J. Ramon Gil-Garcia is an assistant professor in the Department of Public Administration and the director of the Data Center for Applied Research in Social Sciences at Centro de Investigación y Docencia Económicas (CIDE) in Mexico City. Currently, he is also a research fellow in the Center for Technology in Government at the University at Albany, State University of New York and faculty affiliate in the National Center for Digital Government at the University of Massachusetts–Amherst.

Pamela J. Jenkins is a professor of sociology and faculty member in the women's studies program at the University of New Orleans (UNO). She is a founding and associate member of UNO's Center for Hazard Assessment, Response, and Technology. Dr. Jenkins has published on first responders and faith-based communities' response and the experiences of the elderly during and after Hurricane Katrina.

John J. Kiefer is an associate professor of public administration and the director of the master's of public administration program at the University of New Orleans (UNO). He is also a faculty associate at the Center for Hazards Assessment, Response, and Technology, UNO's applied hazards social science research center. His current research interests include hazard policy, emergency management, program evaluation, and the development of outcome-focused collaborative networks to create disaster resilience.

Hyuckbin Kwon is a Ph.D. candidate in public administration at the University at Albany, State University of New York and a graduate assistant in the Center for Technology in Government. His research interests include freedom of information policy, interorganizational collaboration and information sharing, and electronic government.

Shirley Laska is a professor of sociology and the director of the Center for Hazards Assessment, Response, and Technology (CHART) at the University of New Orleans. Her research interests include environmental, risk, and community dynamics using a participatory approach for CHART collaborations with coastal Louisiana communities to support their assessing and responding to coastal storm risk and other natural hazards. She was named the 2008 recipient of the American Sociological Association's award for Public Understanding of Sociology.

Sarmistha R. Majumdar is an assistant professor in the master's of public administration (MPA) program in the Department of Political Science at Sam Houston State University in Huntsville, Texas. She specializes in analysis of public policies related to transportation, environment, and other social issues.

Cindy Martin is a research analyst in the Office of Institutional Research at the University of Memphis. Her project development, implementation, and evaluation experience focuses on the application of geographic information systems to the analysis of issues impacting community development, health, and safety. She worked for 15 years in the private sector as a computer systems analyst. Martin is currently completing her doctorate in educational research at the University of Memphis.

Colleen Moynihan earned her bachelor of science degree at Ohio University and a master of science degree in geography from the University of North Texas. She was a Peace Corps volunteer in Cameroon, Africa, and worked as a community organizer in Cleveland, Ohio. Moynihan currently works for the U.S. Environmental Protection Agency.

Theresa A. Pardo is the director of the Center for Technology in Government at the State University at Albany. She is also a faculty member in public administration and policy and informatics at the university. Ms. Pardo has written extensively on a range of topics related to information technology innovation in government including cross-boundary information sharing, trust and knowledge sharing, and preservation of government digital records. She was recently appointed a senior adviser to the Information Research Institution at the State Information Center in China.

Dana J. Patton is an assistant professor in the Department of Health Services Management in the College of Public Health at the University of Kentucky. Previously, Dr. Patton taught political science and public administration courses at Eastern Kentucky University. Her research interests include reproductive health policy, public health systems and services research, the politics of health policy, and implementation and evaluation of health policies.

Jason Pierce received his master's degree in public administration from the University of North Texas in Denton. He was an active participant in creating the Denton County Transportation Authority. Mr. Pierce is currently involved in other collaborative efforts, working to provide regional water and wastewater services to cities and utilities in Denton County.

Susan Tomlinson Schmidt is the campus director of the American Humanics Nonprofit Management Certificate Program in the Division of Public and Nonprofit Administration at the University of Memphis. Her outreach focus is on administrative systems development and documentation.

Kendra B. Stewart is an associate professor and the director of the master's of public administration program at the College of Charleston in Charleston, South Carolina. Her research interests include state government reorganization, nonprofit networks, homeland security, and women in politics. Prior to her current position, Dr. Stewart was a faculty member at Eastern Kentucky University and worked for the State of South Carolina in a variety of capacities.

Amy D. Sullivan is an epidemiologist for the Multnomah County Health Department. She works with the county's communicable disease prevention and control programs and is a member of the health department's emergency response incident management team. Previously, Dr. Sullivan served as a Centers for Disease Control and Prevention (CDC) Epidemic Intelligence Service officer and worked extensively overseas, primarily in Bangladesh and Malawi.

Christopher M. Wirth manages the Multnomah County Vector Control and Code Enforcement programs, which serve the Portland, Oregon, metro area with an integrated public health vector surveillance and control program, after successful careers in museum entomology, invertebrate zoological curation, and pest control. Additionally, Dr. Wirth works as part-time research assistant for the State of Oregon Department of Human Services public health veterinarian.

Chapter 1

The Promise of Strategic Collaboration

Dorothy Norris-Tirrell and Joy A. Clay

Contents

1.1 Introduction

Skillfully managing, leading, facilitating, and negotiating collaboration is difficult. Satisfying mixed, and often conflicting, demands for significant innovation and change makes it just that much more complicated and taxing. To be more successful, we must transform our way of thinking—our mind-set—about *how* we collaborate.[1] This book is for public and nonprofit managers and other community leaders who seek effective collaborative practice. Strategic collaboration is a proactive and concrete approach for policy makers, agency administrators, and providers to engage in collaboration creatively and successfully, across all kinds of boundaries, in a systematic, intentional, and inclusive manner.

Almost any problem today is too complex for individuals or agencies working alone only in their silos.[2] What in the past would have appeared as a straightforward administrative problem now more than not requires working with other programs, agencies, citizens, and multiple stakeholders across policy arenas. For example, consider a school system with truancy problems. In the past, the expectation would have been for the school system to develop and implement policies in its silo. Today, this same school system might find that the police or sheriff's departments, parent–teacher organizations, the district attorney's office, juvenile court judges, youth-focused nonprofit agencies, local foundations interested in education quality, and community advocates vocal about community issues would expect to be involved since changes in truancy policies are recognized to have a ripple effect across the community. Moreover, democratic norms and the political nature of consequential public problems demand the inclusion of and collaboration with concerned and affected stakeholders.[3] Funders, agency leaders, and community stakeholders expect to be involved in the analysis and policy design process and press for the authentic inclusion of citizens and advocates.[4] As a result, public and nonprofit managers find themselves in the middle, safeguarding professional expertise and responding to norms of inclusion while balancing expectations for thoughtful processes with public pressure for expeditious results.[5]

Strategic collaboration is an intentional, collective approach to address public problems or issues through building shared knowledge, designing innovative solutions, and forging consequential change. When used strategically, collaboration produces positive impacts, stakeholders committed to policy or program change, and strengthened capacity of individuals and organizations to effectively work together. Strategic collaboration offers the promise of addressing difficult public problems:

- Citizens, local government managers, elected officials, business leaders, community development corporations, neighborhood associations, design experts, and environmental advocacy groups can use authentic and inclusive economic development decision-making processes to plan and implement smart growth to assure a sustainable future that has far-reaching impacts across a city, region, or even the globe.

- Scientists, health providers, school leaders, and employers can work together nationally, locally, or internationally to reduce the spread of a dangerous virus, to protect lives, and to assure economic continuity.
- Cross-county collaboration among a broad range of criminal justice professionals, administrators, elected officials, and researchers can address growing public safety threats as gangs, opportunistic criminals, and drug cartels quickly respond when crime deterrence and detection are not coordinated regionally.
- A broad-based effort to prevent child abuse and domestic violence can engage government, nonprofit, and private organizations, the faith-based community, advocates, and professionals to address not just the problem but also the underlying causes of these problems.
- Collaboration across states and regions can address intergovernmental issues (e.g., water scarcity, air quality, traffic congestion, access to tertiary health care, economic development).
- Community leaders, medical providers, local foundations, community-based organizations, insurance companies, and researchers can collaborate together to address rising rates of infant mortality, diabetes, obesity, adolescent pregnancy, HIV/AIDS, and more.

All of these policy challenges demand a strategic approach to collaboration if they are to have positive outcomes. Working in silos or muddling through will likely fail. Government and nonprofit managers must work together with leaders and citizens more intentionally to collaboratively deliver results and transform public service practice.

1.2 Silo-Oriented Lens

Early in the history of public administration, creating hierarchically structured units to accomplish the tasks of government made sense. Agencies formed around a specific public problem or function allowed employees to specialize and grow needed expertise—including the technical, administrative, legal, and political competencies—germane to the task at hand. For example, faced with growing environmental issues, federal and state governments formed units specifically focused on environmental protection or regulatory programs. Conventional wisdom viewed modern silo-based, hierarchically organized structures as the optimal means of efficiency, effectiveness, and oversight.[6] Many of these agencies remain dynamic and are recognized centers of expertise in particular problem or issue areas.

Everyday agency responsibilities still require that public and nonprofit managers appropriately work within their agency boundaries. When problems or issues are not sufficiently weighty to warrant the time and effort required by collaboration and the agency has the resources or expertise to satisfactorily address the issue, silo-based approaches remain an effective and efficient approach. Working in silos does not mean that cooperation and coordination are absent. Systems and processes develop to assure both vertical and lateral coordination inside the agency but also with stakeholders outside the agency. Experts within public and nonprofit agency silos build their knowledge not only of program eligibility and requirements but also of the organizations that administer or advocate for relevant programs; likewise, stakeholders outside the agencies build their knowledge of constituent concerns, how relevant programs function, and how to influence decision making.[7] Clearly, silos play an essential role in structuring how units accomplish their everyday tasks and responsibilities, coordinate, and cooperate across organizational and sector boundaries.

1.3 New Governance—From Silos to Collaborative Activity

The governance system that appeared to work in the 20th century, however, is no longer sufficient; an era of new governance has emerged[8] as public programs are increasingly more complex and interconnected. Emphasizing tools of coordination and collaboration, new governance is marked by a reliance on a dynamic collection of third parties and governmental units because problems have become too difficult and controversial for the government to act alone:

> Today's problems are "too complex for government to handle on its own, because disagreements exist about the proper ends of public action, and because government increasingly lacks the authority to enforce its will on other crucial actors without giving them a meaningful seat at the table"[9]

An important tool in new governance is collaboration, commonly defined as "a process in which those parties with a stake in the problem actively seek a mutually determined solution."[10] While Lester Salamon, director of the Center for Civil Society Studies at Johns Hopkins University, agrees that the need for coordination and collaboration is not novel, he convincingly argues that these collaborative approaches must be addressed in a new, more coherent manner.[11]

Collaborative activity falls on a continuum that integrates the perceived significance of the problem that is "on the table" (or the stake of the issues being considered) with an assessment of the perceived expectations about decision-making processes (or the need for inclusiveness) (Figure 1.1). On the far left of the continuum are pure silo-based activities, where issues are seen as solely and appropriately placed with the agency. As boundary-spanning functions increase in magnitude, the activities move to the right along the collaborative continuum, from simple collaborative

Figure 1.1   The continuum of collaborative activity.

activities to full-blown, strategic collaboration. The issues at hand may require only a minimal level of collaboration that is more short term in nature and simpler in its purpose. In contrast, thorny problems that are interconnected with other policy arenas and have high investment on the part of other agencies, sectors, and interests may require a strategic approach to forming and building collaboration.

All too often, decisions about building or joining a collaboration are not strategic in nature and lead to what can be labeled *ad hoc* collaboration—that is, a group of well-intentioned participants working together but with limited forethought about the purpose, structure, processes, and outcomes of the collaboration. This common approach mirrors the notion of "muddling through" and "hoping for the best." With the right circumstances, luck, and persistence, such collaborations may have positive results. Unfortunately, collaborative inertia, fatigue, and frustration are the more likely outcomes from this nonstrategic approach.

Moreover, when the collaboration has high political stakes and serious consequences or crosses multiple policy and sector boundaries, *ad hoc* collaboration has less likelihood of success. To advance public service practice and reach longer-term solutions, collaborative activity needs to be appreciably more strategic in its approach to assure intentional, systematic, and inclusionary collaboration, as public and nonprofit managers wrestle with trying to manage upward, downward, and outward within their particular context.[12]

Working in silos succeeds when the issue, problem, or task at hand does not warrant significant "outside-the-silo" collaborative activity. The challenge for public and nonprofit administrators is in knowing when it is more appropriate to stay within the boundaries of their home agency, when to proceed ahead with a collaborative activity, and what intensity of collaboration is required.[13] Given the time, resources, and attention that an effective collaboration takes, public and nonprofit managers must be methodical about determining the optimal institutional choice ranging from "pure" silo to a major collaborative undertaking. Public and nonprofit managers and community stakeholders must question when collaboration is the best tool for a problem, the costs and benefits of participating (or not), and the potential for positive and substantial outcomes.

1.4 Defining a Strategic Collaboration Approach

Strategic collaboration is an intentional, collective approach to address public problems or issues through building shared knowledge, designing innovative solutions, and forging consequential change.

While frequently used by public and nonprofit managers to tackle today's public problems, too often collaboration becomes an impromptu tool for meeting immediate funder and community demands. In contrast, strategic collaboration raises the tool of collaboration to an advanced level of practice to assure that those with a stake in a problem engage together to develop mutually determined goals and solutions. Crossing organization, sector, and discipline boundaries, strategic collaboration is a valuable approach for public and nonprofit administrators as they seek to advance their agencies' missions and to serve the best interests of the community at large. Strategic collaboration has several purposes. The first is to bring to the table the knowledge, ideas, and perspectives of a diverse set of participants. The second purpose is to encourage this group to move out of its status-quo-focused silos so that it can begin to identify and navigate the social, political, and economic hurdles of creative public problem solving. Third, strategic collaboration advances individual and organizational legitimacy while making progress on the targeted policy issue. Beyond the specific collaboration activity, the resulting collective intelligence can have long-lasting positive effects on organizations, policy networks, and communities. Framing strategic collaboration as a deliberate approach helps public and nonprofit managers better understand how to first examine various conditions that will likely affect the collaboration's success and then how to act strategically as they work with and through the collaboration to bring about change.

The decision to undertake strategic collaboration is a choice for a nonpermanent, although possibly long-term, effort on a particular public problem. Strategic collaboration at inception does not create a new permanent organization or system to replace or duplicate what currently exists, although this may be the result as the collaboration matures; rather, the approach is about creating an organic and fluid structure to encourage change, innovative thinking, and new actions that lead to problem resolution. The strategic approach is about building on the strengths of existing organizations and systems while nurturing new practices that emerge. The nonpermanent status reduces the barriers related to competition and turf protection.

Successful strategic collaboration requires an intentional decision to collaborate that includes thinking through commitments carefully and strategically. It purposefully designs flexible and responsive structures, processes, and outcomes that coincide with the collaboration's stages of development. It supports implementation processes that are inclusive and authentic. Finally, strategic collaboration focuses on short- and long-term outcomes that lead to change.

1.5 Impacts of Strategic Collaboration

As in organizational settings, strategic collaboration leaders must examine the expected and unexpected effects of the effort's work. Answering the explicit question of "what difference will the collaboration make" identifies the anticipated

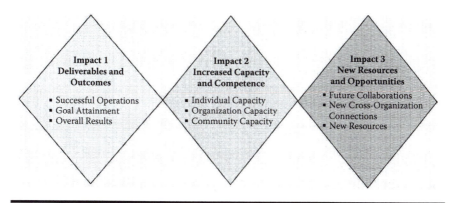

Figure 1.2   Collaboration impacts.

direct and indirect results of the collaboration. Some impacts are clearly identifiable in the maturation process of strategic collaboration (e.g., goal-related outcomes). Other impacts emerge gradually over time or may not occur until after the collaboration ends. Impacts can be immediate, short term, or longer term and positive or negative. The focus of this book is to help the reader maximize positive impacts.

As illustrated in Figure 1.2 the positive impacts resulting from the strategic collaboration's work include the direct deliverables and outcomes specific to the collaboration's mission and goals, participants who increase their capacity for collaborative work, and new collaborative opportunities. Recognizing the multidimensional impacts that can result from a strategic collaboration is an important component of creating a meaningful overarching agenda for the effort.

1.5.1 Impact 1: Deliverables and Outcomes

Strategic collaboration deliberately focuses on desired outcomes, products, or results throughout the collaboration's evolution or life cycle. To enhance accountability, goals and expected outcomes should result from transparent processes and be clearly articulated. Strategic collaboration produces three typical outcomes: (1) outcomes related to the successful operation of the collaborative effort; (2) deliverables and outcomes related to the established goals of the collaboration; and (3) overall results.

The first type of outcomes assesses the utility of the processes, procedures, and activities necessary to create and implement the collaboration. Early and important success in this category of outcome is the positive functioning of the collaboration itself: a synergy of interaction that creates a positive culture and effective relationships. These new formal and informal relationships are often built through the sharing of information that was previously not easily accessible to the broader group. Additional success measures related to the collaboration's operations include (1) the acquisition, leveraging, and continuance of resources needed for collaboration progress and (2) evidence of innovative thinking and programming that influences funders and policy decision makers. As the collaboration evolves, outcomes become a regular and ongoing point of discussion with internal and external stakeholders.

The second category of outcomes focuses on goals specific to the collaboration's planned actions and can be wide-ranging, including tangible deliverables such as research project reporting, implementation of new programs and services, community-wide dialogue, changes in local, state, or national policy, or enhanced public awareness campaigns. The benefits of these deliverables are often the most visible, concrete outcomes from the work of the collaboration and, therefore, should not be underestimated. The use of collaborative strategies to develop products and programs has been found to increase the likelihood that results will be used.[14]

A third category of outcomes relates to the impact of the collaboration's cumulative set of activities. Specifically, have the strategic collaboration's overall efforts produced the anticipated changes in the target population or policy area of focus? Measurement of this impact area is often difficult and costly and requires a long-term orientation. However, strategic collaboration emphasizes agreed upon measurement processes to evaluate progress and overall outcomes. Other examples of potential results include modifications in agency decision-making processes or structuring (e.g., agencies or programs merging, interlocal agreements), broad introduction of new program design or service delivery mechanisms, and passage of comprehensive public policy.

Continued focus on deliverables and outcomes is essential to the success of strategic collaboration. The collaboration's goals, data definition and collection processes, and assessment criteria must assure reliability, standardization, and meaningfulness to participants and key stakeholders. Benchmarking, comparative data, and dashboards are useful tactics to build a common understanding of and expectations about outcomes, thus fostering accountability[15] and building a track record of success.

1.5.2 Impact 2: Increased Capacity and Competence

In addition to the external benefits, the experience of successful collaboration allows all participants to develop and extend important knowledge, skills, and abilities.[16] The challenging work of strategic collaboration is the ideal setting for individuals to try on new skills, to expand current competencies outside of their home organization, and to deepen their knowledge about specific policy arenas.[17] Participants can come away from a collaboration experience with new skills such as facilitation, conflict management, and program evaluation as well as a more comprehensive understanding of a particular issue. This new knowledge and ability is useful to the collaboration and to the participant's home organization. While collaboration processes benefit from participants who bring appropriate knowledge and skills to the table, new experiences also provide an important venue for further development and the opportunity to exercise creativity.

Collaboration-related competencies include the ability to work skillfully both within and outside of hierarchy and to frame the environmental context of the situation and the nimbleness to work with an emerging set of norms, roles, and values. As public and nonprofit managers ramp up this set of competencies, their capacity for future successful collaborative work, in both single- and cross-organizational settings, is increased. Moving beyond turf protection, participants increase their ability to collaborate effectively and thereby grow the pool of potential participants for future collaboration work. In addition, the trust built through a positive collaborative experience can strengthen existing relationships and repair fractured relationships.[18] As the number of individuals in a given community or policy arena with skills and values needed for successful strategic collaboration increases, the opportunities for using the approach for significant change also increase.

In agencies, supervisors have the responsibility for assuring the professional development of their staff members. Collaboration conveners and leaders also need to assess and identify development needs of participants. Professional development focused on collaborative competencies will build capacity for future collaborative efforts as well as advance public service practice overall.

1.5.3 Impact 3: New Resources and Opportunities

The third impact of strategic collaboration moves beyond the specific collaboration and its participants to identify new opportunities that result including future collaboration and new resources. Regardless of the specific deliverables and results of a given strategic collaboration, the relationships, outcomes, and resources it has nurtured can be used as a foundation for future collaborative efforts. The groundwork is laid for further formal and informal information sharing, improved coordination, and a progression of organizational relationships.[19] These future efforts may be related to the original policy area or evolve into collaborating with other networks. For example, a disaster preparedness collaboration might lead to a new effort focused on long-term recovery, an important phase following a catastrophic event, or a seemingly unrelated topic such as food insecurity or school truancy. Thus, the "socially embedded relationships"[20] created through the collaborative processes are an important "take away" no matter the tangible outcomes of the collaboration. The result is a cultural shift in how agencies connect to each other, ideally moving from a perspective of competition to one of cooperation or at least laying the foundation for future positive dialogue and cooperation. In addition to the possibility of new strategic collaborations, these relationships may lead to previously unexplored interorganizational connections, such as alliances, coalitions, and partnerships.

Finally, the strategic collaboration's efforts may bring new resources to the public problem of focus. Significant results, greater visibility for the problem area, and new relationships with key funders and stakeholders improve the opportunity for funding. Moreover, new government, foundation, or corporate resources may be targeted to an existing agency or program to create a new agency or program, for the work of the collaboration itself, or for a new collaborative effort. The processes, capacities, products, and resource impacts of strategic collaboration thus become the catalyst for future transformational opportunities.

1.6 Transferring Organizational Expertise to Collaboration Practice

From simple to highly complex settings, public and nonprofit managers have been practicing collaborative public management for years. As illustrated in the case narratives in Chapters 5 through 13, public and nonprofit managers collaborate with federal, state, and local officials as well as community advocates, working in policy networks from regulation of the environment to protecting public health to influence policy formulation, adoption, implementation, and evaluation. Similarly, political officials, government agency administrators, and nonprofit leaders join together in various ways to wrestle with wide-ranging municipal and regional problems from public safety responsiveness to preparing communities for natural disaster response.

Although not as intentional and purposefully strategic as described in the upcoming chapters, everyday skills needed to manage public and nonprofit agencies and their interagency connections are already readily transferrable to collaborative work. McGuire argues that managerial skills such as managing human and financial resources, managing the structure and rules that guide operations, and designing and implementing effective communication, information management, strategic management, and conflict management practices are common in both hierarchical organizations and collaborative contexts.[21] Consequently, the translation of such skills from everyday organizational settings into a collaboration context requires that public and nonprofit managers thoughtfully interpret this new orientation and adjust their conduct and behaviors appropriately since collaborations are inherently more unstable, fragile, and idiosyncratic than hierarchical settings. The ability to reflectively read a situation as it unfolds and to be instinctively resourceful as collaborative structures and processes evolve requires that public and nonprofit managers act both deliberately and strategically. Moreover, in a collaborative setting, the everyday skills of negotiation, communication, conflict resolution, and facilitation take on added complexity as the degree of control is decreased and engagement levels vary.

Three knowledge areas, illustrated in Figure 1.3, important to effective collaboration build from organizational expertise, likely familiar to public and nonprofit managers. Collectively the three broad knowledge areas—getting things done with and through people, using analytic methods, and managing boundary-spanning activities—serve as a foundation for collaboration practice but, as discussed in Section 1.7, need to be transformed to result in effective strategic collaboration practice.

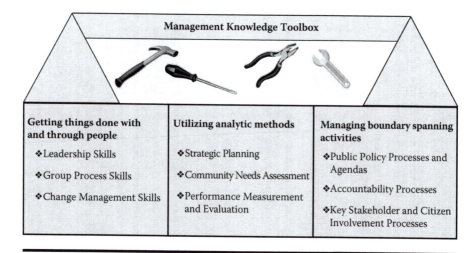

Figure 1.3 **Three knowledge areas transferable to collaboration.**

1.6.1 Expertise Related to Getting Things Done with and through People

In this knowledge area, three sets of highly interconnected skills are essential to effective organization management: leadership, group process, and change management. These same skills are critical to collaborations. Just as in organizations, leadership builds and sustains commitment, facilitates group interactions, and negotiates the natural resistance to change. Effective leaders strengthen relationships and bring cultural competence to their diverse organizations. Importantly, public and nonprofit managers build agendas, work plans, and performance systems that further their organization's mission and priorities. Strong communication skills facilitate information exchange, ease work tensions, and build trust.

Translating to the collaborative context, personal characteristics such as flexibility, patience, and a cooperative spirit are important to success.[22] As in organizations, differences among individuals participating in the collaboration clearly affect interpersonal interactions as individuals develop trust and shared understandings of expectations or conversely create conflict and struggles over priorities and direction.[23] Organizational policies and agendas, especially related to funding decisions and control locus, also influence intergroup dynamics.[24] Further, differences in priorities and expectations can negatively impact intergroup dynamics.[25] Understanding how to introduce change and then to manage both the human and political reactions to change is critical to achieving positive collaboration outcomes.[26] Achieving success and mutual benefit sustains continued participation in a collaborative effort. Elaborating on collaboration processes, researchers Thomson and Perry note that "collaboration occurs over time as organizations interact

Table 1.1 People Skills Essential for Collaboration

- Build and sustain relationships with people at all organizational levels.
- Facilitate group processes as a leader or team member to accomplish tasks.
- Cultivate support for vision and desired outcomes.
- Listen to understand and value diverse perspectives.
- Communicate effectively in writing and in person.
- Create agendas to organize projects, manage meetings, coordinate assignments, and navigate change.
- Use transparency and accountability to mediate and negotiate conflict.

---

formally and informally through repetitive sequences of negotiation, development of commitments, and execution of those commitments."[27]

In summary, the people skills used in organization and collaboration are a mix of both informal and formal leadership and program/project management skills. To navigate the more heterarchical and fluid dynamics of collaboration, public and nonprofit managers must adeptly transfer the appropriate leadership and people skills and abilities used in their organizational, hierarchical contexts. Table 1.1 lists the people skills important to collaboration effectiveness.

1.6.2 Expertise Related to Embracing Analytic Methods

This knowledge area focuses on the expertise needed for analytical decision making. Analytic processes commonly used by public and nonprofit managers to inform their decision making and strategy setting, such as strategic planning, needs assessment, performance measurement, and evaluation, lend themselves to use in collaborative settings.[28]

Although typically organization driven, strategic planning is a common practice used by public and nonprofit managers to set an agency's trajectory as well as to articulate measureable and realistic goals.[29] Strategic planning generally includes analytic steps that focus on developing or refining a mission or vision for the organization, environmental or situational analysis (e.g., strengths, weaknesses, opportunities, threats), and results in priority and goal setting as well as resource allocation. Needs assessment is another helpful technique used by a variety of administrators. Public health and social service practitioners use needs assessment techniques to comprehensively identify needs in a community and to set organizational or program priorities[30] Training professionals use needs assessment to identify human resource development needs

Table 1.2 Analytic Skills Essential for Collaboration

- Facilitate groups to develop shared knowledge and goals.
- Perform environmental or needs assessment analysis.
- Identify and collect relevant data.
- Conduct key stakeholder analysis.
- Develop and implement performance measurement and program evaluation processes.
- Use a variety of methodologies for analysis.

in an organization. In general, needs assessment steps include first exploring what is known and articulating issues and concerns, gathering, and analyzing data relevant to the needs; benchmarking what is to existing or new standards; and then identifying priorities and possible solutions to address the identified needs.[31] Similarly, professionals engaged in community and economic development use analytic methods to integrate and build consensus for community-based planning. For example, land-use planning uses systematic processes to comprehensively examine future needs and impacts, trends, and policy alternatives, often involving communities in the analysis and prioritization processes.[32] Community-building processes such as those described by Kretzmann and McKnight[33] and supported by the Community Development Block Grant Program[34] emphasize grassroots and asset-based perspectives to problem definition, asset mapping, and community-based strategy formulation important to analytic decision making.

In addition, public and nonprofit managers incorporate analytic skills for performance management and program evaluation using methodologies such as cost-benefit or cost-effectiveness analysis, benchmarking, dashboards, balanced scorecards, social return on investment indicators, and other quality improvement tactics. Existing models of analysis, both quantitative and qualitative, used by public and nonprofit managers to assess problems, needs, and opportunities can transfer to collaborative settings but must be refined to assure information produced is meaningful and accessible by a diverse set of potential users.[35] As summarized in Table 1.2, a wide range of common analytic skills prove useful to the collaboration setting.

1.6.3 Expertise Related to Boundary-Spanning Activities

This knowledge area includes attention to public policy processes and agenda, accountability processes, and key stakeholder and citizen engagement processes

Table 1.3 Boundary-Spanning Skills Essential for Collaboration

- Scan environment for relevant political, social, and economic forces.
- Develop and coordinate cross-agency action plans, assignments and timetables, and budgets resources.
- Solicit feedback to revise or refine plans and implementation processes
- Ensure accountability.
- Perform regular reality check for alignment of expectations and priorities.
- Consider roles for citizen, client, and consumer participation.
- Communicate with external stakeholders.

that require informed boundary-spanning activity. The organizational skills that relate to this knowledge area include influencing and informing policy formulation and implementation, stakeholder management, reporting and dissemination mechanisms, and public relations.

As summarized in Table 1.3, many typical organization-based boundary-spanning skills translate to the collaboration setting. As organizations use feedback to revise programs, collaborations also need to regularly assess relevant external perspectives and factors to coordinate and update goals, timetables, and work plans. Given the increasing demand for transparency, reporting processes that focus on the review of status reports, budgets, and performance data and provide critical information for a range of internal and external stakeholders are a necessary management responsibility. Determining how citizens, clients, and consumers will be involved in agency planning processes and preparing information for a diverse set of external stakeholders are familiar tasks for contemporary public and nonprofit managers.

1.7 The Translation to Strategic Collaboration Practice

Public and nonprofit managers at all levels need to know how to get "multiple heads" working together well. The list of competencies and skills identified for effective collaboration are wide-ranging.[36] The three knowledge areas described in the previous sections provide a general lens for more systematic thinking about how everyday organizational expertise can be transformed for success in collaborative settings.

Getting people and organizations with different or competing values and priorities to work effectively together, outside of hierarchy, requires that public and nonprofit administrators be effective facilitators and communicators as well as politically astute.[37] Developing shared understanding about authority, resource sharing, responsibility, and rewards in collective settings is hard but essential work.[38] Emergency management collaborations offer helpful examples. The potential participants for this type of collaboration often bring diverse expertise and expectations. The more traditional "command and control" leadership style of public safety participants is likely to conflict with a consensus-building group-process format, highlighting the need for savvy leadership and management practice that includes transparent communication. Strategic collaboration people skills ensure that the collaboration addresses the core structural components of the collaboration, especially how the collaboration is purposefully created and organized, vision and goals articulated, processes planned and executed, and roles and responsibilities defined and managed. Additionally, people skills are key to building group trust and negotiating resistance to change.

In strategic collaboration, the analytic knowledge area grounds the effort's work in methods and analysis that are both more intentional and inclusive. Intentionality speaks to the need for a systematic examination of the forces calling for a collaborative effort, while inclusivity speaks to the need to actively engage stakeholders to build or enhance shared understandings and elicit commitment to the collective effort. Moreover, to achieve positive outcomes, stakeholders involved in the collaboration should not just passively receive data but should actively engage in the process of data collection and analysis. Introducing nontraditional discipline or policy arena participation in strategic collaboration processes not only broadens the data and methodologies used but also results in a more holistic examination and definition of the problem. For example, collaborations focused on infant mortality should include not only a wide range of medical and health professionals but also representatives from education, social services, insurance providers, and faith-based communities. This example also illustrates the potential for collaboration with higher-education social scientists, who bring not only disciplinary knowledge but also insights into underlying conditions and how to better link data to action.

Following from analytic processes and knowledge building, strategic collaboration stakeholders must also be authentically engaged in boundary spanning, priority setting, and resource allocation. For participants, the interaction between functional and mission-based considerations serve as an impetus for collaborative action, including the desire to exchange and create shared knowledge, coordinate planning and decision making, pool resource capacity or increase the ability to shape policy processes and decisions. Researchers Bingham and O'Leary argue that collaboration plays out differently depending on where it is in the policy process.[39] Consequently, strategic collaboration participants must consider the timing of public policy processes since organizations and political entities have norms for how issues get on action agendas as well as set calendars for undertaking policy changes and formulating budgets. Strategic collaborations must be explicit about the results anticipated from the collective effort, must ensure that they align with political, regulatory, legal, and external expectations, and must communicate with both agency stakeholders and external stakeholders about progress and outcomes. Proactive attention to environmental dynamics that underlie collaboration, including the social, economic, and political influences beyond the control of individual actors, is also essential for strategic collaboration success. Exceedingly complex, these environmental dynamics often require an examination of "under-the-surface" values, rights, and expectations. While statistical and policy tools can measure and analyze many environmental forces such as general public opinion, economic conditions, and racial or cultural tensions, it is also important to gather the perspectives of key stakeholders through interviews, focus groups, and surveys of opinion leaders, clients, and funders for a more holistic analysis. For example, the many studies of New Orleans post-Hurricane Katrina have added new dimensions to our understanding of how poverty and race shape political, social, and economic dynamics. Clearly, aligning context and consequence to guide action is critical.

Realistically, not everyone can collaborate. The lack of skills in any of the three knowledge areas can paralyze strategic collaboration processes. Certain "negative" behaviors and attitudes hinder collaboration interpersonal dynamics, including communication patterns dependent on position and rank, an inability to integrate knowledge outside of an individual's expertise, and a personal focus centered on individual achievement, turf protection, and conflict avoidance.[40] Analytic weaknesses include narrow thinking, inadequate methodology skills, a predisposition to overemphasize methodological purity and expect data perfection, and the inability to think creatively about when and how to use data. Limitations in the boundary-spanning knowledge area include excluding stakeholders in the quest for efficiency, paying insufficient attention to changing contextual forces, and failing to manage the message to external stakeholders.[41]

While experienced and educated public and nonprofit managers may already possess needed organizational expertise, they need to effectively transfer and translate this expertise and create new collaborative knowledge, skills, and competencies to be effective strategic collaboration practitioners. This new collaborative capacity enables them to strategically design collaborative structures and processes to ensure authenticity and inclusivity; to elicit and facilitate creative energies to strengthen and evolve the collaborative; to harness the energies of those involved to work together and stay on task; to facilitate what can be "messy" group dynamics and processes; and to purposefully assess their performance. Further, effective practitioners must be skillful in managing the additional complexity and uncertainty inherent in collaborative activities as the collaboration's goals may conflict with existing home-agency priorities, threaten power bases, introduce more politics into administrative processes, and fragment organizational resources.

Thus, the challenge is in knowing what skills readily transfer from everyday organizational work life and what skills need refinement or a fresh approach for a specific context. To advance their skills, public or nonprofit managers can draw on many professional development programs and materials available to further their collaborative skills.[42] Managers can also access a growing literature to further their skills for effective collaborative practice. See Appendix A for a recommended set of readings that focus on collaborative practice and lay a helpful foundation for advancing collaborative practice. Clearly, the ability to effectively (and patiently) manage and lead collaborations requires extensive people, technical, and administrative skills. To transform collaboration to effective strategic collaboration practice, however, requires the refinement and expansion of these skills in new ways. By more intentionally and systematically managing the organic and fluid collaborative processes, public and nonprofit managers can increase the likelihood of success, can balance competing pressures, can match effort with results, and thus can realize positive community and societal change.

1.8 Purpose of the Book and Overview of Remaining Chapters

Although collaboration reigns as today's leading public policy approach, it is not without critics as both practitioners and researchers question when to use collaboration and whether any real results can be attributed to collaborative effort. This book argues that the problem is not with collaboration as an approach but in how it has been framed and practiced and sets out to fill this gap with a focus on the knowledge and skills needed for collaboration leaders, facilitators, and participants. Thus, the purpose of strategic collaboration is to move policy makers, program administrators, and service providers outside of the typical fragmentation of silos to explore opportunities and to creatively work with others to address higher-order issues and to advance public service practice.

This chapter introduced the strategic collaboration approach and the expertise that grounds the development of more refined, nuanced, and specific knowledge and skills for success. The chapters that follow focus on how public and nonprofit managers can use strategic collaboration as a public problem-solving approach and, when chosen, how to nurture, shape, and align effort and results for positive impact. Being more strategic will help public and nonprofit managers juggle the collaboration workload with their ongoing internal, agency duties and performance expectations. With a more strategic perspective, a powerful tool emerges. Chapter 2 introduces the *collaboration life cycle model* to understand the evolutionary nature of strategic collaborative practice. The chapter describes the five stages of collaboration, noting the differences between conventional and strategic collaboration. Chapter 3 discusses *collaboration readiness*, with a focus on answering the key question of "when to collaborate." Both of these chapters use a brief scenario to illustrate and reinforce key concepts. Whether the community is struggling with the appropriate means to be proactive about litter and garbage reduction (Chapter 2) or to increase the quality and years of healthy life and to eliminate health disparities (Chapter 3), the brief scenarios demonstrate strategic collaboration in action. Chapter 4 provides six key principles for public and nonprofit managers to successfully use strategic collaboration and a framework of strategic collaboration that pulls together the key components discussed in the first four chapters.

The case studies in Chapters 5 through 13 describe strategic collaborations that have a broad focus, that cover multiple policy arenas, that involve participants that cross organizations, sectors, and disciplines, and that include high-stakes community expectations about outcomes (Table 1.4). The cases illustrate the various contextual factors that can lead to a strategic decision to collaborate, how context shapes collaboration structures and processes, and how success is increased if decisions are strategic and systematic. Each case describes the complex and intentional involvement of government agencies, nonprofit organizations, individuals, interest groups, disciplinary experts, and funders from the relevant policy arenas. In some case chapters, the collaborations operated within an established framework, such as those formed according to established state or federal guidelines, mandated requirements, or funding source. Even so the collaboration's leaders had to strategically engage participants in the collaboration if they were to be successful. Other case collaborations emerged from grassroots efforts to address an immediate and pressing community need. Some of the cases describe the critical role of a champion (individual or committed group) throughout the evolution of the collaboration. Other cases examine how collaborations change over time, from formation to ending point. What raised the cases from *ad hoc* to strategic collaboration is that the resulting multilayered, multidisciplinary, and high-stakes community efforts operated in a manner more systematic than in conventional collaborations and resulted in innovative or creative approaches to public problems.

Chapter 14 summarizes the lessons of the cases and provides practical perspective on building a successful strategic collaboration and the roadblocks and pitfalls to avoid. The appendices provide a useful set of resources for public and nonprofit managers to support the implementation of strategic collaboration, including sample collaboration operating guidelines (Appendix B), participant agreement (Appendix C), a matrix of collaboration participant roles (Appendix D), a checklist for strategic collaboration meetings, and a collaborative analysis of a contested policy issue checklist (Appendix G). To further advance practice, Appendix H includes a review of current collaboration literature from relevant research published in the American Society of Public Administration (ASPA)-sponsored journals.

Strategic collaboration is a systematic and practice-based approach to working with others to find new and improved solutions for problems of concern to public and nonprofit managers, leaders, and citizens. Chapter 2 introduces the collaboration life cycle model as a lens to help practitioners move from conventional collaboration to strategic collaboration practice.

Table 1.4 Overview of Cases

Chapter	Case	Location	Primary Policy Arenas	Initiating Forces
5	Attending to the Forgotten: The Elderly, Collaborative Practice, Evacuation	Louisiana: New Orleans	Emergency management	Event triggered: Hurricane Katrina
6	Running Out of Classrooms! Solving School Overcrowding through Collaborative School Planning	Florida: Palm Beach County	Education/ economic development	State-mandated interlocal agreement
7	Moving beyond Hierarchies: Creating Effective Collaboration Networks for West Nile Virus Biosurveillance in Oregon	Oregon	Emergency management/ public health	Event triggered/ state funded: public health threat
8	Information Stewardship and Collaboration: Advancing Evidence-Based Public Policy Decision Making	Tennessee: Memphis/ Shelby County	Information technology	Event triggered/ foundation funded: public safety failure
9	Choices and Challenges: Sustaining a Rural Health Network When Funding Vanishes	Kentucky	Community health	Federal funded: rural health services provision
10	Collaboration, Citizen Participation, and Environmental Protection in the Marine Oil Trade of Alaska	Alaska: Prince William Sound	Environment/ trade	Federally mandated: *Exxon Valdez* oil spill

(continued)

Table 1.4   Overview of Cases (Continued)

Chapter	Case	Location	Primary Policy Arenas	Initiating Forces
11	Paving the Way for Public Transportation in Texas through Public Collaboration	Texas: Denton County	Transportation/ environment	Federally mandated: public participation
12	Cape Fear Healthy Carolinians: Taking Risks, Crossing Boundaries	North Carolina: Wilmington	Community health	State funded: community health and safety
13	Building a Community–Higher Education Collaboration to Meet the Needs of the Local Nonprofit Sector	Tennessee: Memphis/ Shelby County	Higher education/ nonprofit sector	Foundation funded: developing local capacity

Endnotes

1. The public and nonprofit literature suggests that collaborative efforts have intensified over the last two decades as "organizations made a commitment to address social issues in new ways." P. Mattessich, M. Murray-Close, and B. Monsey, *Collaboration: What Makes It Work* (2d ed., St. Paul, MN: Wilder Foundation, 2001) p. 2. Gray posits that collaboration occurs when organizations are faced with turbulent conditions, such as rapid economic or technologic change, shrinking funding for programs, and competitive pressures. B. Gray, *Collaborating: Finding Common Ground for Multi-Party Problems* (San Francisco: Jossey-Bass, 1989), p. 29. We argue not only that should the decision to engage in collaboration be accomplished in a strategic, intentional manner but also that decisions about how public and nonprofit agencies engage in collaborative activities should also be intentional and strategic within their particular context. See L. O'Toole, K. Meier, and S. Nicholson-Crotty, Managing Upward, Downward and Outward, *Public Management Review, 7* (1): 45–68, 2005; L. Bingham and R. O'Leary, Conclusion: Parallel Play, Not Collaboration: Missing Questions, Missing Connections, *Public Administration Review, 66* (Supplement): 161–167, 2006; T. Koontz and C. Thomas, What Do We Know and Need to Know about the Environmental Outcomes of Collaborative Management, *Public Administration Review, 66* (Supplement): 111–121, 2006.
2. Weber describes this as bureaucratically defined, jurisdictional stovepipes. E. Weber, Explaining Institutional Change in Tough Cases of Collaboration: "Ideas" in the Blackfoot Watershed, *Public Administration Review, 69* (2): 321, 2009.

3. Huxham and Vangen suggest that those demanding collaboration often view it as a moral imperative, indicating that people want to come together to work on the important societal issues. This then inherently requires collaboration since "these issues have ramifications for so many aspects of society that they are inherently multi-organizational." C. Huxham and S. Vangen, *Managing to Collaborate: The Theory and Practice of Collaborative Advantage* (London: Routledge, 2005), p. 7. Also see L. Salamon, *The Tools of Government: A Guide to the New Governance* (New York: Oxford University Press, 2002); D. Kettl, Managing Boundaries in American Administration: The Collaboration Imperative, *Public Administration Review, 66* (Supplement): 10–19, 2006; E. Boris and C. Steuerle, Eds., *Nonprofits & Government: Collaboration and Conflict* (2d ed., Washington, DC: Urban Institute Press, 2006); R. Agranoff, Inside Collaborative Networks: Ten Lessons for Public Managers, *Public Administration Review, 66* (Supplement): 56–65, 2006; M. McGuire, Collaborative Public Management: Assessing What We Know and How We Know It, *Public Administration Review, 66* (Supplement): 33–43, 2006; Meier and O'Toole, Managerial Strategies and Behavior in Networks: A Model with Evidence from U.S. Public Education, *Journal of Public Administration Research and Theory, 11* (3): 271–293, 2001; J. Bryson, B.C. Crosby, and M. Stone, The Design and Implementation of Cross-Sector Collaborations: Propositions from the Literature, *Public Administration Review, 66* (Supplement): 44–55, 2006.

4. Collaboration may be brokered by various stakeholders, individuals, or organizations, acting as champions of collaboration or mediating agents. See R. Keast, M. Mandell, K. Brown, and G. Woolcock, Network Structures: Working Differently and Changing Expectations, *Public Administration Review, 64* (3): 363–371, 2004; Agranoff, Managing Collaborative Performance, *Public Performance & Management Review, 29* (1): 18–45, 2005; Bryson et al., Design and Implementation; P. Kathi, T. Cooper, and J. Meek, The Role of the University as a Mediating Institution in Neighborhood Council–City Agency Collaboration, *Journal of Public Affairs Education, 13* (2): 365–382, 2007; M. Rhodes and J. Murray, Collaborative Decision Making in Urban Regeneration: A Complex Adaptive Systems Perspective, *International Public Management Journal, 10* (1): 79–101, 2007. Collaboration also may be explicitly mandated by funders or authorities. See S. Page, Measuring Accountability for Results in Interagency Collaboratives, *Public Administration Review 64* (5): 591–606, 2004; S. Selden, J Sowa, and J. Sandfort, The Impact of Nonprofit Collaboration in Early Child Care and Education on Management and Program Outcomes, *Public Administration Review, 66* (3): 412–425, 2006; Agranoff, Enhancing Performance through Public Sector Networks: Mobilizing Human Capital in Communities of Practice, *Public Performance & Management Review, 31* (1): 320–347, 2008.

5. Collaborative public and nonprofit functions add to management complexity and uncertainty as these activities may conflict with existing priorities, threaten power bases, introduce more politics into administrative processes, and fragment organizational resources. Keast, Brown, and Mandell, Getting the Right Mix: Unpacking Integration Meanings and Strategies, *International Public Management Journal, 10* (1): 9–33, 2007; T. Bryer, Explaining Responsiveness in Collaboration: Administrator and Citizen Role Perceptions, *Public Administration Review, 69* (2): 271–283, 2009; K. Callahan, Citizen Participation: Questions of Diversity, Equity and Fairness, *Journal of Public Management and Social Policy, 13* (1): 53–68, 2007;

K. Yang and Callahan, Citizen Involvement Efforts and Bureaucratic Responsiveness: Participatory Values, Stakeholder Pressures, and Administrative Practicality, *Public Administration Review, 67* (2): 249–264, 2007. The pressure on public and nonprofit managers to collaborate can create a situation marked by an intense clash of competing values, producing confusion about when and how to respond. Consequently, they are not necessarily strategic about their decision to collaborate or not and then not strategic in how they then manage collaborative processes. For example, Agranoff and McGuire posit that collaborative management in economic development presents a continuum of activity level and strategic degree. In their insightful study, these researchers found that lower levels of collaborative activity may or may not have been overtly strategically decided by the cities in their study. Agranoff and McGuire, *Collaborative Public Management: New Strategies for Local Government* (Washington, DC: Georgetown University Press, 2003).

6. Not that other structural forms are not in place, but bureaucracy and hierarchy continue to be the popular form of organizing public service agencies, as leaders struggle with balancing differentiation and integration of roles and responsibilities and are held accountable to political officials or board members. See L. Bolman and T. Deal, *Reframing Organizations: Artistry, Choice and Leadership* (3d ed., San Francisco: Jossey-Bass, 2003). Also see Salamon, *Tools of Government*.

7. Policy and issue networks have tended to become quite complex. For example, policy networks concerned about environmental issues are broad based, reaching across sectors, intergovernmental boundaries, and national boundaries. Thus, networks have become recognized as an important feature of public policy and governance processes. For example, see Salamon, *Tools of Government*; S. Goldsmith and W. Eggers, *Governing by Network: The New Shape of the Public Sector* (Washington, DC: Brookings Institution Press, 2004).

8. Researchers have recognized that collaborative activities involving a diverse set of actors are increasingly used to address a wide range of public problems. There is a growing body of research literature on collaboration governance and collaboration processes. Regarding furthering the understanding of interorganizational collaboration see, for example, E. Bardach, *Getting Agencies to Work Together: The Practice and Theory of Managerial Craftsmanship* (Washington, DC: Brookings Institution Press, 1998). Regarding how local governments seek and implement collaboration, see, for example, Agranoff and McGuire, *Collaborative Public Management*. Regarding governance through networks, see, for example, Mandell, *Getting Results through Collaboration: Networks and Network Structures for Public Policy and Management* (Westport, CT: Quorum Books and Goldsmith, 2001); Goldsmith and Eggers, *Governing by Network*. Regarding understanding how collaborations improve policy outcomes, see, for example, Weber, Explaining Institutional Change; M. Imperial, Using Collaboration as a Governance Strategy: Lessons from Six Watershed Management Programs. *Administration & Society, 37* (3): 281–320, 2005. A summary of recent collaboration related articles in ASPA-sponsored journals is provided in Appendix H at the end of this volume.

9. Salamon, *Tools of Government*, p. 8.

10. B. Gray, *Collaborating: Finding Common Ground for Multi-Party Problems* (San Francisco: Jossey-Bass, 1989), p. xviii.

11. Salamon, *Tools of Government*.

12. See O'Toole et al., Managing Upward; Bingham and O'Leary, Conclusion: Parallel Play; Koontz and Thomas, What Do We Know.

13. Not all collaborative relationships have the same intensity. This dimension of collaboration should be strategically decided upon as the collaboration is formed and entered into by each of the participants. Sowa found that "the more that is shared between organizations in an interagency collaboration, the more intense that relationship becomes and the more value is created by the collaboration." J. Sowa, Implementing Interagency Collaborations, *Administration & Society, 40* (3): 318, 2008.

14. M. Berner and M. Bronson, A Case Study of Program Evaluation in Local Government: Building Consensus Through Collaboration, *Public Performance & Management Review, 28* (5): 309–325, 2005.

15. Callahan and K. Kloby, Collaboration Meets the Performance Measurement Challenge, *Public Manager, 36* (2): 11–24, 2007.

16. L.M. Takahashi and G. Smutny, Collaborative Windows and Organizational Governance: Exploring the Formation and Demise of Social Service Partnerships, *Nonprofit and Voluntary Sector Quarterly, 31* (2): 165–185, 2002; Berner and Bronson, Case Study of Program Evaluation.

17. Of interest, Agranoff found five types of personal benefits resulting from collaborative participation, including enhancement of scientific and technical knowledge, development of interdisciplinary cultures and exposure to different organization cultures, enhanced abilities to work across boundaries and with different publics, enriched networking opportunities and opportunity to learn about other programs, and (lowest in priority) increased access to decision makers and the opportunity for serving the public. Agranoff, Enhancing Performance, p. 329.

18. Alexander and Nank indicate that trust is the precursor, "if not the single most important component of stable interagency partnerships" and that for nonprofit organizations, "trust is the defining element of organizational survival. J. Alexander and R. Nank, Public–Nonprofit Partnership: Realizing the New Public Service, *Administration & Society, 41* (3): 364–386, 2009. Also see Bryson et al., Design and Implementation; R. Seppanen, K. Blomqvist, and S. Sundquist, Measuring Inter-organizational Trust—A Critical Review of the Empirical Research in 1990-2003, *Industrial Marketing Management, 36:* 249–260, 2007; C. Ansell and A. Gash, Collaborative Governance in Theory and Practice, *Journal of Public Administration Research and Theory, 18* (4): 543–571, 2008.

19. See A. Vogel, P. Ransom, S. Wai, and D. Luisi, Integrating Health and Social Services for Older Adults: A Case Study Interagency Collaboration, *Journal of Health and Human Services Administration, 30* (2): 199–228, 2007; S. Gardner, *Beyond Collaboration to Results: Hard Choices in the Future of Services to Children and Families* (Phoenix: Arizona Prevention Resource Center, Center for Collaboration for Children, 1999).

20. P. Ring and A. Van de Ven, Developmental Process of Cooperative Interorganizational Relationships, *Academy of Management Review, 19:* 10–18, 1994.

21. McGuire categorizes the distinctive collaborative skills needed as those related to activation (identification and integration of the appropriate participants and necessary resources), framing (facilitating roles and responsibilities as well as procedures and structures), mobilizing (eliciting commitments), and synthesizing (facilitating productive and intentional interactions to build relationships and information sharing. McGuire, Collaborative Public Management, p. 37.

22. S. Goldman and W. Kahweiler. 2000. A Collaborator Profile for Executives of Nonprofit Organizations, *Nonprofit and Voluntary Sector Quarterly, 10* (4): 435–450, 2000.

23. See D. Evans and D. Yen, E-government: An Analysis for Implementation: Framework for Understanding Cultural and Social Impact, *Government Information Quarterly, 22*: 354–373, 2005; J. West and E. Berman, The Impact of Revitalized Management Practices on the Adoption of Information Technology: A National Survey of Local Governments, *Public Performance and Management Review, 24*(3): 233–253, 2001.

24. M. Minkler and N. Wallerstein, *Community Based Participatory Research for Health* (San Francisco: Jossey-Bass, 2003).

25. A. Schulz, B. Israel, and P. Lantz, Assessing and Strengthening Characteristics of Effective Groups in Community-Based Participatory Research Partnerships. In *Handbook of Social Work with Groups*, ed. M. Galinsky and L.M. Gutierrez (New York: Guilford Publications, 2004), pp. 557–587; Evans and Yen, E-government.

26. For example, see R. Kearney and Berman, Eds., *Public Sector Performance: Management, Motivation, and Measurement* (Boulder, CO: Westview, 1999). Berman, *Performance and Productivity in Public and Nonprofit Organizations* (2d ed., Armonk, NY: M. E. Sharpe, 2006). A helpful handbook of planned change challenges and strategies is described in R.T. Golembiewski, *Handbook of Organizational Consultation* (2d ed., rev. and exp., New York: Marcel Dekker).

27. A. Thomson and J. Perry, Collaborative Processes: Inside the Black Box, *Public Administration Review, 66* (Supplement): 21, 2006.

28. For example, see H. Hatry *Performance Measurement: Getting Results* (2d ed., Washington, DC: Urban Institute, 2007); T. Poister, *Measuring Performance in Public and Nonprofit Organizations* (San Francisco: Jossey-Bass, 2003); W. Shadish Jr., T. Cook, and L. Leviton, *Foundations of Program Evaluation: Theories of Practice* (Newbury Park, CA: Sage, 1991); C. Weiss, *Evaluation: Methods for Studying Programs and Policies* (2d ed., Upper Saddle River, NJ: Prentice Hall, 1998); J. Wholey, Hatry, and K. Newcomer, Eds., *Handbook of Practical Program Evaluation* (2d ed., San Francisco: Jossey-Bass, 2004).

29. For example, see Bryson, *Strategic Planning for Public and Nonprofit Organizations: A Guide to Strengthening and Sustaining Organizational Achievement* (3d ed., San Francisco: Jossey-Bass, 2004). The associated handbook is also a useful resource. Bryson, *Creating and Implementing Your Strategic Plan: A Workbook for Public and Nonprofit Organizations* (2d ed., San Francisco: Jossey-Bass, 2005). Insights in general about strategic planning are discussed in H. Rainey, *Understanding & Managing Public Organizations* (3d ed., San Francisco: Jossey-Bass, 2003); M. Moore, *Creating Public Value: Strategic Management in Government* (Cambridge, MA: Harvard University Press, 1995).

30. B.R. Wikin and J.W. Altschuld, *Planning and Conducting Needs Assessments: A Practical Guide* (Thousand Oaks, CA: Sage, 1995). See also publications describing community-based participatory research, such as Minkler, Using Participatory Action Research to Build Healthy Communities, *Public Health Reports (Washington, D.C.: 1974), 115* (2-3): 191–197, 2000; Minkler and Wallerstein, *Community Based Participatory Research*.

31. Wikin and Altschuld, *Planning and Conducting Needs Assessments*.

32. P. Berke, D. Godschalk, and E. Kaiser with D. Rodriguez, *Urban Land Use Planning*, (5th ed., Urbana: University of Illinois Press, 2006). Also see Rhodes and Murray, Collaborative Decision Making; M. English, J. Peretz, and M. Manderschied, Building Communities While Building Plans: A Review of Techniques for Participatory Planning Processes, *Public Administration Quarterly, 28* (1–2): 182–221, 2004.

33. J. Kretzmann and J. McKnight, *Building Communities from Inside Out: A Path toward Finding and Mobilizing a Community's Assets* (Evanston, IL: Asset-Based Community Development Institute, ACTA Publications, 1993).

34. See the U.S. Department of Housing and Urban Development's community development program website, http://www.hud.gov/offices/cpd/communitydevelopment/programs/.

35. D. Norris-Tirrell and J.A. Clay, The Production of Useable Knowledge, In *Handbook of Organization Consultation*, ed. Robert T. Golembiewski (New York: Marcel Dekker, 2000), pp. 829–834. The notion of creating new knowledge from shared, collective, and emergent processes positions expert knowledge as just one factor in creating useable knowledge. Weber found that either the scientific data needed to assess the environmental issues being addressed by the Blackfoot Watershed collaboration did not exist or, if databases existed, that they were incomplete, fragmented, too specific to a particular interest, or based on incompatible scientific protocols. He reports that the "stakeholders believed that the traditional bureaucratic and interest group repositories of information that tend to dominate formal problem-solving exercises needed leavening with the local, practical expertise," which was accomplished through the inclusion of social science and community knowledge being added to the problem-solving processes. Weber, Explaining Institutional Change, 317, 321–322. Leach also found in environmental collaborations that an assessment of the representativeness of stakeholders required that local versus national, urban versus rural, and environmental versus economic perspectives all needed to be included. W.D. Leach, Collaborative Public Management and Democracy: Evidence from Western Watershed Partnerships. *Public Administration Review, 66* (Supplement): 102, 2006.

36. Researchers and theoreticians in this area use different terms and labels for organization and collaboration skills. For example, as mentioned in note 21, McGuire suggests that skills such as managing human and financial resources, managing the structure and rules that guide operations, and designing and implementing effective communication, information management, strategic management, and conflict management practices are common in both organizations and collaboration. In addition, he identifies distinctive collaborative skills related to activation, framing, mobilizing, and synthesizing. McGuire, Collaborative Public Management. Similarly, Goldsmith and Eggers argue that networked managers need different competencies and capabilities including "negotiation, mediation, risk analysis, trust building, collaboration, and project management. They must have the ability and the inclination to work across boundaries and the resourcefulness to overcome all the prickly challenges to governing by network." Goldsmith and Eggers, *Governing by Network*, pp. 157–158. Getha-Taylor adds the concept of "interpersonal understanding" for collaboration competence. H. Getha-Taylor, Identifying Collaborative Competencies, *Review of Public Personnel Administration, 28* (2): 103–119, 2008.

37. P. Mattessich, M. Murray-Close, and B. Monsey, *Collaboration: What Makes It Work* (2d ed., St. Paul, MN: Wilder Foundation, 2001), p. 4. See also Vangen and Huxham, Nurturing Collaborative Relations: Building Trust in Interorganizational Collaboration, *Journal of Applied Behavioral Science, 39* (1): 5–31, 2003; Huxham and Vangen, *Managing to Collaborate.* Lessons learned from collaboration experience are described in W. Waugh and G. Streib, Collaboration and Leadership for Effective Emergency Management, *Public Administration Review, 66* (Supplement): 131–140, 2006;

Bryson et al., Design and Implementation; K. Thurmaier, High-Intensity Interlocal Collaboration in Three Iowa Cities, *Public Administration Review, 66* (Supplement): 144–146, 2006.

38. R. Wells, M. Feinberg, J.A. Alexander, and A.J. Ward, Factors Affecting Member Perceptions of Coalition Impact. *Nonprofit and Voluntary Sector Quarterly, 19* (3): 327–348, 2009.

39. Bingham and O'Leary, Conclusion: Parallel Play.

40. This list highlights the negative indicators from Getha-Taylor's competency model of effective collaborators. Getha-Taylor, Identifying Collaborative Competencies, p. 116.

41. How collaborations seek, add, or hinder knowledge transfer and learning affects collaborative capacity and is integral to collaborative performance and effectiveness. Bryson et al., Design and Implementation; M. Feldman, A. Khademian, H. Ingram, and A. Schneider, Ways of Knowing and Inclusive Management Practices. *Public Administration Review, 66* (Supplement): 89–99, 2006; S. Dawes, A. Cresswell, and T. Pardo, From "Need to Know" to "Need to Share": Tangled Problems, Information Boundaries, and the Building of Public Sector Knowledge Networks, *Public Administration Review, 69* (3): 392–402, 2009; Agranoff, Enhancing Performance; Van Buuren, Knowledge for Governance, Governance of Knowledge: Inclusive Knowledge Management in Collaborative Governance Processes, *International Public Management Journal, 12* (2): 208–235, 2009.

42. Professional development opportunities are provided by the American Society of Public Administration, International City Managers Association, American Management Association, and other similar professional associations. Local nonprofit organizations also may provide developmental opportunities. For-profit companies may also offer management training programs in your locality.

Chapter 2

A New Lens: The Life Cycle Model of Collaboration

Dorothy Norris-Tirrell and Joy A. Clay

Contents

2.1 Introduction

While shaped by the political, social, and economic landscape, the path to collaboration often emerges from initiating forces such as events[1] (e.g., disasters or high-profile tragedies), mandates from governments or funders,[2] and ideas for social service delivery or technical innovation generated from a range of variables including constrained fiscal environments, changing leadership, or energized community advocates.[3] A life cycle model provides a new way to understand and shape what happens as collaboration processes begin. Just as organizations commonly follow a predictable pattern of development, collaborative efforts evolve through a series of stages as illustrated in the following scenario:

> In response to international headlines, fluctuating oil prices, and increasing utility demands, a local family foundation takes on the issue of environmental sustainability. Determining that all types of businesses, nonprofit organizations, schools and universities, and government agencies need to "reduce,

reuse, and recycle," the foundation president calls a meeting of representatives from this wide range of local organizations to brainstorm a plan of action. The possibility of potential funding brings everyone invited (and some who weren't) to the table. The early meetings produced a laundry list of ideas, activities, and tactics and a beginning set of priorities, but the group quickly turned their attention to implementation, asking whether an existing organization could take a lead role or if a new organization was needed.

To avoid competition for funds, volunteers, and political clout, the convening group decided on a collaboration structure. They recruited a recently retired news anchor to serve as champion of the group's mission, enlisted a nonprofit environment group to serve as fiscal agent, developed a process for making initial decisions and setting goals including a Saturday retreat at a nearby state park, and began recruiting additional participants. Initial implementation was highly successful with XYZ Computers sponsoring an equipment recycling initiative, another local corporation kicking off a competition for high school students to develop creative reuse ideas for automobile tires, and a new community calendar of environment-focused events highlighted on local media websites. The effort continued to grow as new participants joined bringing fresh ideas, more opportunities, and needed energy. To make sure all participants were meaningfully involved and to balance the competing demands for the group's time, the group restructured, forming a steering committee to serve as the leadership team and a set of task forces to perform specific roles, including governance, calendar and events, advocacy, and marketing.

While the collaboration participants struggled during a few tense meetings over how to prioritize resources, the clearly focused mission and measureable goals kept the effort on task. The programs and activities were embraced by elected officials and community leaders as funding opportunities grew. As the success of the group's efforts became well known throughout the region and state, founding members were asked to advise others about replicating the effort and new funding sources approached them about adding programs. Now, the group had to decide whether it was time to become a formal nonprofit organization or to continue with the collaboration structure. After a series of meetings with all participants, the group celebrated its success, thanked its membership, and transitioned to nonprofit organization status.

Conceptualizing collaboration as an evolutionary process offers public and nonprofit managers fuller, deeper, and practical insights into planning and diagnosing collaboration. The collaboration life cycle model presented in this chapter provides a practical lens for understanding both the explicit and implicit processes that are common to collaborative efforts. In addition, the chapter discusses the knowledge, skills, and abilities that evolve strategic collaboration practice.

The collaboration life cycle model builds on research suggesting that organizations tend to move through human-like stages of development. These stages include conception or formation; puberty and growth where they struggle with internal coordination; adulthood and mastery of the organization's internal and external environments; and, finally, old age where choices are made regarding revitalization, atrophy, survival on the margin, or death.[4] Collaborative activity also follows a similar life cycle of development,[5] moving from exploration to maturity and eventually reaching a formal end point. Unlike organizations where the goal is almost always maturity and long-term success, not all collaborative efforts have the goal of long-term sustainability. In fact, strategic collaborations are inherently temporary in nature. For example, some collaborative efforts may find interested parties coming together for a short series of meetings sufficient to address an issue with no decision to formalize the collaboration any further. Other collaborations lasting a decade or more are still thought to be transitory structures. As illustrated in the previous scenario, collaboration was initially the appropriate approach for this venture. With growth and increased programming demands, a more formal structure became necessary. Thus, the temporary nature of collaboration, where the dissolution of the collaboration at some point is inevitable, creates a more nuanced notion of a life cycle.

The stages of collaboration follow an expected pattern, with each stage shaping collaborative structure, processes, and outcomes (Figure 2.1.) The sections that follow describe each of the five stages and the types of decisions and behaviors for effective strategic collaboration practice. At each stage, collaboration participants face a new set of challenges and opportunities. How leaders and participants transition the collaboration from one stage to the next greatly influences the potential for overall success. The transitions are not necessarily obvious, and the same tactics that produce success in one stage can create frustration and failure in the next:

- ◾ Stage 1: Exploration—Conveners examine, formally or informally, the tool of collaboration.
- ◾ Stage 2: Formation—Initial structures and processes are developed.
- ◾ Stage 3: Growth—Participants struggle to build consensus on goals and begin implementation.
- ◾ Stage 4: Maturity—Ideal state of collaboration with participants actively engaged, resources available, and results shared.
- ◾ Stage 5: Ending:
  - – Stage 5a: Ending/dissolution—The collaboration's work is done and, ideally, celebrated.
  - – Stage 5b: Decline—An intermediary stage that may lead to renewal or dissolution based on participant and stakeholder perception of need for continued effort.

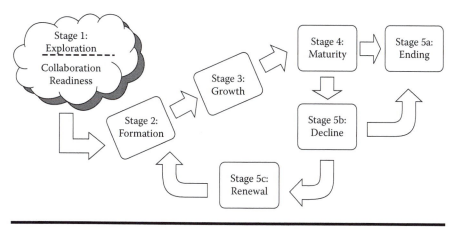

Figure 2.1 Life cycle model of collaboration.

■ Stage 5c: Renewal—Reinvention of structure, processes, and outcomes with goal of reentry into healthy collaboration life cycle.

Figure 2.1 represents the "ideal" progression allowing the collaboration to fully develop before ending or renewal is considered. In reality, the stages do not necessarily follow this pattern. Ending or dissolution can come during the growth stage, before the collaboration has reached a point that might produce the best success story. Also not easily seen in the figure is the ongoing influence of the collaboration's context, particularly the political, social, and economic dynamics that continually shape decision making and implementation.

Each stage is discussed next. The tables that follow each section compare conventional collaboration activities with strategic collaboration practice.

2.2 Stage 1—Exploration: Setting the Stage for Strategic Collaboration

Participants in Stage 1 explore whether collaboration is an appropriate approach given the collaboration context and focus on whether to proceed with a formal collaboration endeavor. The stage begins with informal and formal meetings held about the specific public problem that may lead to collaboration. These small or large meetings may be called by a convener or may start as side conversations at gatherings called for other purposes. In the exploration stage, interested parties tend to emphasize brainstorming and information gathering through informal discussions and reviewing opinions and expectations. While a collective effort may already be predetermined as the tactic of choice, collaboration may also emerge as shared expectations are created and participant relationships are established and strengthened among the organizers.

2.2.1 Implementing Strategic Collaboration Practice

The decision for strategic collaboration is made collectively and intentionally identifying the transition from exploration to formation stages. At this stage, individual organization leaders and individuals assess participation. Decisions to engage continue on an ongoing basis as organizations and individual participants make intentional and systematic choices about the level of effort and how long to remain active in the collaborative effort.

2.2.1.1 Intentional Decision for Strategic Collaboration

The intentional decision to create a formal collaboration is pivotal in Stage 1. Intentional decisions require "useable knowledge" as the foundation for information-based action.[6] Several types of useable knowledge are important in determining when to engage in and throughout the evolution of the strategic collaboration including contextual knowledge, technical knowledge, analytical knowledge, relational knowledge, and strategic knowledge (Table 2.1). The success conditions for collaboration discussed fully in Chapter 3 inform the initial decision about whether to engage in a strategic collaboration.

2.2.1.2 Suitable Participants and Resources Are at the Table

A sufficient number of participants are required to have the needed conversations about problems and gaps, existing programs, and shared priorities. Initial participants must be willing to spend the necessary time to collect and process needed information before the formal decision to collaborate can be made and to deliberate about shared risks and rewards. The exact number of initial participants depends on the number of key stakeholders in the policy area and geographic parameters of interest. Importantly, organizational representatives must see the connection between their organization's mission and goals and that of the collaboration and must bring the support of their organization's leadership.

The participants in early exploration meetings typically have a lot in common, particularly in the way they are defining "the agenda," thus raising the need to encourage diversity and inclusion when recruiting the next set of participants. A history of effective partnering enhances the early stages of collaboration. Conversely, a history of mistrust or system inequities related to race and class can have a negative influence. The key is to take the time to examine the important contextual factors pertinent to the potential collaboration. Who needs to be at the table is determined largely by the public problem focus and the context of the geographic area of concern. In general, a more inclusive approach produces the best strategic collaboration

Table 2.1   Usable Knowledge for Strategic Collaboration Practice

Type of Knowledge	Definition
Contextual	Knowledge related to the (1) pertinent history of collaboration including the existing nonprofit and government relationships and "turf" issues; (2) the political context including opinions of professional, political, and the general public that may openly or covertly block collaborative efforts; and (3) the current status of relevant programs and projects related to the collaboration's focus.
Technical	Knowledge related to the areas of expertise important to the proposed collaboration's focus or purpose, including relevant policy arenas.
Analytical	Knowledge related to framing problems and using analytical methods for decision making and problem solving to assess the utility of the proposed collaboration.
Relational	Knowledge about fostering and maintaining personal and institutional relationships needed for successful collaboration.
Strategic	Knowledge that assesses the connection of the potential participant organizations' missions, values, and priorities to that of the collaborative effort. Implicit is the ability to be reflective and realistic about access to and availability of resources, including social and human capital for the collaboration.

group. Therefore, examining a full range of possible participants is essential, including those agencies not typically at the table (e.g., faith-based agencies), those that are essential for implementation, and especially those that oppose change. Whether and how citizens will be involved should be carefully considered.[7] Whatever the decision, bridging cultural gaps in our diverse communities and integrating local knowledge is often critical for the collaboration's progress. While intentionally recruiting for broad representation is essential, participants also need to have interpersonal skills and a problem-solving perspective.[8]

Often the founding participants provide all or a large part of the resources required for start-up of the collaboration such as in-kind donations of employee time, space, and equipment. In addition, participants should be recruited who bring resources, broadly defined to include access to dollars or policymakers, skills and expertise (e.g., grant writing or current trend information), and the possibility of in-kind support.

2.2.1.3 A Champion Leads the Effort

Leadership is important throughout the collaboration's life cycle; however, in the early stages, an identified leader or champion can bring legitimacy and access that could otherwise take significant time to build. At the exploration and early formation stages, the champion plays the role of neutral convener or trusted broker in reframing issues, facilitating dialogue, and promoting the collaboration's efforts. This may be a person who was initially involved in the start-up or someone who is recruited to play the role. Of course, the "wrong" champion can step forward or be recruited. Thus, the rules and procedures established in the next stage, formation, are important to ensure that leadership transition is expected and occurs routinely.

Information gathering and brainstorming are key activities of the exploration stage (Figure 2.2). The amount, scope, and depth of information can be overwhelming. In the environment-focused scenario introduced earlier, the exploration stage was initiated and facilitated by a local foundation. The early discussions focused the group's priorities and expectations for a potential collaborative effort with an energetic leadership team emerging and the recruitment of a champion. Just as appropriately, the group might have determined that a collaborative effort was not needed. Successful transition to the next life cycle stage requires participants who maintain the collaboration's focus while encouraging new ways of thinking and doing as the design of the collaboration is developed.

2.3 Stage 2—Formation: Shaping the Strategic Collaboration

In Stage 2, the collaboration becomes reality. The common steps in this stage include the creation and approval of the collaboration's operational structure and procedures by the start-up or convening group. The structure provides the skeleton or frame of the collaboration for governance and decision making. In this stage, goals are also established, and action steps are developed. Finally, implementation begins.

Conventional Collaboration Activities		Strategic Collaboration Practice
• Conversations/meetings on a specific public problem or issue • Brainstorming and information gathering • Relationships established or continued with a focus on shared expectations		• Intentional decision for strategic collaboration. • Suitable participants and resources at the table. • A champion leads the effort.

Figure 2.2   Collaboration life cycle Stage 1: Exploration.

ASSIGNING THE COLLABORATION PARTICIPANT ROLE

One important question for collaborative participants is whether organizations should send a specified representative to the collaboration. While sending different representatives increases exposure of the collaboration to the organization (and vice versa), the use of a specific representative for as long a time period as possible allows for greater trust. As such, the practice of strategic collaboration requires organization leaders to carefully assign the participant role to individuals who not only have the capacity to "report back" to the organization as appropriate but also offer needed skills for helping the development of the collaboration.

2.3.1 Implementing Strategic Collaboration Practice

Decision-making processes in Stage 2 launch initial actions. At this stage, establishing a permanent organization structure (e.g., incorporating as a separate 501(c)(3)) is not typically recommended. Rather, the initial collaboration structures should design flexibility to respond to changes in the collaboration context and to further negotiate roles and responsibilities as the collaboration develops. Again, strategic collaboration takes an intentional and systematic approach to the design of collaboration structure, processes, and outcomes that is all too often missing when collaborative effort proceeds in an *ad hoc* manner.

2.3.1.1 Sharpen Mission/Vision during Process-Oriented Planning

As the collaboration begins, the important processes of articulating desired results through planning and goal setting, ongoing processes such as periodic retreats, revisiting priorities at each meeting, and regular written and verbal reporting related to outcomes are keys to a strategic orientation. In the formation stage, participants must clarify the collaboration's vision, mission, and expected outcomes if longer-term success is to be achieved. While these visioning processes are time-consuming, they are essential. If not handled sufficiently with skilled facilitation and patience, the lack of consensus on important priorities will frustrate the work of the collaboration. Participants may come and go throughout the collaboration life cycle, but a clearly defined mission and goals that plan success at multiple achievement points (e.g., early, short term, long term) keep the effort focused. Deliberately created agendas for meetings and overall collaboration planning are useful for focused and productive processes. (See Appendix E as a resource for meetings and agendas.)

2.3.1.2 Create Structures and Processes That Ensure Broad Stakeholder Participation

In strategic collaboration, founders should attend carefully to the development of the collaboration's structure, focusing on the rules of governance and decision making, role and responsibilities of key individuals and organizations, and important timeframes while at the same time ensuring diverse and representative participation. Documents such as bylaws, organizing principles or guidelines, and organization charts should answer essential questions about leadership (e.g., officer selection, committees and subcommittees), decision-making processes, authority and accountability, resource availability and allocation, membership or participant eligibility, and staff selection and oversight. Importantly, at this stage the criteria and expectations for participation (or membership) should be clearly articulated. As structure and operations are designed and implementation is begun, the role of primary and secondary stakeholders must be detailed and risks and rewards explicitly considered. (See Appendix D for a matrix of collaboration participant roles.)

In the initial stages of collaboration, a smaller group may be more useful, allowing for increased nimbleness. As the formation stage concludes and inclusiveness becomes important, the number of participants will increase. Tactics such as snowball recruitment can help broaden the pool of potential participants. In snowball recruitment, current participants are asked to identify possible recruits based on certain criteria such as expertise or experience. If the collaboration is large, the creation of an advisory committee or steering group with delegated authority and time limits for office, similar to a board of directors, can be a useful design. If this model is used, strategies for assuring that all participants are informed and engaged, such as newsletters, regular larger group meetings, and committee assignments, must be developed.

Collaboration relationships can be facilitated with letters of commitment, participant agreements, or memorandums of understanding from each of the participating organizations. These documents articulate the organization's and individual's commitment to the collaboration, specify expectations of benefits and allocated resources (e.g., representative's time), and clarify authority.[9] (See Appendix B for a collaboration operations guidelines sample and Appendix C for a participant agreement.)

2.3.1.3 Build Trust through Ethical Communication and Operations

With the processes essential to the formation stage comes a certain amount of tension requiring participants to understand and embrace change processes and exercise good judgment. The relationships and trust built among participants in the formalization stage allow the collaboration to weather the transition to the next stage and to achieve success. Thus, an emphasis of strategic practice is the creation of mutually beneficial relationships that shape the culture and norms of the collaboration. Trust is argued by many as a key ingredient in successful collaborations. The development of trust is complex, is influenced by many factors including individual personalities, past experiences with collaboration, and previous relationships with other participants, and is often gained by taking small successful steps leading to more ambitious opportunities. Very important at this stage is the development of the collaboration culture, through paced discussions at retreats and planning meetings, so that leaders and participants quickly address inappropriate or negative behavior such as bullying or power plays and assure that turf protection and other hidden agendas are faced rather than ignored.

The knowledge, skills, and abilities that each individual brings to the collaboration greatly influence the process. Reciprocity, or a shared stake, is another important component of a successful collaborative process. All participants should share the costs and benefits (although not necessarily equally) of the collaboration's success or failure. Trust is further enhanced by the use of ongoing control and accountability tools for budgeting and performance measurement. Strategic collaboration practice emphasizes open communication of expectations, risks and rewards, the appropriate management of conflict, and inclusive decision making to assure that shared understanding, ownership, and transparency create an ethical foundation for the development of trust. Again, meeting agendas can be useful tools for the leadership team in assuring that time is allocated for addressing these important points.

2.3.1.4 Identify and Foster Early Success

Initial planning processes should build in early, achievable goals. Success via the tactic of identifying "low-hanging fruit," including process-oriented goals as initial outcome measures, provides a positive reward for the early hard work of establishing a strategic collaboration. Examples of early success vary widely from attracting new stakeholders to the table or securing financial support to media attention and publishing an initial website. These early successes not only allow participants to recognize that their labor can bring positive results but also offer important information for participants to take back to their home agencies and for marketing the collaboration to external stakeholders.

Transitioning from Stage 2 to Stage 3 is straightforward. In the environment scenario, the formation stage (Figure 2.3) began as the group identified a leadership team and recruited an appropriate nonprofit agency to serve as a fiscal agent. The group used planning processes, such as a retreat, and regular meetings to build a common vision for the participants and developed procedures for decision making and participant recruitment. They also began immediately to publicize their initial activities, generating stories on local television and interest by local corporations. When all of the important structure, process, and outcome elements are in place and implementation activity is under way, Stage 3 has begun!

Conventional Collaboration Activities	Strategic Collaboration Practice
• Develop collaborative structure and operating procedures and begin implementation. • Define parameters and expectations of participation. • Develop goals/action plans and begin implementation.	• Sharpen mission/vision during process-oriented planning. • Create structures and processes that ensure broad stakeholder participation. • Build trust through ethical communication and operations. • Identify and foster early success.

Figure 2.3   Collaboration life cycle Stage 2: Formation.

2.4 Stage 3—Growth: Strengthening Collaboration Processes

In the growth stage (Figure 2.4), planning and priority setting continue to be emphasized, but operational processes, such as participant recruitment and monitoring, are routinized. Common at this stage is the introduction of new participants, either due to growth in the number of participants or as original participants choose to step out and new members are recruited. As a result, this stage can be one of frustration and unrealized opportunity as the group appears to be inefficient in rehashing priorities and processes. Just as adolescents test boundaries and struggle to identify what they will "be when they grow up," at this stage the collaboration is verifying its vision, mission, and priorities.

2.4.1 Implementing Strategic Collaboration Practice

The collaboration's authenticity or legitimacy is of vital concern at this stage. As tensions emerge, persistent "nay-sayers" and "fence-sitters" must be dealt with head-on and systematically by building and managing the agenda, facilitating participant involvement and engagement (and disengagement when necessary), assuring effective communication, and balancing risk and reward.

Conventional Collaboration Activities	Strategic Collaboration Practice
• Continued planning and priority setting. • Operation implementation and monitoring strategies routinized. • Ongoing cycle to participant recruitment and exit.	• Foster innovation and creativity. • Emphasize cooperation and new, shared understanding • Focus on information dissemination and feedback

Figure 2.4   Collaboration life cycle Stage 3: Growth.

2.4.1.1 Promote Innovation and Creativity

Strategic practice focuses on continual reflection and assessment, emphasizing new ways of thinking and acting rather than creating another static bureaucracy or silo-based structure that may stifle innovation. As the group grows in size, the temptation is to build a hierarchy that resembles traditional organization structures, assuming this will increase efficiency and accountability. However, at this point, leaders must concentrate on how to facilitate the collaboration as an organic and temporary entity, keeping the boundaries open to encourage flexibility so that redesign can occur and innovation is cultivated. Redesign may include changes in the governance structure, creating or redefining task forces, introducing new activities, or hiring staff. Thus, ongoing planning and priority setting processes, such as retreats and fact-gathering sessions, can be used to maintain the collaboration's vibrancy. Attention to ongoing priority setting allows new ideas and opportunities to surface while openly maintaining focus on agreed upon priorities. For example, as new program opportunities arise, decisions must be transparent and inclusive to maintain trust and to keep the collaboration moving forward. As a result, decision-making processes shape and sharpen the collaboration's culture, values, and norms.

2.4.1.2 Emphasize Cooperation and New, Shared Understandings

Essential at this stage are continuing processes that ensure open and ethical communication, cooperation rather than competition, and the creation of new, shared priorities and understandings. Because participants have little experience in this more fluid setting and new participants with new ideas and priorities are joining the collaboration, conflict often emerges. New participant orientation processes, regular retreats, and productive, open meetings are key platforms for creating authentic and shared understandings about the mission, and goals of the collaboration enable conflict to be managed. Sufficient process time to develop a common and shared vocabulary around desired results, to clarify decision-making rules, and to provide opportunity for input, feedback, and analysis is needed to lay the groundwork for creative thinking and innovation.

Another opportunity for building cooperative relationships is in the intentional promotion of the collaboration and its results. "Taking the collaboration public" may at first create a competitive tension with questions about who or what organization gets credit. Deliberate work to include all participants in the collaboration's visibility efforts increases trust and cooperation and consequently leads to greater overall impacts. Promotional tactics include press releases, regular public meetings, newsletters to key external stakeholders, and public forums.

2.4.1.3 Focus on Information Dissemination and Feedback

As the backbone of strategic collaboration operations, regular communication systems that disseminate important and timely information as well as provide avenues for meaningful feedback are critical. Redundant information sharing by using multiple strategies (e.g., e-mail, other Web-based means such as Google Sites, newsletters, and in-person meetings) is necessary to maximize internal communication. In addition, information dissemination addresses accountability, stakeholder management, and collaboration legitimacy needs. Budgeting and performance measurement tools can be used to ensure control and accountability. The resulting processes and findings become vehicles for ongoing discussion and further collaboration program development. If the outcomes are not met or the investment is not viewed as mutually and appropriately shared, then participants will reduce their involvement or exit the collaboration. Time-limited task forces, workgroups, or committees with concrete deliverables are useful for involving many people in the work of a collaboration. As participants engage in activities that lead to shared and expected outcomes, their commitment to invest continues and strengthens, and, importantly, the groundwork for innovative thinking and acting is created.

Defining the transition from Stage 3 to Stage 4 is subtle. While Stage 3 "works through" reiterative disagreements, Stage 4 embraces necessary conflict as important to enhancing vibrancy and innovation. In the environment scenario, the leadership team members recognized that their early success in recruiting a large number of active participants meant they needed to restructure to a steering committee and task force model. This restructuring allowed participants to focus their energies and activities on activities that were the most meaningful to them individually and to their home organizations, while the steering committee was charged with assuring that the overall collaboration remained focused. As expected, conflict occurred at both the steering committee and task force levels, but the time put into developing shared goals and priorities paid off in keeping the effort productive and cohesive. While at Stage 3 operations and processes become routine, Stage 4 fights complacency to assure meaningful results.

2.5 Stage 4—Maturity: Making a Difference

The maturity stage (Figure 2.5) is the ideal state of development for any collaboration. As the collaboration achieves this stage, resources including funding, participation, and access are stable, while strategies are in place for ongoing planning, evaluation, and quality improvement. Collaboration results are shared with stakeholders, and collaboration purposes are assessed.

Conventional Collaboration Activities		Strategic Collaboration Practice
• Resources stabilized. • Planning, evaluation, and revision strategies continued. • Collaborative activity visible.		• Balance stability with innovation. • Remain mission-driven and results oriented. • Build a deeper bench.

Figure 2.5   Collaboration life cycle Stage 4: Maturity.

2.5.1 Implementing Strategic Collaboration Practice

Challenges for strategic practice at this stage focus on decision making that balances the current stability and success with the anticipated future steps required to maintain vibrancy.

2.5.1.1 Balance Stability with Innovation

Just as organizations seek an equilibrium state for continued survival, strategic collaborations also seek stability. In the maturity stage, successful collaboration operations bring expected resources and outcomes; however, this sense of stability must be balanced with continued outward-looking assessment processes that scan the collaboration context and with internal processes that encourage innovative thinking and action. New information and ideas must be valued to assure currency of continued decision making and implementation. Tactics such as site visits and guest speakers can energize participants to think in new ways (see Principle 5 in Chapter 4). This balance of maintaining while creating is essential to keep the collaboration vibrant. Given the inherent temporary nature of collaboration, the appropriateness of ending (Stage 5 discussed herein) is also explicitly on the table.

2.5.1.2 Remain Mission Driven and Results Oriented

The challenge for collaboration leaders is to maintain a sense of urgency related to the problem area of focus so that participants continue to understand their role of "revolutionary" rather than caretaker, the role typical in mature organizations. The situation or context that originally instigated the collaboration may have evolved, calling for revision of the overall mission and goals of the collaboration to keep in step with the changing context. Regular attention to performance assessment and progress toward goals with sufficient time for meaningful dialogue with participants and stakeholders is crucial (see Principle 6 in Chapter 4).

2.5.1.3 Build a Deeper Leadership Bench

The structure of a strategic collaboration should identify officers and terms of office in its operating guidelines. (See Appendix B for an example of collaboration operating guidelines.) As the collaboration progresses, the guidelines related to the leadership structure may need new attention. If a steering or advisory committee is used, it may need to change in size related to the number of active participants (i.e., more participants typically require a larger governing body or integrated committee structure) and to create a more clear-cut path of leadership (e.g., chair of the nominating committee raises to the chair-elect role). To assure strong leadership, a nominating committee may need a clearly defined role so that consideration is given to a variety of factors in building a leadership team, including enthusiasm for the collaboration, success in a committee role, and time/energy commitments. A governance committee may also be necessary to develop an integrated committee structure that encourages the involvement of all current collaboration participants and thoughtfully enlarges the leadership pool. Participant training, site visits, or expert consultations in technical, legal, or policy areas related to the collaboration's focus or in the skills of collaboration may prove useful.

The strategic collaboration may remain at Stage 4: Maturity for an indefinite period of time until key stakeholders determine that goals have been reached or will never be reached. In the environment scenario, the collaboration moved quickly to the point of maturity implementing innovative programs, bringing in new funding, and involving a wide range of stakeholders. As opportunities increased, the collaboration leaders and participants determined that greater success could be achieved by transition to permanent nonprofit organization status.

2.6 Stage 5—Ending: The Mortal Nature of Collaboration

Following Stage 4: Maturity, the collaboration moves into one of three ending stages: dissolution, decline, or renewal. These are the least studied stages of the collaboration life cycle. The decline stage is an intermediary step resulting in dissolution or reinvention. With strategic collaboration viewed as a temporary means for reaching desired ends, mortality is assumed. In fact, the dissolution of the existing collaboration structure may be its most critical accomplishment toward achieving more far-reaching impacts. The environment scenario introduced one type of ending with the collaboration converting to nonprofit organization status. Another ending story could be a local government agency taking on the mission and activities of the earlier collaboration. A less satisfactory ending can also be envisioned if the participants stopped attending meetings and following through on committee assignments, if events no longer attracted interested community members, and if the once-innovative programs such as the high school competition no longer received entries. With the declining path, leaders must determine whether the collaboration's mission remains relevant enough to attract a new set of stakeholders adequate for renewal or the time is right to officially dissolve the collaboration.

Too often, a collaboration fades away with no intentionality. Tackling each ending stage path deliberately brings symbolic closure to the current effort and lays the foundation for a new collaboration to emerge when needed.

2.6.1 Stage 5a—Ending

Ending or dissolution may result because (1) the collaboration has successfully resolved the problem or issue that it was formed to address, or (2) participants/stakeholders determine that the current collaborative effort has gone as far as it can go. Both of these are a satisfactory ending (Figure 2.6). Regardless of why the collaboration is dissolving, the collaborative effort should recognize individual effort and share results broadly. More commonly, the collaboration would experience a level of decline that would lead participants to implicitly question its continuing value (see Stage 5b: Decline) and would begin to exit, either explicitly through resignation or implicitly by reducing participation.

2.6.1.1 Implementing Strategic Collaboration Practice

Strategic collaboration practice stresses deliberate and open processes in the decision to dissolve, emphasizing that the collaboration was one step in addressing the problem area of focus. Dissolution may lead to a reinvention of the collaboration's structure, processes, and outcomes in the form of a new collaborative effort or a totally different form such as permanent organization or a formalized partnership. Strategic practice for the dissolution stage requires consideration of the possible long-term impacts of the collaboration as well as opportunities for new funding and new collaborative opportunities.

2.6.1.1.1 Act with Intentionality

Facilitating future collaboration and furthering relationships should be the driving force as the collaboration ends. The participants and important stakeholders should

Conventional Collaboration Activities		Strategic Collaboration Practice
• Recognition • Sharing results	⟹	• Act with intentionality. • Seek expert assistance. • Archive processes, participants, and impacts. • Be transparent.

Figure 2.6   Collaboration life cycle Stage 5a: Ending/Dissolution.

make the intentional decision to end the collaboration and to develop ending processes that reflect open, ethical decision making to formalize closure of the effort. The topic of ending the collaboration should be on the formal agenda with current leaders specifically invited and fully engaged in the deliberations. Recognition and celebration events are essential to acknowledge the effort of individuals and organizations as well as the results and impacts achieved.

2.6.1.1.2 Seek Expert Assistance

As the dissolution decision is made, specific experts may be needed including lawyers, accountants, or marketers. Collaboration participants and leaders should not hesitate to bring in required knowledge and skill so that the ending process is handled with appropriate attention.

2.6.1.1.3 Archive Processes, Participants, and Impacts

To set the groundwork for future success in related collaborative efforts, the processes, participants, and impacts of the collaboration should be documented in an accessible format. Meeting notes, reports, and other products should be gathered. A local public library or a website may be appropriate archival locations. A final report that highlights, summarizes, and celebrates the effort and impacts can record important details, participants, and recommendations. Events may be held to recognize key participants and to publicize the overall impacts of the group's work. Importantly, archiving documents allows future interested parties to learn from the collaboration's work and to avoid unnecessary pitfalls.

2.6.1.1.4 Be Transparent

Finally, collaboration operations should conclude with honor by informing current and past participants and stakeholders, including funders, of the collaboration's dissolution and by emphasizing positive impacts, lessons learned, and recommendations for future action.

2.6.2 Stage 5b—Decline

In the decline stage, the collaboration has lost its focus and energy. It may now exist in "name only" or on the margin with membership numbers decreasing, meeting attendance dropping, resources uncertain and constrained, and participants frustrated. The emphasis of meetings is survival with a status quo vision.

Table 2.2   Diagnosing Collaboration Decline

• Meeting attendance decreases.
• Participants frustrated and dropping out.
• Resources uncertain and constrained.
• Status Quo emphasized in decision making.

2.6.2 *Implementing Strategic Collaboration Practice*

Strategic collaborative practice does not take a passive posture, which has the collaboration fading away with loose ends. Rather, the ending stage of decline becomes an intermediate step as participants intentionally choose closure or renewal.

2.6.2.1 *Diagnose Collaboration "Pathologies"*

The strategic task at this point is to investigate why the collaboration is failing by examining the "pathologies" of the participants, processes, and external context. This discovery process requires participants to communicate openly and to brainstorm all possible failure reasons. The intent is not to place blame but to understand what happened (Table 2.2; Figure 2.7) and to plan next steps. One tool for beginning this type of discussion is "Taking the Collaboration Temperature: Assessing Level of Frustration" (Chapter 4, Table 4.6). This diagnosis of possible pathologies is essential to determine whether the collaboration should dissolve or entertain renewal.

2.6.2.2 *Create Reality-Based Analysis Processes*

After the problems and barriers are recognized, collaboration leaders and participants must move beyond normative and "wishful" thinking. Although potentially time-consuming, a return to the design processes of the formation stage is necessary before a grounded decision about the future directions of the collaboration can be made.

Conventional Collaboration Activities		Strategic Collaboration Practice
▪ Meeting attendance drops		▪ Diagnose "pathologies."
▪ Participants frustrated		▪ Seek "outside" perspective.
▪ Resources uncertain		▪ Create reality-based analysis processes.
▪ Emphasis on status quo		▪ Be purposeful about what's next.

Figure 2.7   Collaboration life cycle Stage 5b: Ending/Decline.

2.6.2.3 Seek Outside Perspective, When Appropriate

Often outside experts or facilitators are needed early in this stage. Participants have lost a rational perspective and can "no longer see the forest for the trees." Outsiders bring an important neutral perspective to identify barriers, problems, and opportunities.

2.6.2.4 Be Purposeful about What's Next

As with every part of the strategic collaboration process, the deliberate and intentional decision about the next step is critical. Will the collaboration move to formal dissolution and closure or will a conscious effort be given to renewing the collaboration toward identified outcomes? With an understanding of the "pathologies" of the existing collaboration, a real-world perspective on alternatives, and, if necessary, the assistance of an outside expert, collaboration leaders and participants can explore options—including the costs and benefits, both short term and long term, of continued operation. One crucial assessment is assessing the extent of reinvention necessary to continue the collaboration. If major reinvention is required, it may be better, particularly for longer-term impacts, for the current collaboration to consciously dissolve (see Stage 5a, previously discussed) and for a new, restructured effort to be purposefully initiated.

2.6.3 Stage 5c—Renewal

While organizational renewal or turnaround is commonplace, comprehensive collaboration reinvention occurs infrequently. Because collaborations are temporary structures where participants must juggle their other responsibilities and often experience collaboration fatigue, dissolution is more likely. However, collaboration participants may make the active choice for reinvention. If renewal is intentionally determined, steps are taken to prepare the collaboration for reentering the active collaboration life cycle. This may include the recruitment of participants, often those previously connected to the collaborative effort as well as new participants, and the initiation of processes for examining and revising the mission (Figure 2.8). If renewal is not successful, the decision to end the collaboration remains an option.

Conventional Collaboration Activities		**Strategic Collaboration Practice**
• New participants recruited/previous participants re-connected • Purpose is clarified or revised		• Bring new perspective to the table. • Hold periodic "retreats". • Deliberate redesign of structure and processes. • Restore legitimacy.

Figure 2.8   Collaboration life cycle Stage 5c: Ending/Renewal.

2.6.4 Implementing Strategic Collaboration Practice

Setting the groundwork for successful renewal of strategic collaboration mirrors earlier work in building the collaboration, particularly attention to who is at the table and what they bring, restructuring operations and processes, and bringing newfound credibility to the effort.

2.6.4.1 Bring New Perspective to the Table

Key to a successful renewal is the commitment level of collaboration participants and leaders. Typically new participants and leaders are needed for successful renewal. Ideally this is done in a way that honors past leaders, participants, and funders. Recruitment processes should emphasize enlisting individuals to the collaboration who bring creative thinking and a willingness (and courage) to move out of the status quo and commitment to revisiting the collaboration's mission and priorities.

2.6.4.2 Hold Periodic Retreats

Group renewal processes, such as retreats, will be necessary for building trust, furthering shared understanding, and reenergizing commitment to priorities. Starting out with these important processes can put the collaboration on the fast track in preparation for reentering the early life cycle stages.

2.6.4.3 Deliberate Redesign of Structure and Processes

The new direction typically requires an intentional and systematic rethinking of operational processes. This major restructuring should be deliberate with a focus on innovative thinking and desired outcomes or results.

2.6.4.4 Restore Legitimacy

The final step for successful renewal is the rebuilding of key stakeholder's perception of legitimacy about the collaboration. Demonstrating the positive turnaround to previous participants, funders, and other key stakeholders sets the opportunity for restoring credibility and opening doors for future relationship development.

2.7 Concluding Points

The environmental scenario used at the beginning of this chapter illustrates how conveners interpreted their context to decide that a collaborative structure was the most appropriate organizing model to energize the community to adopt environmental activities. With success, the collaborative structure no longer fit with the growing demands and a more formal, permanent structure was needed to guide the growing diversity of environmental programming. The scenario demonstrates the need to carefully align approach to context while reinforcing the essential premise that strategic collaboration is a nonpermanent arrangement that evolves in concert with goals and priorities of leaders, participants, and external stakeholders.

The collaboration life cycle model provides an evolutionary perspective useful for public and nonprofit managers. The model discusses core decisions and dynamics to be addressed at each stage. Table 2.3 sequentially summarizes the important activities throughout a collaboration life cycle. Of course, the steps may occur out of order and may need to be repeated to achieve collaboration success.

The collaboration life cycle model is also useful when analyzing or diagnosing an existing collaboration to systematically introduce changes to achieve success. In addition to emphasizing the actions and perspectives required to move from conventional collaboration to strategic collaboration, the model highlights two important insights for success. First, prior positive relationships among the participants allow the collaboration to progress quickly through the early stages. When participants already know each other and have a common understanding of relevant contextual and issue-based factors, the time necessary to develop shared purpose and goals is reduced while commitment to the effort is increased. The second insight emphasizes the importance of keeping participants engaged throughout the collaboration's evolution, recognizing that the knowledge, skills, and abilities and the related participant roles change at each stage. In addition to open and regular communication processes, successful transitioning between stages often requires training and development for participants. The leadership role may need to evolve as well. While in the early stages an idea champion is important for bringing people together and energizing the effort, a different type of leader—one more focused on process—becomes essential for assuring that the needs of all participants are addressed and that the effort maintains a focus on reaching designated outcomes.[10]

The periods of transition from one collaboration life cycle stage to the next are opportunities for participants to assess progress, to reconsider commitment, and to shift priorities as necessary. However, the first key transition point in the exploration stage is the decision about whether to use strategic collaboration. Chapter 4 examines the important factors for collaboration readiness to assist conveners with this crucial decision.

Table 2.3   Steps of Strategic Collaboration

1. An idea emerges:

   • From an informal group or a champion.

   • Related to a public problem, issue, or need.

   • Requiring cross-organization, cross-discipline, or cross-sector perspective and action.

2. Recruit a set of individuals and hold meetings to discuss the idea.

3. Group brainstorms and gathers useful information about:

   • Related efforts locally, regionally, nationally, and globally.

   • Current constraints and opportunities.

   • Desired and expected results.

4. Group decides whether strategic collaboration is appropriate (see Chapter 4 for discussion of collaborative readiness).

If the Decision Is Yes:

5. Recruit champions as chairs or conveners:

   • from existing convening group or new to the effort

   • to serve as visible face for the collaboration

6. Identify and recruit participants for collaboration with attention to creating a group that is

   • diverse and inclusive

   • offers needed expertise and resources

   • possesses skills and time for collaborating

7. Hold meetings, retreats, workshops, conferences, and/or public forums to

   • Gather information.

   • Make decisions about vision, mission, goals, and priorities.

   • Establish operating guidelines including structure and decision-making procedures.

   • Develop and sign initial letters of commitment, participant agreements, or memorandums of understanding.

(continued)

Table 2.3   Steps of Strategic Collaboration (Continued)

> - Build and strengthen participant relationships through orientation sessions and professional development exercises related to collaboration.
>
> - Identify measures for success: early, intermediate, and long term.
>
> - Keep the focus on mission and expected results.
>
> 8.   Work of the collaboration is under way through staff, committees, and task forces.
>
> 9.   Assess implementation progress through:
>
>   - Monitoring processes and outcomes.
>
>   - Reporting processes and results to participants and stakeholders via meetings, mailings, website, press releases.
>
>   - Creating feedback opportunities so that interested parties can comment, reflect, and offer input.
>
> 10.   Hold periodic site visits, public forums, expert presentations, and conferences to:
>
>   - Stimulate creative thinking.
>
>   - Share new information and learning.
>
>   - Build external stakeholder interest and commitment.
>
> 11.   Hold annual (or regular) sessions and/or retreats to
>
>   - Revisit the collaboration's vision, priorities, and goals using results and new information to inform processes.
>
>   - Revise organization guidelines as appropriate.
>
>   - Revise mission, priorities, goals, and action plans as appropriate.
>
>   - Assure productive leadership transitions.
>
>   - Continue new member orientation as needed.
>
> 12.   Celebrate successes internally and externally (early and ongoing).
>
>   - Recognize the accomplishments and lessons learned.
>
>   - Recognize new collaboration members.
>
>   - Disseminate broadly to participants, stakeholders, and media.

Table 2.3   Steps of Strategic Collaboration (Continued)

13.   Reach the end of the collaboration:

- Dissolving the collaboration:

  o Meet to decide to end the collaboration.

  o Hold event to celebrate accomplishments.

  o Document and archive processes, results, and learning.

  o Inform participants, funders, and other stakeholders.

- Recognizing decline:

  o Hold meetings to diagnose the causes of decline.

  o Invite consultant or expert to assist in understanding the decline.

  o Evaluate whether the decline can or should be reversed or whether the collaboration should end.

  o Inform funders, participants, and other stakeholders.

- Choosing renewal:

  o Recruit new leaders and participants for the collaboration.

  o Hold retreats and forums to develop shared understanding of collaboration's role.

  o Redesign operating guidelines for new mission, priorities, structure, and processes.

    ▪ Use experts and consultants.

    ▪ Review professional practice and research literature.

  o Develop and implement strategies to reconnect with funders, participants, and other stakeholders regarding new vision and plans.

Endnotes

1. For examples, see J.J. Kiefer and R.S. Montjoy, Incrementalism before the Storm: Network Performance for the Evacuation of New Orleans, *Public Administration Review* 66 (Special Issue on Collaborative Public Management): 122–130, 2006; A.K. Donahue, The Space Shuttle Columbia Recovery Operation: How Collaboration Enabled Disaster Response, *Public Administration Review 66* (supplement): 141–142, 2006; G. Simo and A.L. Bies, The Role of Nonprofits in Disaster Response: An Expanded Model of Cross-Sector Collaboration, *Public Administration Review 67* (Supplement): 125–142, 2007.

2. Private foundations in particular have played a significant role in influencing collaboration. For examples, see F. Delfin and S. Tang, Philanthropic Strategies in Place-Based, Collaborative Land Conservation: The Packard Foundation's Conserving California Landscape Initiative, *Nonprofit and Voluntary Sector Quarterly, 35* (3): 405–429, 2006; L. Silver, Negotiating the Antipoverty Agenda: Foundations, Community Organizations, and Comprehensive Community Initiatives, *Nonprofit and Voluntary Sector Quarterly, 33* (4): 606–628, 2004. Funding from advocacy organizations also has political implications as they inherently represent particularistic interests. See C. Brecher and O. Wise, Looking a Gift Horse in the Mouth: Challenges in Managing Philanthropic Support for Public Services, *Public Administration Review, 68* (Special Issue): S146–S161, 2008.

3. See S. Goldsmith and W. Eggers, *Governing by Network: The New Shape of the Public Sector* (Washington, DC: Brookings Institution Press, 2004); J. Bryson, B.C. Crosby, and M. Stone, The Design and Implementation of Cross-Sector Collaborations: Propositions from the Literature, *Public Administration Review, 66* (Supplement): 44–55, 2006; R. O'Leary and L. Bingham, Conclusion: Conflict and Collaboration in Networks, *International Public Management Journal, 10* (1): 103–109, 2007; E. Weber and A. Khademian, Wicked Problems, Knowledge Challenges, and Collaborative Capacity Builders in Network Settings, *Public Administration Review, 68* (2): 334–349, 2008; Weber, 2009, Explaining Institutional Change in Tough Cases of Collaboration: "Ideas" in the Blackfoot Watershed, *Public Administration Review, 69* (2): 314–327, 2009.

4. The organization life cycle research is a part of a larger research theme: organization ecology. Focused mainly on commercial organizations, the research looks at why new organizations form and why old ones die using a selection and adaptation or environmental vulnerability lens. See C.R. Carroll and M.T. Hannan, *The Demography of Corporations and Industries* (Princeton, NJ: Princeton University Press, 2000); I. Adizes, *Corporate Life cycles: How and Why Corporations Grow, Die and What to Do about It* (Englewood Cliffs, NJ: Prentice Hall, 1988); D.A. Whetten, Issues in Organization Decline, In *Readings in Organizational Decline: Frameworks, Research and Prescriptions,* ed. K.S. Cameron, T.I. Sutton, and Whetten (Cambridge, MA: Ballinger Publishing, 1988), pp. 3–19; H. Mintzberg, Power and organization life cycles, *Academy of Management Review, 9,* 207–224, 1984; R. Quinn and K. Cameron, Organization Life Cycles and Shifting Criteria of Effectiveness: Some Preliminary Evidence, *Management Science, 29*: 33–51, 1983; J.R. Kimberly and R.H. Miles, *The Organizational Life Cycle* (San Francisco: Jossey-Bass, 1980); S.K. Stevens, *Nonprofit Life cycles: Stage-Based Wisdom for Nonprofit Capacity* (Long Lake, MN: Stagewise Enterprises, Inc., 2003); M. Archibald, An Organizational Ecology of National Self-Help/Mutual-Aid Organizations. *Nonprofit Voluntary Sector Quarterly, 36* (4): 598–621, 2007.

5. Winer and Ray suggest four stages of collaboration progression. Stage One focuses on individual-to-individual achieved results and describes the very beginning work of collaboration including bringing participants together around a shared vision, building trust among those participants, and specifying the separate desired results of participation. Stage Two moves from individual to organization requiring the original participants involved to work with the other organization members toward the collaboration effort. Stage Three highlights organization-to-organization work as joint systems are established, results are evaluated, and renewal activities are undertaken to implement the shared vision. Finally, Stage Four assures the continuity

of efforts through collaboration to community work, as activities shift to creating visibility of the collaboration and to changes that bring new individuals and organizations to the collaboration to address changing problems and opportunities. M. Winer and Ray, *Collaboration Handbook* (St. Paul, MN: Amhurst H. Wilder Foundation, 1994).

6. D. Norris-Tirrell and J. Clay, The Production of Useable Knowledge, In *Handbook of Organization Consultation*, ed. R.T. Golembiewski (New York: Marcel Dekker, 2000), pp. 829–834.

7. The design of citizen engagement requires a strategic perspective. Cooper, Bryer, and Meek describe five dimensions of citizen engagement in collaboration that address key questions that should be considered: (1) who is involved; (2) who initiates civic engagement; (3) why are citizens involved; (4) where does the engagement take place; and (5) how are citizens involved. T.L. Cooper, T.A. Bryer, and J.W. Meek, Citizen-Centered Collaborative Public Management, *Public Administration Review,* 66 (Supplement 1): 76–88, 2006. There are also inherent tensions in choices about citizen engagement with no one approach likely able to satisfy legitimacy, justice, and effectiveness. A. Fung, Varieties of Participation in Complex Governance, *Public Administration Review,* 66 (Supplement): 66–75, 2006.

8. E. Bardach, *Getting Agencies to Work Together: The Practice and Theory of Managerial Craftsmanship* (Washington, DC: Brookings Institution Press, 1998); Goldsmith and Eggers, *Governing by Network*; M. McGuire, Collaborative Public Management: Assessing What We Know and How We Know It, *Public Administration Review,* 66 (Supplement): 33–43, 2006; H. Getha-Taylor, Identifying Collaborative Competencies, *Review of Public Personnel Administration,* 28 (2): 103–119, 2008; Weber and Khademian, Managing Collaborative Processes: Common Practices, Uncommon Circumstances. *Administration & Society,* 40 (5): 431–464, 2008.

9. Winer and Ray, *Collaboration Handbook*, p. 74.

10. Takahashi and Smutny refer to these different leadership roles as the collaborative entrepreneur and the collaborative manager. L.M. Takahashi and G. Smutny, Collaborative Windows and Organizational Governance: Exploring the Formation and Demise of Social Service Partnerships, *Nonprofit and Voluntary Sector Quarterly,* 31 (2): 165–185, 2002.

Chapter 3

Assessing Collaborative Readiness: The Missing Strategic Step

Joy A. Clay and Dorothy Norris-Tirrell

Contents

3.1 Introduction

When to employ a strategic collaboration approach is a critical question for community leaders, public and nonprofit managers, funders, and citizens as they wrestle with the many problems on the public agenda. As illustrated in the following scenario, the challenge is in being systematic and purposeful about the decision to plunge into collaboration.

The key is to be purposeful about the decision to jump into a community-wide strategic collaboration. This requires potential collaboration participants and leaders to be insightful about the history of past collaborative efforts, how the agency is perceived as a collaborator within the community, the risks of proceeding (or not proceeding) with involvement, and the level of commitment that is most appropriate at this time. Although the description presented is a public health scenario, the implications apply broadly across public policy arenas. This chapter guides conveners in the collaborative readiness analysis process.

Healthy People 2010 is an example of a strategic collaboration at a national level. Building from earlier national health promotion efforts, a wide-ranging network has been created to guide the national health promotion effort to increase the quality and years of healthy life and to eliminate health disparities. Using a collaborative process with the U.S. Department of Health and Human Services (DHHS) as the lead agency, government, nonprofit, and private organizations, professionals, and advocates from around the country developed a list of health indicators to strategically focus the effort. Integrating accountability, the National Center for Health Statistics has implemented a supporting collaborative process to monitor and report on progress of each of the indicators, collecting data from a broad array of collaborating agencies and organizations.[1]

The two broad goals and more specific health indicators or benchmarks are intended to serve as a basis for local-level community planning and action. Moving the Healthy People 2010 initiative to the local level requires public health directors to determine the extent of the leadership and support role the agency should take in creating a community-level collaboration. While concerned whether other key stakeholders will agree to collaborate on an extensive community effort and will provide resources as well as visible buy-in, the director also must assess the internal receptivity since a coordinated community effort will significantly add to the agency's workload. Also, access to expertise and specific local data may prove to be a major hurdle. Each health indicator can have its own set of advocates, who, of course, see "their" indicator[2] as having primacy. Recruiting collaboration participants who will patiently dig into data[3] can also be a challenge as participants often prefer to proceed to action rather than struggle with scientific knowledge and investigate best practices. At the same time, sensitivity to the political environment, including potential turf issues and avoiding duplication with other community health efforts, is required. Alternatively, the director may decide that the agency would be better off with a very minimal leadership role, perhaps providing data while encouraging others to take the leadership and convening role. Either decision may be appropriate for the director's specific context.

3.2 Collaborative Readiness

As illustrated in the opening scenario, systematic analysis of collaborative readiness helps public and nonprofit managers in their roles of collaboration conveners and as potential collaboration participants know when strategic collaboration is the appropriate tool for the public issue at hand. Too often, public administrators engage in collaborative activity unwisely, before they have had a chance to adequately assess the factors and dynamics that will directly and ultimately shape the collaboration's effectiveness. By making these preconditions explicit, managers can be more deliberate both in their decision to proceed but also in proactively guiding the operations of the collaboration. Collaborative readiness analysis should occur as the collaboration context is assessed and the convening group transitions out of the collaboration life cycle Stage 1—Exploration (see Chapter 2).

Building from Evan Berman's research on organizational change preconditions[4] as well as insights from research on planned change[5] and strategic planning,[6] collaborative readiness analysis incorporates the specific assessment of the five preconditions of collaborative success:

1. Legitimate and pressing need to collaborate
2. Critical mass and sufficient representativeness
3. Skilled and committed leadership
4. Competence for collaboration
5. Reasonable probability of consequential change

Collectively, the five preconditions described in this chapter provide important clues as to collaborative readiness and should underlie the "go," "no go," or "proceed with due caution" decision as the convening group explores the formation of a collaboration. The results of the collaborative readiness analysis also enable the convening group to proactively predict stumbling blocks that will need to be considered during the initial design of collaborative structures and processes. Although each collaboration context has differing dynamics that make it easier (e.g., a prior history of successfully collaborating together) or more difficult (e.g., a prior history of conflict and resistance) to succeed, public and nonprofit managers should examine the broad range of success preconditions to be able to make prudent decisions about using their individual and agency resources in collaborative activities.

Assessing collaborative readiness using the preconditions explained in this chapter is also useful for the individual public and nonprofit manager in determining whether his or her agency should participate in the collaboration and, as described earlier in the public health scenario, the extent of collaborative leadership involvement. Although the individual manager's analysis will likely be informal, this exercise can help managers avoid "group think" or "going along to get along" pressures that can commonly occur when working with groups. Once the exploration stage is moving forward, managers may find it difficult to disembark. The public or nonprofit manager must then exercise judgment to determine the cost, risk, and potential benefits of involvement in the collaboration.

This chapter identifies key signals and associated analytical tasks for each of the five preconditions. While this analysis can range from highly informal, on the back of an envelope, to a more formalized structure, the collaborative readiness assessment is a concrete aid for improving the probability for successful strategic collaboration. The analytic structure to assess each precondition signal can be a simple metric of high or low or "strong versus weak," a more nuanced five-point Likert scale (e.g., very likely, likely, neutral, unlikely, or very unlikely), or a ranked value of 1–10 to scale the assessment. Whatever analytic structure is used to assess the precondition signals, it needs to be straightforward and explainable to others and support dialogue among the conveners.

Finally, this chapter combines the individual precondition assessments to propose a summary assessment method of collaborative readiness. Using this analytic frame, conveners can reach a well-thought-out decision regarding the likelihood of successful strategic collaboration. As illustrated in the public health scenario, the key for the public and nonprofit manager is in assessing what is most appropriate for his or her context.

3.3 Precondition 1: Legitimate and Pressing Need to Collaborate

The first precondition is the attributed importance, consequence, and urgency of the problem driving the collaborative effort's formation—or, in shorthand, "collaborative salience": *Is the need important enough to carry the collaboration forward?* If the initiating problems, events, requirements, or opportunities are perceived to have the necessary and sufficient degree of collaborative salience, the collaboration is more likely to receive support, resources, and acknowledged legitimacy from key stakeholders such as elected officials and funders. Similarly, busy public and nonprofit managers are much more likely to expend their time, attention, and energy on a collaborative effort if they perceive that the call for collaborative action has public legitimacy, urgency, and visibility.

How legitimate and pressing does it have to be? The short answer is "enough!" Clearly, no one answer will fit every situation. If the strategic collaboration is to consider an issue that is pervasive such as poverty or infant mortality, the framing and contextual analysis of the issue is particularly crucial. When the collaboration is addressing politically divisive or controversial issues such as family planning or immigration policies, sufficient levels of support become essential. Sometimes the question is whether the needed legitimacy can be created because the issue is not yet on a larger public agenda. Hence the concern here is whether key stakeholders believe in or can be convinced of the issue's importance. Conveners must deliberately think their way through this critical precondition, wrestling with questions such as the following:

- Does sufficient political support exist to sustain the work of the collaboration?
- Is the issue adequately urgent to displace other priorities?
- Does the driving issue have public visibility?

■ How likely will the key stakeholders and community be willing to accept or implement the results?

The assessment of the need to form a new collaborative effort should also explicitly examine the potential for duplicating or competing with similar efforts. Questions to pursue from this perspective would include the following:

■ What other projects are currently under way related to this issue?
■ Is the proposed collaboration duplicative of these efforts?
■ What agencies are involved and how?
■ How will the collaboration relate to these efforts?
■ How much resistance will this new effort face?
■ Why bring added focus and energy to the issue now?

Duplication of effort in itself is not sufficient to stop exploring the feasibility of forming a new collaboration, but it should give the founding group pause.

Overall, the assessment of this first precondition should proactively estimate whether a valid gap in collaborative action exists and where turf protection issues may surface (i.e., where other entrenched groups may view the collaboration as interfering or meddling with their work or goals). Further, the processes associated with collaboration rely on the goodwill of participants and thus will not always be the highest priority of every participant at every stage. If participants view the issues addressed as urgent, legitimate, significant, or politically visible, the collaboration has a greater likelihood of sustaining commitment and achieving positive outcomes. This critical precondition assessment of need adds fundamental information for conveners to consider before embarking on a collaborative effort and as they move through the collaboration life cycle stages.

3.3.1 Precondition 1 Signals: Assessing Need

Signal 1.1: Issue Is Important to Key Stakeholders

> **Task:** Identify key stakeholders and estimate the level of collaborative salience that each would place on the issue driving the collaboration.

Key stakeholders include opinion leaders (those who tend to have influence within the community or network), elected and appointed officials, as well as funders such as foundation and grant-making organization executives. Collaborative salience is a measure of the importance, urgency, and visibility that each stakeholder would likely assign to the problem driving the collaboration formation. In the public health scenario, key stakeholders could include a broad range of health providers, medical association representatives, school health nurses, restaurant owners, members of the faith community, nonprofit agencies, neighborhood activists, architects and planners involved in healthy community design, university researchers, and grassroots advocates concerned about breastfeeding, smoking cessation, biking, and so forth.

Signal 1.2: Need for and Purpose of the Collaboration Is Clearly Articulated; Purpose Does Not Unnecessarily Duplicate Other Efforts

> **Task**: Draft a statement of purpose for the collaboration, identify key projects and agencies that relate to this purpose, and estimate the degree of overlap with already existing collaborations.

The purpose statement articulation is an essential step to assure that there will be focused agreement among the convening group and a cogent vision for the collaborative effort. Although some duplication of purpose may be acceptable, conveners need to assess whether the degree of overlap presents a significant barrier to proceeding, from both a resource and political perspective. In the public health example, Healthy People 2010 provides guidance for how to build a community coalition, to prioritize objectives, and to measure results.

3.4 Precondition 2: Critical Mass and Sufficient Representativeness

This second precondition has to do with assuring that the collaboration will have enough, and the right kind, of people power to do what needs to be done to move the collaboration forward in a timely manner: *Are the right people at or willing to come to the table?* The challenge is in predicting that the collaboration will attract and retain the necessary number of individuals and organizations to commit to be directly and actively involved in the collaboration. The quantity and quality of those involved must be sufficient both to do the work of the collaboration and to adequately represent key stakeholders, including key organizations, policy arenas, perspectives, expertise, and demographics to assure a multidisciplinary, multilayered effort. How many? The critical number needed and sufficiency of representativeness is situational and, thus, is a judgment call.

Important questions include the following:

- Is the convening group sufficiently knowledgeable about the set of "must be at the table" participants?
- Can the collaboration count on key people or agencies to carry their part of the burden?
- Will agencies be willing to add this as an important expectation for their staff?

■ Will the set of participants collectively and legitimately represent the varied and competing interests?

■ Will the people who have the knowledge and expertise that is needed for the collaborative issue be willing to commit to the collaboration?

■ Can the collaboration balance the needs for both professional expertise and local knowledge?

■ How much direct participation of elected or community leaders is necessary?

To be successful in the long term, collaborations will also need to include the relevant minority, grassroots, and end-user groups.[7] For strategic collaboration, an important stakeholder question is "if, when, and how" to involve citizens. This decision needs to be intentional. While adding a level of complexity, citizen engagement has the potential "to build citizen efficacy, citizen trust in government, and citizen competence."[8] Consequently, a level of forethought should be applied to the decision to undertake citizen involvement in the collaboration and also to the processes of citizen engagement in the collaborative activities. Thus, collaboration convening groups need to consider which citizens, how many, and through what process will they be engaged? Will citizens represent a group or special interest, or are they serving solely as an individual? Is the agenda of the collaborative so controversial that only polarizing advocates will step up for participation and dominate the collaborative proceedings? Will this be authentic participation or just to gloss over what's already decided? The public health scenario is an excellent illustration of the tension that can occur between essential scientific and medical expertise while also needing community-level input and buy-in as priorities and benchmarks are set.

Although the degree of involvement may vary over time, at any point in the collaboration's life cycle a sufficient number of participants must be willing to add to their workload and share resources while accepting added responsibility, risk, and the potential for an uneven distribution of rewards. Busy people are more likely to commit to the collaborative if they think that other relevant stakeholders will help shoulder the various responsibilities. Thus, assuring a sufficient number and representative "mass" is an essential precondition of strategic collaborative readiness.

3.4.1 Precondition 2 Signals: Assessing Critical Mass and Representativeness

Signal 2.1: Individuals and Agencies That Have a Stake in the Purpose and Anticipated Outcomes of the Collaboration Are Likely to Engage in the Work of the Collaboration

Task: Identify the key interests that must be represented and the extent of overall engagement that can be anticipated from these key interested parties.

Conveners need to carefully think through who should be at the table, not just who is likely to show up. The level of participation necessary to assure that a sense of being represented during the collaboration's deliberations also needs to be assessed, including whether citizens or citizens groups should be included, whether citizens (or their representatives) will be willing to engage in the work of the collaborative, and whether participants will engage authentically with citizens and stakeholders external to their organizations. Reflecting back on past collaboration experience may give clues as to the likelihood of participants' willingness and capacity to deliver on their promised level of involvement and commitment.

Signal 2.2: *The Set of Key Agencies and Participants with Needed Expertise Are Likely Willing to Actively Engage in the Work of the Collaboration*

Task: Identify the essential tasks that need to be done, and then predict the willingness of key agencies or participants to be engaged and their expertise areas.

At this early stage, this could just be a draft list of tasks and responsibilities, including agenda setting, meeting logistics and documentation, data analysis, planning, reporting, policy analysis, legal requirements analysis, and media communications that will be needed to be accomplished during the life of the collaboration. The list should then be matched with a subjective assessment of the likelihood of who might "volunteer" for the responsibility and their qualifications for the tasks. In the public health example, the director may be aware of the most appropriate representatives from a community agency or the recognized leader on a priority issue (e.g., a group tasked with physical activity would likely want to consider including the highly vocal advocate on biking trails). See Appendix D for a tool to use in developing a matrix of responsibilities that might also be useful in thinking through roles and responsibilities.

3.5 Precondition 3: Skilled and Committed Leadership

This precondition relates to the leadership skills and expertise of participants who will be guiding the progress of the collaboration: *Will people step up and exercise shared leadership?* Group collaborative processes require that an individual (or small group of individuals) take ownership of the collaboration and champion its development and evolution. Getting people and organizations with different or competing values and priorities to work effectively together, outside of hierarchy, is a leadership and managerial art form that marries skills in communication, facilitation, and negotiation with the necessary expertise in the policy arena. The existence of a champion or highly visible and well-known leader or leadership group helps the collaboration persuade participants to join and engage, inspires participants and agencies to stay committed, and articulates the mission and goals of the collaboration to participants as well as to external audiences to sustain legitimacy and community support of the collaboration's efforts.

Yet, beyond this reliance on the existence of a champion, the convening group should estimate how the leadership process will play out before embarking on a collaborative effort. Questions that should be considered include the following:

- Is there an obvious designated lead or coordinating organization or individual?
- Would this assumption of the leadership role be helpful or problematic?
- Will the initial leadership structure be in place only for start-up, or will it continue for a set period or indefinitely?
- Will the founding group be able to develop an agreed upon leadership plan if leadership is shared among multiple participants?
- Does the leadership team possess the skills to facilitate participants through the collaboration process?
- Will it be clear who has the power to set the rules on accountability and who would be responsible for assuring and monitoring outcomes?

Clearly, the collaboration's leadership group will have to skillfully balance the need for clarifying roles and responsibilities in the initiating stage while leaving adequate flexibility for further refinements and to generate group buy-in. The more controversial the driving force for collaboration or the more barriers that are anticipated, the greater the need for the conveners to think through their assignment of the leadership roles.

3.5.1 Precondition 3 Signals: Assessing Leadership Capacity

Signal 3.1: Key Participants Have the Necessary Leadership and Facilitative Skills to Guide the Design and Evolution of the Collaboration and Are Willing to Serve in Leadership Roles

Task: Identify the participants who are likely to lead the collaboration, and assess their leadership skill level.

Leaders with a past history of collaborative leadership could be assessed for their ability to communicate, problem solve, diagnose resistance, negotiate, and energize a group. Potential leaders with limited collaborative experience could be assessed for their commitment level to the collaboration, ability to work with and empower others within their context, and ability to communicate effectively.

Signal 3.2: Prospective Leaders Have Adequate Community Connections and the Skill Level to Recruit Participants and to Generate Resources

> **Task:** Assess the capability of the anticipated leaders of the collaboration to obtain resource commitments and to enlist support.

Leaders with a past history of successful networking or collaborating with others may be more likely to have the connections to elicit support. Leaders who have personal or organizational power and status are also more likely to be able to elicit support. It is important at this step to broadly estimate the resources that will be needed and make explicit the anticipated source of these resources, indicating the likelihood of the source committing these resources.

3.6 Precondition 4: Competence for Collaboration

This precondition relates to whether the people who are likely to get involved in the collaboration actually have group process skills (or are willing to learn them) and the personal characteristics that enable them to be productive in collaborative settings: *Do the people likely to be at the table know how to "play well" with others in a collaborative setting?* The founding group must understand that collaborating together can be a scary proposition as participants become anxious about the likelihood of success after expending a great deal of effort, about the potential risk to their career or self-interest or their agency if significant change results, about whether there will be a fair sharing of risks and rewards for cooperating, or about whether leaders have a hidden agenda that runs counter to the stated goals. Member anxieties about collaborating will be increased if participants have experienced a failed history of collaboration within their community or network. Thus, this precondition recognizes the limits on even the most skilled leader to overcome structural and historical barriers to effective collaboration.

While the quality of leadership can facilitate relationship building, the success of the collaboration rests on the ability of participants to develop sound relationships and to create a climate that allows for the open exchange of ideas and critique. Thus, the convening group needs to ask the following:

- Do the likely participants have the skills and personal characteristics that will foster and enhance trust so that the collaboration can be successful?
- If they do not, will they be willing to work together to develop these skills?

- Will they be able and willing to cooperate together to overcome issues that may arise to hinder trust?

For example, collaborative efforts are vulnerable to toxic personalities and self-serving agendas. A toxic environment is especially damaging when groups are struggling to sustain creative energy, to work through uncertainty, and to bring about change. While strong leadership can help to contain the damage, the group itself must be willing to expend sufficient energy to building and sustaining interpersonal trust dynamics and to assert itself if necessary to overcome this hurdle. Consequently, other key collaborative climate questions that should be asked include the following:

- Of those likely to want to engage in the collaboration, can they suspend self-interest in the pursuit of a collective goal?
- Are they respected in their relationship network?
- Can they trust others sufficiently to work through what may be difficult, controversial, or threatening issues?

The processes of collaboration create shared understandings and norms. To be successful, the participants themselves must be willing to create an environment that nurtures the exchange of ideas.

While legitimacy of the issue will open the door, trust is essential in keeping the door open so that participants will continue to work together effectively and collaboratively. In the Healthy People 2010 example, the federal leadership to improve the nation's health establishes legitimacy of the associated community efforts, but the keys to local success rest with community relationships and effective collaboration processes. Trust is an essential ingredient in the ability to bring about change. Berman convincingly argues that "managers must do things that are likely to inspire trust in others to give people a reason to trust them."[9] This same insight relates to the participants involved in a collaborative effort. Also, successful collaborative participation requires that sufficient trust be built and maintained so that individuals and agencies involved agree to accept evolving roles and nonhierarchical relationships and to work through competing and conflicting values and demands. Public and nonprofit managers committed to having a successful strategic collaboration will need to know how to build and manage trusting relationships, sustaining strong relationships already existing while nurturing new ones. Constructive attention to relationship and trust building among the participants will directly affect how well people work together, the level of buy-in of the collaboration's work and products, and the degree of agreement over the expectations about what the collaboration will or can accomplish.

3.6.1 Precondition 4 Signals: Assessing Openness to Collaboration

Signal 3.1: Positive History of Productive Relationships and Collaboration

> **Task:** Identify the examples of recent collaboration efforts within the community, and assess whether the experience was positive or negative.

A positive history of collaboration lays the foundation for positive future collaboration efforts. Be careful, since a positive history of collaboration may also lay the foundation for greater expectations than can realistically be delivered by this specific collaboration. Very importantly, this step in the assessment should specifically identify organizations or individuals likely to participate who have a history or reputation for not being effective in collaborative settings and estimate the challenges that they bring. If these more "negative" organizations or individuals are essential to the collaboration's success, the collaboration faces a significant obstacle.

Signal 3.2: Key Participants Have Sufficient Levels of Trust within the Group to Work through the Initial Steps of Forming a Collaboration and to Sustain the Collaboration

> **Task:** Identify the participants who are likely to be involved in the collaboration and assess the strength of their relationships with each other.

This signal differs from the previous one because it focuses on the current quality of relationships and dependencies among the potential participants. Assess whether the likely participants already have relationships with each other and how strong or weak the ties are. For example, consider whether the participating agencies are dependent upon one another for delivering programs and whether the success of the collaboration will directly affect the agency. Already existing ties, strong or weak, lay a foundation that can be more readily built upon to yield a "safer, more open" climate for the exchange of ideas and to encourage creativity and questioning of the status quo. The lack of ties will mean that more proactive work will need to be done to develop productive relationships and to create a productive environment for authentic communication.

3.7 Precondition 5: Reasonable Probability of Consequential Change

This precondition pointedly addresses whether the time is right for the collaboration effort: *Have the stars aligned to engender innovation and change?* Since the ultimate goal of strategic collaboration requires some kind of change, and typically multidimensional change, convening groups must assess the existing system-level barriers and the prospects for meaningful innovation and results. The system-level barriers vary by the issue driving the collaboration but commonly include an entrenched, agency or discipline-based silo perspective that fuels turf protection; societal and historical conditions that further complicate the collaborative context such as social and racial inequality; and local-, state-, and federal-level policies and structures that confound change. The greater the system-level resistance to change, the greater persistence and innovation required to achieve any level of results.

Good intentions and commitment to public service aside, a successful strategic collaboration requires participants who come to the table with a commitment to the issue at hand and to the change effort needed. At the same time, participants should bring a willingness to think creatively, to encourage the often time-intensive processes that nurture innovation, and to weather the failed paths and projects necessary to reach long-term success. However, a reality-based approach recognizes that collaborative energy will be nourished if participants and external supporters perceive that the collaboration is successful (e.g., goals reached, change adopted). Success, particularly visible achievements early in the collaboration's history, will inspire continued commitment as well as counter any naysayers. Since it is human nature to want to be on a "winning team," success will also energize other individuals or organizations to join or support the collaboration. Therefore, a focus upon innovation and change must be carefully balanced with the expectations of participants. While the processes of collaboration create shared understandings and norms that directly affect how well people work together and continued buy-in of the collaboration's work and products, the initial collective direction or shared understanding of what needs to be done and how it should be done is foundational.

Essentially this precondition examines the timing or timeliness of the collaboration itself and the anticipated outcomes. Is there an appropriate confluence of internal and external factors to create the window where collaborative action can bring about significant change? The challenge for public and nonprofit managers who choose collaboration is to match the collaboration's design, processes, and outcomes to the problem addressed while fostering innovation so that positive impacts are realized.

3.7.1 Precondition 5 Signals: Assessing the Window for Change

Signal 5.1: The Timing Is Right

> **Task:** Articulate the pressing reasons or forces that justify proceeding now. List the key environmental conditions, initiating forces, and tactical drivers that are propelling collaboration.

Match the reasons for proceeding with an assessment that the timing is right to press for change. In addition, identify the people who are pushing for action, and match this with their power or status to drive collaborative formation. Each member of the convening group may assess this very differently since the potential positive or negative impact if the collaboration is successful will vary.

Signal 5.2: System-Level Barriers Can Be Identified to Become Targets of Opportunity

> **Task:** Identify key obstacles specific to the issue driving the collaboration, and estimate the likelihood of innovation or reinvention.

List the predicted (and those that would be serious) obstacles, and then match them against the likelihood of their occurrence. Key obstacles could include entrenched silo perspectives and jealously guarded turf, societal or historical conditions such as social and racial inequalities and tensions, or existing local, state, and federal policies and requirements. The assessment should make explicit the level of effort that will be needed to overcome these barriers. In the public health example, statistical analysis of health data and identification of best practices are critical steps in thinking through the extent of the challenges and obstacles that will be faced. For example, realistically assessing the political will to change tobacco policies, nutrition ratings of restaurant menus, and child abuse policies present very real obstacles to likely health promotion targets.

3.8 The Overall Assessment of Collaborative Readiness

After reviewing each precondition, collaboration conveners must perform a summative assessment of collaborative readiness. By examining the signal strength for each respective precondition, the conveners can more explicitly estimate the collaboration's likelihood of and obstacles to success. A suggested approach is for each convening group member to assign a general ranking of readiness to each of the five preconditions. Strategies for ranking include assigning values of high, medium, or low, using a five-part Likert scale to allow greater nuance (i.e., very likely, likely, neutral, unlikely, very unlikely), or giving a ranking from 1 to 10 (high likelihood to negligible likelihood). A rigid rule on how to assign the rating is not possible because of the vast number of factors, many of which are highly subjective, that will shape the precondition's assessment.

As individual assessments are discussed, conveners develop a shared understanding of collaborative readiness. Table 3.1 illustrates one method to use this analytic frame. Ideally all of the preconditions signals clearly indicate "proceed" or "don't proceed." However, a mixed assessment of signal vitality is more likely, with some preconditions ranking more positive or negative than others, requiring conveners to deliberately weigh the relative likelihood of success and benefits anticipated against the risk of proceeding or not proceeding. The more signals without adequate evidence of success, the greater consideration should be given to not proceeding at this time with collaboration—unless other influences such as a stakeholder with high political clout and status suggest that some level of collaboration is unavoidable. If the decision is to proceed, then conveners should pay particular attention to the identified weaknesses and should deliberately attend to them to evade predictable obstacles in the formation. Serious weaknesses in any of the five preconditions may justify a negative decision—that is, to not collaborate or to minimize involvement as much as is politically possible.

Table 3.1 Collaborative Readiness Assessment and Decision to Proceed or Not

Likelihood of Collaborative Success	*Collaboration Decision*
High (All signals for all five preconditions suggest optimal collaborative readiness.)	Proceed with forming the collaboration.
Medium (Signals suggest a mixed picture of collaborative readiness.)	Proceed with caution, realizing that the lack of readiness of the preconditions provide important clues as to roadblocks that will likely appear and interfere with success.
Low (All signals suggest inadequate collaborative readiness.)	Do not proceed.
	OR
	Proceed only if other considerations trump the assessment and then proceed with great caution.

This deliberative and analytic step, however, provides a frame that articulat the thought and decision process that underlies the choice to pursue forming a co laboration. The very act of engaging in a dialogue about the preconditions shoulu enable the conveners to more systematically and strategically structure their collaborative decision process.

3.9 Conclusion

This chapter discussed the five preconditions required to increase the likelihood of strategic collaboration success. Using this analytic technique, collaboration conveners can carefully analyze collaborative readiness. This analytic process will enable the conveners to make a more informed decision about whether to proceed with the collaboration. By addressing the key readiness questions raised in this chapter (Table 3.2) and assessing the strength of the signals associated with each precondition, the collaboration is more likely to be designed and managed in a strategic and systematic manner. Collaborative readiness analysis also serves as an important foundation for rich communication among the founding group. The signals, with their respective analytic tasks, provide a concrete vehicle for assessing collaborative readiness and identifying areas of vulnerability.

Table 3.2   Key Readiness Questions to Be Addressed Prior to Forming a Strategic Collaboration

- Is the need important and legitimate enough to carry the collaboration forward?
- Are the right people at or willing to come to the table?
- Will people step up and exercise shared leadership?
- Do the people likely to be at the table know how to "play well" with others in a collaborative setting?
- Have the stars aligned to engender innovation and change?

s

extensive website that has been made available for more information on this
al health promotion effort: http://www.healthypeople.gov. The Healthy People
Toolkit is an excellent resource for communities engaging in health planning
includes guidance on leadership and structure, securing resources, engaging part-
ers, setting objectives and targets, sustaining the process, and communication. Public
Health Foundation (PHF). Healthy People 2010 Toolkit. Washington, DC. August
1999. http://www.health.gov/healthypeople/state/toolkit (accessed May 24, 2009).

2. The 10 leading health indicators are (1) physical activity, (2) overweight and obesity, (3)
tobacco use, (4) substance abuse, (5) responsible sexual behavior, (6) mental health, (7)
injury and violence, (8) environmental quality, (9) immunization, and (10) access to
health. Determining priorities is a challenge since all of the potential targets, whether
it is cardiovascular health or adolescent sexual behavior, warrant attention.

3. More than 450 objectives are being tracked by almost 200 data sources. Two examples
of major data sources are the National Health Interview Survey and National Health
and Nutrition Examination Survey. For more information on the data systems, see
PHF. Tracking Health People 2010. Washington, DC. August 1999. http://www.
healthypeople.gov/document/html/tracking/THP_PartC.htm (accessed September
19, 2009).

4. E. Berman, *Performance and Productivity in Public and Nonprofit Organizations* (2d ed.,
Armonk, NY: M.E. Sharpe, 2006).

5. R. Golembiewski, *Handbook of Organizational Consultation* (2d ed., rev., exp., New
York: Marcel Dekker, 2000); M.A. Griffin, A.E. Rafferty, and C.M. Mason, Who
Started This? Investigating Different Sources of Organizational Change, *Journal of
Business and Psychology, 18* (4): 555–570, 2004; J. Kotter, 1995, Leading Change: Why
Transformation Efforts Fail, *Harvard Business Review, 73* (2): 59–67, 1995.

6. See J. Bryson, *Strategic Planning for Public and Nonprofit Organizations: A Guide to
Strengthening and Sustaining Organizational Achievement* (3d ed., San Francisco: Jossey-
Bass, 2004); H. Rainey, *Understanding & Managing Public Organizations* (3d ed., San
Francisco: Jossey-Bass, 2003); M. Moore, *Creating Public Value: Strategic Management
in Government* (Cambridge, MA: Harvard University Press, 1995).

7. M. Winer and K. Ray, *Collaboration Handbook: Creating, Sustaining, and Enjoying the
Journey* (St. Paul, MN: Amherst H. Wilder Foundation, 1994), p. 49.

8. T. Cooper, T. Bryer, and J. Meek, Citizen-Centered Collaborative Public Management,
Public Administration Review, 66 (Supplement): 79–80, 2006; Also see A. Fung,
Varieties of Participation in Complex Governance, *Public Administration Review, 66*
(Supplement): 66–75, 2006.

9. Berman, *Performance and Productivity*, p. 50.

Chapter 4

Strategic Collaboration in Action: Six Principles

Dorothy Norris-Tirrell and Joy A. Clay

Contents

4.1 Introduction

Moving from silos to collaboration requires public and nonprofit managers to think differently about working beyond discipline, organization, and sector boundaries. As Chapter 1 discussed, *strategic collaboration is an intentional, collective approach to address public problems or issues through building shared knowledge, designing innovative solutions, and forging consequential change.* The knowledge, skills, and abilities of effective practice related to any collective effort—such as the importance of recruiting and retaining participants, facilitating meetings, and group

73

problem solving—remain essential and ground the practice of strategic collaboration. However, as the short scenarios about environmental awareness and building healthy communities initiatives demonstrate, strategic collaboration can take collective endeavor to a new level, yielding results outside of the command and control context so that new ways of thinking, innovation actions, and unimagined-before outcomes result. While contexts, participants, and processes are unique to every effort, six overarching principles define the distinctive core of successful strategic collaboration practice:

- **Principle 1:** Choose strategic collaboration wisely.
- **Principle 2**: Understand the strategic collaboration life cycle.
- **Principle 3:** Strengthen leadership capacity.
- **Principle 4:** Balance risk and reward transparently.
- **Principle 5:** Cultivate innovation for meaningful change.
- **Principle 6:** Emphasize outcomes and impacts.

This chapter begins with a discussion of each principle and includes a tool for implementation or furthering thinking on key practice elements of strategic collaboration. Following the discussion of the principles is a set of questions and answers that summarizes key components of strategic collaboration implementation. Finally, a framework of strategic collaboration connects the pieces presented earlier. Together the principles and the framework can transform the hard work of collaboration into workable strategies for resolving complex public problems and advancing public service practice.

4.2 Principle 1: Choose Strategic Collaboration Wisely

Although collaboration is an important public policy approach today, Chapter 1 presents current public problem-solving activity as a continuum of collaboration, with silos at one end and strategic collaboration at the other and more modest forms of collective action in between. Thus, Principle 1 recognizes a contingent model of collaboration—in other words, public and nonprofit managers should understand that silo-based work is best used in some situations while *ad hoc* collaboration or strategic collaboration will be more appropriate for others. Any of these choices may be a suitable or best choice dependent on contextual conditions and the overall state of a potential group's collaborative readiness.[1] The challenge is in systematically matching the purpose of the collective action with the appropriate level of collaboration, ranging from none to a fully developed strategic collaboration.[2]

If problems can be addressed within the agency, discipline, or sector by simply cooperating with another entity, there is little justification for formal collaboration.[3]

THE CHALLENGE OF LABELS

Part of the challenge facing public and nonprofit managers is the lack of clarity over labels that are used to describe collective activities. Collaboration can mean the actual structure created to gather people to collaborate or work together on shared goals. The term, however, can also be used to describe the collective, collaborative processes used by individuals as they work together. To ensure effective communication, public and nonprofit managers should avoid using the term *collaboration* when they mean coordination or cooperation. Is it a distinction without a difference? No, because words matter when people come together from different value, experience, and educational orientations. Such differences create the potential for both conflicting expectations and frames of reference. Moreover, how participants perceive they will be working together lays the groundwork for building commitment, facilitates the ability to reach agreement, and frames understandings and norms.

Serendipitous or *ad hoc* collaborations may be sufficient for informal discussion or information exchange. With the right circumstances, luck, and persistence, such collaborations may have positive results.

The best use of strategic collaboration results from a deliberate decision that it is the appropriate approach to use for the public problem or issue at hand. Public and nonprofit managers should take this leap thoughtfully and not engage in collaboration simply because it is the popular approach or the preferred choice of funders. If the public problem has a limited shelf life and calls for an immediate fix, then strategic collaboration is not the tool to choose. Strategic collaboration is also not a permanent method; rather, it is organic, temporary, or at most semipermanent. It is more likely to be successful when the structure has no formal status (e.g., it does not incorporate as a separate 501(c)(3) nonprofit), emphasizes a neutral role to facilitate dialogue and planning, and embraces an advocate role serving as a catalyst for change. One important advantage of strategic collaboration, then, is to avoid competing with existing organizations for funding, instead serving as an incubator for new financial and other resources.

The preconditions for collaboration success presented in Chapter 3 can be used to assess collaboration readiness. The precondition signals create a checklist (Table 4.1) for public and nonprofit managers and collaboration convening groups to use to guide the determination of whether or not to move forward with strategic collaboration. In summary, choosing when to use a strategic collaboration approach is critical in ultimately reaching success.

Table 4.1   Collaborative Readiness Checklist

Precondition 1: Legitimate and pressing need to collaborate.

- Signal 1.1: Issue is important to key stakeholders.

    Task: Identify key stakeholders, and estimate the level of collaborative salience that each would place on the issue driving the collaboration.

- Signal 1.2: Need for and purpose of the collaboration is clearly articulated; purpose does not unnecessarily duplicate other efforts.

    Task: Draft a statement of purpose for the collaboration, identify key projects and agencies that relate to this purpose, and estimate the degree of existing overlap with the proposed collaborative purpose.

Precondition 2: Critical mass and sufficient representativeness.

- Signal 2.1: Individuals and agencies that have a stake in the purpose and anticipated outcomes of the collaboration are likely to engage in the work of the collaboration.

    Task: Identify the key interests that must be represented and the extent of overall engagement that can be anticipated from these key interested parties.

- Signal 2.2: The set of key agencies and participants with needed expertise are likely willing to actively engage in the work of the collaboration.

    Task: Identify the essential tasks that need to be done, and then predict the willingness of key agencies or participants to be engaged and their expertise areas.

Precondition 3: Skilled and committed leadership.

- Signal 3.1: Key participants will be willing to lead and have the necessary leadership and facilitative skills to guide the design and evolution of the collaboration.

    Task: Identify the participants who are likely to lead the collaboration, and assess their leadership skill level.

- Signal 3.2: Prospective leaders have adequate community connections and the skill level to recruit participants and to generate resources.

    Task: Assess the capability of the anticipated leaders of the collaboration to obtain resource commitments and to enlist support.

Table 4.1   Collaborative Readiness Checklist (Continued)

Precondition 4: Competence for collaboration.

- Signal 4.1: Positive history of productive relationships and collaboration.

    Task: Identify the examples of recent collaboration efforts within the community, and assess whether the experience was positive or negative.

- Signal 4.2: Key participants have sufficient levels of trust within the potential group to work through the initial steps of forming collaboration and to sustain the collaboration.

    Task: Identify the participants who are likely to be involved in the collaboration, and assess the strength of their relationships with each other.

Precondition 5: Reasonable probability of consequential change.

Signal 5.1: The timing is right.

    Task: Articulate the pressing reasons or forces that justify proceeding now. List the key environmental forces or tactical drivers that are driving collaboration.

- Signal 5.2: System-level barriers can be identified to become targets of opportunity.

    Task: Identify key obstacles specific to the issue driving the collaboration, and estimate the likelihood of innovation or reinvention.

4.3 Principle 2: Understand the Strategic Collaboration Life Cycle

Chapter 2 presented the conceptual framework of collaboration life cycle, suggesting that a strategic approach to collaboration emphasizes the evolutionary nature of collective activity. By understanding the collaboration's life cycle stages, participants will better understand the dynamics of formation and more fully estimate the resources and commitment required to make a collaboration successful. Moreover, a richer understanding of what it takes to yield effective collective action will enable managers to align their decision-making and problem-solving processes to the respective life cycle stage. Understanding that an ending may actually mark the beginning of a new collective activity also highlights the importance of knowing when to end a collaboration and how to end it well.

Just as understanding organizational life cycles helps us to better understand how agencies evolve over time, Principle 2 emphasizes that high-functioning strategic collaborations must attend to changing needs and dynamics as collective effort progresses throughout the collaboration life cycle. Crucial to the smooth passage at each stage are the transitions from one stage to the next, each creating a window of opportunity. The first life cycle stage, exploration, is about knowing when to consider and when to jump into strategic collaboration. When contextual factors converge to create the needed problem legitimacy for strategic collaboration, intentional choices can be made. As Principle 1 indicates, the choice for strategic collaboration should be made carefully and with intentionality.

The formation stage centers on the creation of nimble structures and rules of engagement that (1) address leadership roles, (2) define participants, and (3) clarify authority and decision-making processes. The transition to the growth stage introduces new tensions among the participants, as evolving expectations and conflicting agendas emerge. Attention to the clarification of goals and anticipated outcomes becomes critical at this stage. Similarly, fuller awareness of the advantages and challenges of the maturity stage enables participants to be more proactive and strategic in how they manage their collaborative commitments and predict the consequences of their actions and to balance demands for stability and innovation.

The final life cycle stage, ending, recognizes strategic collaboration as a temporary medium and, therefore, that dissolution should be anticipated. However, to end well, the disbanding should be explicitly planned to address the practical, emotional, and symbolic needs of the participants and stakeholders. At the same time, while planning the ending, changes in the collaboration context may require that participants refocus and reengineer the strategic collaboration. New research findings and funding priorities, economic conditions, or political leadership changes may lead participants to support renewal or reinvigoration with a revised focus. Other external factors, however, may argue for the more final ending of the collaborative effort due to loss of salience.

Understanding the common challenges and opportunities at each life cycle stage allows participants to recognize the windows for transition and to create an effective and productive strategic collaboration. Table 4.2 summarizes the conventional and strategic practice activities throughout the collaboration life cycle, identifying the different tasks and outcomes common for each stage. Taking advantage of these opportunities to build sustained commitment and to push the collaboration's evolution is crucial to the ultimate success of the effort.

4.4 Principle 3: Strengthen Leadership Capacity

In strategic collaboration, *leadership matters*—both the structures that set up the leadership roles as well as the individuals who take on these roles. In a nutshell, the leadership team makes sure the collaboration creates (and continually recreates) a shared agenda and then intentionally manages the work of the collaboration around that agenda—in a context not the traditional hierarchal organization model

Table 4.2 The Stages of Collaboration: Conventional Activities and Strategic Practice

Collaboration Stage	Conventional Collaboration Activities	Strategic Collaboration Practice
Stage 1: Exploration and Formation	• Conversations and meetings on a specific public problem or issue. • Brainstorming and information gathering. • Relationships established or continued with a focus on shared expectations.	• Intentional decision for strategic collaboration. • Critical mass of engaged participants. • Suitable participants and resources at the table. • A champion leads the effort.
Stage 2: Formalization	• Develop collaborative structure and operating procedures, and begin implementation. • Define parameters and expectations of participation. • Develop goals and action plans, and begin implementation.	• Sharpen mission and vision during process-oriented planning. • Create structures and processes that ensure broad stakeholder participation. • Build trust through ethical communication and operations. • Identify and foster early success.
Stage 3: Growth	• Continued planning and priority setting. • Operation implementation and monitoring strategies routinized. • Ongoing cycle of participant recruitment and exit.	• Avoid bureaucratic thinking. • Promote innovation and creativity. • Emphasize cooperation and new, shared understanding. • Focus on information dissemination and feedback.

(continued)

Table 4.2 The Stages of Collaboration: Conventional Activities and Strategic Practice (Continued)

Collaboration Stage	Conventional Collaboration Activities	Strategic Collaboration Practice
Stage 4: Maturity	• Resources stabilized. • Planning, evaluation, and revision strategies continued. • Collaborative activity visible.	• Balance stability with innovation. • Remain mission driven and results oriented. • Build a deeper leadership bench.
Stage 5: Ending A. Ending/ Closure	• Recognition. • Sharing results.	• Act with intentionality. • Seek expert assistance. • Archive processes, participants, and impacts. • Be transparent.
B. Decline	• Meeting attendance drops. • Participants frustrated. • Resources uncertain. • Emphasis on status quo.	• Diagnose "pathologies." • Seek "outside" perspective. • Create reality-based analysis processes. • Be purposeful about what's next.
C. Renewal	• New participants recruited and previous participants reconnected. • Purpose clarified or revised.	• Bring new perspective to the table. • Hold periodic retreats. • Deliberate redesign of structure and processes. • Restore legitimacy.

nor from a posture of professional expert.[4] In a strategic collaboration, the leader's approach is not "command and control" but rather focuses on building common purpose (e.g., shared vision of desired results) and a common base of knowledge including a shared vocabulary, shared understanding of facts, and shared information regarding the work of the collaboration and resulting outcomes.

Pulling this off successfully requires leaders to use some of the same tactics that are smart practice in any group setting, but with particular attention to the larger

LEADERS ARE NOT FOREVER

Good operating guidelines create term limits for leadership roles. Even the champion who invested heavily in the exploration and formation of the strategic collaboration must eventually move out of the primary leader role. Establishing a time frame and tenure of office early in the formation stage avoids the frustration of a leader who stays too long due to founder syndrome.

At the same time, operating guidelines should provide a leadership progression path so that upcoming leaders serve in key roles that allow them to learn about the role and expectations before stepping up.

outcomes of building the collaborative capacity of all participants and preparing others to assume designated leadership roles. For example, a skilled leadership team will explicitly plan an overall agenda. This requires time, attention, and forethought both to assure steady progress and also to be respectful of participant energy and time. Meeting agendas should align with the overall life cycle stage of the collaboration, aligning milestones for meetings to the relevant stage dynamics (Appendix E). The sequence of major tasks should strategically address requirements or commitments. Thus, the comprehensive agenda becomes a way to organize and manage the collaboration's work.

In particular, the leader must negotiate the collaboration's context of shared power, limited hierarchy, and competing tensions to build collective buy-in. The effective leader must build collaborative decision-making processes as well as engender group commitment to manage conflict. Formalized structures and operating guidelines are essential tools for leadership and governance in defining power and decision-making rules.[5] (See Appendix B for sample operating guidelines.)

Effective decision making in the strategic collaboration setting requires a sufficient, yet not overwhelming, process-oriented perspective. Building trust and sustaining commitment to collaborative goals requires that participants have opportunities to provide authentic and inclusive feedback and analysis in a neutral arena.[6] Naysayers and participants who do not engage authentically in the collaboration (e.g., bickering, turf protecting, jealously vying for power) must be managed so that they do not thwart progress. These "thorns in the side" will always exist; therefore, skilled leaders must tactically and tactfully handle problem personalities and other distracters through reorienting meeting agendas, new small-group assignments, and individual conversations. Making progress on the collaboration's established and shared agenda requires discipline and multiple, redundant communication mechanisms so that in-person meetings can become the central place for real discussion that leads to decision making and innovation (see Principle 5).

Working across organizational, sector, and disciplinary boundaries—a corner-stone for most strategic collaboration—is challenging for many public and non-profit managers. Given the already stretched resources of most public and nonprofit agencies, adversarial posturing is not uncommon. Unfortunately, this often leads to a competitive "us" against "them" attitude, a serious impediment to effective collaboration.[7] Without experience and the requisite skills in conflict management, collaboration participants may resort to inappropriately interjecting status or exper-tise or to withdraw in a passive-aggressive manner. As each participant brings his or her own interests, experiences, and priorities to the table coupled with the power imbalances that are common in every group, conflict is inevitable—and poten-tially useful. Consequently, a key role of collaboration leaders and facilitators is to minimize disruptive conflict, reducing the discomfort that it typically produces, nurturing open communication, and modeling effective interactions. The healthy sharing of points of friction is often the catalyst for innovation (see Principle 5). If organizational status, turf, or competition is the cause, emphasizing the collabora-tion's competitive advantage can overcome the negative friction.[8]

Tensions between experts and community participants also require special attention by leaders.[9] Feedback opportunities can provide important cues about how conflict affects relationship and trust building. In strategic collaboration, managing conflict is facilitated by proactively creating structures and processes that strengthen relationships, build trust, and yield new opportunities such as increased access to funding, expertise, and legitimacy.

Leaders must facilitate the "everyday" work of the strategic collaboration so that participants are willing to sustain their commitment to the collaboration, must understand the overall purpose of the collaboration, yet must have patience to work through any glitches that lead to frustration. The Collaboration Temperature Tool (Table 4.3) provides leaders one way to assess the collaboration's process and to diagnose where points of frustration may be occurring and where new tactics are needed to reinvigorate the collaborative dynamics. Another possible instrument that could be used is Thomson, Perry, and Miller's 17-indicator scale of collabora-tion that helps to surface underlying tensions and explore the state of interorgani-zational relationships.[10]

4.5 Principle 4: Balance Risk and Reward Transparently

Principle 4 is about aligning the various purposes and missions of participants, par-ticipant organizations, and the collaboration itself; clarifying expected and desired outcomes; and reaching shared agreement on participant obligations. Authentically and transparently addressing "what's in it for me (or my agency)" and "how much will it cost" questions are essential. As a first step, conveners should clearly commu-nicate the purpose and anticipated outcomes of the strategic collaboration so that participants can compare their investment of resources (e.g., time, energy) with the

Table 4.3   Taking the Collaboration Temperature

1.	Overall, the collaboration's goals are clearly understood and agreed upon by participants.				
	1	2	3	4	5
	Strongly Disagree		Agree	Strongly Agree	
2.	Overall, collaboration participants can be counted on to deliver on their commitments.				
	1	2	3	4	5
	Strongly Disagree		Agree	Strongly Agree	
3.	Overall, the collaboration leaders are effective communicators and facilitators.				
	1	2	3	4	5
	Strongly Disagree		Agree	Strongly Agree	
4.	Overall, participants can be counted on to regularly show up for collaboration meetings				
	1	2	3	4	5
	Strongly Disagree		Agree	Strongly Agree	
5.	Stakeholders consider the collaboration to be important and publicly support it.				
	1	2	3	4	5
	Strongly Disagree		Agree	Strongly Agree	
6.	Overall, meetings are effective and productive with participants energized.				
	1	2	3	4	5
	Strongly Disagree		Agree	Strongly Agree	
7.	Overall, the collaboration is likely to be successful in meeting its purpose before it ends.				
	1	2	3	4	5
	Strongly Disagree		Agree	Strongly Agree	

(continued)

Table 4.3 Taking the Collaboration Temperature (Continued)

8.	Overall, the group is supportive of bringing about change even if it negatively affects their agency.				
	1	2	3	4	5
	Strongly Disagree		Agree	Strongly Agree	
9.	Overall, the amount of effort spent on collaborating is worth the anticipated outcomes.				
	1	2	3	4	5
	Strongly Disagree		Agree	Strongly Agree	
10.	Overall, the collaboration climate is positive, strengthening relationships and trust.				
	1	2	3	4	5
	Strongly Disagree		Agree	Strongly Agree	

value and probability of anticipated results. This "return on investment" exercise is crucial for public and nonprofit managers and community volunteers. Not only are resources tight and therefore every allocation decision crucial, but busy professionals and volunteers are also often overextended, limiting their ability to make a real contribution to any effort. Thus, public and nonprofit managers' decisions to participate in a collaboration should include systematically thinking through whether they can provide agency resources (e.g., staff time, energy) that will likely be needed and expected for success and whether they have or can afford to assign appropriately skilled staff to represent their agency and interests. An honest "no, not at this time" is better than agreeing to participate and then not delivering on the commitment.

One tool for clarifying potential rewards and risks for participants is the use of a formal document such as memorandum of understanding (MOU) or a letter of commitment. Table 4.4 provides standard elements of an MOU for collaborative participants. Often highly technical and legal, the formal document can require extensive negotiation. The MOU should include as much detail as is known at the time of execution. Of course, things will change as the collaboration evolves, but spelling out these issues avoids dysfunctional expectations, charges of inefficiency, and squandered time. A participant agreement (Appendix C) or matrix of collaboration participant roles (Appendix D) can assist in clarifying the specific expectations and responsibilities of individuals. The MOU or letter of commitment should be renewed at least annually to remind participants of their commitments and to give the opportunity for renegotiation based on changing conditions and opportunities. This formal document and process lays

Table 4.4   Key Elements of MOU or Letter of Commitment

- Mission or purpose of the collaboration.

- Expected outcomes or results.

- Structure and processes of the collaboration (leadership assignments; decision-making procedures, revision procedures).

- Participant identification (either by individual name or position, e.g., executive director or human resources manager).

- Responsibilities and obligations of participants (meeting attendance—how often are meetings; committee work; outreach; proposal development; supervision; leadership roles).

- Time frame of commitment, including termination procedures.

- Financial commitments.

- Other resource commitments such as administrative support, technical support, Web page space, office space, meeting room space.

- Reporting and monitoring format and time frame.

- Recognition methods.

the groundwork for open and real conversations throughout the collaboration's life cycle.

More information available up front allows better decisions about whether the balance of resource investment to anticipated results is "right" for each participant. Although not the norm for recruiting people to join a collective effort, founding the strategic collaboration on an openly honest foundation is more likely to produce the desired outcomes. Similarly, it is important that participants have a sense of reciprocity or shared risk and reward, although not necessarily equal across all participants.[11] Depending on the context, the resources that participants or participating agencies bring to the table and what they hope to receive from the effort will vary greatly. At the same time, those invited were invited for a reason; each participant plays an important role in the overall success of the collaboration, whether to provide financial resources, expertise, political connections, or legitimacy in the community.

Ultimately, participants must determine if the intended benefits and outcomes are important, visible, or legitimate enough to warrant the necessary investment. One essential question for participants should be about the correlation of their agency's mission with that of the collaboration effort. The more direct the connection, the more likely that participation will be mutually beneficial.

4.6 Principle 5: Cultivate Innovation for Meaningful Change

A strategic collaboration is about forging meaningful change that addresses the problem area of focus, ultimately rethinking and transforming the related status quo systems. Therefore, Principle 5 is about nurturing groundbreaking thinking and action. This requires asking new questions, seeing boundaries in different and multiple ways, and encouraging diverse perspectives. From the point of formation on, the promotion of a creative and innovative collaboration mind-set or culture is vital to strategic collaboration. In contrast, organizational managers are often encouraged to focus on efficiency and quality control. The result is a culture that values routinization, rules, stability, and "product" consistency. Instead the mind-set of strategic collaboration turns these on end and calls for public and nonprofit managers to explicitly value and nurture innovation dynamics:

- Hopefulness: Overall positive sense that the collaboration's efforts will produce meaningful results that impact the problem area of focus.
- Transformational thinking: New ways of doing, both incremental and radical, are embraced as the collaboration explores the obstacles and opportunities related to the problem area of focus.
- Moving beyond the status quo: Willingness to question and challenge current practice.
- Multidimensional perspective: Values working across discipline, organization, and sector boundaries and proactively seeks to break down existing barriers to change.
- Ongoing learning: Willingness to invest in new learning and to see mistakes or failures as learning opportunities.

Creating a collaborative mind-set of innovation can hit many barriers related to structure (e.g., restrictive policies, rules and procedures, long chain of command), process (e.g., demands for consensus, slow approval mechanisms), and individual concerns including fear of failure, prejudging ideas, and disparaging remarks. Strategic collaboration requires participants to be imaginative, to envision a future different from the present, to work collaboratively to advantage, and to be change agents.[12]

To counter the sometimes overwhelming barriers, six steps are important to building a collaborative mind-set centered on innovation and results:

1. Expect high-quality innovation and meaningful change.
2. Foster open communication and value creativity.
3. Encourage informal relationships and learning from each other.
4. Provide participants the tools and opportunities for learning and innovation.

5. Explore complex issues from multiple points of view.
6. Keep stakeholders informed of potential recommendations.

The first step in establishing an innovative mind-set is to positively and optimistically anticipate that high-quality innovation and meaningful change will result. Conveners should set high expectations for the collaboration's efforts, recruiting participants who connect to the desired goals but also leaders who can bring the group together to obtain optimal outcomes. Of course, what is meant by these terms *high-quality innovation* and *meaningful change* will vary greatly across any problem area and collaborative group. Consequently, the participants will need to regularly revisit their respective definitions of innovation and change, keeping their key stakeholders informed.

Fostering open, two-way communication and valuing creativity is the second step. Communication strategies and processes should be transparent yet not burdensome. All participants need easy access to all information. Technology can play an important role here today with the advent of Google groups and Web-based tools that make electronic communication easier. All participants should view creative and innovative thinking (no matter how radical) as their responsibility. Finally, communication processes must be safe so that ongoing dialogue is productive. In particular, all participants must protect the process from "naysayers" who can quickly derail creative discourse.

The third step is to nurture informal relationships and ongoing learning from each other. The tried and true tool of brainstorming, "a family of methods that allows noncritical generation of ideas prior to analysis and selection of the best idea,"[13] is a particularly effective method for meeting the multiple goals of developing relationships built on trust while generating ideas and information useful to the overall purposes of the collaboration. Table 4.5 lists common tools for stimulating group-based creativity and innovation.

The fourth step is providing participants with the tools and opportunities for learning and innovation. While participants may come to the table with expansive knowledge related to the collaboration's purpose, cultivating creativity often requires time, training in new methods such as benchmarking or trend analysis, and exposure to new information. Site visits, experts (e.g., researchers who can raise questions in new ways), consultants, and guest speakers may provide the needed stimulus for creative discourse.

The fifth step is to explore complex issues from multiple points of view, communicating assumptions openly but suspending judgment in the first stages of discussion. The evaluation of alternatives and a decision for the best course of action comes later. Conflict is inevitable and must be kept constructive by showing respect for every team member, encouraging expression of feelings as well as ideas, but limiting criticism to ideas and positions rather than individuals.

The final step is to keep stakeholders, including participating agency's leaders, informed of potential recommendations to increase broad consensus on the

Table 4.5 Tools for Group Creativity and Innovation

- Brainstorming

- Nominal group technique

- Group passing technique

- Team idea mapping method

- Directed brainstorming

- 6-3-5 Brainwriting

- Mindmapping

- Delphi processes

- Productive thinking models

proposed innovations. Resistance to change must be anticipated, but information sharing along the way is an important tool for enlarging the base of support while gathering useful feedback.

4.7 Principle 6: Emphasize Outcomes and Impacts

While recognizing critical processes that nurture innovation and creativity (see Principle 5), Principle 6 embraces a results orientation that keeps the collaboration focused on goal achievement:

- Returning regularly to the collaboration's goals, priorities, and desired results.
- Setting criteria for measuring and monitoring.
- Using existing data and analysis when available, but with a critical eye.
- Considering experimentation and pilot studies and projects to test models.
- Creating and sharing useable knowledge.
- Rewarding and recognizing accomplishments.

Collective agreement on what is important and on what should be tracked to identify successful results requires ongoing attention. Desired results or the strategies for measuring results can vary by participant and by stakeholder group, making it essential that collaboration time is spent on exploring the range of possible measurements and articulating a shared understanding around the measures selected. The agreed upon results should be large and small, short term, intermediate, and long term in nature. Importantly, collaborative goals and priorities should identify early results so that participants see positive benefits, both tangible and intangible, from their effort. Early success further engages participants and sets an important tone for the collaboration's developing culture.

The use of previously collected data or data collected for purposes outside of the collaboration's purview should be considered for efficiency purposes. These data can raise new questions that lead to new possibilities. For this strategy to be effective, however, participants must understand data limitations such that available databases may be insufficiently comparable, current, or complete. Research suggests that collaboration decision making based on data, however, is important to participants' perceptions of community impact.[14] Grounded in data, analysis, and evidence-based methods, participants should entertain the use of rigorous evaluation, perhaps on a small scale or pilot basis, to test innovations and to build the case for larger resource investments. To support effective evidence-based decision making, strategic collaboration participants will often require additional training.

Sharing results with appropriate stakeholders in a format that is useful and relevant is also essential. Although creating knowledge that can be used by a wide range of users takes time and attention, adopting this posture to stakeholder management increases the likelihood that the collaboration's voice will be heard, that the work will be valued in the short and long term, and that meaningful change will result. Therefore, choosing dissemination strategies requires attention and intentionality as to who the ideal users are, an understanding of the formats that would be most useful to those users, and identification of the time sensitivity for information sharing. (See Table 4.6 for a sample list of dissemination methods.)

Principles 5 and 6 encompass the art and science of the strategic collaboration as change agent. The art is in the innovation and creativity to envision and build

Table 4.6   Collaboration Dissemination Methods

- Written report
- Issue report card
- Issue dashboard
- Press release
- Press conference
- Research report
- Community event
- Workshop or training sessions
- Website
- Conference presentation

new solutions to public problems while social science data and understanding provide analytical tools for assessing opportunities and outcomes.

4.8 Implementing Strategic Collaboration

While the skills demanded for effective strategic collaboration practice are similar to those used by public and nonprofit administrators in everyday management of organizations, the principles presented here argue that there is a significant difference in the application of these skills to a context inherently more unstable, fragile, and idiosyncratic. The need to work skillfully both within and outside one's hierarchy, to frame the environmental context of the situation, and to work with an emerging set of norms, roles, and values is magnified for public and nonprofit managers in the collaboration setting. Moreover, negotiation, communication, conflict resolution, and facilitation skills must be practiced in an environment that is marked by institutional and individual competition for resources, turf, and status; participant commitment levels that wax and wane with little consequence; and an overarching context that is inherently uncertain. Therefore, collaboration participants must develop and strengthen a broad range of strategic skills to be effective in this different role. Ideally, participants also possess personal traits that foster effective collaboration (Table 4.7).

To explicitly tie the six principles to practice, the following questions and answers identify and summarize key components of successful strategic collaboration practice:

- **What resources are required for strategic collaboration?** The key resource required is engaged participants. Other resources (e.g., paid staff, meeting space, equipment) will be determined as the collaboration's goals and processes evolve. Optimal versus feasible decisions regarding resources will be needed as the collaboration moves to implementation. The lack of sufficient resources may be an indication that the collaboration is doomed from the start. Determining sufficiency requires an open and realistic discussion and assessment by conveners.
- **What is the role of leadership in strategic collaboration?** At the onset, a neutral, trusted leader can play an important role in convening a strong set of participants. Universities are also useful in this role due to their perceived impartial and nonpartisan position. Importantly, the leaders should possess political acuity and cultural competence to recruit, develop, and work with a diverse set of participants.
- **Who should be involved in strategic collaboration?** The public problem or issue at hand provides the information for identifying the set of appropriate participants. In addition to bringing related knowledge, skills, abilities, and needed resources, conveners should set out to create a diverse group that crosses

Table 4.7   Personal Traits for the Ideal Strategic Collaboration Participant

- Competent (technical knowledge, analytical capacity).

- Effective communication skills (both sending and receiving).

- Self-aware (comfortable with self and understand how behaviors affect others in collective situations).

- Disciplined curiosity (alert to new information; variety of sources yet can make sense of situation with incomplete or limited data).

- Optimistic (belief that positive outcomes will result).

- Reality-based, catalyst for action (when to stay with process and when to make a decision).

- Team player (comfortable with group process and possess skills to build trusting relationships, not always be in control, negotiate conflict, and navigate connection to home organization).

organizations, sectors and disciplines, politics, and individual characteristics (e.g., education, experience, perspectives, race, culture, socioeconomic status). Having at least a few participants with significant and positive experience in a collaborative setting is very useful to advancing the effort. Another dimension to consider is expertise knowledge versus "on-the-ground" experience. To fully understand the problem of focus and to create new strategies for change, many different experiences and expectations will prove useful.

■ **What is the role of participants in strategic collaborations?** Participants must be engaged in the work of the collaboration: Participants come prepared to meetings by reviewing materials and completing assignments; they participate fully in decision making and creative processes; they report back to important stakeholders laying the foundation for the larger impacts of the collaboration's work.

■ **How are citizens involved in strategic collaboration?** The level and specific role of citizens varies by the purpose of the strategic collaboration. Regardless of whether citizens or nonprofessionals are regular participants in the collaboration, the results will affect citizens, making their direct and indirect input essential. This input must be carefully planned and valued.

■ **How many participants are required for strategic collaboration?** Specific advice on an adequate number cannot be provided. The number of participants should parallel the scope of the problem being addressed by the collaboration's efforts. At the exploration stage, a smaller number of participants increase nimbleness while laying the groundwork for the greater inclusiveness and participant numbers as the collaboration evolves to the growth stage. If a large number of participants are appropriate, methods such as a steering committee and a set of working taskforces may be useful for best using the talents and knowledge of all participants. As participant numbers and complexity increase, the challenges for maintaining effective processes and expected results also increase.[15] Geographic proximity is another challenge in recruiting participants. When distance becomes a challenge, ever improving technology may provide new methods for active communication (e.g., telephone and videoconferencing, group work software such as Google Documents, Microsoft's SharePoint software).

- **How can a collaboration be sustained?** A strategic collaboration is time limited from onset. This defining characteristic allows participants to engage in a more focused way than in a nebulous collective effort that participants fear will become a competitor for their respective organizations. Nevertheless, specific attention is required to structures, processes, and outcomes that are responsive to participant and stakeholder expectations for the necessary level of engagement to move the collaboration toward its overall goals. Each collaboration stage should have outcomes that can be celebrated or recognized so that next steps can be planned.

- **How can the collaboration's effort stay on track?** Ongoing assessment of processes and activities is key to the progress of strategic collaboration. From a process standpoint, rules of engagement and risks and rewards should be explicit. In addition, methods that create accountability streams for participants and stakeholders related to outcomes will focus the group's work.

- **What impacts can be achieved with strategic collaboration?** Established goals should inspire the collaboration to reach for consequential change—to make a real difference—while being feasible for the time, resources, and capacities of the current context. Revolutionary change may be required to resolve many of today's public problems. Strategic collaboration can lay the groundwork for larger, transformational change while successfully achieving smaller goals.

Strategic collaboration can accomplish what could never be achieved in a silo. Not only can strategic collaboration create new solutions to public problems, but as a byproduct participants become stronger players in their own organizations and communities. The collaborative intelligence produced by engaging in effective strategic collaboration practice increases the knowledge, skills, and abilities of participants, thus increasing their capacity to (1) work meaningfully with others to develop innovative projects and programs; (2) compete better for external funding; and (3) contribute to and lead new collaborative efforts.

Much like learning organizations, a successful strategic collaboration will thrive in a dynamic environment, will develop structures and rules only as necessary to meet process and accountability demands, and will focus on creating strong informal relationships that lead to synergistic innovation and become a catalyst for change.

4.9 Tying the Pieces Together: A Framework of Strategic Collaboration

Moving *ad hoc* collaboration to a level of strategic practice requires purposeful decision making and systematic action throughout the evolution of the collaboration. A more strategic perspective increases the likelihood of positive outcomes for those involved in the collaboration and, most importantly, for the public problems targeted. The framework of strategic collaboration provides public and nonprofit managers valuable guidance to advance effective public service practice and to play key roles in public problem solving. Building from a growing research and practice literature (see Appendix G for a summary literature review of American Society of Public Administration [ASPA]-sponsored journals),[16] the framework identifies the critical components of strategic collaboration:

- Understanding the collaboration context.
- An intentional decision for strategic collaboration.
- Considering the collaboration's life cycle of development, including the time to end.
- Using appropriate organizational expertise and adding enhanced strategic collaboration knowledge, skills, and abilities.
- Acknowledging and endorsing a multifaceted view of desired impacts.

The framework builds on what we know to help public and nonprofit managers considering or planning to use strategic collaboration as well as those seeking to analyze or diagnose an existing collaboration to enhance successful outcomes from collaborative activities.

The framework integrates the pieces presented earlier to coherently organize the essential features of strategic collaboration practice, including when leaders and managers should use strategic collaboration; what expertise, processes, and resources will be needed at each stage of the collaboration's development; and how to know if collaboration is successful. Figure 4.1 graphically illustrates the key components of the framework. On the far left side of the figure, the collaboration context includes the factors (e.g., complex problems, events, government or funder requirement, ideas or opportunities) that "push and pull" public and nonprofit managers out of their individual agencies, to cross organizational boundaries and sectors and to forge connections to other policy arenas.

Given the right confluence of contextual factors, the initial stage of a strategic collaboration life cycle emerges. Just as organizations follow a predictable pattern of development, collaborative efforts evolve through a series of stages that offer public and nonprofit managers insights into better understanding, planning, diagnosing, and administering collaboration. The collaboration life cycle model presented in Chapter 2 begins with the exploration stage, which includes the decision point: to collaborate or not? The explicit determination of collaboration readiness identified

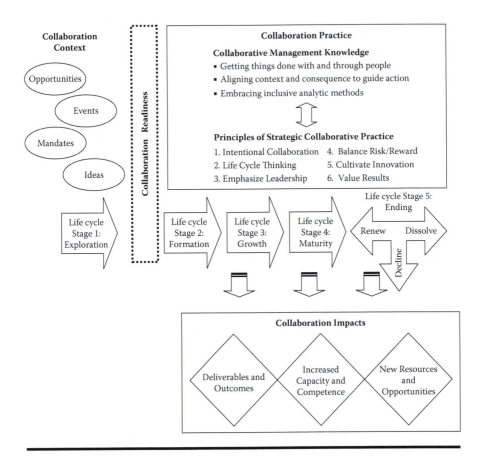

Figure 4.1 Framework of strategic collaboration.

in the starred box in Figure 4.1 requires deliberate knowledge gathering and decision making identifying whether the five conditions are met: (1) legitimate and pressing need to collaborate; (2) critical mass and sufficient representativeness; (3) skilled and committed leadership; (4) competence for collaboration; and (5) reasonable probability of consequential change. If the decision is to proceed, the life cycle stages that follow—formation, growth, maturity, and ending—have a significant and ongoing interaction effect fueled by feedback opportunities and the environmental dynamics (social, economic, and political) constantly flowing into the open system operations of strategic collaboration, allowing for adaptation as the external or internal conditions change.[17] The collaboration life cycle model offers practitioners an organizing scheme that captures the knowledge, skills, and abilities needed at each of the five stages to move the collaboration toward success and desired impacts.

Another key element of the framework is collaboration practice, identifying both the expertise about effective organizational management that participants bring to collaboration and the more specific knowledge, skills, and abilities required for strategic thinking and acting identified in the six principles presented earlier in this chapter. The final component of the framework of strategic collaboration is impact, including the collaboration specific deliverables and outcomes, increased capacity of participants, and the future resources and opportunities. These impacts may begin as soon as the strategic collaboration's work is under way and may continue long after its official work is ended. As described in Principle 6, a results orientation is critical to the success of strategic collaboration.

4.10 From the Field: Nine Cases and Implications for Strategic Collaboration Practice

The nine case studies that follow in Chapters 5 through 13 examine strategic collaborations that have a broad focus, cross multiple policy arenas, and use multiorganizational representatives as participants. The cases represent a variety of geographic locations, policy arenas, and collaboration contexts and as a group comprehensively cover the promises and realities of strategic collaboration. An overview of the case and strategic collaboration lessons learned are presented in a case brief at the beginning of each case.

Each of the case collaborations brings together agencies with competing interests and individuals with very different areas of expertise, experiences, and expectations. At the same time, all sought to influence the outcome and affect public policy processes, with leaders attempting to strategically manage the collaborative processes. Each case had high-stakes implications and articulated a shared mission and set of goals and priorities that served as a strategic focus of the collaboration.

Chapter 14 summarizes the practical lessons from the cases to highlight key implications for how to create strategic collaborations, discusses the fundamentals of mastery, and identifies roadblocks for collaboration success.

Endnotes

1. Ansell and Gash reviewed 137 collaboration case studies and found that five factors influence whether collaboration governance will be successful: (1) prior history of cooperation or conflict (and how this is worked through to either facilitate or hinder collaboration); (2) stakeholder incentives; (3) presence of imbalances in resources and power; (4) quality of leadership skills to steward the process; and (5) the basic procedures and collaboration protocols that shape and guide collaboration processes. In addition, these researchers found that collaboration processes needed to include face-to-face dialogue and the building and development of trust, shared understanding, and commitment to create a virtuous cycle of collaboration. They concluded that three core contingencies—time, trust, and interdependence—apply that should be considered before embarking on collaboration. C. Ansell and A. Gash, Collaborative Governance in Theory and Practice, *Journal of Public Administration Research and Theory, 18* (4): 543–571, 2008.

2. The degree of collaboration, coordination, or cooperation needed to yield the desired outcomes needs to be weighed prior to embarking on collaboration. These decisions thus affect selecting collaboration as a strategy as well as the design of the collaboration effort. See L. Bingham and R. O'Leary, Conclusion: Parallel Play, Not Collaboration: Missing Questions, Missing Connections, *Public Administration Review*, 66 (Supplement): 161–167, 2006; R. Keast, K. Brown, and M. Mandell, Getting the Right Mix: Unpacking Integration Meanings and Strategies, *International Public Management Journal*, 10 (1): 9–33, 2007; Mandell and Keast, Evaluating Network Arrangements: Toward Revised Performance Measures, *Public Performance & Management Review*, 30 (4): 574–597, 2007.

3. Based on his analysis of a comparative cross-case analysis, Imperial argues that the challenge facing public managers "is to identify opportunities for collaboration that create public value while simultaneously minimizing problems and transaction costs," further suggesting that "when used inappropriately, it can create more problems than it solves." M. Imperial, Using Collaboration as a Governance Strategy: Lessons From Six Watershed Management Programs, *Administration & Society*, 37 (3): 312, 2005.

4. From their review of nine community-based nonprofits over a 10-year period, Alexander and Nank found that collaboration was fostered through sharing of information, integrating responsibilities, and collaborative decision making. To accomplish this, they advise that public service administrators need to shift from a professional role to a facilitative-leadership posture to successfully collaborate with members of the community to identify problems and solutions. J. Alexander and R. Nank, Public–Nonprofit Partnership: Realizing the New Public Service, *Administration & Society*, 41 (3): 364–386, 2009.

5. K. Babick and L. Thibault, Challenges in Multiple Cross-Sector Partnerships, *Nonprofit and Voluntary Sector Quarterly*, 38: 177–143, 2008; D.R. Connelly, Leadership in the Collaborative Interorganizational Domain, *International Journal of Public Administration*, 30: 1231–1262, 2007.

6. Building trust is consistently repeated in the collaboration research literature as a key factor in collaboration success. For example, see Imperial, Using Collaboration; J. Bryson, B.C. Crosby, and M. Stone, The Design and Implementation of Cross-Sector Collaborations: Propositions from the Literature, *Public Administration Review*, 66 (Supplement): 44–55, 2006; A. Thomson and J. Perry, Collaborative Processes: Inside the Black Box, *Public Administration Review*, 66 (Supplement): 20–32, 2006; M. McGuire, Collaborative Public Management: Assessing What We Know and How We Know It, *Public Administration Review* 66 (Supplement): 33–43, 2006; W.L. Waugh and G. Streib, Collaboration and Leadership for Effective Emergency Management, *Public Administration Review*, 66 (Supplement): 131–140, 2006; Keast et al., Getting the Right Mix; P. Kathi, T. Cooper, and J. Meek, The Role of the University as a Mediating Institution in Neighborhood Council–City Agency Collaboration, *Journal of Public Affairs Education*, 13 (2): 365–382, 2007; J. Alford and O. Hughes, Public Value Pragmatism as the Next Phase of Public Management, *American Review of Public Administration*, 38 (2): 130-148, 2008; Alexander and Nank, Public–Nonprofit Partnership; and Thomson, Perry, and T. Miller, Conceptualizing and Measuring Collaboration, *Journal of Public Administration Research and Theory*, 19 (1): 23–56, 2009.

7. K. Babiak and L. Thibault, Challenges in Multiple Cross-Sector Partnerships, *Nonprofit and Voluntary Sector Quarterly*, 38: 117–143, 2008.

8. C. Huxam and D. Macdonald, Introducing Collaborative Advantage: Achieving Interorganizational Effectiveness through Meta-strategy, *Management Decision, 30* (3): 50–56, 1992.

9. Importantly, government managers are advised not to take on the role of "expert" or attempt to hierarchically "manage" the process if the collaboration is to be successful and create processes that adopt more inclusive interactions and have an emergent posture. See T. Bryer, Explaining Responsiveness in Collaboration: Administrator and Citizen Role Perceptions, *Public Administration Review, 69* (2): 271–283, 2009; M.S. Feldman, A. Khademian, H. Ingram, and A.S. Schneider, Ways of Knowing and Inclusive Management Practices, *Public Administration Review, 66* (Supplement): 89–99, 2006; J. Kiefer and R. Montjoy, Incrementalism before the Storm: Network Performance for the Evacuation of New Orleans, *Public Administration Review, 66*: 122–130, 2006; H. Getha-Taylor, Learning Indicators and Collaborative Capacity: Applying Action Learning Principles to the U.S. Department of Homeland Security, *Public Administration Quarterly, 32* (2): 125–146, 2008; A. Van Buuren, Knowledge for Governance, Governance of Knowledge: Inclusive Knowledge Management in Collaborative Governance Processes, *International Public Management Journal, 12* (2): 208–235, 2009.

10. In their exploratory research, a 56-item questionnaire was developed by Thomson et al. to address five dimensions of collaboration: (1) governance; (2) administration; (3) autonomy; (4) mutuality; and (5) norms. The instrument was mailed to 1,382 directors who participated in AmeriCorps in 2000 and 2001 and had a 32% response rate. The specific questions include items that ask about how much partners' opinions matter or are appreciated or whether there is agreement on goals as well as asking whether the organization involved in the collaboration knows why other participating organizations belong to the collaboration (the questions are provided in their article). The 17-indicator scale that resulted from this effort offers another instrument that could be used to surface underlying tensions and take the "temperature" of the collaboration. From their analysis, Thomson et al. found that the 17 indicators were valid measures of the five dimensions and are determining whether the 17-item collaboration scale is useful in examining outcomes. Although still needing further empirical testing, the instrument offers a way for collaboration participants to start a dialogue and reflection process. Thomson et al. Conceptualizing and Measuring Collaboration. See also the collaborative leadership tools, self-assessment tools, and skill-building exercises offered by the Turning Point Leadership Development National Excellence Collaborative, a partnership of local, state, and national public health organizations, supported by The Robert Wood Johnson Foundation. Turning Point. Leadership Development. February 10, 2006. http://www.turningpointprogram.org/Pages/leaddev.html.

11. B.G. Peters, "With a Little Help from Our Friends": Public–Private Partnerships as Institutions and Instruments, In *Partnerships in Urban Governance,* ed. J. Pierre (New York: St. Marten's, 1998), pp. 11–33.

12. See B. Gray, *Collaborating: Finding Common Ground for Multi-Party Problems* (San Francisco: Jossey-Bass, 1989), p. 5; J. McKnight, *The Careless Society: Community and Its Counterfeit* (New York: Basic Books, 1995); E. Goldman, Strategic Thinking at the Top, *MIT Sloan Management Review, 48* (4): 75–81, 2007; R. Ireland and M. Hitt, Achieving and Maintaining Strategic Competitiveness in the 21st Century: The Role of Strategic Leadership, *Academy of Management Executive, 13* (1): 43–57,

1999; C. Huxham and S. Vangen, *Managing to Collaborate: The Theory and Practice of Collaborative Advantage* (London: Routledge, 2005); J. Camilus, Strategy as a Wicked Problem, *Harvard Business Review*, 99–106, May 2008.

13. M. Van Wart, *Dynamics of Leadership in Public Service: Theory and Practice* (Armonk, NY: M.E. Sharpe, 2005), p. 41.

14. R. Wells, M. Feinberg, J.A. Alexander, and A.J. Ward, Factors Affecting Member Perceptions of Coalition Impact, *Nonprofit and Voluntary Sector Quarterly*, *19* (3): 327–348, 2009.

15. B. Gazley and J.L. Brudney, The Purpose (and Perils) of Government–Nonprofit Partnership, *Nonprofit and Voluntary Sector Quarterly*, *36*: 389–415, 2007.

16. Also see P. Foster-Fishman, S. Berkowitz, D. Lounsbury, S. Jacobson, and N. Allen, Building Collaborative Capacity in Community Coalitions: A Review and Integrative Framework, *American Journal of Community Psychology*, *29* (2): 241–261, 2001, for a review of literature published 1975–1997, on community-based collaborations. These authors identify emerging themes related to critical elements of collaborative capacity and strategies for building core collaborative capacities. See Turning Point's review of the collaborative leadership literature 1985–2001. Turning Point Leadership Development National Excellence Collaborative. Collaborative Leadership and Health: A Review of the Literature. 2001. http://www.turningpointprogram.org/toolkit/content/cllit-review.htm (accessed July 12, 2009). See also Ansell and Gash's meta-analysis of 137 collaboration case studies to identify contingent conditions that affect collaborative success, such as leadership and power. Ansell and Gash, Collaborative Governance.

17. E. Mulroy, Community as a Factor in Implementing Interorganizational Partnerships: Issues, Constraints, and Adaptations, *Nonprofit and Voluntary Sector Quarterly*, *14* (1): 48–66, 2003.

Chapter 5

Attending to the Forgotten: The Elderly, Collaborative Practice, and Evacuation

Pamela J. Jenkins, John J. Kiefer, and Shirley Laska

Contents

Case Brief

Background and Purpose of the Collaboration: The impact of Hurricane Katrina on the Gulf Coast region, and particularly New Orleans, clearly demonstrated serious flaws in the evacuation of vulnerable citizens. More than 1,000 people perished in the storm, most of them seniors. The City of New Orleans and many nonprofit organizations were fiscally challenged in Katrina's wake. A long history of distrust existed in the region: distrust between local government and citizens, between different levels of government, between government and nonprofit organizations, and even among citizens of different ethnicities and socioeconomic status. In addition, the elder population faced a myriad problems that involved their displacement, return, and possible recovery. As an essential part of their recovery, the question of evacuation safety persisted. This collaboration brought together key agencies and stakeholders to identify needed resources for ensuring a responsible evacuation for New Orleans's most vulnerable citizens. Funded by the Grantmakers in Aging Hurricane Fund for the Elderly, the collaboration was initiated by the University of New Orleans Center for Hazards Assessment, Response and Technology (CHART), a center focused on community-based disaster response for resiliency, and the Greater New Orleans Regional Planning Commission. The initial group structured the project to examine how to incorporate the knowledge and capacity of nongovernmental stakeholders into the planning for elderly evacuation.

Current Status: This collaborative network, centered on the Elderly Evacuation Working Group, continues to meet periodically to assist and assess local evacuation plans. In the wake of Hurricane Gustav, the authors were contacted by the city and asked to provide information about what worked well and what problems took place during the evacuation. The research team designed a detailed survey that asked questions about the evacuation experience and administered that survey to a random sample from over 18,000 citizens who participated in the City Assisted Evacuation Program (CAEP). The results were provided to the mayor and the city's Office of Emergency Preparedness as well as to members of the Elderly Evacuation Working Group. The lessons reported through the survey will serve as a strong foundation for improving the city's evacuation of its most vulnerable citizens.

Lessons for Strategic Collaboration Practice: In this case, a team of university researchers acted as the issue catalyst. The team had a long history of community involvement, and the university was regarded as apolitical by key stakeholder agencies. A community champion was recruited and played a key role in gaining support from potential participants. The champion's role as broker was essential in fostering a sense of shared commitment across a diverse group of stakeholders, identifying needed resources, and developing a realistic plan for linking extant resources with a myriad of shortfalls. Trust was built through attention to paced, inclusionary conversations to build shared perspectives. Early in the process, negative reaction to the role and style of government experts required a regrouping. Ultimately, the strategic collaboration approach not only increased the visibility of the elderly population's need in the time of emergency but also repaired and strengthened stakeholder relationships for broader community-building efforts.

As with all of us who speak and write on Katrina, we use an exemplar to show the complexity of the event. One of the authors begins each talk on Hurricane Katrina with the story of her friend's mother. Her mother did not evacuate because she was in a wheelchair and had lived through previous storms. Several members of her family were with her, and she thought she was safe in her house. But the waters came, and her family tried to get her to safety. First, they pushed her to a school where they were told rescuers were coming. No one came. Then, they pushed her to a nursing home where they were also told people would come. No one came. Then, they pushed her to I-10 where they were assured help would come. No one came. A friend of her grandson "borrowed" a water truck and drove her to the Superdome. She finally got on a plane to San Antonio, and then her family got her to Las Vegas, where one month later (in October 2005) she died. She did not die because she was 78 years old—she was still active, connected to her church, family, and community. She died because no one came.

5.1 Introduction

The introductory story, in some version, was repeated over and over in the first week after Hurricane Katrina. The story of the elderly did not end as the waters receded. The elder population faced problems that involved displacement, return, and possible recovery. As an essential part of their recovery, the question of evacuation safety persists.

This case illustrates the importance of an issue "champion" in acting as a catalyst for bringing together and gaining the support of a variety of players that are essential to developing a viable solution to a problem. In this case, a team of university researchers acted as the catalyst. The team had a long history of community involvement, and the university was regarded as apolitical by stakeholder agencies. Essential in this case was the fostering of a sense of shared commitment, identification of needed resources, and development of a realistic plan for linking extant resources with a myriad of shortfalls. To do this, the team identified best practices in elderly evacuation, capitalized on the local experiences suffered by vulnerable citizens during Hurricane Katrina, and implemented a collaborative network of stakeholders to craft workable solutions for reducing risk. To be effective, the network had to be viewed by all stakeholders as inclusionary, and one that was built with a shared sense of trust and commitment.

The chronology of events that the elderly faced is one of the most critical and underreported problems of Hurricane Katrina.[1] If the elderly evacuated, they faced, along with the others, hours on the road with few amenities and anxiety of the unknown. They also had to very quickly adjust and adapt to new surroundings such as a shelter in an evacuee city, a stranger's home, or the home of a family member.

For those who stayed, the experience was life-threatening and sometimes fatal. As the waters rose, many elderly found themselves caught in their attics or abandoned in hospitals or nursing homes. Many of the frail had successfully negotiated their living spaces pre-Katrina. They could live in their homes, knowing where everything was, who their neighbors were, and how to ask for help. In the first week after the storm, as 80% of the city flooded, nearly all of the infrastructure was destroyed, and, in effect, so was their world.

The elderly experienced significantly higher rates of mortality from this event relative to any other age group. Although elderly age 60 and older comprised only 15% of the population, 60% of Katrina deaths were in this age group.[2] The world tragically witnessed the inadequate evacuation and sheltering plan for New Orleans during Hurricane Katrina. Complicated medical conditions, transportation debacles, and the often extreme stress of uprooting regular routines were just a few of the reasons that forced some elderly to choose to stay behind or to evacuate too late. It was evident that a disproportionately larger amount of attention and resources directed at evacuating senior citizens was critical to ensuring acceptable outcomes in subsequent evacuations.

During the recovery, the elderly have also found their lives still disrupted. Even if they were homeowners, the amount of paperwork involved in claiming benefits was difficult. Applying for Federal Emergency Management Agency (FEMA) grants, insurance, American Red Cross benefits, and other funding was time-consuming and often unsuccessful. The amount of work to rebuild their lives after the storm continues to be unrelenting. All of the events of the recovery—families dispersing, senior centers closing, congregations not returning—have made the elderly in the city more vulnerable than before the storm.[3] As each hurricane season approaches, the needs of the elderly increase, and the ability of the New Orleans's community to reach and respond to them remains a critical issue.

In lieu of providing a *shelter of last resort*, the focus before and during Katrina, the city of New Orleans and the state of Louisiana are now developing *evacuation plans of last resort* for the most vulnerable populations: the "special needs" and the elderly. Although this top-down approach to evacuation planning is necessary, as this case will illustrate, it is not sufficient to address the complex needs and barriers in the community or to accommodate the entire elderly population.

5.2 Establishing an Effective Collaborative Structure

5.2.1 The Role of Public Administrators (Government and Nonprofit) in Forming and Convening the Collaboration

The collaboration described was initiated as part of a university project funded by the Grantmakers in Aging Hurricane Fund for the Elderly. When the facts about what had happened to the elderly began to emerge after the hurricane, the University of New Orleans Center for Hazards Assessment, Response, and Technology (CHART), a center focused on community-based disaster response for resiliency, collaborated with the greater New Orleans Regional Planning Commission to reframe the elderly issues. The initial group structured the project to examine how to incorporate the knowledge and capacity of nongovernmental stakeholders into the planning for elderly evacuation. The goal throughout the project was to build on the strengths and efforts already existent in this group of stakeholders. The other critical task was to facilitate how to combine the more top-down efforts of the government with those of the more neighborhood- and community-based elderly services agencies.

To identify the most important nonprofit organization leaders on elderly issues, the initial group talked with several community leaders and then selected one of the first stakeholders to discuss the project. Selection of the "entrance point" into the nonprofit community was extremely important because it set the stage for building the rest of the collaboration. The person selected held a key position in that nonprofit organization network. During this first meeting, additional names were requested of other nonprofit personnel from other organizations that also had a commitment to ensuring safe elderly evacuation. Identifying the initial group began the process of purposively snowball sampling elderly stakeholders. Each of these individuals was then contacted in person to discern if he or she would be interested in participating and also was asked to recommend others. Given that the end goal was to strengthen the overall success of the evacuation of the elderly from New Orleans, city officials were invited to participate. Also, representatives of the American Red Cross, the large, quasi-government disaster agency, were invited. While this group of nonprofit organization and government representatives certainly knew each other, they had not ever been asked before to participate in this manner.

5.2.2 Negotiating Purpose and Mission

At the beginning of each meeting, we restated our purpose to create further understanding about increasing safe elderly evacuation, building a working relationship with city and nongovernmental agencies, and building on local knowledge with national best practice. Each of the individual meetings and the larger workshops began with recognition of respect for the local knowledge of the stakeholders. It was very important to create a conversational environment that would permit the evolution of the initial idea with input from the practitioners. As the challenges of the elderly and those of the public agencies to assist in solving them have become increasingly clear, the purpose and mission of the collaborative effort have evolved.

5.2.3 Structures Created: Rules of
Participation, Roles Defined

The primary rule of participation for those invited to join the project was that they be willing to participate in the bimonthly meetings that would be held throughout the year of the project. The group committed to a number of meetings for the length of the project. The group established a collaborative process in the meetings. There was always a facilitator, but participation was the most important factor in all meetings. As much as possible, the director of the Council on Aging took the leadership role in a very inclusionary way rather than in a vertical, hierarchical manner.

5.2.3.1 Phase II of the Stakeholders Project

Following completion of the first year's efforts, a broader recruitment and participation process evolved as the purpose of the group changed. The second year's goal was to refine the needs that came out of the first year and to define actions that could support addressing the needs. It became evident that the nonprofit organizations representing the elderly stakeholders were addressing some of the core needs but that the next step had to be an inclusionary one, bringing the other *general* disaster response agencies to the table so that the efforts of all could inform the discussion about the most pressing needs and their solution. Of course, the initial participants were encouraged to continue, and many of them did. The wider net was cast of both nonprofit and various government organizations (Table 5.1).

5.3 Attending to Process and Procedures

5.3.1 Process to Establish Purpose, Rules, Policies

Great care was taken during the initial conversations with the nonprofit organizations representing the elderly stakeholders. We felt it extremely important to describe the tentative structure and process right at the beginning of our initiative. The initial ideas were modified through these conversations, but little more

Table 5.1 Elderly Evacuation Working Group Participation

Original, Phase I Participants	Phase II Participants
University of New Orleans	Original members, plus:
New Orleans Council on Aging	New Orleans Fire Department
American Red Cross	Volunteers of America
Catholic Charities	Mercy Corps
Central City Senior Center	New Orleans Police Department
City of New Orleans Office of Emergency Preparedness	New Orleans Emergency Medical Services
Kingsley House	St. Tammany Parish Office of Homeland Security
Operation Brother's Keeper	Cox Communications
Social Security Administration	Regional Transit Authority
Uptown Shepherds' Center	Louisiana State University

was needed for the group to effectively function throughout the first phase of the project. During the second expanded stakeholder phase, similar purpose and rules were eventually implemented, but at the outset all participants were not so directly informed on an individual basis. Refinement and consensus were reached during the first meeting of the group. The unfortunate result of this less structured process was that more control was assumed initially by specific individuals. Yet we knew it would be important to ensure a balanced conversation among participants. This was accomplished at the second meeting of the Elderly Evacuation Working Group, where careful attention was given to organizing the meeting in such a way that the more balanced conversation resulted, stimulating the collaborative environment and eliciting a broad range of topics for truly interactive discussion.

5.3.2 Leadership, Trust, Communication, Sharing Investment and Risk

Throughout the project, we exercised participatory leadership with careful attention to inclusivity of the players. This resulted in very little "turf" negotiation in the initial phase. The conversations engendered full participation and encouraged the sharing of investment and risk—important considerations for the establishment of a functional collaborative network. Some agencies rotated their respective agency's participants rather than having the same representative each time. This had the unfortunate effect of diminishing the "bonding" that might have occurred if the same person had been able to attend each meeting. But an unintended positive benefit was that the group enjoyed a somewhat broader variety of ideas and opinions. We felt that the considered pace of the meetings, the inclusionary conversations, the shared commitment to goals, and the resulting shared perspective on the issues appeared to engender trust among the participants.

5.4 Assuring Accountability

This unique stakeholder group was not formed in the traditional sense of collaboration but in the hope that we could better understand the process of the elderly issues in evacuation. Thus, as already described, the members were carefully chosen to represent the voices of the elderly as well as the elderly themselves. Accountability was achieved in the first phase by continually doing a member check of the organization. As we worked through best national practices as a group, we verified the points that were most salient for the entire group. This involved discussion and rewording of the document as it progressed. Each participant was continually asked to comment on drafts and to provide feedback on the process. Finally, two different meetings were held: one at the Senior Center for the Council on Aging and another at a senior center connected with a congregation. At each of these meetings, local best practices were presented, and the group members (all elderly or working with elderly) were allowed to comment on the findings. In each case, we modified our local knowledge to reflect the input from the community.

The measurable objectives of the process were as follows:

- Identify and recruit community leaders and stakeholders who are either elderly themselves or individual caregivers.
- Identify and recruit organizational leaders among the stakeholder agencies and nonprofit organizations, including faith-based organizations, who work with the elderly.
- Form a working group of leaders and stakeholders that will develop an evacuation action plan for community-based organizations and recommendations to the city.
- Engage the public at large in the planning process through a series of community meetings that inform the working group and give a noninstitutional perspective to the challenges of evacuation of elderly and infirmed populations.
- Produce recommendations for the city.
- Produce an action plan for mobilizing nongovernmental resources, and coordinate community-based evacuation efforts.

The program was evaluated by whether the following benchmark activities were completed to a satisfactory level:

- Identifying barriers to evacuation by the elderly. Through this community-based planning process, the working group consortium did identify the barriers that had previously dissuaded or prevented the elderly from evacuating in a hurricane. The barriers were explicitly stated in the action plan. The measure of whether the list is comprehensive comes from the response by the citizens at the final community meeting where the action plan is unveiled.
- Creating short- and long-term solutions to these barriers. The working group identified short- and long-term solutions to the barriers to evacuation among the elderly. As with the previous outcome, the measure of whether these solutions are appropriate comes from the response by the citizens at the final community meeting when the action plan is unveiled.
- Creating a time frame for the implementation of the evacuation plan. Included in the action plan was a time frame for implementation.
- Identifying local leadership. The planning process allowed individuals from stakeholder organizations and the general public to take leadership roles in the creation of a city-wide nonprofit organization evacuation plan. This leadership was crucial to pressing for implementation of the plan. The success of this outcome was measured by the number of highly active participants in the working group and the number of individuals recruited from the general meetings to participate in the working group.

■ Creating a standing working group. This process created the Elderly Evacuation Working Group, which will continue to work on the issue of elderly evacuation. Success was measured by the number of participants who explicitly agreed to continue working on the implementation phase of this plan once this grant was complete.

■ Building trust in the community through transparency. An evacuation plan is good only if individuals trust that it will work for them and are willing to participate in the evacuation process as outlined in the plan. Given the challenges that the carless citizens experienced in evacuating from Katrina, building trust in the plan is both extremely challenging and vital to its success. By holding community meetings to engage the public in the decision-making process, the working committee gained the trust of the citizens that it was forming a plan that is in their best interest. The measure of this success was from feedback forms at the community meetings, especially the final presentation of the action plan.

■ Documenting the planning process. It is part of the ongoing work of CHART to determine effective models for hazard preparedness; therefore, the method for contacting organizational stakeholders and for organizing the community meetings was thoroughly documented.

5.5 Lessons Learned to Build Conceptual Knowledge

One of the most important goals of this group of stakeholders was to work through the local issues of evacuation using national best practice. Over the course of the first phase of the collaborative, the group worked through the issues of elderly evacuation. The work of disaster planning occurs through the development of action plans aimed toward reducing the impact of disaster on communities, preparing for risks that cannot be eliminated, and directing the actions needed to deal with the consequences of and recovery from actual events. We organized the discussion around the four phases of emergency management: mitigation, preparedness, response, and recovery. At first, we asked the group to identify the issues from Katrina and then to address the most salient best practice for the local area.

Mitigation is any sustained action taken to reduce or eliminate long-term risk to life and property from a hazard event. The goal is to decrease the need for response instead of to increase the response capability. Specifically, the stakeholders mentioned over and over again that the elderly did not have access or knowledge about evacuation planning and preparation, including making their own plans and being aware of the governmental plans. Further, the memories of prior evacuations played an important part in the decision-making process for the elderly. Many had evacuated for Ivan, only to return to their unaffected home. Others had stayed through Betsy and Camille and had survived. The elderly experience with prior evacuation often led many to believe that it was better to stay.

After working through national best practices concerning mitigation, the stakeholders came to the following conclusions. Effective planning for the elderly around natural and man-made disasters has one factor in common: the recognition that the plans and tools need to be consistently reviewed and revised. The assumption of these plans, as well, is that there are wide-ranging differences in the elderly population. If elderly service organizations strengthen the ability to maintain their provision of services during a disaster, it will increase the likelihood that the elderly will continue to have access to crucial services.[4]

The group thought that it was critical to build on the strengths of the elderly and disabled.[5] They have experience and had roles throughout their lives working with others. Consequently, they have knowledge about what works best for them. For example, in preparing for, or sheltering, during a disaster, the elderly may be able to assist family and community members in caregiving, planning, cleaning, and other proactive activities.[6]

The group also thought it was critical that elderly education about planning and evacuation be consistently done as part of their family and social networks.[7] They emphasized that many elderly are connected to their families and neighborhood and that this must be taken into account in planning. For example, a good project would be to work with the elderly and their families to continually update their supply checklists of goods.[8] Checklists could include items such as medication supplies, special dietary supplies, basic hurricane supplies, and family contact number list.

Preparedness focuses on plans and preparations made to save lives and property and to facilitate response operations. Again, the issue of communication about the issue came to the forefront, especially about transportation. Moreover, many of the elderly and their families did not have either transportation or the resources to evacuate. On another level, the elderly thought it would be safer to stay home with their medications and familiar setting than to risk the unknown, and they were afraid that they would not be taken care of if they left.

After identifying the local issues during Katrina and thinking about the local elderly population, the stakeholders began the process of identifying the issues they thought most important for preparedness. For planning, the group thought that community vulnerability maps should be created to pinpoint where high-risk groups are concentrated including elderly group living facilities, elderly communities, and senior centers. Shelters, parks, community centers, churches, and response networks are useful community resources that can be included in these maps as well.[9] In addition, they thought that the city should plan for as little sheltering as possible. Mitigation and preparedness optimally should be accomplished before a storm that allows individuals, particularly the elderly, to avoid shelters. Shelters can lack the intensity of care that some elderly need to be comfortable and to maintain optimal health, both physical and mental. This would mean, of course, that the planning around transportation is carefully thought out and tested before hurricane season. At the same time, planning needs to consistently ensure continuity of services for the elderly.[10] One way to accomplish this is to work with other cities regarding their sheltering services and to create ways to ensure a transition of services for specific elderly needs.

Another area that came up was to anticipate the psychosocial trauma associated with a disaster. Research needs to document the impact of grief and trauma on the elderly from disaster and to distinguish this impact from the disabling effects of aging. Further, disaster planners need to develop psychosocial programs that involve and support the elderly specifically. Displacement may mean dealing with issues such as the fear of death and burial in a foreign place. This means that reunification plans should be established to facilitate evacuees finding each other after a disaster, especially caregivers finding seniors and people with disabilities. For example, locations of shelters need to be well publicized so that family, friends, and caregivers can search more effectively for elderly loved ones.

Communication issues were central to the recommendations of the group. First, the group recommended the use of memorandums of understanding (MOUs) or some type of operational relationship with the city emergency management system to facilitate cooperation and funding.[11] As well, there should be a hotline specifically for elderly populations to quickly and simply obtain information concerning disaster planning. And, finally, public service announcements should be created in a variety of media to remind the community to get to know and to check on their elderly neighbors.[12]

Another issue of major concern to the stakeholders was financial preparedness. Planning should include elderly persons in credit and savings plans before a disaster. The elderly are among the most consistent and reliable in management of savings and return of loans. Lists of potential sources of financial assistance should be compiled by local elderly service agencies, along with simple information on how to contact such sources. These lists then can be provided to the elderly before a disaster. Also, stakeholders should facilitate the elderly in creating a way to safely have cash-on-hand in their homes for these events. Oftentimes, credit cards and checks may become useless after a disaster. Service agencies should incorporate this information into other preparedness material often supplied to the elderly before a disaster (with the caution to not tell strangers that cash is in their home).

Response relates to the actions taken to provide emergency assistance, to save lives, to minimize property damage, and to speed recovery immediately following a disaster. Specifically, the group thought that elderly issues for the response phase were most egregious of all. The major issue that emerged was the feeling of abandonment that the elderly experienced. Shelters of last resort had difficulty caring for the elderly. Many of the elderly thought that they were abandoned by those programs and individuals assigned to help them. For example, some nursing home staff left their clients at the airport on their way out of town, and other nursing home staff also left the elderly in the home as they made their way to safety. Many of the elderly knew other elderly who died because no one knew where they were or could not reach them. For many of the elderly, their life span was shortened by the culmination of their experiences during and after Katrina.

After much discussion, the group focused on activities that may lessen the sense and actual abandonment of the elderly during and after a catastrophe. One of the strongest recommendations involved the use of technology to identify the elderly before a storm, particularly the use of geographic information system (GIS)/Internet technology to find information about elderly population concentrations. Senior communities, senior living complexes, and nursing homes should be mapped and then referenced by emergency responders and community workers to more efficiently locate and evacuate or to provide supplies to elderly populations.[13] In addition, there is a recommendation to use GIS/Internet technology to find information about open and closed shelters.[14] This can greatly improve the ability to find appropriate sheltering for specific elderly needs. The availability of space at special needs shelters and other relevant details can be viewed in real time to find what is full, open, or damaged, in state as well as out of state.

During the initial disaster phase, the community should implement previously created MOUs that outline member responsibilities. Involved parties should have an intimate understanding of the specific tasks they have to accomplish in relation to each other during response and recovery.[15] Another tactic is to take advantage of the upsurge in cell phone usage by elderly populations. Weather updates, sheltering information, and personal location can be text messaged to and from the elderly who are sheltering in place or in shelters.

There are two other issues that directly related to elderly lives lost in Katrina. Because pets were such a hindrance to evacuation, the change in law concerning pet evacuation to concerned elderly evacuees needs to be clarified and communicated. Federal law passed in 2006 states that pets are to be evacuated and sheltered upon the owner's request. Shelters must now provide alternate shelter for evacuees' pets. Also, in shelters, cognitive impairments of the elderly evacuees need to be addressed. Many elderly may have diminished sight or hearing or suffer from Alzheimer's and other debilitating diseases. Emergency information should be provided to the elderly in accessible formats to cope with new surroundings and to minimize confusion.[16] And finally, immediately after the storm, there is a need to dispatch city workers to preassigned areas (e.g., neighborhoods or zip codes) where the elderly are known to be sheltering in place to deliver food and water.[17]

Recovery focuses on actions taken to return to a normal or improved operating condition following a disaster. Specifically, we found that the physical and emotional toll on the elderly continues in the recovery phase. Many elderly have experienced an overwhelming sense of loss. While the experience of loss is a constant factor in the lives of the elderly in general, the loss experienced in Katrina continues to be extraordinary. The loss is defined in terms of entire neighborhoods, friends, and family. Many elderly are too frail to be able to rebuild their homes and to participate in the rebuilding of their community. As a consequence, some elderly have told agency personnel, "I should not have left; I should have died in New Orleans," and "I want to come home to die." Identifying specific mental and other social support for the elderly and their caretakers is a continual crisis and currently difficult to achieve.

The strongest recommendations were concerned with the physical and mental health of the elderly. The group recommends that city and nonprofit agencies proactively find elderly disaster victims through their corresponding aid agencies before the stress of recovery and rebuilding becomes debilitating. Family physicians, critical stress counselors, and clergy are sometimes available and accessible through senior service center personnel and involved aid agencies.

Another recommendation revolved around financial and relief issues. The elderly receive less proportionate aid in the aftermath of a disaster than their younger counterparts.[18] Economic recovery appears to be the area where the elderly fare worse than the nonelderly, and the inability to recover financially can and does result in a change in an individual's standard of living and should be examined closely.[19] Therefore, the shelters and aid agencies should make available updated elderly-specific packets of potential sources of financial assistance, including simple information on how to contact important sources. Senior service agencies could create follow-up programs for their members to ensure applications were filled out correctly and in a timely manner.[20]

The consensus of the stakeholders is that planning with the local elderly about evacuation in New Orleans can be successful only in conjunction with confronting the everyday life issues of recovery. These sets of assumptions were agreed upon by the stakeholders and verified by the meetings and interviews with the elderly. The themes that are dominant in this discussion continually refer to working with existing agencies to build on the strengths of the elderly. Overwhelmingly, the stakeholders did not want a new agency created; they wanted to work with the already established nonprofit and government agencies.

With this new agreement about the phases of evacuation for the elderly, the group made recommendations for local agencies to do the following:

1. Identify and address their own agency hazards and vulnerabilities.
2. Ensure their capability to continue services throughout the disaster incident.
3. Prepare to receive technical and other assistance from public agencies during the disaster to maintain operations.
4. Develop procedures to enhance the organization's recovery from the event incident.
5. Create an inventory of local elderly services that then can be integrated into the city's plan.

The next step was the formation of a collaboration of agencies including city, state, local, and appropriate stakeholder groups to define special needs and to develop an evacuation and shelter plan that supports special needs people. This knowledge led to the work in the next phase.

5.5.1 Implementation

As we began to move toward implementing the initiatives developed during the first year of the project, we realized that we could not go any further with the rather limited pool of stakeholders involved in the first phase. It would be necessary to involve a much broader range of government, private, and nongovernmental agencies to ensure effective implementation. Using the information obtained in the first year of the project, we identified regional stakeholders that would have both the knowledge and capacity to implement acceptable modifications to the city's evacuation plan.

In fall 2007, public, private, nonprofit, and academic agencies met to form the city's Elderly Evacuation Working Group. We began with an understanding that the city lacked resources. Post-Katrina New Orleans still suffered from significant fiscal challenges. It would be necessary to determine what resources would be necessary to ensure an inclusive evacuation process.

To stimulate this process, a tabletop exercise was developed and facilitated by the CHART team. The team had significant experience in facilitating prior homeland security and disaster-related exercises, and this exercise used a hurricane scenario to encourage thoughts and ideas about needed resources as a hurricane approached the city. We wanted each of the participating agencies to understand what others would be doing as a disaster approached, and then struck, the region. It was of utmost importance to us that public agencies learned from and worked with nonprofit organizations. We knew we needed to build a better relationship between these two sectors, as the Katrina experience caused many nonprofit organization representatives to feel that in an emergency the city would need to partner with the nonprofits in order to have a successful evacuation of the elderly.

As a result, we included participation by the state, hospitals, religious congregations, AARP, the American Red Cross, universities, the regional transport authority, cable companies, public utilities, the military, law enforcement, Amtrak, bus companies, nursing homes, Community Emergency Response Team (CERT), Society for the Prevention of Cruelty to Animals (SPCA), the Association of Community Organizations for Reform Now (ACORN), and AmeriCorps.

Meetings were scheduled on a quarterly basis, based on the need to disseminate, digest, review, and revise source material that emerged during the meetings. Reference documents and plans were often mentioned tangentially in the meetings, and participants expressed a need to review these documents in light of the group discussions. Throughout the time between meetings, small groups of actors often conferred and refined their understanding of relevant documentation in preparation for a subsequent group effort.

At the first meeting of what became known as the Elderly Evacuation Working Group, city agencies set what would be a problematic tone by adopting an "instructional," emergency-planner-dominated approach. Most of the nonprofit agencies attending this first meeting did not know that the city's evacuation plan had undergone significant revisions post-Katrina. Indeed, the plan had not been made publicly available. The effect was to initially alienate a large portion of the other agencies that attended the meeting and that expected to be able to offer their diverse expertise as full, collaborative partners in shaping the city's evacuation plan.

To gain the maximum number of ideas while promoting opportunity for interaction in a relatively small group and to counter the attempt at expert dominance, the participants were directed to four separate conference rooms. The groups were preselected by the CHART team to ensure adequate agency representation and diversity of ideas, and each team was facilitated by a "senior mentor," a practitioner or academic with significant disaster planning experience. Each of the four teams was to address the scenario independently, reporting back at the end of the day where ideas would be compared, consolidated, and prioritized for action. This first meeting of the Elderly Evacuation Working Group resulted in an agenda for further implementation:

■ To encourage congregations to become more involved in the evacuation of the elderly population.
■ To clearly identify the locations of the elderly populations.
■ To prepare the population year-round for evacuation.
■ To use a positive approach to informing the elderly population of evacuation requirements.
■ To use a "family plan" approach to evacuating the elderly.
■ To gain the trust of the elderly by emphasizing dignity.
■ To convince the elderly populations that their pets will be appropriately cared for.
■ To encourage citizens to register with the city through dialing 311.
■ To familiarize the elderly with where they are going, what the facilities will be like, and the plan for return.
■ To develop a special plan to reach out to the elderly who have shunned interaction with others.
■ To disseminate messages out to the deaf population and those who speak other languages and to get them to register with 311.

At the subsequent meeting of the Elderly Evacuation Working Group, held three months later in early 2008, we were determined to keep the discussion "fair and balanced." As a productive outcome of the earlier meeting, the city had made available to all working group members a copy of the current evacuation plan and invited review and comment. The city also took on a much more receptive approach, inviting informed discussion and input. This was a significant step forward in opening a meaningful and interactive learning process for all participants. It was only then that realistic action steps could be developed, including the following:

- Negotiating a partnership with the local Meals on Wheels program to aid in registering the elderly for the City's 311 Citizen Assistance Evacuation Program.
- Developing an elderly-sensitive presentation regarding evacuation procedures to be presented at local congregations, senior centers, and community fairs.
- Providing appropriate information to potential elderly evacuees about how their pets will be evacuated.

5.6 Linkages to the Literature on Emergency Planning

Elderly and other special needs populations require a proactive approach in pre-disaster planning. While as much as possible disabled persons must be prepared to help themselves in a disaster, it is important to raise awareness about the ways the elderly can be helped during emergencies. Specifically, Parr recommended that disabled persons should be centrally involved in disaster planning and preparedness.[21] One of the challenges faced by evacuation planners is that the older a person is, the less likely he or she is to respond to a warning message.[22] Therefore, it is essential that the process of communicating risk to seniors be explored and existing barriers such as lack of trust in the authorities, access to new technologies, physical and mental problems, tendencies toward greater isolation in aging, and, thus, unreachable in group outreach activities and other related issues be understood and addressed. Identifying that there are vulnerable groups with disparate needs is a solid first step. Willing "issue champions" must be identified and act as subject matter experts across the whole spectrum of planning, drills, and exercises.[23]

5.7 Lessons Learned Specifically Related to Collaborative Practice

Several important lessons from this case are applicable to collaborative processes in general. While we present each in more detail in the following paragraphs, an important finding is that public managers are often important catalysts for community change. Through careful management of collaborative processes, they can effectively strengthen or even repair fractured stakeholder relationships to promote effective community outcomes. Public managers can focus attention on marginalized stakeholders and can coordinate a process of identifying resource limitations useful to (often fiscally challenged) government agencies in other planning processes. Finally, effective public managers should become adept at identifying resources within a community and should assist in developing partnerships that will ensure that those resources can be committed when needed.

5.7.1 Best Practices in Meeting the Needs of the Elderly Population during an Evacuation Were Identified

As with most research, any initiative should begin with an assessment of best practices. The UNO-CHART researchers, were able to effectively identify best practices from a wide variety of sources. In addition to research on a national scale, it was also extremely important that the research team tapped into the local experience of Katrina. This, combined with significant primary research centered on identifying the needs of elderly populations, provided a sound framework for subsequent collaboration among diverse groups of stakeholders.

5.7.2 The Relationships between the Stakeholders Were Undoubtedly Strengthened

Some stakeholders had a long history of established relationships among their agencies, while others were relative newcomers. UNO-CHART researchers in collaboration with other stakeholders, brought agencies and individuals to the table who had rarely worked together prior to these meetings. In a few instances, there was a limited history of active relationships directed toward common solutions to the challenges of the elderly. The city, while having ultimate responsibility for the evacuation of citizens, has limited resources. Prior to this initiative, the city had a utilitarian perspective of an evacuation—it was prepared to do all it could with its limited expertise and resources to ensure a successful evacuation for the majority of the population. Yet, undoubtedly, additional resources would be needed to ensure an effective outcome in evacuating the city's most vulnerable populations.

The collaboration showed city evacuation planners that a broad range of community resources could be enlisted to aid in the development of inclusive and more effective evacuation outcomes for stakeholders. The process helped identify the special needs of the elderly population during an emergency evacuation. A broad range of best practices in evacuating vulnerable populations was identified by the academic stakeholders. The unique challenges of communicating risk to elderly populations were presented by appropriate advocacy groups. Resources for communicating risk through existing community channels were identified by private and nonprofit sector participants. As the collaborative process evolved, city officials were sensitized to the special needs of the elderly and their families in an evacuation.

5.7.3 Getting on the Calendar of Very Busy Individuals after a Catastrophe Required a Great Deal of Time

Graduate students involved in the project worked diligently to arrange a time when individuals would feel committed to attend. After a catastrophe of the magnitude of Hurricane Katrina, the time constraints on the stakeholders were enormous. The consistent attendance during both phases speaks to the value of the method and the content.

5.7.4 The Collaboration Increased the Visibility of the Elderly Population

Prior to Hurricane Katrina, elderly advocacy groups enjoyed little or no representation in a variety of local and regional emergency exercises and drills. They were a largely invisible group that needed representation to ensure an optimal evacuation outcome. Some degree of pressure was needed to bring attention to this marginalized population. This pressure came from the academic community, which employed collaborative theory to create an effective network. The academic team realized that external pressure was an essential first step.

To illustrate the importance of pressure as the initial step in creating a collaborative network, we refer back to the evacuation of New Orleans during Hurricane Katrina. One segment of the population—the middle and upper socioeconomic classes of the area—could be counted on for political pressure. These were the people who had the economic resources to self-evacuate. They had cars, money for fuel and lodging, and access to a variety of communications tools. During previous hurricane evacuations, they successfully brought pressure on local and state officials to refine the highway-reversing incoming-lane evacuation system known as "contra flow," to minimize delays and coordinate for effective outcomes. During Hurricane Katrina, contra flow indeed was viewed as highly successful.

On the other hand, the elderly and other special needs populations were largely hidden and certainly not active on the issue of evacuation. While the objective probability of an evacuation was much greater than the probability of an actual hit by a major hurricane, a Katrina-like disaster was beyond anyone's experience, so the threat was easier to ignore. Bardach points out that external pressure can significantly affect network performance, and this appears to be a case in point with regard to the Katrina evacuation.[24]

5.7.5 The Collaboration Increased Stakeholder Involvement

The lack of pressure on behalf of the elderly and special needs population was also a symptom of "closedness," the exclusion of important or potentially important actors.[25] In the case of disaster evacuation, everyone in the area is a stakeholder, but getting all of their attention and involvement is problematic. This was certainly the case in the City of New Orleans before Katrina, and it remains a challenge. The planning and implementation of the pre-Katrina exercises were largely confined to professionals in the disaster management network, with limited external stakeholder participation. Certainly, the elderly population of New Orleans was not directly represented. The network eventually identified the elderly as an evacuation problem, but it did not generate pressure for quick and decisive action either before or as Katrina struck the city.

In most of the network literature, the participants come together to solve problems that they cannot solve alone. Although the definition of the problem and acceptable solutions may change as a result of the collaboration, the impetus for action usually comes from the outside, as it does in this case study. When the network has to identify the problem and then stimulate action, the problem of implementation is much greater. The nature of a network is the absence of authority to compel action by its members.

The goal of successful evacuation of New Orleans's elderly population represents a special case for the study of collaborative public management. The shared threats and the potential for mutually beneficial coordination and resource sharing call for sustained interaction among a variety of stakeholders. Yet the lack of immediacy in the threat coupled with the higher transaction costs in networks lessens the probability of decisive action in the preparation phase of disaster management. Broad collaborative agreements are not enough because there is no time in the response phase for extensive negotiation and adjustment.

In one of the few articles to directly address the use of networks in disaster management, Louise Comfort makes a number of useful recommendations.[26] Among them are frequent exercises with diverse scenarios and wide publication of the results. The experience of Hurricane Katrina lends support to these recommendations. Exercises are important for testing plans and capacity. They are also important for identifying and defining new problems. Thus, there is a need for imaginative and varied scenarios that include elderly evacuation problems.

Comfort's admonition to widely publicize results addresses the issue of "closedness" discussed above. It is critical that citizens understand the threats under which they are living. No advocates of the elderly population in New Orleans were ever included in any of the exercises prior to Katrina.[27] Whether they might have made a difference in pushing for more attention to the elderly population or in devising innovative strategies for dealing with the problem is unknown, but at least they would have had an opportunity.

As research on networking and collaboration continues, it is important to recognize the various contexts in which it may take place and to look for opportunities to evaluate results as well as process. The case of the elderly population suggests that networks tend to move slowly, especially in the absence of a strong external stimulus. It is also difficult to sustain momentum. The lesson is not that we should avoid using networks in disaster preparation but that we should recognize their incremental tendencies and should take steps to increase the awareness and participation of affected populations.

5.7.6 *It Was Important to Emphasize a Team Approach*

The UNO-CHART team, in facilitating the collaborative process, was careful to foster the development of a climate of collaboration. No one actor or agency was allowed to dominate. Even the facilitators were intentionally chosen from a variety of neutral organizations and were trained to both foster a collaborative environment and be vigilant for single or multiple agency domination of discussions. Several key skill sets were present in the facilitating team that were essential to guiding an effective collaborative process:

- Familiarity and experience with collaborative networking processes.
- An established reputation as politically neutral actors—this included fostering an environment of "no finger pointing" for past mistakes, looking forward instead to future outcomes and impacts.
- A reputation for a high degree of professional competence among the stakeholder agencies.

5.8 Remaining Questions

Several important challenges remain. Probably the most important challenge is how to sustain the stimulus to address the needs of the elderly during evacuations. The current trend in fiscally constrained governments is that many disaster networks are formed through sponsorship by entities outside traditional government, although they do include participation by various governmental agencies and may even be partially sponsored by government agencies. They are most often sponsored by either quasi-governmental bodies or the private sector and are formed to address specific and often narrow dimensions of disasters such as critical infrastructure interdependencies, cyber security, tourism, maritime security, and banking. Stakeholders representing elderly needs are not included in these special interest networks.

Another remaining question is how to best communicate risk and appropriate evacuation action to the elderly population. The elderly and their families need better information regarding evacuation resources and procedures. Yet communication is often clouded by lack of trust in government, by lack of access to communications technology, or even by barriers such as language or physical handicaps. How to foster a greater level of trust between the elderly community and the city of New Orleans remains a significant challenge and will likely take years to improve. Finding the best way to communicate with a dispersed and often isolated population is problematic. Future research may be helpful in identifying appropriate communications media.

5.9 Conclusion

Planning for the evacuation of vulnerable populations, at least in the southeastern region of Louisiana, required the collaboration of a wide range of diverse players. Prior to Katrina, the planning process could best be described as a "silo," with government emergency planners dictating an emergency plan with little input from segments of the community that would be most affected by an ill-conceived plan. While preparation for emergencies that impacted critical infrastructure, tourism, and ports or those directly caused by terrorism were well funded and responses practiced, the largely invisible vulnerable population did not enjoy a seat at the planning table. Evacuation planning used a "one-size-fits-all" approach, with little sensitivity to special needs (other than for residents who needed special medical, life-support equipment, and even with the pre-Katrina attention to such needs many, many severely ill residents died because the evacuation plans were not sufficient or sufficiently practiced).

In the New Orleans region, the University of New Orleans and particularly its Center for Hazard Assessment, Response, and Technology (CHART) served as the catalyst for creating an inclusive collaborative network of community stakeholders. Management and leadership of an effective collaborative process took place without the appearance of managing or leading. First, through identifying national best practices for evacuating vulnerable populations, next by applying those best practices to the New Orleans region's unique population mix and distribution, and finally through an aggressive implementation plan that relied upon a solid collaborative structure, stakeholders were able to create and refine an inclusive evacuation plan that was socially equitable and responsible for vulnerable populations.

Endnotes

1. M. Gullette, Katrina and the Politics of Later Life, In *There Is No Such Thing as a Natural Disaster,* ed. C. Hartman and G.D. Squires (New York: Routledge, 2006); P. Sharkey, Survival and Death in New Orleans: An Empirical Look at the Human Impact of Katrina, *Journal of Black Studies, 37* (4): 482–501, 2007.
2. R. Knowles and B. Garrison, Planning for Elderly in Natural Disasters, *Disaster Recovery Journal, 19* (4): 1–3, 2006.
3. P. Jenkins, S. Laska, and G. Williamson, Connecting Future Evacuation to Current Recovery: Saving the Lives of Older Adults, *Generations, 31* (4): 49–52, 2008.
4. L.S. Fernandez, D. Byard, C.C. Lin, S. Benson, and J.A. Barbera, Frail Elderly as Disaster Victims: Emergency Management Strategies, *Prehospital and Disaster Medicine, 17* (2): 67-74, 2002.
5. Ibid.
6. Older people in disasters and humanitarian crises: Guidelines for best practice, *HelpAge Internationsl,* 2005–2007, p. 67–74, Saffron&Hill, London, UK: accessed online. http//helpage.org/resources/manuals, 12-16-09.
7. Fernandez et al., Frail Elderly.

8. Ibid.
9. B.H. Morrow, Identifying and Mapping Community Vulnerability, *Disasters, 23* (1): 1–18, 1999; L. Comfort, B. Wisner, S. Cutter, R. Pulwarty, K. Hewitt, A. Oliver-Smith, et al., Reframing Disaster Policy: The Global Evolution of Vulnerable Communities, *Environmental Hazards, 1* (1): 39–44, 1999.
10. J.J. Clinton, B.R. Hagebak, J.G. Sirmons, and J.A. Brennan, Lessons from the Georgia Floods, *Public Health Reports, 110* (6): 684–688, 1995.
11. Fernandez et al., Frail Elderly.
12. Comfort et al., Reframing Disaster Policy; A. McCampbell, *Best Practices Model: Including the Needs of People with Disabilities, Seniors, and Individuals with Chronic Mental Illness in Emergency Preparedness and Planning* (Report to the New Mexico Department of Health, 2003).
13. Morrow, Identifying and Mapping; Comfort et al., Reframing Disaster Policy.
14. Fernandez et al., Frail Elderly; Comfort et al., Reframing Disaster Policy.
15. Fernandez et al., Frail Elderly.
16. Ibid.
17. Ibid.
18. Ibid.
19. Ibid.
20. Ibid.
21. A.R. Parr, Disasters and Disabled Persons: An Examination of the Safety Needs of a Neglected Minority, *Disasters, 11*:148–159, 1987.
22. C.E. Nelson et.al., *Post-Hurricane Survey of Evacuees Sheltered in the Tampa Bay Region during Hurricane Elena in 1985* (Tampa: Department of Community Affairs, Division of Emergency Management, with support of the Tampa Bay Regional Planning Council, University of South Florida, 1988).
23. J.J. Kiefer and R.S. Montjoy, Incrementalism before the Storm: Network Performance for the Evacuation of New Orleans, *Public Administration Review, 66* (Special Issue on Collaborative Public Management): 122–130, 2006.
24. E. Bardach, *Getting Agencies to Work Together: The Practice and Theory of Managerial Craftsmanship* (Washington, DC: Brookings, 1998).
25. L. Schaap and M.J.W. van Twist, The Dynamics of Closedness in Networks. In *Managing Complex Networks. London,* ed. W. Kickert et al. (Thousand Oaks, CA: Sage, 1997), pp. 62–78.
26. L.K. Comfort, Risk, Security, and Disaster Management, *Annual Review of Political Science, 8*: 335–356, 2005.
27. Kiefer and Montjoy, Incrementalism before the Storm.

Chapter 6

Running Out of Classrooms! Solving Overcrowding through Collaborative School Planning

Esteban Dalehite

Contents

Case Brief

Background and Purpose of the Collaboration: Florida legislators in 1985 invited jurisdictions to develop means to help school districts deal with population growth. Palm Beach County faced several obstacles: Developers and cities were concerned growth could be stifled; elected officials were concerned that resources would not be allocated equitably between old and new development areas of the county; municipalities distrusted the school district; and commissioners found the plan's mechanics confusing. Palm Beach County's burgeoning population growth created overcrowded schools. A plan was needed to provide new classrooms to meet the demands of 30 years of steadily increasing enrollments. The school district needed the county and municipalities to include education planners in decisions on new developments, and governments needed to assure prospective migrating companies that Palm Beach County had desirable schools. The heads of the school board and county commission joined forces for a long collaboration to establish the state's first approved school concurrency policy.

Current Status: The effort covers more than two decades: Local-option school concurrency introduced to state's growth management laws (1985); Palm Beach County began joint school concurrency effort (1993); Palm Beach County Commission approved school concurrency Inter-Local Agreement (ILA) (2000); School District of Palm Beach County achieved the ILA's level-of-service benchmark (2004); and the state legislature overhauled state growth management laws and made school concurrency mandatory (2005). While 2008 was the deadline for all Florida counties to implement a school concurrency policy, Palm Beach County reached, and has maintained, a 110% maximum level of service at the opening of school year 2004–05. The state, following trials in a few counties to individually craft policies, mandated that all counties implement school concurrency by December 2008.

Lessons for Strategic Collaboration Practice: This case emphasizes the important role of trust in moving toward a viable solution, even when the collaborative effort is mandated by government. In addition to geographic size and demographic diversity, system inequities often heighten tensions for key stakeholders, requiring conveners to negotiate competing needs. In this case, a trusted broker played a key and persistent role in establishing the strategic collaboration in a context with a long history of mistrust. Overcoming the hidden agendas and negative participant behaviors to build trust and shared understanding required patience and perseverance. Mutually beneficial agreements with unique incentives for reaching performance benchmarks were particularly important for potential participants who thought they would suffer financially from collaboration. The sustained catalytic leadership ultimately led to success in accessing new resources and negotiating the competing needs of developers and the school system.

In 1993, Jody Gleason was chair of the school board in Palm Beach County, Florida, representing District 3, a predominantly low-income urban territory. The State Constitution required a uniform system of public schools. However, Jody witnessed a diverging reality where school facilities in the district she represented were poorly cared for and capital dollars were flowing to build new schools in up-sprouting, relatively well-to-do suburban developments. Even then, to her dismay, resources were grossly inadequate to build enough school seats to meet demand. A dual crisis of failing old facilities and insufficient new schools had arrived and was festering. Population growth had outrun school expansion. Development regulations had been wholly inadequate and could not come close to paying for what schools actually cost. Lack of collaboration among county, school district, and cities stood as a main obstacle to solving the school overcrowding problem. Yet the state legislature had recently offered a glimmer of hope, a way out of the problem. It had just approved amendments to state statutes governing local planning that allowed jurisdictions to establish collaborative school planning processes through interlocal agreements. Drawing inspiration from the state amendments, Gleason took the initiative and found a willing partner in Karen Marcus, chair of the county commission. Together they led the way through a thicket of complications—poor reputation, mistrust, lack of resources, resistance—to fashion, after nine years of negotiations, a collaborative school planning process with the necessary resources to keep school construction up with the county's perennial rapid growth while modernizing obsolete facilities.

6.1 Introduction

Relentless urban sprawl has steadily raised the premium on establishing successful "smart growth" policies to mitigate or solve the most ubiquitous social problems associated with this phenomenon, including environmental degradation, traffic congestion, rising infrastructure costs, declining central cities, and the decreasing supply of affordable housing.[1] However, the implementation of smart growth policies has been difficult to achieve largely due to political resistance from groups that bear the costs associated with these policies and opposition to the transfer of power from local to regional bodies.[2]

Collaborative public service networks have become increasingly popular as a viable alternative for the joint provision of services that allows governments involved to retain autonomy and to avoid the transfer or loss of power. This chapter presents a case study of the Palm Beach County collaborative school planning (CSP) process that arose from implementing Florida's school concurrency policy, a unique form of smart growth policy that aims to solve the school overcrowding problem. The term *school concurrency* refers to the policy objective of ensuring that the supply of school seats concurs with the demand generated by new residential development.

In particular, this chapter focuses on the voluntary phase of Florida's school concurrency policy that took place from 1993 to 2005 and consisted of a local option encouraging local governments to subscribe to an interlocal agreement (ILA) with a financially feasible solution for the school overcrowding problem. During this period only 1 of 67 counties in Florida—Palm Beach—was successful in subscribing to the ILA and establishing and maintaining a collaborative school planning process. CSP helped achieve not only concurrency and the solution of the school overcrowding problem but also modernization of existing schools and equality of facilities across the county.

This chapter investigates the context and process that led to the establishment of CSP, as well as its structure and spin-off benefits. The case provides the following six lessons for practitioners who are currently engaged in or may be planning to engage in collaborative agreements:

1. Mistrust generates resistance to collaboration, even when all parties stand to benefit from collaboration.
2. Collaboration can be established in the context of mistrust if the mistrusted actor exerts sustained catalytic leadership over a long period of time, seeks a trusted broker to mediate with parties, accepts conditional or tentative commitments to collaboration by mistrusting parties, and is prepared to shoulder a greater share of the financial burden necessary to underwrite the mutually beneficial outcomes of collaboration.
3. Trust can be regained through effective collaboration.
4. Successful collaborative public service networks can help secure additional revenue sources.
5. Collaborative public service networks provide unique incentives to meet performance benchmarks to continue to receive the benefits from collaboration.
6. Mutually beneficial agreements are an important factor underlying the establishment and sustainment of collaborative public service networks.

These lessons are discussed in the concluding section of the chapter.

The research presented in this chapter is derived from periodicals, public documents, and semistructured interviews with diverse public officials conducted by George Solli and the author. The interviews were structured using Nunn and Rosentraub's model of interjurisdictional cooperation[3] and Anthony Down's economic theory of democracy.[4]

6.2 Understanding the Situational Context

The Palm Beach CSP process was established in a politically heated context of overcrowded schools. In fact, CSP was an important part of the solution to overcrowded schools. This context also included serious obstacles to collaboration: mistrust, inequity, and the perception that collaborative school planning implied growth controls. This section describes in detail these aspects of the context in which CSP emerged as well as the main actors involved and their positions vis-à-vis CSP.

6.2.1 School Overcrowding

The emergence of CSP in Palm Beach County begins with a problem: crowded schools getting more crowded. Overcrowding can be defined as the excess of enrollment over the capacity for which schools have been built and is typically measured as the ratio of enrollment to capacity. Thus, school overcrowding is determined not only by the rate of enrollment growth but also by the ability of school construction to keep up with that growth. In the case of Palm Beach County and Florida in general, school-building efforts were unable to keep up with the state's dramatic rates of enrollment.

Fueled largely by interstate and foreign immigration, Florida has been one of the fastest growing states in America for more than 100 years. According to the Census Bureau, it has gone from a population of 528,542 in 1900 to 17,516,732 in 2004, growing at an average rate per decade of approximately 40%. This rate contrasts starkly with the average growth rate per decade of approximately 14% for the nation as a whole over the same period. Florida is now the fourth largest state and, according to U.S. Census Bureau projections, is expected to continue to grow from 2000 to 2030 at an average rate per decade of approximately 21.5%—the third largest growth rate in the nation—and to surpass New York and become the third largest state in the nation behind California and Texas.

Naturally, student enrollment at the K–12 level has mirrored the general population pattern. According to the National Center for Education Statistics, 6 of the 20 largest school districts in the nation were located in Florida during the 2003–2004 school year, with Miami-Dade ranking 4th, Broward 5th, Hillsborough 10th, and Palm Beach 11th. Figure 6.1 shows the pattern of student growth for Florida's largest school districts from 1987 to 2004 and contrasts them to a hypothetical average

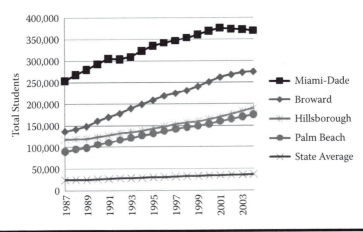

Figure 6.1   Enrollment in Florida's largest school districts, 1987–2004. (This figure was constructed by the chapter author with data from the National Center for Educational Statistics Common Core of Data.)

Table 6.1 1994 Descriptive Statistics for School Crowding (Enrollment/Capacity) in Palm Beach County, Florida, by Type of School

	Mean (%)	Median (%)	S.D. (%)	Min. (%)	Max. (%)
Elementary	141	140	52	65	463
Middle	124	127	21	86	164
High School	98	98	21	56	134

Data source: This table was constructed by the chapter author with unpublished data provided by the Palm Beach County School Board.

school district in the state. The graph shows the large variation in size and growth patterns across school districts and the trend faced by the largest school districts. During this period the number of total students in Palm Beach County grew at a steady rate of approximately 5,000 students per year or, in relative terms, at an approximate average rate of growth of 4% per annum or 48% per decade.

Large rates of enrollment growth led to school overcrowding. Table 6.1 provides descriptive statistics for school overcrowding in Palm Beach County schools for 1994, the year after the local ILA option was established in statute. This information shows that the problem was worst for elementary schools, followed by middle and high schools. On the average, elementary schools were 41% over capacity, and middle schools were 24% over capacity. High schools were roughly at capacity on the average. More insight into the school overcrowding problem can be obtained by looking at the top half of the distribution. Roughly 50% of elementary schools were 40% to 363% over capacity; 50% of middle schools were 27% to 64% over capacity; and 50% of high schools were between 2% under capacity and 34% over capacity. The minimum values contained in Table 6.1 show that Palm Beach County faced problems of underuse in addition to overuse (overcrowding).

A 1993 memo prepared by the Legal Counsel of the Broward County Planning Council depicts the situation in vivid terms:

> The crisis of financial shortfall and overcrowding is here and it is festering. Growth has outrun school expansion and most schools in new residential areas are severely and dangerously overcrowded. Although the problem is one of longer duration, state legislators have three times rejected adding public educational facilities to concurrency requirements, such as water, sewer, traffic, drainage and environmental concerns .... Development regulations have been wholly inadequate and have fallen far short of paying for what schools actually cost, including site acquisition and construction of facilities. (P. 2)

Alternative solutions were proposed or implemented to solve the problem, including busing, redistricting, portable school stations, concurrent sessions in the same classroom, and all-year schooling with double daily and summer sessions. However, these alternatives were either insufficient or politically unpalatable. In the tradition of smart growth policies, *school concurrency* was advanced as a solution. School concurrency made reference to the broad objective of putting school seats in place prior to or concurrent with new development. However, the actual road map to achieve this end was not immediately obvious to state or local officials, nor was it without risk.

Other services subject to concurrency—such as roads, sanitary sewer, solid waste, drainage, potable water, parks and recreation, and mass transit—are all capital intensive and can be provided with flexibility. For example, special districts can be created for their provision, and they can ultimately be paid by user charges or special levies. Public K–12 education, on the other hand, is considerably more labor-intensive and much harder to provide through entities other than the established school districts. Moreover, school concurrency required the integration of school district, county, and city planning processes and thus CSP.

6.2.2 Collaborative School Planning: An Important Component of the Solution to School Overcrowding

At one extreme, the solution to school overcrowding consisted of limiting new development and growth, with no action taken on the rate of school construction. Although eight decades of runaway urban sprawl had spawned supporters of such a policy, this solution would have met the opposition of developers and very likely reduced the supply of housing while increasing the price, with possible negative economic and political ramifications. The state was very careful to guard against this potential solution by retaining and exercising the power to approve school concurrency plans developed at the local level.

At the other extreme, the solution consisted of simply embarking on an ambitious school construction program to catch up and keep up with development, with no action taken to rationalize real estate development. Assuming the existence of the necessary resources, this extreme was also unsatisfactory. As long as real estate development (i.e., city and county planning) and school planning were separate processes, the provision of quality education, including matching students and school capacity, stood little chance of being rational and of adequately solving the school overcrowding problem. Thus, CSP emerged as an important component of the solution to school overcrowding. The ideal policy was to put an aggressive school construction program in place while also integrating the city and county planning processes with the school facilities planning processes implemented by school districts.

6.2.3 Stakeholders and Their Position vis-à-vis Collaborative School Planning

Establishing CSP involved the participation of the following stakeholders: the school district, county, cities, state, real estate developers, and citizens. The position that each of these actors held vis-à-vis CSP is introduced in this section and further elaborated in later sections. Table 6.2 provides a summary of these stakeholders and their basic position.

The school district was the actor most interested in achieving a CSP process that would help solve the overcrowding problem, modernize existing facilities, and integrate city, county, and school planning. It was the direct responsibility of the district to provide uniform education in the county and thus ensure the necessary facilities, in number and quality. CSP was an instrument to fulfill this responsibility and also to satisfy voters concerned with school overcrowding.

Cities in the county were the parties that most opposed CSP. It is not that they did not benefit from CSP. In fact, cities stood to benefit from CSP for at least three reasons. First, the provision of quality K–12 education is an important location factor and driver of economic development. Second, integrating the city and school planning processes would help rationalize city planning as well. Lastly, school overcrowding was an important political issue for voters even in city elections. However, cities were also the actors that most stood to lose. Cities are charged with planning within their jurisdiction, which is where most schools are constructed. Integrating city and school planning processes meant that they would henceforth share their planning authority with the school district, especially with regards to issuing permits for new residential developments. This loss of power, mistrust of school authorities, and the political pressure exerted by real estate developers were the main sources of city opposition to CSP.

Contrary to cities, the county favored and championed CSP. The county, contrary to cities, is charged with planning in unincorporated areas where little if any school construction takes place. Thus, the negatives from integrating county and school planning processes (loss of power, possible growth controls) were minimal, allowing the county to clearly appreciate the benefits of CSP and act accordingly.

Table 6.2 Key Stakeholders and Position vis-à-vis Collaborative School Planning

Stakeholder	Position
School board and school district	Support
County	Support
Cities (new and old)	Opposition
Real estate developers	Opposition
State	Promotion and approval

The state appreciated the benefits of solving school overcrowding from the political and economic development standpoints. However, it was also aware of the economic and political importance of real estate development and wanted to make sure that solving overcrowding did not entail growth controls. Formally, the state could issue statutes governing county, city, and school planning to solve the overcrowding problem. However, simply mandating a solution to the overcrowding problem had its obvious perils. Hence, the state amended state statutes to promote local solutions to the problems until a clearer statewide policy could be mandated.

Real estate developers played an indirect yet powerful role that impacted state and city decisions. A sufficient supply of good schools and rational school and city planning would certainly make real estate developments more attractive for prospective homeowners. Thus, real estate developers stood to benefit from CSP as well. However, this important private interest group was much opposed to CSP primarily on grounds that it could entail growth controls.

Lastly, citizens played a double role. While they may have not had a specific position with regards to CSP, they placed pressure on elected officials at both the state and local levels to solve the school overcrowding problem. They also exerted the powerful role of approving bond issues or sales tax surtaxes at the local level to pay for schools.

6.2.4 Mistrust, Inequity, and Resistance to Collaboration

Several obstacles stood in the way of achieving CSP. The first of these was mistrust. Concurrency required a tremendous construction program as well as CSP. In turn, CSP required giving the school district some enforceable level of influence in the process of issuing permits to new development. For cities, this implied sharing power they had hitherto exercised autonomously. For developers, it implied an additional layer of bureaucracy as well as costs in terms of resources, time, and loss of influence. If cities and real estate developers were going to allow the school district's participation in the real estate planning process, they needed to trust the ability of the school district to deliver new schools and to employ qualified staff to engage effectively in joint planning activities.

However, the School District of Palm Beach County had a poor reputation among citizens and county and city officials. They were considered underqualified and known for not delivering schools on time. One particular event weighed heavily in the mind of parties. In 1986 the school district obtained approval from citizens through a referendum to issue bonds and to increase the tax rate to pay for these bonds. Bond proceeds were for school construction. Regardless of what the truth is on the use of bond proceeds, the public perception was that the school district misspent bond proceeds, using the money for the construction of a headquarters and the purchase of computers and unneeded parking lots, leaving schools unfinished.[5] Under these circumstances cities and real estate developers had little incentive to support CSP.

The second obstacle to CSP took the form of inequity. Whereas the county government and the school district serve the entire county, cities serve different communities within the county. The school crowding problem took place mostly in newly developed, relatively well-to-do areas. Solving the school crowding problem implied taking resources form the entire county and redirecting them to these newly developed areas. At the same time, however, older communities were experiencing a problem of obsolete schools that also placed a demand on resources. Given that facilities were underused in many of these obsolete schools, concurrency policy did not, in principle, consider assigning resources to these older communities to solve the obsolescence problem. Thus, solving the overcrowding problem through concurrency was perceived as inequitable by older communities with obsolete school facilities, who naturally opposed the concurrency policy as well as CSP. Jodie Gleason, school board chair and champion of concurrency and CSP in Palm Beach County, represented an underprivileged district with obsolete, underused school facilities.

The equity issue had two dimensions. The first was equity from the benefits received perspective (commutative justice). Solving the school overcrowding problem implied making individuals in older communities pay for goods that they would not consume (schools in high-growth areas). The second was equity from the ability to pay or redistributive perspective (distributive justice). Solving the school overcrowding problem implied taking money from all, including the low income, to pay for schools for the well-off while ignoring the problem of obsolescence, particularly in low-income areas.

Finally, a third obstacle was the perception that CSP would imply growth controls. Concurrency and collaborative school planning were not well-defined concepts or policies, and there was no shortage of public opinion that painted these policies as growth controls. As a result, real estate developers as well as state and high-growth city officials had serious concerns. CSP could imply conditioning the housing supply to the will and ability of the school district to raise revenues and build schools. In other words, instead of increasing the rate at which schools were being built, local authorities could slow down the rate at which new development permits were issued. This would dampen home construction, raise real estate prices, and lower future property tax revenues. The only approach that real estate developers could ever fully support was for CSP to entail an ambitious construction program of school facilities that caught up and kept up with the supply of housing as determined by the marketplace.

6.3 The Process of Establishing Collaborative School Planning

Establishing CSP took nine long years of consistent efforts to overcome resistance. The state played an important role in amending state statutes to provide a way for local authorities to channel their efforts. Most of the hard work, however, was left to local entities. The underlying factors of the successful establishment of CSP at the local level included the catalytic leadership of two public officials, the brokerage of a third party, certificates of participation to finance school construction, and equity and escape clauses. These roles and key factors are discussed in this section.

6.3.1 The Role of the State in Convening School Concurrency

Interest in solving school overcrowding existed at both the state and local levels. The state government had a clear stake and responsibility in finding a solution for several reasons: (1) The issue was politically important; (2) quality education is a driver of economic development; (3) local planning was governed by state statutes; and (4) the solution to school overcrowding was beyond the authority of any specific local jurisdiction. However, the state did not have the necessary resources, nor were the necessary policies and expected outcomes clear. State lawmakers decided that studies based on local-option school concurrency agreements were necessary before a uniform statewide policy could be mandated.[6] The state would have to find a framework to encourage, guide, support, and approve the differing solutions developed at the local level until a clearer blueprint on how to solve the problem emerged.

Florida statutes had for many years contained statutory language empowering local governments to establish collaborative mechanisms that could have been used to solve the school crowding problem.[7] However, such provisions were weak and had not been effective at propelling local governments into action. In 1993, however, the state legislature amended the statutes governing local comprehensive plans to strengthen the legal basis for collaboration. The new language can be seen in italics in Table 6.3. These amendments allow local entities to establish, by interlocal agreement, processes of collaborative planning and decision making on population projections and location of public schools. They also allow local entities to extend the concurrency requirement to public schools.

Language governing school concurrency has multiplied since these amendments were approved. However, these 1993 amendments were the legislative innovations that set in motion, catalyzed, or otherwise gave direction to the efforts of several counties to establish CSP and solve the school overcrowding problem, particularly in Palm Beach County. This new law provided not a solution to the problem but rather a process to find a solution to the problem for willing parties. The language of the 1993 amendments highlights that the lack of collaboration among county, school district, and cities was perceived as one of the main obstacles to solving the school overcrowding problem.

6.3.2 The Role of Local Governments in Palm Beach County

Concern over school crowding had been brewing at the local level as well, particularly in large, high-growth school districts, such as Palm Beach County. The growing

Table 6.3   1993 Amendments Strengthening Collaboration Provisions

163.3177 Required and Optional Elements of Comprehensive Plan

(...)

(6) In addition to the requirements of subsections (1)-(5) and (12), the comprehensive plan shall include the following elements:

(...)

(h) (...)

2. The intergovernmental coordination element shall further state principles and guidelines to be used in the accomplishment of coordination of the adopted comprehensive plan with the plans of school boards and other units of local government providing facilities and services but not having regulatory authority over the use of land. *Each county, all the municipalities within the county, the district school board, and service providers in that county shall establish by interlocal or other formal agreement executed by all affected entities, and include in their respective plans, joint processes for collaborative planning and decision making on population projections and public school siting, the location and extension of public facilities subject to concurrency, and siting facilities with countywide significance, including locally unwanted land uses whose nature and identity are established in the agreement.*

163.3180 Concurrency

(1) Roads, sanitary sewer, solid waste, drainage, potable water, parks and recreation, and mass transit, where applicable, are the only public facilities and services subject to the concurrency requirement on a statewide basis. No additional public facilities and services shall be made subject to concurrency on a statewide basis without appropriate study and approval of the Legislature; however, any local government may extend the concurrency requirement so that it applies to additional public facilities within its jurisdiction. If a local government elects to extend the concurrency requirement to public schools, it should first conduct a study to determine how the requirement would be met and shared by all affected parties. The state land planning agency may provide technical assistance to local governments that study and prepare for extension of the concurrency requirement to public schools.

(...).

Note: New language is in italics.

motivation to find a solution in this county finally found a channel or framework in the 1993 amendments. Public officials at the Palm Beach County School Board and District unanimously credit the hard-fought success of their interlocal agreement and financially feasible school construction plan to three factors: (1) the leadership of two public officials; (2) the mediation of a broker; and (3) the unabashed use of certificates of participation (COPs) to underwrite school construction.

6.3.2.1 Catalytic Leadership and Brokerage

The process of reaching the CSP-ILA in Palm Beach County was not easy and took approximately nine years, from 1993 to 2001. Interviewees unanimously credit the leadership and perseverance of two persons—Jody Gleason, chair of the school board, and Karen Marcus, chair of the county commission—for starting the process, keeping it on the front burner, presiding over periodic meetings, and infusing the process with a win–win philosophy that eventually gained purchase with critics and led to the signing of the ILA in 2001. According to Gleason, who first brought the proposal to a joint school board and county commission meeting in 1993, there was considerable skepticism about whether CSP could work, and many sat perfunctorily in the initial task force, waiting for it to fail. In the words of Marcus, "Even starting a study of school concurrency was not popular."[8] The two boards cocreated a 21-member educational response committee (later renamed task force) with representatives from parents, real estate developers, and the legal field, as well as members of both boards.[9]

The process of reaching an agreement went through three phases. The first phase took place from 1993 to 1995. Initial efforts during this period failed, in part due to a lack of funding for school construction. Nevertheless, the task force met biweekly during this phase, gaining momentum and bringing to light many good ideas.[10]

The second phase is the period 1996–1998 in which the state legislature declared a moratorium on school concurrency efforts and created a commission to study the policy and make a decision about whether to allow its continuation. This moratorium came in the wake of Broward County's controversial efforts to establish concurrency. This case ended up in litigation and an eventual finding that Broward's proposed comprehensive plan amendments were not in compliance with state law.[11] In July 1998 the state legislature lifted the moratorium, after the Public Schools Construction Study Commission recommended continuation of school concurrency as a local option.[12] The lifting of the moratorium marks the beginning of the third and conclusive phase for Palm Beach County.

Once the moratorium was lifted in 1998, the Palm Beach County School Board and County Commission made a move that is widely credited as another main factor in reaching the agreement: They hired retired engineer and consultant Leo Noble, who had previously helped develop transportation concurrency plans and was well regarded and trusted in private and public circles. It was his job to educate recalcitrant cities and real estate developers on the proposed concurrency policy and negotiate the terms of the ILA. However, Noble faced stiffer resistance than originally envisioned. The following is a summary of events provided by Scott Travis[13]:

> The idea of school concurrency first was studied in 1994 and has faced numerous obstacles since then. Developers and some cities feared the proposal would stifle growth. Cities in the western part of the county worried the district wouldn't build schools fast enough. Coastal cities

were afraid the district would let their schools deteriorate. Many cities also didn't trust the school district after it failed to build all the schools promised when a 1986 bond referendum passed.

Although the concurrency plan would require the school district to build schools based on projected growth, officials from some cities doubted the district would do that. Former Delray Beach Mayor Tom Lynch, who is now chairman of the county school board, was one of the skeptics.

In 1998, the county and the school board hired retired engineer Leo Noble to oversee the concurrency effort. Noble said he thought it would take about six months to draft a document that everyone would support. Instead, it took two years. "There were so many competing interests," Noble said, adding that some municipalities, which he wouldn't identify, tried to use the plan as political leverage.

Nearing the end of the negotiations, the League of Cities demanded a harsh clause allowing one-third of the municipal signatories to end the concurrency plan without cause and not even a recommendation from the CSP-ILA's controlling body, the Technical Advisory Group (TAG). In addition, the Gold Coast Builders Association, representing 1,000 home builders in Broward and Palm Beach Counties, wanted the county's Development Review Committee, not the school district, to sign off on new development requests. It also wanted a seat on the TAG. The reaction of the Board of County Commissioners was to pull the interlocal agreement off the May 16, 2000 agenda.[14]

Noble negotiated a final draft in which the CSP-ILA could be suspended if 33% of the parties to the agreement concurred with a recommendation from the TAG to suspend and in which a business person representing the for-profit sector would be one of the five members of the TAG. On June 6, 2000, a spent Noble told a county commission split on whether to accept the League of Cities' weakening compromises, "The negotiations that got us to this point [have] been, needless to say, very long and tense; and what I'm presenting to you is what I think is the best shot we have of getting this thing through...."[15] He told reporters, "I think most people will hold their nose and sign it. No one's going to like everything in it."[16]

Nearly 280 officials were a part of the approval process. By January 2001, approximately nine years after the initial task force meetings, representatives from the school board; county; 32 cities, towns, and villages; 5 special districts; and 1 airport authority had signed the ILA.[17] "All I can say is this is the best Christmas and Hanukkah present to all the students in the county," said county commissioner Burt Aaronson. "It should have happened earlier, but I'm elated it's happening now."[18]

6.3.2.2 Financial Feasibility

Underwriting a major school construction and modernization program in a context of rapidly increasing construction costs was a difficult challenge. However, it was ultimately necessary for the school district to deliver on its end of the bargain. Financial feasibility was necessary for the state government to approve the CSP agreement and a precondition of trust in the school district's ability to deliver. Table 6.4 contains a catalog of the different revenue sources available to the School District of Palm Beach County, with an indication of the two major revenue sources used to underwrite the program as well as those that were made possible or enhanced by collaboration.

State grants were an irregular drop in the bucket. Impact fees covered roughly one elementary school per year. Mitigation, a form of impact fee established in the ILA, was a positive spin-off from collaboration but ultimately was insufficient to underwrite an ambitious construction program. Municipal bonds were not an option, given the voter referendum requirement established in Article VII, Section 12 of the Florida Constitution, and the school district's poor reputation derived from the 1986 bond issue. A local option sales surtax also required voter approval and was unviable for the same reason. The use of property tax revenues to pay for school construction was limited. According to Florida Statutes, sections 1011.71 and 1011.715, no more than 2 mills (property tax millage of 2) could be used for capital facilities and buses. Property tax revenues, practically speaking, could be used to service debt but not to pay for school construction up front.

Thus, Palm Beach County turned to the only option available to underwrite a large construction program: certificates of participation. The use of COPs was an idea that took time to mature and execute, and it was made possible thanks to the efforts of another school board member—Bill Graham. COPs are a relatively

Table 6.4 Revenue Sources Used to Finance Concurrency and Modernization

Revenue Source	Contribution	Enhanced by Collaboration?
State grants	**Minor**	–
Property tax	–	–
Sales tax	**Major**	**Yes**
Municipal bonds	–	–
Certification of participation	**Major**	–
Impact fees	**Minor**	–
Mitigation	**Minor**	**Yes**

well-known means of acquiring debt financing without complying with voter referendum or debt limit requirements applicable to municipal bonds. They can imply higher interest rate costs and, if used irresponsibly, could lead to overindebtedness. For these reasons, there is a negative stigma attached to their use. However, COPs were the only viable alternative for the school district, and the school board did not hesitate to use them. Nevertheless, the Palm Beach School District operated responsibly and self-limited COP issues to what could be serviced with a property tax millage rate of 1.

6.3.2.3 Equity and Escape Clauses

Interviewees in Palm Beach County generally stress the three foregoing factors as the main determinants of the successful establishment of CSP. However, two ILA clauses should be considered important factors as well. The first is the equity clause or provision in the ILA that gave equal weight to modernizing old school facilities and to building new school facilities in overcrowded areas.[19] This clause turned the ILA into a mutually beneficial agreement for all parties involved. Without this clause, it is hard to imagine older cities with obsolete school facilities having anything to gain with the agreement and thus signing the agreement.

The second is the escape clause mentioned previously allowing only 33% of parties to suspend the ILA if the TAG found the agreement to be ineffective. Such was the cities' mistrust for the school district that it was important for them to have a flexible clause enabling them to undo the agreement if the school district did not deliver on the promised construction program.

6.4 The Structure of Collaborative School Planning

The structure of CSP is relatively simple and consists of three parts. The first is the main exchange agreed to by school board, county, and cities—that is, the most important commitment that the school board wanted from cities and county and what the latter wanted from the school district. These commitments are the essence of CSP. The second part consists of the supporting clauses that further define CSP, and the third part is the controlling body created by the agreement to evaluate its effectiveness and recommend suspension. These three parts are discussed in this section.

6.4.1 Main Exchange

The structure of collaborative school planning contained in the ILA is depicted in Figure 6.2. This figure outlines what can be termed the main exchange between the signatory parties. On the one hand, the school district agreed to produce a five-year capital improvement plan (CIP) that solves the school overcrowding problem and in addition modernizes old, obsolete school facilities. Solving the

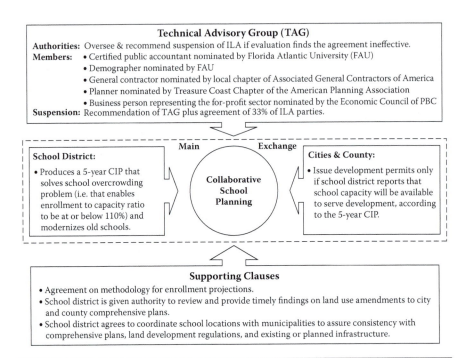

Figure 6.2   Structure of collaborative school planning.

school overcrowding problem is defined as meeting a particular performance benchmark, which consists of staying at or below an enrollment to capacity ratio of 110%. In fact, this benchmark had to be reached by 2004 in each of 21 specified concurrency areas within the county. In essence, the school district agreed to catch up and keep up with development. To meet this benchmark, the school district also agreed to make program and boundary adjustments as necessary to maximize the use of existing capacity. This commitment entailed, of course, securing the necessary resources to execute the ambitious construction and modernization program.

On the other hand, cities and county agreed to issue development orders only after the school district has reported that school capacity was available to serve a new development, according to the five-year plan. To strengthen this commitment, county and cities agreed to add a Public School Facilities Element to their comprehensive plans consistent with the school district's five-year plan and to implement this element by ordinance. A three-year rule applied: If a proposed development brings the enrollment to a capacity ratio over 110% and new capacity will be in place within the next three years, this expected capacity is added to existing capacity to determine whether the student impacts from a new development causes capacity to be exceeded.

6.4.2 Supporting Clauses

As shown in Figure 6.2, the main exchange rests on three important additional clauses contained in the ILA that enhance and further define CSP:

- An agreement on the methodology for enrollment projections—the importance of this agreement cannot be stressed enough, given that both the five-year plan and the 110% performance benchmark were based on enrollment projections.
- The commitment of cities and county to give the school district the opportunity to review and provide timely findings and recommendations on proposed land use amendments to comprehensive plans.
- The commitment of the school district to coordinate the location of educational facilities with each municipality to assure consistency with comprehensive plans, applicable land development regulations, and existing or planned infrastructure, including parks, libraries, and community centers—cities and the county can propose alternative locations.

6.4.3 Technical Advisory Group

Lastly, Figure 6.2 shows another important part of the structure of CSP, specifically the creation of an independent controlling body called the Technical Advisory Group with authority to oversee compliance with the ILA and to recommend suspension of the agreement. The TAG has the following membership:

- A certified public accountant nominated by Florida Atlantic University (FAU).
- A demographer also nominated by FAU.
- A general contractor nominated by the local chapter of the Associated General Contractors of America (AGC).
- A planner nominated by the Treasure Coast Chapter of the American Planning Association.
- A business person representing the for-profit sector nominated by the Economic Council of Palm Beach County.

One of the charges of the TAG is to carry out, every two years or when requested, an evaluation of the effectiveness of the ILA and, if findings are negative, to recommend suspension of the CSP-ILA. If this were the case, the ILA provides that a minority of 33% of the parties to the agreement can suspend the agreement. As mentioned already, this harsh suspension clause was necessary to get the support of the League of Cities.

6.5 Reaching Benchmarks and Reaping Additional Benefits from Collaboration

Once the ILA had been signed, all eyes were on the school district to see whether it could deliver on its end of the bargain. First and foremost, it had to put a construction plan in place that would catch up and keep up with development in a context of escalating construction costs. The school district did just that. However, short of reaching this goal, the school district realized that even COPs were not enough to finish the job. Fortunately, the positive synergies and renewed trust derived from CSP and the school construction and modernization program allowed the school district to tap into the necessary resources to finish the job. This section discusses the results of the school construction plan and these additional revenue sources made possible by CSP.

6.5.1 Reaching Performance Benchmarks

The Palm Beach CSP-ILA established a mandatory performance benchmark. By August 2004, approximately four years after the ILA had been signed by all parties, the enrollment-to-capacity ratios in each of the 21 concurrency service areas established in the agreement would have to be at or below 110%. After nine years of negotiations to get all jurisdictions in the county to join the agreement, the ball was in the school district's court. Successful execution of the new collaboration was achieved, in part, by the school district professionalizing its planning staff. Several important hires were made: a full-time demographer; an additional senior planner; and a planner for concurrency. Additionally, boundaries and finance committees were established and a mantra was developed to keep politics out of the determination of priorities in the five-year plan (the "CIP rules" mantra).

Very importantly, a vigorous school construction process was put into high gear rigorously exercising real estate, architect, engineer, and construction management staffs to deliver on the five-year capital improvement plan. Figure 6.3 shows public school-building activity in Palm Beach County from 1910 to 2006. The remarkable pace of construction at the turn of the century is readily viewed.

Figure 6.3 clearly shows school construction and modernization peaking in 2000, the year the ILA was being signed, and in 2003 and 2004, years in which the school district's deadline to deliver on the 110% benchmark was closing in. The year in which watershed Florida collaboration and concurrency legislation was enacted, 1993, no new schools were completed in Palm Beach County. Thus, for comparison purposes, three periods are distinguished. The first is the seven-year period leading up to the 1993 amendments (1986–1992). This is a period in which the state unsuccessfully invited local jurisdictions to form collaborative school planning and concurrency agreements. The second is the seven-year period (1994–2000) where the state amended with specific rules its permission for collaborative school planning

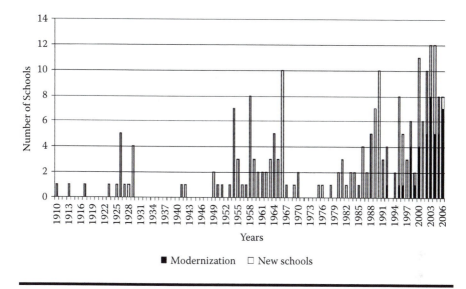

Figure 6.3 New and modernized schools. (*Source:* This figure was constructed by the chapter author with unpublished data provided by the Palm Beach County School Board.)

and concurrency. In this period Palm Beach County officials held collaboration negotiations. The third is the four-year period (2001–2004) leading from signature of the ILA to the deadline for meeting the 110% performance benchmark. Table 6.5 summarizes some of the main contrasts between these periods.

The first important insight provided by Table 6.4 is that the rate of school construction and modernization per year did not change much in the periods before and after the 1993 amendments. The Palm Beach County School District built or modernized roughly five schools per year before and after the important amendments. However, the rate of school construction and modernization nearly doubled in the period following signature of the ILA. Ten schools per year were either built or modernized in the 2001–2004 period. This shows the powerful effect of the

Table 6.5 Trends in New and Modernized Schools

	Period		
	1986–1992	*1994–2000*	*2001–2004*
Average number of schools built and modernized per year	5.00	5.30	10.00
Ratio of modernized to new schools	0.03	0.42	0.82

110% benchmark as well as the determination of the school district to preserve the authority it had gained in the CSP-ILA.

The second important insight provided by Table 6.4 is the change in the mix of new and modernized schools. Clearly, the ratio of modernized to new schools increases from one period to the next. Whereas this ratio is only 0.03 in 1986–1992, it increases to 0.42 during 1994–2000 and to 0.82 during 2001–2004. The increase in school modernizations could be partly coincidental; that is, it could be explained by many schools coincidentally becoming obsolete. Nevertheless, the data show a distinct acceleration in school building when the ILA came into effect and, in particular, a distinct effect of the modernization clause contained in the ILA.

Reaching performance benchmarks by 2004 led to renewal of the Palm Beach CSP-ILA in January 2006. In addition, based on the success in Palm Beach, the state legislature passed the 2005 Growth Management Bill, which ended the voluntary phase of school concurrency and collaborative school planning, making it mandatory by December 1, 2008.

6.5.2 Revenue Sources Made Possible by Collaborative School Planning

The synergies and renewed trust derived from CSP helped secure two additional revenue sources. The first—a voter-approved local sales surtax—was fundamental for the continuation of the five-year plan once COPs proceeds proved to be insufficient. The other was less important in terms of amount but ultimately made possible thanks to CSP.

6.5.2.1 Voter-Approved Sales Surtax

During the first years of CSP the school district had managed to regain trust and to establish a reputation for building quality schools on time and on budget. It had successfully recovered from a scandal for misspending referendum money. The construction program was now reviewed by multiple citizen oversight committees that had lent their endorsements as had the press. New schools could be seen throughout the county. The county, cities, developers, and citizens were happy. The best measure of the regained trust was voter support and approval of a half-penny on the dollar sales tax surcharge in the November 2004 general election intended to raise $560 million to supplement the five-year budget to build new schools.[20] City officials and even developers actively campaigned in favor of this surtax.

6.5.2.2 Mitigation

CSP made possible a revenue source of its own: mitigation. This novel revenue source is conceptually akin to impact fees. If the latter represent an opportunity and means of passing the bill of infrastructure construction (including schools) directly to users, mitigation represents a second opportunity of doing the same.

Mitigation is established in the ILA. In a nutshell, it operates as follows. If a developer submits a new residential development project and the additional demand for school seats causes the enrollment/capacity ratio to exceed the 110% benchmark considering current and planned school seat capacity for the next three years, a developer must offer mitigation through the following alternatives:

> (1) Donation of buildings for use as a primary or alternative learning facility; and/or (2) Renovation of existing buildings for use as learning facilities; or (3) Construction of permanent student stations or core capacity; or (4) … the developer may build the school in advance of the time set forth in the SCHOOL DISTRICT's Five-Year Capital Facilities Plan. The SCHOOL BOARD shall enter into an agreement to reimburse developer …; or (5) Charter school; or (6) Private School.[21]

6.6 Conclusions and Lessons Learned

The case study presented in this chapter has found many of the same factors underlying the creation and effectiveness of collaborative networks described in the literature, such as trust, reciprocity, brokerage, intractable problems, performance benchmarks, and mutually beneficial agreements.[22] Moreover, it provides a fresh, practical, detail-rich look at many of these factors and the relationships among them. In particular, the Palm Beach CSP case provides the following valuable lessons about the centrality of trust in collaborative public networks for practitioners who are currently engaged or may be planning to engage in collaborative agreements: Mistrust can generate resistance to collaboration even when all parties stand to benefit; overcoming mistrust requires considerable effort over a long period of time; and collaboration itself provides the process for regaining trust. In addition, the case study provides lessons about the importance of mutually beneficial agreements, the incentives provided by collaboration to achieve performance benchmarks, and the additional revenue sources made possible by regained trust through collaboration. These lessons are discussed in the following paragraphs.

6.6.1 Lesson 1

Mistrust generates resistance to collaboration, even when all parties stand to benefit from collaboration. As previously discussed, once the equity clause was part of the agreement, all parties involved in the Palm Beach County CSP-ILA stood to gain from school construction and modernization. However, even so, some parties fiercely resisted CSP simply because they did not trust the ability of the school district to follow through on its end of the bargain. Mistrust can be seen as a discount factor for benefits expected by parties in the agreement. If mistrust is large, the discount factor is large, discounted benefits are small, and net benefits are possibly negative or negligible.

In the case of the School District of Palm Beach County, mistrust came from underqualified staff and public perception that voter-approved bond proceeds had been misspent. The school district learned the hard way that, if voters approve a bond issue to build schools, these schools better be built, even if bond proceeds are insufficient and additional revenue sources are required.

6.6.2 Lesson 2

Mistrust can be overcome. However, to establish a collaborative public service network in the context of mistrust, the actor that is mistrusted must exert sustained catalytic leadership over a long period of time, must seek a trusted broker to mediate with parties, must accept conditional or tentative commitments to collaboration by mistrusting parties, and must be prepared to shoulder a greater share of the financial burden necessary to underwrite the mutually beneficial outcomes of collaboration.

In this case study, the financial burden of school construction and modernization was placed fully on the school district. This could not have been any other way leading up to the signing of the CSP-ILA or even until the 110% performance benchmark had been reached and trust had been regained. Today, however, the distribution of the financial burden is an issue for the school district, which considers that a greater share of the burden can and should be borne by developers. The school district has learned that, by being overly eager to add capacity to the five-year plan, developers often use this capacity to avoid offering mitigation. Under the agreement, developers can also use capacity in a neighboring concurrency area to avoid offering mitigation. Thus, the school district would like to take measures to shift some of the financial burden to developers, and the question is whether regained trust will give it the necessary leverage to do so.

6.6.3 Lesson 3

Trust can be regained. One of the pluses of overcoming mistrust to establish collaboration is that collaboration itself offers a way for trust to be regained. To do this the mistrusted actor must deliver on commitments acquired under the collaboration agreement.

6.6.4 Lesson 4

Successful collaborative public service networks can help secure additional revenue sources. In the case study, two additional revenue sources were made possible thanks to collaboration. First, the school district negotiated a revenue source called mitigation that allowed it in principle to transfer part of the financial burden of school construction to developers. Second, once the school district had delivered on the promised school construction and modernization program and had regained trust with citizens and other stakeholders, it was able to get voter approval for a sales surtax. Cities and developers that had previously resisted CSP campaigned to support the surtax.

6.6.5 Lesson 5

Collaborative public service networks provide unique incentives to meet performance benchmarks to continue to receive the benefits from collaboration. Collaboration is established in agreements where parties make exchanges of value. In the case study, the school board and district offered a construction plan to modernize old schools and build enough new schools to solve the overcrowding problem. In exchange, however, it got from cities the authority to approve permits for new residential developments. However, if it did not meet its end of the bargain—that is, if it did not meet the 110% benchmark—it would lose the authority to approve permits for new residential developments. Thus the collaborative contractual arrangement provided a unique incentive to reach the performance benchmark.

6.6.6 Lesson 6

Mutually beneficial agreements are an important factor underlying the establishment and sustainment of collaborative public service networks. In the case study of Palm Beach County, school construction and modernization benefited all parties involved directly and indirectly in CSP. The case of neighboring Broward County may help to illustrate the point. Broward County faced a similar or worse school crowding problem than Palm Beach and tried to reach a school concurrency solution for six years. However, Broward met state government disapproval and the fierce opposition of home builders, which even took the county to court over its concurrency plan. Even after rewriting its concurrency plan several times, the State Department of Community Affairs repeatedly rejected it on grounds that it was not realistic or incomplete. In 1999, after spending roughly $1 million on establishing school concurrency, Broward County finally gave up. The difference between the approaches of both counties was that, while the Palm Beach CSP agreement determined that school construction would have to keep up with development, the Broward proposal, in contrast, limited development to the construction of schools.[23] Under the Broward proposal, developers stood to lose—hence, their opposition and that of the state. The Broward proposal did not provide benefits to all parties involved. Thus, credit is due to those unwavering leaders of Palm Beach for imbuing their process with a win–win philosophy that allowed them to be the first county in Florida and perhaps the nation to establish a novel collaborative school planning process.

Endnotes

1. A. Downs, Smart Growth, *Journal of the American Planning Association 71* (4): 367–380, 2005; R.K. Norton, More and Better Local Planning, *Journal of the American Planning Association, 71* (1): 55–71, 2005.
2. Downs, Smart Growth.
3. S. Nunn and M.S. Rosentraub, Dimensions of Interjurisdictional Cooperation, *Journal of the American Planning Association, 63* (2): 205–219, 1997.
4. Downs, Smart Growth.
5. Leanne Evans (treasurer of the Palm Beach County School District), in an interview with Esteban G. Dalehite on March 27, 2007, states that public perception is erred on this issue. She indicates that bond proceeds were spent on schools but that the funds were insufficient due to escalating constructions costs. The mistake made by the school district, according to Evans, was that instead of using property tax revenues to finish the schools started with bond proceeds, it built a new headquarters instead. The main lesson learned is to always finish the construction of schools.
6. D.L. Powell and M. Gazica, And Now ... School Concurrency, *Florida Bar Journal, 79* (10): 44–47, 2005.
7. Ibid.
8. G.A. Solli and E.G. Dalehite, Interlocal Cooperation to Achieve School Concurrency, Unpublished paper presented at the South Eastern Conference of Public Administration, Athens, GA, September 28, 2006.
9. Ibid.
10. Ibid.
11. Powell and Gazica, And Now ....
12. Ibid.
13. S. Travis, County, Towns, Cities to Tie Development to School Space - The Last of 28 Governments Signed Off on Plan That Will Limit Housing Development if Nearby Schools Are Overcrowded, *Stuart News*, C2, December 23, 2000.
14. Solli and Dalehite, Interlocal Cooperation.
15. Travis, County, Towns, Cities.
16. Ibid.
17. A few small municipalities in Palm Beach County did not have a school within their boundaries, nor were they expected to acquire any in the future, and were exempt from the agreement.
18. Travis, County, Towns, Cities.
19. *Modernization* is a trade term for building a completely new school on the grounds of the old school. Typically, the new school is constructed on the athletic field or playground. When completed, the faculty and students are moved to the new facility, the old school is demolished, and a new athletic field or playground is installed. Modernization should not be viewed as merely building an *addition* to the school or *refurbishing* it. Such events may also occur in a school's desired 40- to 50-year lifetime.
20. F.S. section 212.055(6) allows a voter-approved capital outlay sales surtax that may not exceed 0.5%.
21. Palm Beach County (PBC), Palm Beach County Interlocal Agreement with Municipalities of Palm Beach County and the School District of Palm Beach County to Establish Public School Concurrency, 2001.

22. K. Thurmaier and C. Wood, Interlocal Agreements as Overlapping Social Networks: Picket-Fence Regionalism in Metropolitan Kansas City, *Public Administration Review, 62* (5): 585–598, 2002; A.M. Thomson and J.L. Perry, Collaboration Processes: Inside the Black Box, *Public Administration Review, 66* (December Special Issue): 20–32, 2006; L.B. Bingham and R. O'Leary, Conclusion: Parallel Play, Not Collaboration: Missing Questions, Missing Connections. *Public Administration Review, 66* (December Special Issue): 161–167, 2006.
23. B. Hirschman, Bush Ties Schools to Development—Governor Looks to Link New Homes to Construction of Classroom Space. *Sun Sentinel*, 1A, January 19, 2001.

Chapter 7

Moving beyond Hierarchies: Creating Effective Collaboration Networks for West Nile Virus Biosurveillance in Oregon

G. Brian Burke, Christopher M. Wirth,
Theresa A. Pardo, Amy D. Sullivan,
Hyuckbin Kwon, and J. Ramon Gil-Garcia

Contents

Case Brief

Background and Purpose of the Collaboration: The West Nile virus (WNV) arrived in Oregon in 2004, with confirmed cases reported in humans, horses, and birds. Over the next several years, the virus spread throughout the state. The status of WNV as a new endemic disease in the Western hemisphere required various agencies to collaborate in new ways, using both human and animal case reporting and sharing information across multiple disciplines. The collaborative structure was built by combining resources across multiple domains, formalizing existing agreements and response plans, and supporting informal agreements that leveraged resources based on cross-agency missions to protect the public. The state-level response strategy selected in Oregon was to coordinate WNV-related activities through the state Public Health Veterinarian (PHV), an official within the public health division of the Oregon Department of Human Services (DHS). Initial grant funding from the Centers for Disease Control and Prevention (CDC) to coordinate state-wide WNV surveillance, testing, and education programs officially started the collaborative effort.

Current Status: Given the need to rely on consensus building as much as possible, the PHV and key local partners employed the use of the CDC funding to provide incentives to participate, covering costs various stakeholders would have had to incur for their part of the surveillance network infrastructure (i.e., sample collection equipment and mosquito, bird, mammal, and human testing for WNV). Recognizing the critical role played by professionals, the PHV worked to create a support network and to provide these local government organizations with the resources they needed, including equipment for WNV monitoring (i.e., mosquito traps, microscopes, laboratory equipment, refrigeration equipment, computer hardware, and software tools). While significant success was achieved in building the relationships to support the statewide WNV surveillance system, a number of challenges were faced such as a statewide economic downturn that forced budget cuts to pre-existing human services and public health programs.

Lessons for Strategic Collaboration Practice: Leveraging existing systems and social networks, this case illustrates that sustainable collaboration must attend to participant investment and reward while building a new, shared understanding of the issue. The state-level leader's first task was getting people with an interest in the collaboration's purpose to the table and then formalizing processes and agreements. Initial funding was important to encouraging and retaining participation for the statewide effort. However, long-term commitment requires retention of key participants and participant agency buy-in, as the original purpose can be lost as participants change or leave due to fatigue, as they balance other competing job responsibilities, or as they become disenchanted with the process. Because of power and status issues often seen when multiple disciplines are involved, key to this case's success was a collaboration culture of continuous improvement that focused on regular information sharing and short- and long-term evaluation processes. Further, using existing systems as much as possible was essential. While issues of turf protection and conflicting interests that crossed professional and political domains were obstacles, a strong and capable leadership team can create a collaboration culture of continuous improvement focused on evaluation strategies and shared goals.

"How do we work together to respond to West Nile virus?" This was the question being asked by the Multnomah County Oregon vector control manager as he monitored the movement of West Nile virus (WNV) westward across the United States. By 2001, the virus was infecting mosquitoes, animals, and people, with a number of human deaths reported, from the East Coast past the Mississippi River. As the virus was approaching Oregon, the question about how best to organize a response was being asked by vector control, wildlife, and public health managers across the state. Like other infectious diseases, the spread of WNV was not bounded by geopolitical, agency, or discipline boundaries of public health, veterinary medicine, and agriculture. The WNV's ability to establish itself as an endemic disease required various agencies to collaborate in new ways, using both human and animal case reporting and sharing information across multiple disciplines to control the spread of the virus as much as possible and ultimately to prevent animal and human casualties.

7.1 Introduction

In 1999 West Nile virus (WNV) was spreading westward across the continental United States, starting with mosquitoes and birds and infecting people from the East Coast past the Mississippi River. By 2001 it was clear that WNV would make its way from New York to Oregon; the disease had been detected in 28 states and was moving in an obvious westward pattern across the United States.[2] Though WNV still had to "pass through" 14 continental states before reaching Oregon, the state began to prepare for its arrival.

West Nile virus finally arrived in Oregon in 2004, with confirmed cases reported in humans, horses, and birds. Over the next several years, the virus spread throughout the state and continues to this day to infect humans and animals. Although the number of confirmed cases as of late 2007 was low, the natural history of WNV in other states indicates that the number of human cases may grow over time.[3] Like other infectious diseases, WNV was not concerned with geopolitical, agency, or discipline boundaries of public health, veterinary medicine, and agriculture. However, the status of WNV as a new endemic disease in the Western hemisphere—and in this case, required various agencies to collaborate in new ways, using both human and animal case reporting and sharing information across multiple disciplines. The collaborative structure was built by combining resources across multiple domains, formalizing existing agreements and response plans, and supporting informal agreements that leveraged resources based on cross-agency missions to protect the public. Many challenges were overcome along the way; a few were too great to overcome, and new strategies had to be developed. The state-level response strategy selected in Oregon was to coordinate WNV-related activities through the state Public Health Veterinarian (PHV), an official within

WEST NILE VIRUS

First isolated in the West Nile District of Uganda in 1937, West Nile virus is commonly found in Africa, Eastern Europe, West Asia, and the Middle East. It is a potentially deadly disease that spreads to humans, birds, and mammals via infected mosquitoes. West Nile virus first appeared in the Western Hemisphere in and around New York City in 1999. Since then the virus has spread across North America, infecting 27,573 people and killing 1,083 in the United States between 1999 and 2007.[2]

the public health division of the Oregon Department of Human Services (DHS). Implementation of this strategy got off to a good start when the PHV secured a grant from the Centers for Disease Control and Prevention (CDC) to coordinate statewide WNV surveillance, testing, and education programs.

This chapter[1] presents the story of how Oregon worked across the traditional boundaries and hierarchies of the public sector to leverage existing and build new collaborative capacity to create a statewide biosurveillance network in preparation for the arrival of the WNV. As background for the case study, a brief review of the literature on cross-boundary collaboration, emergency response, public health, and information sharing is presented. The case is then presented in four subsections: The first provides an overview of Oregon's strategy; subsections two through four present the case in terms of the process of establishing an effective collaboration structure, using specific stakeholder strategies for building the network, and finally establishing a culture of continuous improvement. The presentation of the case is followed by a set of lessons learned from the case as well as a set of final conclusions and questions for future research. Four lessons about using collaborative strategies for building effective biosurveillance networks emerged from the case analysis. The lessons learned focus on the importance of context, the value of existing networks and the importance of creating some new ones, the importance of time and money in building new relationships, and the need to focus first on informal relationships that can evolve through a variety of mechanisms into formal agreements. These lessons are relevant to any policy domain in which organizations, public—private, and non-profit—must come together with the responsibility for creating new capability to respond to a pressing public problem.

7.2 Collaboration and Information Sharing: Insights from Current Research

Disease outbreak response involves complex public policy and management challenges that are cross-boundary in nature. These cross-boundary challenges emerge because no single agency or government has the necessary authority or resources to act alone, so these organizations must work together in the public interest. In the case of WNV in Oregon, for example, no one state or local agency acting alone could implement a statewide surveillance network capable of collecting and sharing all of the information needed to respond. As a consequence, collaboration networks are emerging as a core strategy in many policy domains, including public health, as they enable the collection and sharing of information necessary to effectively plan for and carry out broad-based and coordinated response efforts. Research has shown, however, that cross-boundary collaboration and information sharing, particularly in times of crisis, are difficult to achieve. They require unique consideration and significant resources to strengthen existing partnerships and build new relationships among important stakeholders across agencies, levels of government, and even different sectors. The next section draws briefly on what is currently known about cross-boundary collaboration and crisis management, public health, and information sharing to set the stage for drawing lessons from the case of WNV in Oregon.

7.2.1 Cross-Boundary Collaboration and Crisis Management

Disaster and emergency management are beyond the capability and jurisdiction of any single organization. For example, the response to the World Trade Center attack in 2001 involved more than 15,000 volunteers and hundreds of organizations ranging from major humanitarian organizations such as the American Red Cross to catering firms feeding emergency response personnel to animal welfare organizations rescuing abandoned pets.[4] For this reason, the field of emergency management since the 1940s gradually moved from a top-down, command-and-control bureaucratic model to a dynamic and flexible network model that enables collaboration.[5] The Emergency Management Accreditation Program (EMAP), the national standard for public emergency management, states that an emergency management program "encompasses all organizations, agencies, departments, entities, and individuals responsible for emergency management and homeland security."[6]

However, the cross-boundary approach to disaster and emergency management is not without disadvantages. Coordinating multiple organizations in a network incurs higher transaction costs than the operation of a hierarchical organization. Conflicting organizational goals and distrust can hinder effective collaboration.[7] Organizational networks can also diffuse responsibility and complicate the question of accountability.[8] Information sharing across organizations also can be seriously hindered by the lack of data standards, lack of policies about data standards, sharing and coordination, and poor data quality.[9]

Several policy recommendations for making more effective use of networks in disaster response can be found in the literature. First, leadership should be based on a common vision and shared values rather than on hierarchy or control management.[10] Second, efforts should be made to increase awareness and participation in the network through public involvement, open communication, and wide publication of results.[11] Third, agencies should act according to flexible guidelines instead of formal rules and be given enough discretion to respond to specific circumstances.[12] Fourth, a systematic planning process to respond to different scenarios is needed.[13]

7.2.2 Cross-Boundary Collaboration and Public Health

The structural framework of the U.S. public health system includes a network of state and local public health agencies working in partnership with the federal government. The framework is balanced on a legal foundation that grants primacy for health concerns to local or state agencies, a financial foundation that allows the federal government to promote equality and minimum standards across states, and a practical foundation for local public health agencies to serve as the point of contact between communities and governments.[14] One aspect of a public health-care system that particularly calls for collaboration is the creation and implementation of surveillance systems to provide early warning and detection of bioterrorism attacks or outbreaks of infectious disease such as severe acute respiratory syndrome (SARS) or WNV. However, critics have pointed out the inadequate surveillance capability of the U.S. public health system, especially before the terrorist attacks of September 11, 2001. Inadequacies can stem from the lack of coordination among levels of government and across government agencies, fragmented structure and overlapping jurisdictions, and the lack of standards in medical data elements and procedures.[15]

Collaboration in partnership with different levels of government, as well as a wide range of groups from many sectors, has been the central feature of public health practice since the mid 19th century.[16] Rowitz contends that the increasing importance of collaborative relationships is one of the top 10 infrastructure issues in the U.S. public health system in the 21st century.[17] Similarly, Beaglehole et al. regard a multidisciplinary approach to all determinants of health and community partnerships as essential themes of modern public health practice.[18]

7.2.3 Cross-Boundary Information Sharing

Cross-boundary information sharing has become an important topic in the public sector.[19] Rocheleau mentions that the capability to share information across boundaries has become "one of the basic goals of modern information management in government."[20] The need for information sharing in government has been further highlighted since the terrorist attacks on September 11, 2001. The 9/11 Commission regards the lack of information sharing across intelligence agencies as one of the major causes of the failure to thwart the terrorist plot.[21] Previous research has identified important benefits from information-sharing initiatives such as reduction of duplicate data collection, processing, and storage, improving the decision-making processes, improving coordination; more public accountability; and more comprehensive public information.[22]

The benefits of cross-boundary collaboration and information sharing are numerous. However, the need for multiple organizations to work together to create a space where they can effectively work together in these initiatives also creates many challenges such as technological incompatibility, mismatched data structures, conflicting organizational goals, potential misuse of shared information, diversity in organizational cultures, structures, and philosophies, inadequate institutional arrangements, and political pressures.[23] Recent studies have identified a set of strategies that help to overcome some of these challenges and to increase the success of cross-boundary information-sharing initiatives. Examples of those recommendations that best apply to the Oregon WNV case include the following:

1. Pay attention to agency culture.
2. Retain autonomy of involved agencies.
3. Build on long-range and comprehensive planning.
4. Secure adequate financial resources.[24]

7.2.4 Insights from Research: Collaboration Networks, Formation Challenges, and Leadership

The review of the literature shows that while many government agencies are still wrestling with managing in today's environment with top-down bureaucratic management models, many disaster and emergency response agencies have moved to more dynamic network models that depend on multiorganizational collaboration. This shift is attributed, in part, to new understanding of the critical role intergovernmental and public–private collaboration plays in the U.S. public health system, particularly for the surveillance of bioterrorism attacks and infectious diseases. While challenges to these efforts such as conflicting goals, high transaction cost, and diffusion of responsibility are still real in initiatives involving multiple organizations, research further shows that leadership based on common vision and shared values, increased awareness and participation, flexible guidelines, and systematic planning process help make collaboration more effective.

7.3 Creating a Coordinated Statewide Surveillance Network in Oregon

While the probability of the WNV virus coming to Oregon was relatively high in 2001, developing the necessary response capability within the state had to compete for funding with a wide range of other *existing* priorities—public health and nonpublic health. Although creating a coordinated statewide surveillance network in Oregon was a critical component of a WNV response, in the socioeconomic context that existed in 2001, getting the money from inside the state would prove to be problematic. Therefore, the funding from the CDC was essential to efforts to build the necessary relationships with state and local actors for the collaborative statewide surveillance network.

An initial CDC grant of approximately $90,000 was notable but limited, requiring a compromise between an ideal and a realistically sustainable surveillance network. CDC advised states that "in any given jurisdiction, surveillance systems should be tailored according to the *probability of arbovirus activity* and *available resources.*"[25] Oregon's most pressing concern was that the surveillance data needed to estimate the risk of WNV transmission to humans could not be provided by a single agency. The challenge of estimating the risk to people required not only traditional human case reporting but also an understanding of what was happening in animal sentinel populations such as mosquitoes, birds, and horses. Thus, it was imperative that the various surveillance components and their respective data-collection arms actively communicate and exchange information in standard ways.

The PHV, along with some of his key partners at the local government level, saw that the best path to a sustainable WNV surveillance system would be to follow CDC recommendations, building on existing vector control districts (VCDs), veterinary and agricultural reporting networks, and public health surveillance structures. A VCD is a special district established to control vector-borne diseases through a variety of means. MCVNC works in cooperation with surrounding communities and other entities to address emerging vector-borne disease issues." VCDs throughout the state existed with varying capacities. Some communities in Oregon were served by actively engaged programs that had been assessing arboviral disease in mosquitoes for years; others had no vector services at all. VCDs from the former efforts together with the PHV provided some of the key leadership in drawing together the VCDs in support of the WNV surveillance efforts. Reporting veterinary diseases relevant to agriculture, including horses, was generally handled through the state veterinarian in the Oregon Department of Agriculture—a position distinct from the state PHV, who dealt primarily with zoonotic diseases. Human disease reporting was generally handled through local health departments (LHDs), which per Oregon statute are the primary public health authorities in the state. In addition to these individuals and agencies were the laboratories that handled arboviral testing, including the Oregon State University College of Veterinary Medicine Laboratory (a.k.a. Veterinary College Lab) for animal specimens and the Oregon State Public Health Laboratory for both human and occasional animal specimens. To accomplish the necessary information sharing among state and local agencies throughout Oregon, both past and current cross-boundary relationships needed to be strengthened and new relationships created. To this end, the PHV and others in state and local government reached out across agencies to build the collaborative arrangements required for implementing a sustainable WNV surveillance network.

7.4 Establishing an Effective Collaborative Structure

Oregon's WNV public health surveillance network was put in place to provide the infrastructure necessary to collect, analyze, and share virus related information in support of the detection, control, and response to an outbreak of WNV in humans. Key players in this network included state and local agencies with roles and responsibilities related to one or more of the surveillance components (i.e., collecting, analyzing, or testing mosquitoes, birds, mammals, or humans for WNV). To create this network, the PHV reached out to the Multnomah County Vector manager and his peers to begin to shape how Oregon would collaborate to handle WNV emergence in Oregon. The initial collaboration was formalized through response plans and some interagency agreements. However, as time went on less formal agreements negotiated between the PHV and various government stakeholders played an even more important role.

Oregon's PHV was key in establishing an effective statewide WNV public health surveillance network, due in large part to his role in dealing with diseases transmitted from animals to humans (i.e., zoonotic diseases like WNV). Like other public health veterinarians across the United States, in Oregon the PHV's role involves preventing significant diseases that humans can get from animals and controlling them when they do break out.[26] The related veterinary public health activities rely on collaboration with physicians, emergency rooms, legislators, local officials, schools, local health departments, and the general public.

Working in this way created some successes as early as fall 2002. In addition to securing funding from the CDC two full years before the first human case in Oregon, the collaborative formalized the statewide surveillance network design in the State of Oregon Mosquito-Borne Disease Response Plan, subsequently referred to as the 2002 OR WNV Plan. This plan focused on the three surveillance components: mosquito, animal (birds and mammals), and human. For each component,

OBJECTIVES OF THE OREGON DISEASE RESPONSE PLAN

1. Leverage and improve upon the existing statewide system for mosquito-borne disease surveillance information in cooperation with appropriate state and local entities.
2. Develop enhanced encephalitis surveillance systems for humans and horses in cooperation with physicians, veterinarians, and local health jurisdictions.[27]

the roles and responsibilities of each organization in the surveillance network were specified with a particular emphasis on technical infrastructure, data collection, and information sharing.

7.4.1 Mosquito Surveillance

The mosquito surveillance component was based on the understanding that knowledge of local mosquito populations is essential for the control of vector-borne diseases. The 2002 OR WNV Plan identified the collaborative partners as the Oregon DHS's Public Health Division and the local VCDs. Technical infrastructure for mosquito surveillance included resources for mosquito collection and testing equipment, information and communications technology for database management, mapping of mosquitoes, and sharing of results. Data collection and information sharing depend on these resources as well as the collaboration agreements that defined the purpose, rules, and policies for data collecting and sharing.

7.4.2 Animal Surveillance

The animal surveillance component was based on the understanding that bird and mammal sentinels can provide early warning on WNV circulation in an area. This warning allowed for enhanced control measures to prevent human cases and to reduce virus impacts on livestock, pets, and wildlife. As described in the 2002 OR WNV Plan, "avian morbidity/mortality surveillance appears to be the most sensitive early detection system for WNV."[28] Thus, the technical infrastructure for animal surveillance relied on the capability to collect and test dead birds. The Veterinary College Lab was the designated site for WNV serologic testing of collected birds. The collection and transport of dead bird specimens to the Veterinary College Lab was an important logistical piece of the infrastructure that depended heavily on the local government partners. In addition to local partners, this surveillance network expanded to include private-sector partnerships.

7.4.3 Human Surveillance

In Oregon, WNV is an expressly reportable condition within the state's passive surveillance system—thus requiring physician and laboratory reporting of human cases. Case reports made to local health authorities are investigated by LHD community health nurses, who also assure appropriate follow-up based on statewide investigative guidelines. Regarding the technical infrastructure, reports go from the county to the state based on agreed upon timelines. In July 2000, the largest LHD in the state—Multnomah County, which accounts for roughly 30% of disease reports—started sending reports to the state electronically. Expansion of this electronic system to other counties in August 2003 and an electronic laboratory reporting system have improved timeliness of case reporting to the state.

7.4.4 Integrating the Components for a Holistic Surveillance Network

Understanding of the threat of WNV and applying lessons learned from surveillance networks elsewhere, the PHV took the initial steps in outlining the collaborative statewide surveillance structure. The next important step was to transfer that outline from paper to reality, implementing the collaborative system of collecting, testing, and sharing information among the state, local, and nongovernment partners involved (Figure 7.1). While the PHV was the primary leader in coordinating this statewide collaborative structure, implementation was made possible by a small group of key partners at the local government level, including vector control specialists and public health epidemiologists from county health departments who saw the importance of building relationships as imperative to the success of the surveillance system.

7.5 Building the Network through a Range of Stakeholder Specific Strategies

Traditional authority and control relationships in terms of existing agreements between state and local public health agencies allowed for some influence over the formation of the statewide surveillance network. However, in the context of the disease affecting both animal and human health domains, it was impossible for the state to mandate partnerships in the overall collaborative structure. Rather, collaboration needed to be built through new, or at least initially, informal agreements. Given the need to rely on consensus building as much as possible, the PHV and key local partners employed two specific strategies to build the necessary collaborations and infrastructure. One strategy involved use of the CDC funding to provide incentives to participate, covering costs various stakeholders would have had to incur for their part of the surveillance network infrastructure (i.e., sample collection equipment and mosquito, bird, mammal, and human testing for WNV). The other strategy involved using the prevalent scientific understanding of the virus and its public health implications to help build consensus around the need for a statewide surveillance network. As demonstrated in the design of the 2002 OR WNV Plan, the components of the surveillance network were derived from a scientific understanding of the nature of arbovirus activity in general and WNV specifically and how the virus was transmitted. This understanding was widely accepted and shared among the CDC and other state and local animal and human health agencies from across the United States.

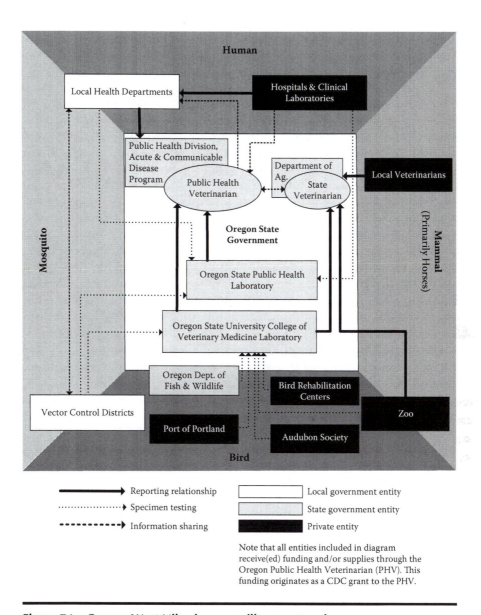

Figure 7.1 Oregon West Nile virus surveillance network.

7.5.1 Activating and Strengthening Existing Networks

Oregon had experience with a statewide surveillance network for arbovirus diseases similar to WNV, specifically Western equine encephalitis and St. Louis encephalitis. For these diseases the state Department of Human Services, VCDs, and LHDs had developed limited surveillance capabilities. However, in areas where VCDs were not part of a local health department, they did not have strong, routine working relationships with their county health departments. Consequently, the event-specific infrastructure developed to address sporadic cases had disappeared by the time the state starting planning for the arrival of WNV. The leaders in establishing the WNV surveillance network set out to reconnect these networks and expand them for WNV. For example, the network among the PHV, county LHDs, and some VCDs needed to be revitalized to establish procedures for reporting, collecting, and testing dead birds. The PHV worked with the local government to put in place procedures by which residents who found a dead bird could notify their LHD. The LHD and VCDs would then collect the dead bird, acquire related information, and send the bird to the designated lab for testing. The cost of shipping and testing was covered by the state through the CDC grant. This process, which played out informally, helped to successfully implement another critical component of the surveillance network by leveraging citizen involvement as well as LHD and VCD resources and CDC funding. It also removed the financial disincentive to local governments, which otherwise would have had to pay for the testing.

Another example of how the state built on previous networks can be found in the human health surveillance activities. When WNV was added to the list of reportable conditions in Oregon, the level of LHD participation in surveillance was required to change; county communicable disease programs were obliged to investigate cases and report them to the state. However, even before this change and beyond minimal mandated participation, most LHDs engaged more fully in understanding the epidemiology of WNV as part of their public health responsibility. This strong commitment to their public health responsibilities was aided by the use of the CDC funding, which made it materially possible for LHDs to encourage physicians to send human samples to the state public health lab for confirmatory WNV testing.

Recognizing the critical role played by LHDs and VCDs, the PHV worked to create a support network and to provide these local government organizations with the resources they needed. Rather than dictate the response, he generally tried to work with local partners through existing channels. For example, there was no formal, regular meeting devoted to WNV, so the PHV used the monthly bioterrorism group meetings as one venue for WNV discussion. National and regional organizations leading WNV response planning such as the American Mosquito Control Association (AMCA) and the Northwest Mosquito and Vector Control Association were also engaged. The PHV regularly leveraged existing resources to provide agencies with equipment for WNV monitoring including mosquito traps, microscopes, laboratory equipment, refrigeration equipment, computer hardware, and software tools.

While there have been significant successes in building the relationships to support the statewide WNV surveillance system, a number of challenges were faced including building relationships between local government organizations, some neighboring LHDs, and VCDs. Breakdowns in the network have been attributed to several issues including differences in agency missions and priorities that precluded negotiation; while WNV was being identified as an *emerging* threat to Oregon, a statewide economic downturn was forcing budget cuts to preexisting human services and public health programs.

The surveillance network formation process also faced other challenges. Unforeseen challenges emerged in the context of new strategies created for dealing with WNV specifically. For example, funneling all human specimen confirmatory testing through the PHV was initially conceptualized as a way to ensure thorough reporting—noting that labs in Oregon are required to supply both negative and positive test results to the "submitter," but only positive results to public health officials. Thus, CDC funds were used to encourage physicians and LHDs to send specimens to the state through the PHV. The unfortunate side effect of this approach was a perception by providers that they could report WNV cases directly to the state PHV rather than to the LHDs as required under Oregon statute. While some understaffed LHDs may have come to rely on the assistance provided, other LHDs considered such outreach efforts as having a negative impact on the existing reporting systems. LHDs were concerned about the state failing to report a case to the county and felt that encouraging physicians to report cases directly to the PHV was undermining their public health authority. This threat to their turf was not just a matter of politics; in fact, county health officials are legally and ethically responsible for the health of their communities. Failure to hear about a mandatory reportable case does not relieve this ethical responsibility for the citizenry and, therefore, makes this concern about being left out of the loop a serious and legitimate one.

7.5.2 *Identifying and Engaging New Partners*

Colleagues from various VCDs frequently worked with the PHV to engage necessary partners from outside of the public health community that were viewed as critical to the overall WNV surveillance system. These organizational partners included other state government agencies such as the Department of Agriculture and the Department of Fish and Wildlife as well as nonprofit organizations such as the Audubon Society. In the OR 2002 WNV Plan, the state Department of Agriculture was recognized as the appropriate agency to notify veterinarians about available WNV testing for pets, livestock, and, very important in Oregon, horses. The availability of free testing provided important input to the surveillance system through the detection of WNV in the animal populations that the veterinarians served. This new centralized testing was previously unavailable to state and local agencies and now provided regular access to information on potentially infected pets, livestock, and horses.

Another "new" relationship was established with the Port of Portland (POP). The POP is a large landowner in Multnomah County and is in charge of biodiversity maintenance at wetland mitigation sites throughout the Portland area. Although the relationship between the PHV and POP was a new one, the POP had a relationship with the Multnomah County VCD long before the arrival of WNV. This relationship was based on a contractual arrangement with the county for integrated mosquito control and surveillance services. After the arrival of WNV in the United States but before its arrival in Oregon, the Multnomah County VCD used the emergence of WNV to engage partners like POP, adding new cooperative activities and expanding existing relationships. An important aspect of expanding the relationship was helping POP see its "public health" role—including its part in a statewide surveillance network. This approach to partnership was characterized by identifying overlapping agency missions and by appealing to a sense of public responsibility.

Most attempts at collaboration were successful when agencies found similarities in their mission and were able to see an appropriate contributory role. As one VCD supervisor saw it, the importance of keeping an open ear in the community for potential stakeholders could not be underrated. However, failure ensued when differences in principles and culture could not be overcome. For example, METRO, a regional infrastructure planning and coordination agency, held a different view of wetlands-related landscape management and development from the VCDs. The main challenges faced were difficulty in educating people on their roles and power relationships. An additional barrier was a lack of historical relationships between agencies. In this instance, funding and appealing to METRO's public health interests were not sufficient to overcome these barriers.

7.6 Evaluation as a Driver for Continuous Improvement and Network Formalization

The success of a surveillance system is broadly understood to depend on whether the right information is being collected, analyzed, and shared in a timely manner with the organizations that need it to plan and respond. Such an evaluation is problematic in any case; evaluating the success of a surveillance system created and managed through a statewide collaborative network is significantly more so. Regardless of the challenges of evaluating such a network, the PHV and key stakeholders in the network recognized the value of such an evaluation process. They determined that a more formalized evaluation process could improve accountability of the relevant stakeholders and improve and sustain—even institutionalize—these relationships over time. To meet the goals they set for themselves in terms of continuous improvement of the network, these stakeholders invested in strategies to leverage existing evaluation practices and models where possible and to build new ones where necessary. Since 2004, Multnomah County has been conducting annual preparatory training to test its surveillance systems for sensitivity and response. Relevant models from existing evaluation efforts used to guide preparation included the incident command system (ICS) and other emergency response approaches. Additionally, since 2006 the VCD in Multnomah County, has incorporated evaluation components in both real time and post event to ensure that the surveillance system is working and is sensitive to a changing community. By 2007, new evaluation frameworks were created; for example, the WNV response component of the 2007 Oregon Emergency Management Plan called for revisions "every other year with the specific attention to comments *from the previous years' exercises or emergencies.*"[29]

As the statewide coordinator of the surveillance network, the PHV is now responsible for reporting on evaluation activity and providing updates on changes to the network to all participants in the network. He does this through a summary year-end report of all WNV surveillance activities. Drawing on the umbrella arrangement with the PHV as the local point person, he is able to collate data from LHDs, VCDs, and other nonhealth agencies such as the Oregon Department of Fish and Wildlife, the local zoos, and other animal-type stakeholders. These efforts are part of an overall strategy to increase the integrity of the surveillance systems and to serve the interests of the collaboration by ensuring that all members, whether central and active or peripheral, are given the chance to reflect on system performance.

Leveraging existing models and creating new evaluation cycles, requirements, and reporting responsibilities are four of the ways Oregon is working to shed light on gaps in the surveillance network and to guide future improvements. The resulting evaluations of the WNV surveillance system focused on two simple but important questions: (1) Are the appropriate data being collected? and (2) Are the right data getting to where they are needed in a timely manner?

Evaluations conducted to determine if the appropriate data were being collected were carried out in a variety of ways. To create these evaluation processes it was necessary for members of the network to gain new understanding about data requirements and data movement through the system so they could develop evaluation models. Case reports of *any* reportable condition in humans, including WNV, are supposed to be reviewed as they are received—first at the local level through the LHD, as the report comes from the provider, and then at the state level, when the report goes from the LHD to the state. In the case of WNV-related illness, this virtually real-time review by the state is particularly important as LHD front-line workers may lack the training to assure that all of the appropriate information is gathered and to deal with variations in the quality of the data collected from county to county. For counties using the Multnomah County Communicable Disease Database, transmission of case reports generally is done at the end of every working day. Personnel at the state review case transmissions and inform counties of any problems encountered. Collaboratively creating a process that delivers valuable and useful data must be based on a shared understanding of the various components of the process.

Other evaluation processes were created to ensure that necessary information sharing and collaboration were occurring during the WNV season as well as between the seasons during which time the mosquito population is inactive. VCDs compile their data for year-end reporting between fall and spring. For example, in Multnomah County, the number of mosquitoes individually analyzed, collected, and speciated in a given year are tracked as one of the Multnomah County VCD's performance measures. Such year-end reporting activities serve a variety of ends including reporting requirements for grants, creating transparency for the public, and allowing for critical review to improve the mosquito surveillance systems. This information is shared with relevant health department, county government, and nongovernment stakeholders and is also available to the state for review.

To ensure that VCDs and LHDs are getting the information they need, the surveillance system is reviewed annually at the Oregon Mosquito and Vector Control Association's annual meeting.[30] These meetings include a stakeholder breakout session to review findings and practices from the previous year of WNV activity, such as the surveillance information previously described and laboratory and field protocols for mosquito, sentinel chicken, and dead bird collection and testing. This meeting allows the PHV to meet with representatives from VCDs, some LHDs, and the state lab to streamline the mosquito, sentinel chicken, and dead bird collection components of the statewide WNV surveillance system. This public meeting also allows a forum for best practices to be developed based on the previous year's successes and challenges.

The state also does an end-of-year assessment of lab reporting times using feedback from the LHDs and VCDs that submitted samples to be tested. Results of this assessment are shared with labs to let them know if they are reporting in the time frame established and to review if other methods of communication (e.g., fax vs. e-mail) would be more efficient for reporting results. Because lab results often guide the response for mosquito control, ongoing review of both testing and communication of test results is also essential. For the bird and mammal surveillance component, annual evaluation focuses on data for dead wild birds and the procedures for collecting and testing them.

An example of a related gap in Oregon's WNV surveillance system was in the area of disease reporting. Systems existed to report surveillance data from the county to the state, but no such systems existed for the state to report back to the counties. In those cases where the data came directly to the state bypassing the county, the PHV has agreed through informal arrangements to get that data to the county as well. Carrying out this agreement, however, was subject to individual availability of the PHV. The evaluation process was able to shed light on this weak link in the reporting system. These stakeholders were aware that much of the network established for WNV surveillance relied on informal agreements between individuals rather than on formal agreements between organizations. Regardless of the efforts of these individual agreements, sometimes they were not enough and fell short of the job at hand.

7.7 Lessons Learned in Building Effective Biosurveillance in Oregon

7.7.1 Lesson 1: Context Matters

Systematically accounting for context in planning for emergencies is broadly recognized as necessary.[31] It is knowledge of context that enables determinations of capabilities for responding to a particular situation and for contingency planning. In the case of Oregon, where efforts were made to develop a statewide WNV surveillance network to collect and share virus-related information, the importance of such contextual factors was very evident. Context issues included state and local government relationships, "turf" (e.g., authority, resources, and organizational interests), and multiple, sometimes conflicting interests among professional (e.g., human health, animal health, wildlife management, environmental protection) and political (e.g., local and state government agencies) domains.

7.7.2 Lesson 2: Leverage Existing Systems and Social Networks

As one of the key linking mechanisms for cross-boundary collaboration, existing networks are vital to future collaboration in terms of the provision of information, resource and expertise sharing, and compensation for organizational and sector shortcomings.[32] In a public health emergency the intensity of the response provides limited time to learn a new system, and those unfamiliar with a system are more likely to make mistakes implementing that system. Tools such as system planning processes[33] and inclusive exercises with diverse scenarios[34] can be very useful under these circumstances. The PHV and the key partners at the local government level worked strategically to strengthen and expand existing relationships and to build new partnerships as needed to implement a working collaborative structure. They did this by negotiating with the necessary actors from the position of shared investment and risk—with, as this case shows, some attempts at collaboration being more successful than others. They demonstrated their commitment to the network rather than their individual agency by being willing to use federal funding to alleviate some of the costs being incurred by local governments to actually participate in the surveillance network and by using the scientific understanding of the virus and its public health implications to help build consensus around the need for a statewide surveillance network.

7.7.3 Lesson 3: Building Sustainable Intergovernmental Collaboration Takes Time and Money

Achieving buy-in from all participants is the most important activity in the initial phase of interorganizational collaborative projects.[35] However, achieving this buy-in can be a difficult and lengthy process, particularly when working with stakeholders who are not required to participate. As this case demonstrates, traditional lines of authority in government often enable the collaborative structures necessary for responding to cross-boundary policy issues such as those represented by WNV. Using funding and appealing to the principles of the public health profession do not always work right away, and stakeholders may need to invest time to build a shared understanding of the issue and to negotiate their own relationship with the network. As more stakeholders, were assembled under the collaborative umbrella particularly those outside of public health such as wildlife managers, a variety of issues around the various processes for WNV response surfaced, which is a common challenge when multiple organizations participate in a disaster management network.[36] For example, notable differences were found among the perspectives on mosquito control and its impact on food sources for other wildlife and how various methods of mosquito control might cause additional health issues. Creating collective understanding around complex issues of public policy and science takes time. All stakeholders bring with them a somewhat unique agenda, and time must be taken to work through the connections between their agenda and the one held by the network so that the overlap can be found. This overlap provides the incentive for committing to the network; finding this overlap takes time and is difficult to do in the middle of a crisis.

7.7.4 Lesson 4: Bring Together Individuals, and Then Focus on Formalizing and Refining Institutional Processes and Agreements

Multiorganizational partnerships usually begin with an informal and personal network of relationships and evolve into more formal partnerships as the initial collaboration gives way to more focused activities.[37] Those leading the organization of the statewide WNV surveillance network in Oregon were well aware that existing lines of authority between and among state and local government agencies were insufficient to mandate participation in the network. External budget and political pressures further limited interest in developing new formal agreements to create the necessary surveillance capability. Therefore, the majority of the collaboration was built on informal relationships among individuals. Strategies that proved successful for sustaining and even strengthening these relationships included finding ways to use existing, institutionalized processes when possible and establishing evaluation mechanisms as a platform for open communication and information sharing and as a foundation for process improvement and formalization. These strategies helped maintain the quality and accuracy of shared information and gave participants the chance to engage in critical reviews of the surveillance system.

7.8 Conclusion

Whether facing a public health crisis, homeland security issues, or environmental conservation, government is about addressing the complex problems of individuals and organizations. In multijurisdictional settings, cross-boundary collaboration and information sharing are essential for effective actions in these complex areas. The case of West Nile virus in Oregon illustrates the importance of building a collaborative structure with defined roles and responsibilities. It also highlights the need for engaging stakeholders informally at first, if necessary with an expectation of formalization over time. These informal and formal relationships provide the critical coordination mechanisms for sharing information across organizational boundaries, policy domains, and levels of government within the context of a crisis. Finally, it is clear from the case of Oregon that the collaborative network was successful, in part, due to the realization by the involved agencies of existing similarities in their missions and an important shared goal: managing the outbreak of WNV. The lessons learned in this case are relevant to any situation in which government must come together with other key stakeholders to create new capability to respond to a pressing public problem.

7.9 Remaining Questions

An examination of the case of Oregon's statewide WNV surveillance network raises a variety of questions including the following:

- How does context influence collaboration and information sharing?
- When and how should a collaborative network shift from informal, individual leadership to formal institutionalized agreements?
- How do the conditions endemic to crisis situations influence multiorganizational collaboration and information sharing?
- How do differences in professional cultures influence the nature of the collaboration process?

These questions provide an agenda for future research of value to practitioners as well as to researchers exploring the complex phenomenon of multiorganizational collaboration and information sharing in the public health arena and in other complex public policy domains.

Acknowledgment

This chapter is based in part on research funded through a grant from the National Science Foundation, grant number ITR-0205152.

Endnotes

1. Centers for Disease Control and Prevention (CDC), *West Nile Virus—Statistics, Surveillance, and Control,* May 31, 2007. http://www.cdc.gov/ncidod/dvbid/westnile/surv&control.htm (accessed April 15, 2008); Oregon Department of Human Services (DHS), *Public Health West Nile Virus Emergency Response Plan* (Portland: Oregon Department of Human Services, 2007).

2. CDC, *Preventing Emerging Infectious Diseases: A Strategy for the 21 Century* (Atlanta, GA: U.S. Department of Health and Human Services, 1998); CDC, West Nile Virus—Final 2001 West Nile Virus activity in the United States, May 29, 2007. http://www.cdc.gov/ncidod/dvbid/westnile/Mapsactivity/surv&control01Maps.htm

3. Oregon DHS, *State of Oregon Mosquito-Borne Disease Response Plan* (Portland: Oregon Department of Human Services, 2002). CDC, 2007b. *Public Health West Nile Virus.*

4. S. Lowe and A. Fothergill, A need to help: Emergent volunteer behavior after September 11th. In *Beyond September 11th: An Account of Post-disaster Research,* ed. J.L. Monday (Boulder: University of Colorado, 2003), pp. 293–314; W.J. Waugh Jr. and G. Streib, Collaboration and Leadership for Effective Emergency Management, *Public Administration Review 66* (s1): 131–140, 2006.

5. Waugh and Streib, Collaboration and Leadership.

6. Emergency Management Accreditation Program (EMAP), *EMAP Standard* (Lexington, KY: EMAP, 2006).

7. T.A. Pardo, J.R. Gil-Garcia, and G.B. Burke, *Informal Leadership and Networks: Lessons from the Response to the West Nile Virus Outbreak in North America,* Paper presented at the eChallenges 2007 Conference, The Hague, The Netherlands, October 24–26, 2007. Pardo et al., Sustainable Cross-Boundary Information Sharing, In *Digital Government: E-government Research, Case Studies, and Implementation,* ed. C. Hsinchun, L. Brandt, S.S. Dawes, V. Gregg, E. Hovy, A. Macintosh, et al. (New York: Springer-Verlag, 2007), pp. 421–438.; Gil-Garcia, I. Chengalur-Smith, and P. Duchessi, Collaborative E-government: Impediments and Benefits of Information Sharing Projects in the Public Sector, *European Journal of Information Systems, 16* (2): 121–133, 2007.

8. L.J. O'Toole Jr., The Implications for Democracy in a Networked Bureaucratic World, *Journal of Public Administration Research and Theory, 7*: 443–459, 1997.

9. Dawes, T. Birkland, G.K. Tayi, and C.A. Schneider, *Information, Technology, and Coordination: Lessons from the World Trade Center Response*, June 2004, Albany: Center for Technology in Government, University at Albany, State University of New York. http://demo.ctg.albany.edu/publications/reports/wtc_lessons (accessed April 15, 2008).

10. Waugh and Streib, Collaboration and Leadership; A.K. Donahue, The Space Shuttle Columbia Recovery Operation: How Collaboration Enabled Disaster Response, *Public Administration Review 66* (s1): 141–142, 2006; Pardo et al., *Informal Leadership*.

11. Dawes, A.M. Cresswell, and B.B. Cahan, Learning from Crisis: Lessons in Human and Information Infrastructure from the World Trade Center Response, *Social Science Computer Review, 22*: 52–56, 2004; L.K. Comfort, Risk, Security, and Disaster Management, *Annual Review of Political Science, 8:* 335–356, 2005; J.J. Kiefer and R.S. Montjoy. 2006. Incrementalism before the Storm: Network Performance for the Evacuation of New Orleans, *Public Administration Review, 66* (s1): 122–130, 2006; G. Simo and A.L. Bies, The Role of Nonprofits in Disaster Response: An Expanded Model of Cross-Sector Collaboration, *Public Administration Review, 67* (s1): 125–142, 2007.

12. Donahue, Space Shuttle Columbia.

13. Comfort, Risk, Security; Donahue, Space Shuttle Columbia; Simo and Bies, Role of Nonprofits.

14. B.J. Turnock, *Public Health: What It Is and How It Works* (Gaithersburg, MD: Aspen Publishers, 1997).

15. Institute of Medicine (IOM), *The Future of the Public's Health in the 21st Century* (Washington, DC: National Academy Press, 2003); K. Patel and M.E. Rushefsky, *The Politics of Public Health in the United States* (Armonk, NY: M. E. Sharpe, 2005).

16. R. Beaglehole, R. Bonita, R. Horton, O. Adams, and M. McKee, Public Health in the New Era: Improving Health through Collective Action, *Lancet 363*: 2084–2086, 2004.

17. L. Rowitz, *Public Health for the 21st Century: The Prepared Leader* (Sudbury, MA: Jones and Bartlett, 2006).

18. Beaglehole et al., Public Health in the New Era.

19. National Association of State Information Resource Executives (NASIRE), Toward National Sharing of Governmental Information, February 2000, Lexington, KY: National Association of State Information Resource Executives. http://www.nascio. org/publications/documents/NASCIO-JusticeReport_Feb2000.pdf (accessed April 15, 2008); B.A. Rocheleau, *Public Management Information Systems* (Hershey, PA: Idea Group Publishing, 2006); A. Bajaj and S. Ram, A Comprehensive Framework towards Information Sharing between Government Agencies, *International Journal of Electronic Government Research, 3* (2): 29–44, 2007; Pardo et al., *Informal Leadership*; Pardo et al., Sustainable Cross-Boundary Information Sharing.

20. Rocheleau, *Public Management.*

21. National Commission on Terrorist Attacks upon the United States (NCTAUUS), *The 9/11 Commission Report: Final Report of the National Commission on Terrorist Attacks upon the United States* (Washington, DC: National Commission on Terrorist Attacks upon the United States, 2004).

22. D.F. Andersen and Dawes, *Government Information Management: A Primer and Casebook* (Englewood Cliffs, NJ: Prentice Hall, 1991); L. Caffrey, *Information Sharing between & within Governments: A Study Group Report of the Commonwealth Secretariat* (London: The International Council for Technology in Government Administration, 1998); Pardo et al., Sustainable Cross-Boundary Information Sharing; Gil-Garcia et al., Collaborative E-government.

23. Dawes, Interagency Information Sharing: Expected Benefits, Manageable Risks, *Journal of Policy Analysis and Management, 15* (3), 377–394, 1996; S. Chang, G. Gable, E. Smythe, and G. Timbrell, A Delphi Examination of Public Sector ERP Implementation Issues, In *Proceedings of the Twenty First International Conference on Information Systems* (Atlanta, GA: Association for Information Systems, 2000), pp. 494–500; Gil-Garcia et al., Collaborative E-government; K. Barret and R. Greene, *Powering Up: How Public Managers Can Take Control of Information Technology* (Washington, DC: CQ Press, 2001); J.L. Ambite, Y. Arens, W. Bourne, S. Feiner, L. Gravano, V. Hatzivassiloglou, et al., Data Integration and Access, In *Advances in Digital Government: Technology, Human Factors, and Policy*, ed. W.J. McIver and A.K. Elmagarmid (Boston: Kluwer Academic Publishers, 2002), pp. 85–106; C.W. Tan and S.L. Pan, Managing E-transformation in the Public Sector: An E-government Study of the Inland Revenue Authority of Singapore (IRAS), *European Journal of Information Systems, 12*: 269–281, 2003; Dawes and Pardo. 2002. Building collaborative digital government systems. In McIver and Elmagarmid, *Advances in Digital Government*, pp. 259–274; J. Zhang, A.M. Cresswell, and F. Thompson, Participants' Expectations and the Success of Knowledge Networking in the Public Sector, Paper presented at the Annual Americas Conference on Information Systems, Dallas, TX, 2002; J.E. Fountain, *Building the Virtual State. Information Technology and Institutional Change* (Washington, DC: Brookings Institution Press, 2001); Z. Irani, P.E.D. Love, T. Elliman, S. Jones, and M. Themistocleous, Evaluating E-government: Learning from the Experiences of Two UK Local Authorities, *Information Systems Journal, 15*: 61–82, 2005.

24. Pardo et al., Sustainable Cross-Boundary Information Sharing; Gil-Garcia, Schneider, Pardo, and Cresswell, Inter-organizational Information Integration in the Criminal Justice Enterprise: Preliminary Lessons from State and County Initiatives, In *Proceedings of the 38th Hawaiian International Conference on System Sciences (HICSS'05)* (Los Alamitos, CA: IEEE Computer Society Press, 2005).

25. CDC, *Preventing Emerging Infectious Diseases*; CDC, *Epidemic/Epizootic West Nile Virus in the United States: Guidelines for Surveillance, Prevention, and Control* (Fort Collins, CO: Centers for Disease Prevention and Control, 2003).

26. National Association of State Public Health Veterinarians (NASPHV). n.d. About us, http://www.nasphv.org/aboutUs.html (accessed May 2, 2008).

27. Oregon DHS, *State of Oregon Mosquito-Borne Disease Response.*

28. Oregon DHS, *Public Health West Nile Virus Emergency Response Plan. Annex F, Public Health and Medical Services.* September, 11, 2007, p. 4.

29. Oregon Mosquito and Vector Control Association, http://www.omvca.org/ p. 14.

30. J.M. Bryson, B.C. Crosby, and M.M. Stone, The Design and Implementation of Cross-Sector Collaborations: Propositions from the Literature, *Public Administration Review, 66* (s1): 44–55, 2006; Simo and Bies, Role of Nonprofits.

31. Simo and Bies, Role of Nonprofits.

32. Comfort, Risk, Security; Donahue, Space Shuttle Columbia.
33. Comfort, Risk, Security; Kiefer and Montjoy, Incrementalism before the Storm.
34. M. Bhandar, Pan, and B.C.Y. Tan. 2006. Towards Understanding the Roles of Social Capital in Knowledge Integration: A Case Study of a Collaborative Information Systems Project. *Journal of the American Society for Information Science and Technology, 58* (2): 263–274, 2006.
35. O'Toole, Implications for Democracy.
36. V. Lowndes and C. Skelcher, The Dynamics of Multi-organizational Partnerships: An Analysis of Changing Modes of Governance, *Public Administration, 76* (2): 313–333, 1998.

Chapter 8

Information Stewardship and Collaboration: Advancing Evidence-Based Public Policy Decision Making

Joy A. Clay and Cindy Martin

Contents

Case Brief

Background and Purpose of the Collaboration: The University of Memphis (UM) is a large, urban, comprehensive university with a long history of faculty involvement in the community, driven primarily by individual UM faculty research and outreach interests that were largely *ad hoc* and short-term arrangements. A confluence of events occurred in the 1990s that transformed this fragmented dynamic at the UM into a much more focused initiative: (1) Key external forces in higher education for over a decade had added legitimacy to the push for increased university–community engagement; (2) local government leaders were facing growing fiscal pressures to meet mandated requirements and public demand for services; (3) local foundation leaders recognized the important role the university could play in improving the local community; and (4) new availability of affordable technology, both hardware and software, along with advances in Internet technology that increased the feasibility of providing a shared data system and also increased the demand for such capacity. Funded largely by local foundations, the Shared Urban Data System (SUDS) was a series of loosely connected collaborative relationships built among researchers and public and nonprofit agency information managers and administrators in Shelby County, Tennessee. Each collaborative was formed to create a particular database subsystem but also to enhance data sharing and the broader use of data to address the region's public policy problems including public safety, public health, education, and social services.

Current Status: SUDS was dissolved in 2007 when the focus of the local funder shifted solely to early childhood issues. The termination of SUDS as a formal collaboration did not end information partnering in Shelby County. The infrastructure built by SUDS continues to be used and built upon by the various collaborations. For example, one subsystem has become an exchange tool for issues related to homeland security, annexation, and the Real Time Crime Center.

Lessons for Strategic Collaboration Practice: A high-profile crisis served as the primary force in forming this strategic collaboration; however, technological advances were an important environmental dynamic particularly given competing agency and political leaders' priorities. Due to the technical nature of the projects, specialist level staff had to possess both the appropriate expertise and collaborative people skills to build and sustain key relationships. Memorandums of understanding (MOUs) were a key tool in managing relationships and assuring data security formalizing serial partnerships rather a shared commitment to the umbrella collaboration. The case also illustrates the vulnerability of collaborations to changing interests of stakeholders and the importance of attending to the political realities of elected officials. Finally, this case raises questions about when and how strategic collaborations consider a transition to a more sustainable structure or end and the challenges of university–community relationships.

8.1 Introduction

This case study describes a series of loosely connected collaborative relationships built among researchers and public and nonprofit agency information managers and administrators in Shelby County, Tennessee. Each collaborative was formed around the creation of a particular database subsystem, but also included a longer-term purpose: to enhance (1) data sharing across public and nonprofit agencies and (2) the broader use of data to address the region's public policy problems. The collaborators recognized the need to move from *data ownership*, a silo approach that had each agency highly protective of its own independent and self-sufficient data system, to *data stewardship and collaboration,* an information partnering approach that continued to assure data confidentiality and integrity while enhancing access and usability. The information collaborative became known as the Shared Urban Data System (SUDS).

8.2 The Collaboration

The common purpose that led officials and information specialists to engage in the data partnering effort centered on enriching geographic information quality and access so that better and timelier decisions could be made about public safety deployment and community service delivery. Each database subsystem had its particular focus (e.g., crime hot spots, infant mortality, prenatal care, community

In 2003, Jim Wagner died waiting 30 minutes for an ambulance to arrive at the pool hall located just inside Bartlett, a suburb contingent to Memphis, where he suffered a heart attack. Wagner's friends said they had made a total of nine 911 calls before help finally arrived. It turns out there were four locations with emergency service personnel within a five-minute drive of the dying Wagner. Municipalities in the Memphis area independently operate emergency response units. City borders determine who responds first to the emergency, regardless of the proximity to the nearest emergency vehicle. Calls to 911 are automatically routed to municipal dispatchers based on information in large address databases with the help of automated mapping software. In Wagner's case, the dispatcher of the initial call sent an ambulance to an address 12 miles away from Wagner. The other 911 calls resulted in dispatchers rerouting the calls back and forth from one municipality to another as they argued about who was responsible for that address. Lack of a common data repository and shared mapping system resulted in conflicting, erroneous information and thus confusion among the dispatchers. While waiting for care to arrive, Wagner died.

resources, referral patterns), and the involved partners had to work through their particular technical, administrative, and political challenges to build a shared database. The partnerships included information specialists from the involved agencies, researchers from local higher education institutions, and other potential users of the database, as the partners realized the interconnectedness of community issues (e.g., crime and abandoned housing). Each collaboration required ongoing dialogue to work through technical issues, to make immediate policy decisions, and to plan for future public policy analysis needs. A dedicated staff at the University of Memphis (UM) was responsible for building a shared, Web-based portal to access the database subsystem and work with the various partners as facilitators and technical advisors. The University of Memphis role was not a conventional vendor–client relationship but rather as a technical, policy analysis, and research partner.

Almost 20 data subsystems were developed and implemented using this formula of collaborative activity with the University of Memphis as the common actor. The partnerships covered a range of policy areas including public safety, community health, and children's and youth services and involved 20 data providing partners. The most complex collaboration to administer centered on public safety databases, with data partners numbering as many as 40 agencies. In contrast, the health collaborations were focused around a particular use by the researchers or local funding agency, and thus, were less complex and had only a few data partners.

The collaborative information systems partnership developed between the University of Memphis and various local agency partners existed from 2003 to 2007 until funding for the university administrative/technical support staff was discontinued. What began in the late 1990s as informal and separate discussions between university staff and researchers with (1) agency officials in the Shelby County Assessor's Office and County Mayor's Office, (2) geographical information interest group members, and (3) public safety officials resulted in a complex information support system that provided a portal to interconnected database subsystems, collectively called the Shared Urban Data System (SUDS). Although the university's involvement in SUDS ended when the funding was discontinued in 2007, the subsystems have continued to evolve independently.

8.3 Understanding the Situational Context

The University of Memphis is a large urban, comprehensive university with an enrollment of approximately 21,000 students. Although it serves the West Tennessee region, the main campus is located in the City of Memphis in Shelby County, which provides university researchers with a metropolitan laboratory. With a long history of faculty involvement in the local and regional community, outreach activities in the community had been driven primarily by individual UM faculty research and outreach interests were largely *ad hoc* and short-term arrangements.

A confluence of events occurred in the 1990s that transformed this fragmented dynamic at the University of Memphis into a much more focused and prioritized initiative. Key external forces in higher education for over a decade had added legitimacy to the push for increased engagement of universities.[1] Nationally, various university researchers and administrators were increasingly recognizing the important impact that higher education institutions had on their regions.[2] Some were actively calling for colleges and universities to engage with their communities to renew the civic mission of higher education specifically calling for local partnerships that could "unite town and gown in enriching the common good."[3] Key leadership dynamics within the university also occurred to enhance and clarify its mission, including the decision by the acting president to establish the School of Urban Affairs and Public Policy (SUAPP) to structurally unite a set of academic units known for their engagement in the community and the subsequent appointment of a university president in 2001 who explicitly supported the Boyer model of an engaged university.[4]

At the local level, government leaders were facing new mandated requirements and increasing public demand for services while revenue generation was constrained. Also, important local foundation leaders had begun to recognize the important role that UM could play in furthering their commitments to improving the local community. These leaders also recognized that funding would be necessary if the university was to realize this mission. Important to this collaborative effort was the availability of affordable technology, both hardware and software, along with advances in Internet technology that increased the feasibility of providing a shared data system and the demand for such capacity. For example, the development of new Web-based file security, advanced firewalls, and secure socket layer technology permit secure data sharing across the Internet. At the same time, a number of new software tools provided important visualization capacity for planning and analysis, such as geographic information systems (GISs), pictometry, and the global justice XML data model (global JXDM).

Thus, the groundwork was laid to develop a formalized partnership between UM and various community agencies that would support more effective deployment of agency resources and lead to evidence-based policy decisions through information integration and sharing. These information-sharing partnerships were viewed as key strategies for connecting researchers to the community while furthering research and civic capacity and, conversely, for connecting the community to the university by supporting evidence-based decision making and improved access to community information. The first step was the creation of the Center for Community Criminology and Research (CCCR) in 2001, placed organizationally in the UM Department of Criminology and Criminal Justice. A local foundation provided start-up funding as well as match dollars for some government funding. Naturally, the initial emphasis of the CCCR focused on supporting law enforcement and criminal justice projects through statistical and spatial analysis of their data, along with supporting local demographic and social data.

In 2004, another local foundation provided significant funding to assemble these and other databases into a comprehensive online information system. This system, SUDS, developed into an information portal serving government (e.g., E911 emergency services agencies) and nonprofit agencies (e.g., the Urban Child Institute) as well as university researchers (e.g., UM and University of Tennessee Health Science Center). As community partners increasingly recognized the utility of sharing and linking data, projects began to include issues of importance to public health, education, social service data users, and researchers. Recognizing this broadening of mission and to protect the integrity of the CCCR's focus on criminology, SUDS was moved organizationally from the Department of Criminology and Criminal Justice to the School of Urban Affairs and Public Policy (SUAPP) in 2005 while retaining a strong partnership with the Center for Community Criminology and Research.

8.4 Outcome of the Information System Collaboration

The tangible product of SUDS consisted of multiple database subsystems with data provided by various agencies, research activities, and SUDS staff. The database subsystems were accessed through a single Web portal. Many of the databases resided on a group of integrated physical and virtual servers at UM, but SUDS was dissolved while work was under way to include virtual connections to database servers at community agency locations apart from the university. The system allowed for reduced redundancy, consistent updates across databases, increased access to databases and analytic technology, and improved data consistency. SUDS served as a community resource, serving public and nonprofit agencies, the public in general, and researchers. UM was viewed by the collaborative partners as an impartial public entity, favoring no one agency or agent over another, and was interested in furthering the usefulness of data from all sources. Consequently, the university was able to serve as a facilitator to solicit involvement of community partners to share data, to sensitively address the tension between broadening accessibility and protecting confidentiality, and to serve as a vehicle for technical innovation. Due to confidentiality and security issues, individual subsystems were created, and those subsystems not needing the interconnectedness of SUDS have continued their development even after SUDS itself was discontinued. Table 8.1 summarizes key SUDS database subsystems to provide a sense of the complexity of, and opportunities provided by, this interconnected information system.

Overcoming technical issues intrinsic to data sharing required the marriage of technical expertise and administrative facilitation while building trust and relationships among the data partners. To facilitate data integrity, all agency data were accompanied by current metadata. This requirement assured that agency partners provided "data about their data" including a data dictionary, data creation details, update frequency, data ownership, rules regarding access, how to get permission to access the data, and, if the data are geographic, additional information consistent with the Federal Geographic Data Committee (FGDC) standards. Each of the subsystems required that relationships be negotiated, clarifying the primary purpose for the information partnership and explicitly defining roles and responsibilities of the respective partners. Table 8.2 summarizes the purpose and roles outlined for the key data partners for each subsystem. As can be noted in the table, data partners were actively involved not just in providing the data but also in assuring its quality, accessibility, and security.

The overarching goal for SUDS was to create actionable information—that is, information that could be acted upon for public purpose, including whether to prioritize the deployment of police officers in a crime "hot spot," to enable fire and EMA officials to plan appropriate responses to emergency situations, to facilitate researchers gathering needed demographic information for a grant application and to inform parents of nearby after-school programs.

8.5 The Collaborative Structure

Conceptually, SUDS had six key components that effectively interacted to comprise the collaborative structure (Figure 8.1). Finding solutions to problems faced by governments and agencies was the ultimate goal, of course. The problems to be addressed were defined through collaboration with SUDS staff, researchers, and

Table 8.1 Summary Description of Key SUDS Information Subsystems

SUDS Information Subsystem	Type of Information System	Users	Use	Data Sources	Funding
Operation Blue Crush	Database query and mapping system that ties temporal, spatial, and statistical algorithms to predict high-crime areas based on past crime activity	Law enforcement, at the precinct and ward levels Criminologists to study trends (access is restricted to specified users)	Identifies crime hot spots and likely locations of perpetrators; command staff use the analysis to plan and deploy resources for intensive operations; researchers provide analysis and mapping and work closely with the command staff to plan the operations; researchers also provide evaluation for postoperation debriefing	Police Department (MPD) and Shared Urban Data System (SUDS)/ Crime Research Information and Statistical Portal (CRISP) database	Local foundation and local government

Public Safety Geographic Data Repository (PSGDR)	Secure, centralized repository of geographic data processed and formatted for use in geographic information systems (GISs)	911 dispatchers Regional first responders (emergency management staff, fire departments, police departments, homeland security personnel, airport authority) Local government planning departments Local utility company County property assessor (access is restricted to specified users)	All agencies involved in emergency response activities use this shared geographic data in their GISs to coordinate resources, to coordinate responses, and to plan operations; agencies such as the public utility and the county assessor are major producers of this geographic data—PSGDR provides a vehicle for disseminating the most current data to all emergency response agencies	Approximately 40 agencies participate in PSGDR and either currently share their data or have plans to share their data as soon as possible	Local foundation and local government

(continued)

Table 8.1 Summary Description of Key SUDS Information Subsystems (Continued)

SUDS Information Subsystem	Type of Information System	Users	Use	Data Sources	Funding
The Blues Project	Secure, online records management system for patients participating in the project, focused on at-risk pregnant women living in four targeted Memphis zip codes	Specified clinicians and University of Tennessee physician researchers (access is restricted to specific computers at participating clinics)	Monitor prenatal care and health outcomes of infants; also serves as a records management system for the four participating clinics; provides automated e-mail reminders to case managers to solicit patients for follow-up care	Patient information input by clerical and clinical staff at the participating health clinics	Local foundation

| First Years | Publicly accessible data repository of community programs available for children 0–3 years and pregnant women; interactive resource mapping; repository of related local research reports; links to related websites | Researchers Local grant writers Community agencies | Referrals; identify gaps in services; locate potential partners; identify location of resources; access recent local research findings related to children 0–3 years | Survey conducted to compile resources and researcher-generated reports | Local early childhood agency funded the initial survey, and a local foundation provided funding for system maintenance and updates |

(continued)

Table 8.1 Summary Description of Key SUDS Information Subsystems (Continued)

SUDS Information Subsystem	Type of Information System	Users	Use	Data Sources	Funding
Youth Resources Information System (YRIS)	Publicly accessible data repository of community programs focused on education and workforce development and available for older children up to 21 years, located in Shelby County and Fayette County, Tennessee	Researchers Local grant writers Community agencies University students	Referrals; emphasis is on job training, workforce development, and education; includes information about skills development programs, employment services, mentoring programs to help youth finish high school.	Some data provided by the Memphis Public Library Information Center (LINC); additional information compiled and processed by SUDS staff through multiple public directory sources	State government

EASEE Resources for Youth Enrichment	Publicly accessible directory of education supplementary programs and services targeting specific public schools and secure access to research data about programs and providers; includes query and interactive mapping capability	Public access to directory and interactive map (parents, teachers, program providers, researchers) (access for specified researchers and Partners for Public Education, Inc. [PIPE], a local public education advocacy group to all of the research information)	To provide detailed information about program available at specific public schools; to determine program funders; and to identify public education support trends	Research partner was the University of Memphis Center for Research in Educational Policy (CREP); online instrument to survey different program providers offering services to school children	Local agency

Table 8.2 Summary of SUDS Subsystems: Key Formal Partners and Their Respective Roles

SUDS Subsystem	Primary Purpose	Key Partners	Roles
Operation Blue Crush	Provide incident and arrest data for crime analysis	Memphis Police Department (MPD) University of Memphis (UM) crime analysts Shared Urban Data System (SUDS) staff	Provide data and assist in data analysis; lead analysis of the data; ensure data availability to MPD and analysts
Public Safety Geographic Data Repository (PSGDR)	Provide data for computer mapping to government agencies	Shelby County Assessor Memphis Light, Gas, & Water SUDS staff	Provide county-wide parcel data; provide infrastructure data; develop and administer the system; facilitate the collaboration
The Blues Project	Provide a repository of health records for patients in the project	University of Tennessee Preventive Medicine Blues Project staff Third-party evaluator SUDS staff	Entry and maintenance of patient data; project evaluation using repository data; ensure secure data availability
First Years	Provide community data and information portal	The Urban Child Institute SUDS staff	Provide guidance as to information content; develop or acquire data content and present information via Web pages

Table 8.2   Summary of SUDS Subsystems: Key Formal Partners and Their Respective Roles (Continued)

SUDS Subsystem	Primary Purpose	Key Partners	Roles
Youth Resources Information System (YRIS)	Provide community resource information for youth and agencies that serve them	Southwest TN Community College Workforce Investment Board Memphis Public Library and Information Center (LINC) SUDS staff	Provide guidance as to information content; provide guidance as to information content and publicize the information availability; provide current resource information; acquire additional data; develop and administer the system
EASEE Resouces for Youth Enrichment	Provide information about local youth program resources	Partners in Public Education (PIPE) SUDS staff	Provide guidance as to content and publicize the website; develop and administer the website

other community partners. The SUDS infrastructure and standards ensured data availability and security.

Public administrators at all levels of government increasingly recognize that their ability to address complex policy issues requires improved collaboration among diverse stakeholders and better decision-making processes based on accurate, reliable, and timely data. Local government, nonprofit, and academic leaders in West Tennessee realize that information sharing and integration are critical to building and sustaining community capacity. This approach allows broad but appropriate levels of access to integrated data, enables research activities that support local decision processes, and helps to assure data consistency and interoperability. As an example of this approach, SUDS consisted of multiple subsystems with data provided by various agencies, research activities, and SUDS staff. To facilitate information sharing capability, the data were uniformly formatted (sometimes available in multiple formats) and adhered to established data standards.

Although some databases in SUDS were publicly available, some were available only to specific users. An agency that agreed to share its data and participate

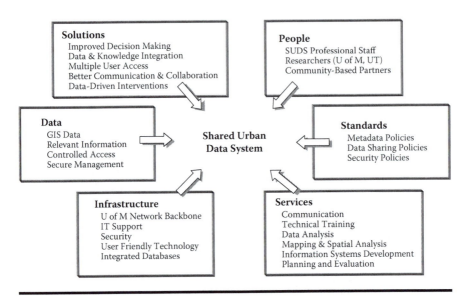

Figure 8.1   Key components in the collaborative structure.

in SUDS was granted access to data from other participating agencies. The SUD's information integration technology made data much more readily available and allowed users access to more sophisticated analytic tools such as complex query interfaces and interactive mapping capable of overlaying diverse data layers. Thus, users of the system were able to ask specific questions of the data or request map overlays using a wide range of data such as bus routes, programs and services, recreational activities, crime, and health statistics.

Each of the major database subsystems included in SUDS had its own history, data challenges, and collaboration challenges ranging from establishing trust among the partners, reaching agreement on the common purpose of the information partnership, to sustaining funding. The information sharing that began through SUDs has continued and evolved for some of the subsystems but ended for others. Table 8.3 summarizes the key subsystems' data-sharing and collaboration challenges as well as the current status of those subsystems now that SUDS funding has ended.

8.5.1 Formalized Data Sharing

Participation varied from one SUDS subsystem to another in terms of purpose, data access, and roles of participating agencies. Creation and maintenance of the data and design of the Web interface and system maintenance also varied from one subsystem to another. At the earliest stage, a common purpose was negotiated, access rights to data and information determined, and participating partners agreed upon. Governance was executed through both formal structures and informal processes.

Table 8.3   Summary of Data Sharing and Collaboration Challenges and Current Status

SUDS Subsystem	Data-Sharing Challenges	Collaboration Challenges	Status since End of SUDS Funding
Operation Blue Crush	Data sensitivity and security Large volume of data Focused need Networking connectivity among Memphis Police Department and University of Memphis (UM) analysts	Trust with UM as data custodian Data ownership and control Shared costs	Analysis function redistributed and data access responsibility shifted to Memphis Police Department
Public Safety Geographic Data Repository (PSGDR)	Data sensitivity and security Focused need Data currency, accuracy, and maintenance	Trust among all partners Expanding partnerships	Data system administration assumed by UM's Center for Community Criminology and Research (CCCR) and collaboration facilitation is shared by remaining partners
The Blues Project	Health data sensitivity and security Assurance of data availability	Trust with UM as data custodian	Databases moved to University of Tennessee Blues Project; computers and administration assumed by Blues Project staff

(continued)

Table 8.3 Summary of Data Sharing and Collaboration Challenges and Current Status (Continued)

SUDS Subsystem	Data-Sharing Challenges	Collaboration Challenges	Status since End of SUDS Funding
First Years	Data currency and accuracy Identification and acquisition of additional data Generation of data analysis	Identification of data users Publicity Clarification of purpose, roles, and content of databases	All functions assumed by the Urban Child Institute
Youth Resources Information System (YRIS)	Data currency and accuracy Identification and acquisition of additional data Promotion of the data availability	Identification of information needs Sustained funding	System administration ended
EASEE Resouces for Youth Enrichment	Assurance of data availability Focused need User tracking	Agreed purpose and avoiding project "scope creep"	System administration assumed by Partners in Public Education (PIPE)

The formal contractual agreement that governed the data partnership occurred through the development of a formalized memorandum of understanding, with technical attachments as needed. This document articulated the partners, named the agency contact person and person responsible for providing the data, detailed each of the partner's (SUDS and agency) responsibilities as well as the University of Memphis' responsibilities, specified any unique requirements that were negotiated, and described a summary of the benefits of the MOU. Included in the MOU was common contractual language, for example, the process for canceling the MOU by either party. The MOUs were approved by the appropriate authorized individual from each of the partnering agencies. In some cases, authorization required approval by various boards and elected officials.

Data/information exchange and access was at the heart of each MOU. In all cases, the data remained the possession and responsibility of the data-owning partner. For example, when the local utility company agreed to share many of their infrastructure-related databases through SUDS, they retained sole responsibility for the accuracy of the data along with responsibility for updating the data and uploading it into the shared repository in a timely fashion. In another example, university researchers interested in collaborative outreach agreed to share their data and research findings through SUDS. They retained ownership of their data and findings and were responsible for maintaining its currency and accuracy. SUDS staff was responsible for maintaining the security of the network, website, and the databases and for providing access according to the data owner's specifications. Clearly stated data ownership and control allayed concerns of data producers over loss of their investments in the creation of their data. Required standard data formats, levels of accuracy, and currency were agreed upon through the MOU.

The data-owning partners were also given the right to limit access to all or some of their data. Thus, for example, some of the utility company's infrastructure data were part of the publicly accessible data, some were accessible by university researchers and community-based agencies that were granted temporary access for limited-term projects, and some were accessible by only designated individuals or partnering agencies that were listed specifically in the MOU. For secured data, SUDS staff granted data access privileges to agencies according to the MOU, and partner agencies controlled access to specific individuals within their own agency. In these cases, each agency specified a data administrator who assigned individual user passwords to people within their agencies.

8.5.2 SUDS Staff Structure

The SUDS office initially consisted of an executive director, a technician, and a graduate research assistant. When the funding support for SUDS was terminated, SUDS staff had grown to 11 and was composed of an executive director, four technicians, a graphics and website designer, and five graduate research assistants. All of the staff had extensive backgrounds in management information systems, GISs, and social science research methodology. SUDS staff formally reported to the SUAPP executive committee. In addition, funders, researchers, and various community stakeholders served in an informal advisory capacity (Figure 8.2).

8.6 Attending to Process and Procedures

SUDS used both formal and informal meetings to build relationships and feedback processes with their stakeholders. During these meetings, SUDS staff sought input and consensus on priorities and strategies, tracking performance to assure effectiveness and accountability of each of the subsystems. Working with a series of advisory groups at the University of Memphis, the SUDS executive director formulated policies, priorities, and strategies for linking SUDS across campus to the community. For example, the SUAPP executive committee provided advice on integrating SUDS in the university and identified potential opportunities for student involvement.

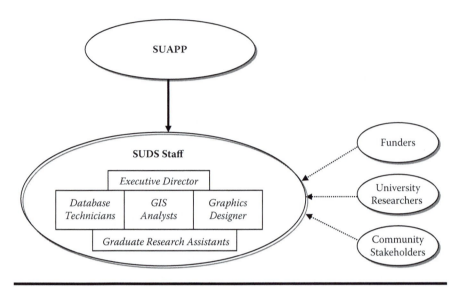

Figure 8.2   SUDS organization structure.

Working through the oversight relationship between SUAPP and SUDS was still in the development stages when SUDS was terminated. Another advisors group composed of UM researchers with active engaged scholarship projects, helped outline strategies for expansion and refinement of the subsystems and analytic tools. The University Center for Partnerships in GIS, composed of major GIS users across campus, provided technical support and assistance. Other research partners from the University of Memphis and University of Tennessee–Memphis provided technical feedback and information, analyzed the data, and identified new database and data opportunities. Informally, the SUDS director solicited feedback from researchers in general as to their respective information needs.

Community partners that provided data met individually with SUDS staff to address their specific issues or as part of a group of providers with shared interests (groups ranged from 3 to 40 partners). Meetings were at least monthly and more frequently in the early stages when forming the information partnership. Meetings with data-providing partners focused on assuring that data were provided and received as agreed upon in the MOU and problem solving as needed. Contacts with other community partners that used but did not provide data occurred primarily through informal meetings and at community meetings.

Final input was from funders and foundations. SUDS staff met individually with each of these key stakeholders. These discussions focused on their specific goals and assurances that the requirements of the funding arrangements were being met.

8.7 Assuring Accountability, Developing Outcomes, and Measuring Impact

SUDS staff members were held accountable for efficiently and effectively managing SUDS technology but also for building the collaborative relationships necessary to sustain the partnerships. Thus, SUDS staff had to demonstrate technical expertise to maintain legitimacy with data partners but also had to attend to the challenging dynamics of building relationships. Respecting the partners' sense of ownership of the database and the anxieties associated with losing control, SUDS staff worked patiently through the process of establishing trust. To sustain relationships, SUDS staff clearly established that data-providing partners had the right to be kept informed of policy and procedural decisions and to be assured that their specific information needs were addressed. The time of first contact to bringing a database online took between two months and one year. The complexity of the database as well as allaying anxieties related to loss of control of a database influenced the time needed to negotiate the contractual arrangement and to move the project to fruition.

The impact of SUDS can be measured in several ways. First, partners were able to demonstrate to their key stakeholders such as mayors, commissioners and aldermen, and nonprofit agency boards of directors improved efficiency and ability due to their participation in SUDS. For example, from experience and explicit feedback from community agencies and data partners, we know that the data were used more effectively to deploy resources, identify gaps in services, identify trends, and coordinate government services. More specifically, the local chapter of the Red Cross partnered with SUDS and UM researchers to develop a process using GISs to track their responses to families who were left temporarily homeless due to house fires. The tracking system was extremely useful to them in demonstrating their effectiveness to their funders. Continued participation of the data collaborators was a measure of the positive value that these agencies placed in the collaboration.

Another criterion used to measure impact was the geographic spread and the number of participating agencies. The system began providing information about crime to law enforcement agencies in Memphis and quickly spread to a broader range of agencies and broader scope of data across Shelby County, including housing and community development, health, community services, and education. Agencies and organizations in neighboring counties in West Tennessee as well as border counties in Mississippi and Arkansas also became active partners in several of SUDS's subsystems, while university researchers further expanded the scope of SUDS data to statewide research projects involving child welfare, health, and law enforcement. A related performance measure was the number of unsolicited requests from additional agencies to participate.

Data access was carefully tracked, updates to the SUDS databases monitored, and system activity logs maintained and reported. These automated logs provided a useful measure of the degree of active participation, and monitoring the system's traffic flow provided some measurement as to the interest in the data contained in the various subsystems. In addition to the number of times individual Web pages were visited, the system automatically tracked who visited, when they visited, where they were located, and the duration of their visit to the SUDS site. These measurements showed rapidly increasing use of some subsystems and steady or decreasing use of other subsystems providing information for decisions regarding expanding or discontinuing particular subsystems.

Certain accomplishments can be viewed as measures of the overall success of SUDS while it was functioning. These include the increasing number of systems, data and information availability, and the level of funding attained. At the time of its termination, SUDS had been successful in serving more than 20 data-providing partners and numerous community information users through 18 subsystems and approximately 250 data files and databases. Funding reached approximately $3.2 million in grants shared with targeted university researchers, and several of the subsystems received growing monetary support from the community partners. Additionally, SUDS staff received steady inquiries from state-level agencies and federal foundations.

Reporting procedures varied widely from subsystem to subsystem based on system complexity, number of partnering agencies, and requirements set forth by funding agencies and partners. Some funding agencies required periodic reports detailing system activity, accomplishments, and outcomes. These generally were in the form of a progress report and distributed only to the funding agency. In addition, SUDS staff met regularly with representatives from partnering agencies. These meetings were usually held monthly and varied in size from three people representing UM and a single agency to approximately 40 people representing public safety and first-responder agencies throughout the area. Meeting notes or minutes were recorded by SUDS staff from all meetings and the minutes were distributed to all members via e-mail. SUDS staff members generally facilitated the meetings, although this responsibility was often shared with other agencies in the larger collaborations.

In addition, SUDS staff representatives served on a number of university and government committees that furthered its mission of broad visibility. For example, the University District Initiative involved a collaborative effort including UM and nine community organizations operating near the university. SUDS was invited to participate in this initiative to provide data support and information regarding data. In another example, SUDS staff served on a committee formed by the Shelby County mayor to improve response to emergency 911 calls. SUDS was quickly identified as a vehicle for data sharing and information dissemination among the E911 agencies and the broader community. This committee met for nearly 18 months and led to additional information-sharing commitments and SUDS partnerships.

8.8 Lessons Learned to Build Conceptual Knowledge

A growing body of literature analyzes both the opportunities and challenges related to community-based collaboration and research. The literature on collaboration[5] and community-engaged research[6] at this point in time remains largely descriptive, often using a case study methodology or other qualitative methodologies, and is not yet fully integrated across disciplinary boundaries. However, progress is being made in better understanding the dynamics of collaboration, intergroup relationships, and academic–community partnerships. The body of literature related to public information management and participatory systems design has also grown as researchers and practitioners respond to the challenges and expectations of more accessible government through e-government.[7] This case study attempts to place the collaboration in a local context and to describe lessons learned to further an understanding of the outcomes of data sharing and collaboration. This case analysis adds to our understanding of the dynamics of collaboration, intergroup relationships among public information managers, and academic–community partnerships.

The growing realization that complex public issues require improved internal collaboration within public agencies and external collaboration with key community organizations and leaders[8] is especially true in the area of public information management.[9] As Gray notes, the involved parties must be able to see different aspects of a problem and "constructively explore their differences and search for solutions that go beyond their own limited visions of what is possible."[10]

To create an effective collaboration, participants must be able to articulate a vision, to define a mission, and to establish concrete goals.[11] Throughout the evolution of SUDS, time and attention were strategically paid to clarify and refine the mission to be responsive to changing circumstances, understandings, and accomplishments. The participants also attended to identifying barriers to participation and worked to strategize ways to successfully overcome technical and policy barriers to further data sharing. In the case of SUDS, success in collaborating on one system led to agreements in working on another; taking on small, distinct tasks and accomplishing them effectively through group effort can set the stage for continuing collaboration. This approach builds momentum for additional joint endeavors and makes "smart" use of "the desire on some people's parts to do good in the world according to their own lights and to participate in the creative challenge of doing it in a nontraditional way."[12]

For this collaboration, intergroup dynamics had not only the usual complex set of interpersonal factors that affect the process of collaboration (e.g., social identity, gender, race, expertise) but also organizational factors (e.g., organizational identity/loyalty, technological capacity). Differences among individuals participating in the collaboration clearly affect interpersonal interactions as individuals develop trust and shared understandings of expectations or conversely create conflict and struggles over priorities and direction.[13] Institutional policies, especially related to funding decisions and control locus, also affect intergroup dynamics.[14] Further, differences in priorities and expectations can negatively affect intergroup dynamics.[15] Achieving both actual and perceived project success and mutual benefit is also important to sustaining continued participation in the project.[16] For SUDS, recognition and branding became an important strategy to sustain participation as well as to grow interest among new potential collaborators.

At the policy level, the trend for improved and direct access to government information relates to the need to both improve governmental transparency and enhance performance.[17] Electronic information systems have become an important strategy to meet this challenge.[18] However, electronic government data is often fragmented and dispersed[19] as well as marked by variation in local conditions, missions, and technical capacity and adaptability[20] and data quality problems, such as being incomplete, inaccurate, and inconsistent.[21] Electronic government researchers argue that effective public managers must balance internal organizational needs with external demands, thus changing their management strategy from centralized control and physical custody to a more distributed and collaborative modality that strategically includes stakeholders and networks[22] and from "owners" to stewards.[23] Researchers note that this challenge requires not only inclusion of specialists in information system design but also users and suppliers and that the design efforts "must be context specific, collaborative ventures."[24] Participatory information systems design also requires that designers understand users' work processes as well as their experience of systems.[25]

Over the past two decades, there has been a call for renewed connection between higher education and the communities in which they are located and serve; *community engagement* has emerged as a label for describing and guiding those interactions. At the core of this call for action is the expectation that community-based researchers will engage in reciprocal relations with their community partners and will build and disseminate new knowledge. There is a growing literature on the changing roles of universities as economic development engines, enhancing the physical development of their geographically close neighborhoods, but also as technological innovators and critical to strengthening (and even globalizing) communities.[26] As described in this case study, universities can play an important role in furthering technological innovation and improving the capacity for policy analysis. Community-based information analysis and development offers the opportunity to bridge research and practice.[27]

8.9 Lessons Learned That Specifically Relate to Collaborative Practice

The specific lessons offered by this case study are as follows:

1. Precipitating events can be critical to launching a collaborative effort and overcoming reticence to participate.
2. Stakeholder needs and expectations are critical drivers to gaining and sustaining active involvement in the partnering activities.
3. Public administrators must have both the requisite technical and administrative skills to build and sustain collaborations.

4. Partners must attend to and regularly refine the institutional structure of the collaboration.
5. Given the fluid nature of collaborations, how we measure success needs to take into consideration both short- and long-term perspectives.

8.9.1 Precipitating Events

Local discussions about the importance of data sharing, especially access to reliable geographical information, had been taking place for several years. Although technical experts advocated partnering, political and agency officials remained focused on the realities of system vulnerabilities and data confidentiality. The media's attention to the death of a citizen caused by poor information sharing created a firestorm that moved the discussions from endless meetings to action, generating not only political but also funding support. Both were critical to being able to move from data silos to more strategic information sharing. Without the firestorm, the discussions may have continued only as "good intentions" meetings (see Figure 8.3).

8.9.2 Stakeholder Needs

The history of SUDS implementation is a lesson in stakeholder management as SUDS attended to the respective data-sharing needs of each of its information partners, adopted marketing techniques to further the relationships, and

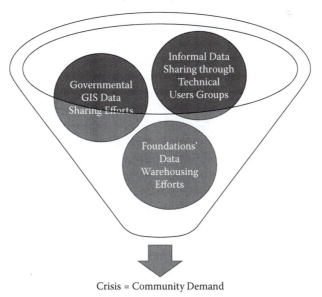

Crisis = Community Demand

Figure 8.3   Community demand.

provided graduate students to assist with system development and research support. Numerous relationships at all levels developed or strengthened subsequent to the implementation of SUDS, including government and nonprofit agency representatives and local university researchers. A ready platform for data and established relationships was provided for researchers from multiple units across UM and the University of Tennessee interested in partnering with local governments, institutions of higher education, nonprofit agencies, for-profit businesses, and other collaborations. For example, researchers from both universities worked together with local law enforcement and justice systems using SUDS to share data and to create data-driven solutions to address issues of domestic violence and crime.

Government and other agencies also worked together through SUDS to eliminate data silos, to share their data and technical expertise, and to develop creative, efficient, and effective strategic plans and solutions to service delivery problems. For example, Shelby County's Division of Public Works, the County Health Department, fire, police, and departments from cities and counties surrounding Memphis now share data for emergency and strategic planning. Also, by using shared GIS data in SUDS's common repository these agencies have effectively addressed problems related to emergency response that were noted in the opening vignette.

From its onset, SUDS employed a couple of marketing techniques to facilitate collaboration among community stakeholders and to allow the respective partners involved in the subsystem to create their own "brand" and thus enable the subsystem to continue apart from SUDS when SUDS lost its funding. First, the SUDS staff "branded" SUDS from the beginning, developing a logo and using it on the website, reports, presentations, brochures, and other promotional materials. At meetings and conferences, SUDS staff marketed and promoted the SUDS brand and concept. The logo became recognizable as SUDS's reputation grew. Attention to this aspect of stakeholder management also allowed each partner to take public credit for involvement in the partnership, an important reality for elected and political appointed officials and for agencies seeking funder support.

A second marketing promotional technique for gaining stakeholder support was the use of loss leaders (providing services at low or no cost to agencies) to garner trust and to build interest in the concept. In many situations, especially early on, government agencies were reluctant to participate in SUDS for fear of high costs, low returns on investment, or loss of control of their data. By providing database services and technical support at no cost, pilot programs were started that demonstrated the value of the agency's participation in SUDS. This promotional approach fostered trust and goodwill and allowed the agency heads to gradually build the relationship with SUDS staff. As the relationships grew, the partnering agencies shared more of their data, and many eventually provided monetary support to the system.

Recognizing the limited resources of partners, the use of graduate students for system development and research support fostered collaboration across UM units and among community agencies. This helped the agencies and provided important learning opportunities for the students. The students performed programming tasks and GIS mapping under the supervision of SUDS staff and assisted researchers as they worked with various agencies. This was cost-effective and provided graduate student support to a range of university departments including computer science, public administration, criminology, health administration, and anthropology. Several internships also developed from these activities, providing further connection between university departments and community agencies.

8.9.2.1 Technical and Administrative Skills

Related to the stakeholder management lesson previously discussed, the public administrators involved in SUDS had to establish their technical "expertise" by providing the requisite technical advice and support to the partnering agencies to establish legitimacy among the participating partners and to elicit new partners. Without this technical knowledge, the partnership would not have been able to grow and evolve. At the same time, technical expertise alone would not have been sufficient. The SUDS staff had to correctly identify representatives who had access to agency decision makers but who also understood how to navigate the complex legal negotiations and approval process needed to bring the data partnership to fruition and to develop and formalize the information-sharing agreements (i.e., MOUs). Both the technical and administrative skills needed in this collaboration helped to generate the trust and legitimacy that kept the information-sharing partners at the table.

8.9.2.2 Institutional Structure

An important decision that needs to be made by those involved in forming a formal collaboration is the appropriate institutional home. The conventional choice generally includes placing responsibility with an existing government or nonprofit agency or deciding to form a new nonprofit to manage and lead the collaboration. SUDS was placed at a university to serve as the technical and administrative facilitator of the information partnerships. Janikowski, a UM criminal justice researcher, notes that universities may not be the best fit for building and sustaining this type of collaboration.[28] He indicates that a 501(c)(3) nonprofit with a broad-based stakeholder board may have been a better vehicle for seeding the information partnership since universities often do not have the crucial infrastructure or staff to sustain this sort of effort in the long term. Alternatively, the seed organization could have been placed in a government agency having a broad-based advisory board. Once developed, Janikowski indicates that the effort should probably be placed in a government agency to assure funding stability and strategic focus—that is, attending to both customer and vision for the information partnering. He advises that foundations have their own priorities and will not fund infrastructure forever. While the university may not be the best institution to seed the partnering infrastructure, Janikowsi further advises that "the network will be people-dependent and benefit from the involvement of individual faculty members." Thus, while the university may not have proven to be the best engine of long-term collaboration in this instance, the involvement of individual faculty members in the collaboration was and continues to be an asset for the community. However, universities may be an appropriate placement for areas requiring neutrality and high access to researchers. Clearly, the institutional home decision is an important one that may need to change as the situational context changes and the collaborative effort matures.

8.9.2.3 Measuring Success

While conventional measures of success (e.g., the number and type of information subsystems involved, number of partnering agencies, types of uses of the information) could be used to assess the success of SUDS, this type of performance management approach neglects an important element integral to collaborations: They are fluid. Prior to SUDS, interest groups had already been meeting and discussed issues of shared concern. SUDS became the technical and governance infrastructure to actualize information sharing and to improve the integration of geographical information into database systems, achieving a laudable degree of information partnering.

Further, loss of funding support does not mean that SUDS was a failure. SUDS was terminated because the local funder was no longer interested in sustaining the collaboration as his foundation's priorities shifted to a focus solely on early childhood issues. Moreover, the termination of SUDS as a formal collaboration did not end information partnering in Shelby County. Janikowski, as a key researcher and the director of the Center for Community Criminology and Research at UM who was involved in developing SUDS, reflected on the collaborations established and noted that the infrastructure built by SUDS is continuing to be used and built upon by the various database subsystem collaborations. For example, the Public Safety Geographic Data Repository (PSGDR) subsystem has become an "essential exchange tool for issues related to homeland security, annexation, and the real time crime center."[29]

Consequently, the lesson for public administrators is to not reify collaborations but to see them as dynamic in nature. The relationships built may lay the foundation for future collaboration. The fall of a collaborative venture may actually lay the groundwork for some other form that addresses the mission and values of the collaboration. The data-driven groundwork laid by SUDS is evolving into an even more sophisticated information collaboration "as the Memphis Police Department is now working to integrate 14 databases so that investigators can more readily query MPD systems, visualize the analysis of linkages among the systems, and assure compliance with national exchange standards for further information sharing."[30] Thus, while in the midst of forming and building a collaborative venture, public administrators should be mindful that funding may end, political support may fade, and participants may lose interest. Lasting success, however, requires strategic analysis that is situationally based, is pragmatic, and takes a long-term approach to opportunities and choices.

8.10 Remaining Questions

This case study raises some interesting questions not just about the collaboration process but also about the role of information technology in democratizing public policy information:

■ How do you balance the need to sustain local focus with the need for broader-based funding to sustain the collaboration? Did the local focus undermine the ability of SUDS in the long term? If SUDS had expanded from a more local-based system to a much broader geographic analysis capacity to support more informed strategic planning, coordination of public services across the Delta region, and design of programs, would state and federal funding have been more realizable and sustainable?

■ What are the key factors that can counter the centrifugal forces that lead agencies to focus on their own needs and interests and not to collaborate and share? By providing data and tools in multiple formats and access modes, assuring a centralized data repository with centralized processing that enables users to query and download data sets, to produce maps, to perform interactive queries, and to execute customized analysis, and by deploying GISs in multiple environments to establish vital redundancy, SUDS had the potential for becoming an important community resource that supported building technical, analytic, and collaborative capacity throughout the region and state. What strategies could have been adopted to expand participation?

■ As Fountain argues, a virtual state "is about the process and politics of institutional change" and requires a "rethinking about the role of the state in relation to the economy and society."[31] In resource-constrained environments, what institution will play the role of convener and facilitator to promote community information sharing and more participatory design processes to broaden access to information of importance to communities and citizens? Is this a key role and opportunity for higher education institutions and faculty members adopting engaged scholarship as a priority for their institution, or is this a more appropriate role for government or nonprofit agencies?

Endnotes

1. Regional and disciplinary accrediting groups, such as the National Association of State Universities and Land Grant Colleges (NASULGC) and the American Association of State Colleges and Universities (AASCU), now include "community engagement" as a component of criteria for assessing performance. Most recently the Carnegie Foundation for the Advancement of Teaching added the category of "community engagement" to its higher education classification system.
2. E. Boyer, *Scholarship Reconsidered: Priorities of the Professoriate* (San Francisco: Jossey-Bass, 1990); D. Perry and W. Wiewel, *The University as Urban Developer: Case Studies and Analysis* (New York: M.E. Sharpe, 2005).
3. M. Brukardt, B. Holland, S. Percy, and N. Zimpher, *Calling the Question: Is Higher Education Ready to Commit to Community Engagement.* (Milwaukee: Milwaukee Idea Office, University of Wisconsin–Milwaukee, 2004), p. ii.
4. Boyer, *Scholarship Reconsidered.*
5. L. Bingham and R. O'Leary, Conclusion: Parallel Play, Not Collaboration: Missing Questions, Missing Connections, *Public Administration Review, 66* (Supplement): 161–167, 2006; L.J. O'Toole, K. Meier, and S. Nicholson-Crotty, Managing Upward, Downward and Outward, *Public Management Review, 7* (1): 45–68, 2005; R. Agranoff and M. McGuire, *Collaborative Public Management: New Strategies for Local Government* (Washington, DC: Georgetown University Press, 2003).
6. Percy, Zimpher, and Brukardt, *Creating a New Kind of University: Institutionalizing Community-University Engagement* (Bolton, MA: Anker Publishing, 2006).
7. J. Fountain, *Building the Virtual State: Information Technology and Institutional Change* (Washington, DC: Brookings Institution, 2001); J. Gil-Garcia and T. Pardo, E-government Success Factors: Mapping Practical Tools to Theoretical Foundations, *Government Information Quarterly, 22* (2): 187–216, 2005.
8. C. Lukensmeyer and L. Torres, *Public Deliberation: A Manager's Guide to Public Deliberation* (Washington, DC: IBM Center for the Business of Government, 2006); T. Cooper, T. Bryer, and J. Meek, Citizen-Centered Collaborative Public Management, *Public Administration Review 66* (Supplement): 76–88, 2006.
9. Gil-Garcia and Pardo, E-government Success Factors; M. Pirog and C. Johnson, Electronic Funds and Benefits Transfers, E-Government, and the Winter Commission, *Public Administration Review* (Special Issue): S103–S114, 2008.
10. B. Gray, *Collaborating: Finding Common Ground for Multiparty Problems* (San Francisco, CA: Jossey-Bass, 1989), p. 5.
11. E. Bardach, *Getting Agencies to Work Together: The Practice and Theory of Managerial Craftsmanship* (Washington, DC: Brookings Institution Press, 1998).
12. Ibid., p. 308.
13. D. Evans and D.C. Yen, E-government: An Analysis for Implementation: Framework for Understanding Cultural and Social Impact, *Government Information Quarterly 22* (3): 354–373, 2005; J. West and E. Berman, The Impact of Revitalized Management Practices on the Adoption of Information Technology: A National Survey of Local Governments, *Public Performance and Management Review, 24* (3): 233–253, 2001.
14. M. Minkler and N. Wallerstein, *Community Based Participatory Research for Health* (San Francisco, CA: Jossey-Bass, 2003).
15. Evans and Yen, E-government: An Analysis.

16. Ibid. The importance of building a culture of shared knowledge is critical in better defining and solving joint problems, in coordinating programs, and in building communities of practice. S. Dawes, A. Cresswell, and Pardo, From "Need to Know" to "Need to Share": Tangled Problems, Information Boundaries, and the Building of Public Sector Knowledge Networks, *Public Administration Review, 69* (3): 393, 2009.

17. Evans and Yen, E-government: An Analysis; Gil-Garcia and Pardo, E-government Success Factors; Dawes, Interagency Information Sharing: Expected benefits, Manageable Risks, *Journal of Policy Analysis and Management, 15* (3): 377–394, 1996.

18. Fountain, *Building the Virtual State.*

19. G. Prokopiadou, C. Papatheodorou, and D. Moschopoulos, Integrating Knowledge Management Tools for Government Information, *Government Information Quarterly, 21* (2): 170–198, 2004.

20. Evans and Yen, E-government: An Analysis.

21. Gil-Garcia and Pardo, E-government Success Factors; T.C. Redman, The Impact of Poor Data Quality on the Typical Enterprise, *Communications of the ACM, 41* (2): 79–82, 1998.

22. Dawes, Pardo, and Cresswell, Designing Electronic Government Information Access Programs: A Holistic Approach. *Government Information Quarterly, 21* (1): 3–23, 2004; Gil-Garcia and Pardo, E-government Success Factors; West and Berman, Impact of Revitalized Management; K. Holtzblatt and S. Jones, Contextual Inquiry: A Participatory Technique for System Design, In *Participatory Design: Principles and Practices,* ed. D. Schuler and A. Namioka (Hillsdale, NJ: Lawrence Erlbaum, 1993), pp. 177–210; Fountain, *Building the Virtual State.*

23. Dawes, Interagency Information Sharing.

24. Dawes et al., Designing Electronic Government, p. 21.

25. Holtzblatt and Jones, Contextual Inquiry.

26. T. Soska and A. Johnson Butterfield, *University–Community Partnerships: Universities in Civic Engagement* (Binghamton, NY: The Haworth Social Work Practice Press, 2004); Perry and Wiewel, *University as Urban Developer*; Percy et al., *Creating a New Kind of University*; W. Wiewel and D. Perry, *Global Universities and Urban Development: Case Studies and Analysis* (Armonk, NY: M.E. Sharpe, 2008); J. Rodin, *The University and Urban Revival: Out of the Ivory Tower and into the Streets* (Philadelphia: University of Pennsylvania Press, 2007).

27. Gil-Garcia and Pardo, E-government Success Factors.

28. R. Janikowski, Interview with the director of the University's Center for Community Criminology and Research, July 2, 2008.

29. Ibid.

30. Ibid.

31. Fountain, *Building the Virtual State.*

Chapter 9

Choices and Challenges: Sustaining a Rural Health Network when Funding Vanishes

Dana J. Patton and Kendra B. Stewart

Contents

Case Brief

Background and Purpose of the Collaboration: Rural communities face specific barriers in health-care delivery due to some common characteristics of nonmetropolitan areas. On average, residents of rural communities are older, less educated, and less likely to be insured, report poorer health conditions, are more likely to be unemployed, and lag behind in their use of technology. Rural communities also face a shortage of health-care providers, leaving residents with fewer options for care as well as transportation challenges in seeking care elsewhere. The federal government has designated the majority of rural communities (especially those in the Southeast) as health professional shortage areas (HPSA). It is predicted that access to health care in rural areas will only get worse as health-care consumption continues to rise due to an aging population while the health-care workforce continues to shrink. In this case, two community nonprofit organizations in Kentucky were awarded a two-year, $1.6 million federal grant to form a health and human services network focused on enhancing community knowledge, improving access to health care, and maximizing coordination of resources and services. The network served an impoverished and predominantly rural five-county service area through a combination of 16 community agencies, physicians, educators, community-based organizations, and faith-based organizations. The network structured activities around four primary goals: (1) increase community knowledge of nutrition and health care; (2) increase the number of trained persons to teach nutrition workshops; (3) improve access to medical benefits programs; and (4) maximize coordination of agency resources and services.

Current Status: The two-year timeline was originally cut to one year due to discontinuation of the funding by the federal government. The network was able to get a six-month no-cost extension, so services were provided for a total of 18 months. The formal network disbanded at the end of the 18-month period. Both nonprofit groups were able to maintain connections to select partners from the network, but on a substantially smaller scale than was originally intended. Some of the toughest challenges the network faced had more to do with the rural areas they were seeking to serve than with the loss of funding.

Lessons for Strategic Collaboration Practice: This case highlights the importance of involving key stakeholders early in the collaboration's exploration and formation stages to create shared understanding and buy-in. By not including faith-based organizations at the table early, important opportunities to build trust with target client populations and to mobilize new resources were lost. Also important to retain active participation is the explicit articulation of each participant's value to the collaboration and the role he or she will play. In this case when federal funding ended, key participants in the collaboration simply stopped attending meetings, illustrating the importance of flexibility to change structures and processes as needed while securing explicit commitment to goals and timelines. Finally, this case illustrates the challenges of collaboration across a large distance and when participants have varying technology access and skills.

9.1 Introduction

Rural communities increasingly face specific barriers in health-care delivery.[1] Many of the problems in nonmetropolitan communities stem from the inadequate financial resources of both the community residents and the local governments.[2] Rural America has experienced a higher rate of poverty since the measure was first captured in the 1960s. Residents of rural communities are older, less educated, and less likely to be insured, report poorer health conditions, are more likely to be unemployed, and lag behind in their use of technology.[3]

Rural communities also face a shortage of health-care providers, leaving residents with fewer options in care as well as transportation challenges in seeking care elsewhere. The federal government has designated the majority of rural communities (especially those in the Southeast) as health professional shortage areas (HPSA) because of very high physician-to-population ratios.[4] Access to

Two community nonprofit organizations in Kentucky were awarded a two-year, $1.6 million federal grant to form a health and human services network focused on enhancing community knowledge, improving access to health care, and maximizing coordination of resources and services. The network served an impoverished and predominantly rural five-county service area through a combination of 16 community agencies, physicians, educators, community-based organizations, and faith-based organizations. Two months into the grant period, notification was received that federal funding for the grant would end after the first year. Choices had to be made by the network regarding the focus of its efforts in the face of waning commitment from some of the participants. Interestingly, some of the toughest challenges had more to do with the rural areas they were seeking to serve than with the loss of funding.

health care in rural areas is predicted to worsen as health-care consumption continues to rise due to an aging population while the health-care workforce continues to shrink.[5]

One way the federal government has attempted to address these serious health-care and access issues in rural communities is through the formation of the Healthy Communities Access Program (HCAP). The HCAP program provides funds to nonprofit organizations to establish networks of care for uninsured and under-insured individuals. In 2005, two community action agencies[6] in Kentucky were awarded a two-year, $1.6 million HCAP grant to form a health and human services network (hereafter referred to as the network) to attempt to address health-care challenges faced by individuals living in rural areas. The network was to serve a five-county service area through a combination of 16 community agencies, physicians, educators, community-based organizations, and faith-based organizations.[7] This represented a unique mix of public, private, religious, and nonprofit groups working together to address serious health issues in a traditionally underserved, poverty-stricken area in Kentucky.

9.2 The Target Population

As already noted, rural populations tend to have lower levels of education and higher rates of poverty and unemployment compared with their more urban counterparts. The counties served by the network fit this description. As shown in Table 9.1, the service region for the network exhibited the expected characteristics compared to the state of Kentucky and to national averages.

In addition to the dire economic conditions in the five target counties, over-weight and obesity-related illnesses were a focus of the HCAP. The Synchronized

Table 9.1   Economic Indicators in the United States, Kentucky, and the Five-County Service Region, 2006

	Per-Capita Personal Income	*Percent of People of All Ages in Poverty*	*Unemployment Rate*	*Percent Receiving Food Stamps*
United States	$36,794	13.3	4.6	8.9
Kentucky	$29,542	17.0	5.9	14.1
Bath	$20,750	21.6	7.9	20.3
Estill	$19,554	26.4	6.7	26.2
Menifee	$17,095	25.6	8.7	23.4
Morgan	$17,168	25.9	9.0	23.0
Powell	$20,397	22.8	7.5	24.6

Source: Data source information for per-capita personal income, percent of people of all ages in poverty, and unemployment rate indicates where data were obtained from the USA Counties website, which is a subset of the US Census. For example, to access per-capita personal income by county, go to the main USA Counties website at http://censtats.census.gov/usa/usa. shtml, select the state and county from the drop down menu. Then, from the "select a table" menu, choose "Personal Income (Bureau of Economic Analysis) – NAICS". Scroll to local per-capita personal income for the desired year.

Per-Capita Personal Income: US Census Bureau, USA Counties, Personal Income (Bureau of Economic Analysis) – NAICS.

Percent of People of All Ages in Poverty: US Census Bureau, USA Counties, Income and Poverty.

Unemployment Rate: US Census Bureau, USA Counties, Civilian Labor Force (Bureau of Labor Statistics).

Percent Receiving Food Stamps: The Data Book, Kentucky Cabinet for Health and Human Services, Department for Community Based Services. Data are percent receiving food stamps in June 2006.

Obesity Awareness & Reduction Outreach (SOAR) program (described herein) was specifically designed to raise awareness about nutrition and the consequences of being overweight. According to the University of Kentucky Prevention Research Center, "Many counties in eastern Kentucky have higher rates of overweight and obesity than the rest of the state."[8] Table 9.2 illustrates how individuals in the five-county target area compare with the United States and Kentucky.

Table 9.2 Adult Overweight and Obesity Prevalence in the United States, Kentucky, and the Five-County Service Region, 2000–2002

	Obesity Prevalence (Percent)	Overweight and Obesity Prevalence (Percent)
United States	21.9	59.7
Kentucky	24.2	62.8
Bath	21.0–24.2	59.4–62.4
Estill	Insufficient Data	Insufficient Data
Menifee	24.3–27.7	66.3–76.2
Morgan	24.3–27.7	62.5–66.2
Powell	Insufficient Data	Insufficient Data

Source: University of Kentucky Prevention Research Center. (Frankfort, KY: Kentucky Department of Public Health.) The Report can be accessed at www.fitky.org. The Kentucky Obesity Epidemic 2004.

Note: Overweight and obesity are determined by body mass index (BMI), calculated as height relative to weight. For adults, a BMI of 18.5 to 24.9 is considered normal weight; a BMI of 25 to 29.9 is considered overweight; and a BMI of 30 or higher is considered obese.

Self-reported data from the service recipients paint an even bleaker picture of the economic, education, and health status of those seeking help from the network.[9] As shown in Figure 9.1, 77% of survey respondents report a monthly income of less than $1,000.

Unsurprisingly, education levels of survey respondents were quite low. A total of 29% of respondents reported an education level of eighth grade or less, and an additional 22% reported some high school but no high school degree, as shown in Figure 9.2. A total of 36% of respondents either completed high school or earned the GED. A small portion reported some college, and two respondents indicated they hold a college degree.

In addition, Figure 9.3 shows the results of the self-reported height and weight of the survey respondents converted to classification as normal, overweight, or obese. Body mass index (BMI) was calculated for each respondent and was used to determine classification.[10] As shown in Figure 9.3, a very high percentage (44%) of the respondents are obese, with the same percentages (28%) classified as overweight and normal.

These characteristics are, most likely, well known among nonprofits building networks to assist underserved rural populations. It is useful, however, to anticipate the unique challenges these and other characteristics may create in building and sustaining a network in rural areas. We return to this idea later in the case study, focusing on five specific challenges the network faced:

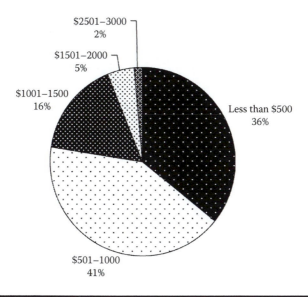

Figure 9.1   Self-reported monthly income of survey respondents.

Question 28. My monthly income (including all sources of income such as spouse's income, welfare, food stamps, SSI, etc.) is...

Respondents were given options in $100 increments from $501–1000, and then responses were grouped into $500 increments (e.g., $1001–1500). Responses between $501–1000 are aggregated for ease of reporting in the figure.

1. Suspicious clientele.
2. Retaining network members after the abrupt end of funding.
3. Serving a large rural geographic area.
4. Lack of technological skills and infrastructure in rural locales.
5. Lack of providers and resistance to buy-in from existing health-care providers.

First, though, we describe the structure, goals, objectives, and assessment of the network.

9.3 Establishing an Effective Collaborative Structure

The simple underlying premise of a network (or community partnership, alliance, cooperative partnership, or integrated service network) is that by forming relationships with other organizations, the needs of the community can be better met.[11] The business of achieving or assessing that seemingly simple premise is hardly straightforward.

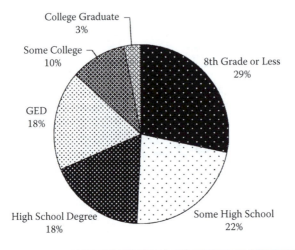

Figure 9.2 Self-reported education level by survey respondents.

Question 25. What was the last grade of school you completed?

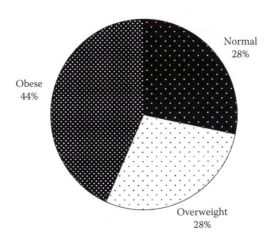

Figure 9.3 Self-reported height and weight by survey respondents converted to three classifications based on body mass index.

Question 22. How tall are you?
Question 23: How much do you weigh?

Ideas abound as to how networks "work," such as pooling resources and expertise within organizations,[12] the benefits of networks at improving efficiency and providing more effective services,[13] and improved planning for dealing with community problems.[14] Some studies confirm the benefits of networks; others, however, raise questions regarding client outcomes,[15] the ability to establish or maintain a network,[16] and O'Toole and Meier[17] reveal the potential "dark side" of network management in the form of politicized decision-making.

In addition, various frameworks, models, analyses, and "lessons" are offered to assist in network building, sustaining, assessing, and more.[18] In the next section, we offer one such model on collaborative community health planning. There are numerous models available to guide organizations seeking to form networks or collaborations in communities to address health issues. We provide several Web sites at the end of the chapter for further exploration of these models.

9.4 A Framework for Community Collaboration on Health Issues

A simple framework for thinking about how a network or collaborative group might approach community health issues was developed by Fawcett et al. and is presented in Figure 9.4.[19]

Figure 9.4   A framework for collaborative public health action by communities. (Reprinted with permission from: Board on Health Promotion and Disease Prevention, and the Institute of Medicine, *The Future of the Public's Health in the 21st Century*, Washington, DC: The National Academies Press, 2002.)

There are several other popular models or frameworks used by groups such as Mobilizing for Action through Planning and Partnerships (MAPP), the Planned Approach to Community Health (PATCH), or the Community Health Improvement (CHIP) model.[20]

Assessing, prioritizing, and planning is the first step in the Fawcett et al. framework and involves setting goals, prioritizing them, and figuring out how to achieve them. The goals of the program, however, should be revisited periodically to determine progress and if changes need to be made.

In the second phase, *implementing targeted action,* the focus should be on high-priority health issues in the community, and a multiprong approach has been found to be most effective.[21] In other words, multiple strategies such as education, legal and political action, and different forms of communication have been most effective in addressing community health issues in a collaborative setting.

The third component of the framework, *changing community conditions and systems*, focuses more on the system level than the individual level, though it has broad implications for individual-level behavior. For example, adopting a city ordinance banning smoking in public places would be an example of a change in the community. In *The Future of the Public's Health in the 21st Century,* this component is described as "…changing aspects of the physical, social, organizational, and even political environments to eliminate or reduce factors that contribute to health problems or to introduce new elements that promote better health."[22]

Achieving widespread change in behavior and risk factors change, the fourth component, should flow directly from the third component. The focus in this component is on individual behavioral changes (e.g., exercising that will have a positive impact on health, but also on the role communities play in facilitating individual behavioral changes (e.g., building walking paths). For example, in the previous paragraph smoking bans were used to illustrate a system change. In addition, workplaces may offer smoking cessation programs or states may tax cigarettes to make buying cigarettes cost-prohibitive in an effort to achieve behavioral changes in individuals.

The final component, *improving the population's health*, is one that is often difficult to assess in the short term. Process evaluations, however, can aid in determining if progress is being made toward the ultimate goal of improved health in a community and often can provide valuable feedback to a program.

9.5 Attending to Process and Procedures

As noted already, the establishment of the network was a collaborative effort by two well-established community action agencies that had served the five-county region for decades. One agency, however, had primary responsibility for administering the grant monies and for hiring the project director, who was paid from the grant. Recruitment of other community agencies, doctors, dentists, and faith-based organizations was finalized upon receipt of the grant. An incentive was offered to participating organizations: Each received a computer, teleconferencing equipment, and Internet service paid for by the grant during the duration of the two years of funding. Meetings were regularly scheduled for all participants but served more as informative gatherings than as collaborative decision-making sessions. Ultimately, the two founding agencies made decisions concerning program administration with the project director taking the lead role in scheduling events and making decisions about how the program would adapt over the course of the grant.

9.5.1 *Grant Goals*

The U.S. Department of Health and Human Services Health Resources and Services Administration (HRSA) has two overarching goals recipients of HCAP grants are expected to accomplish: (1) to further the coordination of services to allow uninsured and underinsured people to gain entry into and receive services from a more efficient, comprehensive, and higher-quality system of care, regardless of ability to pay; and (2) the development of infrastructure that will result in a health-care delivery system characterized by effective collaboration, information sharing, and clinical and financial coordination among providers and organizations in the community.[23]

The network designed its HCAP services around four broad objectives to accomplish the goals set forth by HRSA:

1. Increase community knowledge of nutrition and health care.
2. Increase the number of trained persons to teach nutrition workshops.
3. Improve access to medical benefits programs.
4. Maximize coordination of agency resources and services.

The first objective, to increase community knowledge of nutrition and health care, was pursued in a creative way. Two large recreational vehicles (RVs) were used as mobile education centers.[24] Network members targeted particular events and places to attend (e.g., county fairs, schools, festivals, public libraries, day care centers, health fairs) and provided nutrition information and cooking demonstrations, information about smoking and health, shopping on a budget, eating healthy snacks, and more.

The second objective, to increase the number of trained persons to teach nutrition workshops, was targeted at faith-based groups that were members of the network. Their primary role was to continue the work of the network by providing nutrition workshops and other information sessions through their religious institutions after the end of the grant period.

The third objective, to improve access to medical benefits programs, took a two-pronged approach. First, the network allocated the maximum amount of money allowed under the grant guidelines ($75,000) to be used as vouchers for medical and dental care, pharmacy assistance, and purchasing eyeglasses. Second, when individuals came to the network's central offices requesting a voucher, case workers interviewed them to determine if they were eligible for various government and private programs, such as Medicare, food stamps, heating assistance, or prescription assistance from pharmaceutical companies. If an individual was determined to be eligible, they were provided enrollment assistance.

Finally, the fourth objective, to maximize coordination of agency resources and services, was pursued through Vertical Integration. The network contracted with an information technology company to advise regarding computer programs and other systems of information sharing. In addition, all members of the network received a new computer, teleconferencing capabilities, and Internet service for the length of the grant to facilitate information sharing.

The overarching and broader goal of the network was to develop a sustainable and strategic collaboration that could provide health-related services to a poverty-stricken, rural area in Eastern Kentucky. The ability of the network to achieve this larger goal became questionable when, two months into the grant period, notification was received that federal funding for the HCAP would end after the first year. The project director and network participants had to make choices regarding how funds would be spent and which aspects of the program would be emphasized over others.

9.6 Assuring Accountability, Developing Outcomes, and Measuring Impact

The relative successes and failures of meeting the various objectives outlined by the network illustrate how support by the members without direct affiliation to the founding agencies (e.g., doctors, dentists, faith-based organizations) decreased after the program and funding were cut. Attendance at monthly network meetings, for example, declined precipitously following notification that the program would end a year earlier than expected. Additionally, some participating organizations were so invested in the two-year timeline they believed collaboration would not be sustainable without the second year. Therefore, upon notice of the shortened timeframe, they became disengaged and unwilling to invest time in an effort they did not believe would become long term.

In a survey of network members, 100% of respondents indicated the network was valuable and needed and provided critical services to the population they served. Of the 12 respondents, 10 indicated a desire and willingness to sustain the network following the end of federal funding, yet only 1 of the 12 was willing to provide funding to continue the work of the network. Thus, most network members were willing to continue the efforts beyond the funding period if someone else picked up the tab. In retrospect, it is clear that sufficient investment and risk sharing did not occur with some network members. For example, the project director noted in an interview that some of the smaller organizations "took the computer and ran" when they found out funding would end after the first year.

9.7 Evaluating the Network

The network's HCAP program was evaluated based on both qualitative and quantitative data collected by both program coordinators and the authors of this case study. Four different surveys were designed and used to collect data from individuals served by the various programs as well as the network members. In addition, indepth interviews were conducted of the key personnel involved in the project.

First, we examined how effective the program was at meeting its two "areas of major achievement" selected from the HCAP goals. These two areas are (1) improved access to health care for uninsured and underinsured patients; and (2) improved coordination and information sharing among community safety-net providers. Findings indicate that significant progress was made regarding healthcare access for the uninsured and underinsured citizens in the five-county service region. Additionally, a solid foundation was developed for improved coordination and information sharing among community partners.

Second, we examined the progress made on three of the four specific project goals outlined in the network's federal grant proposal. The first goal, to increase community knowledge of nutrition and health care, changed shape from what was originally proposed due to the shortened timeline and decreased funding. The network did, however, exceed its outreach goal and provided nutrition and health-care education to over 8,100 individuals.

The network fell short of achieving its second goal, to increase the number of trained persons to teach nutrition workshops. The network intended the SOAR component to continue to function through the faith-based organizations that would receive training through the Train the Trainer component of the grant. Once potential participants realized funding was ending, there was a significant decrease in support for these efforts. According to the project director, when the network found out funds and the timeline had been cut, "the wind went out of everyone's sails, and especially the smaller groups." Later we discuss the creative choice made by the network leaders to salvage the Train the Trainer aspect of the program.

Survey responses suggest the network was very successful in achieving the third goal of the project, which was to improve access to medical benefits programs. Many individuals seeking vouchers qualified for social service programs and received assistance from the network completing their applications for benefits. In addition, the network began working with pharmaceutical companies to register participants for free medications. This component of the HCAP has been continued in the work of the agencies and is a critical service to the communities they serve. Finally, there is evidence that progress was made on the fourth goal, to maximize the coordination of agency resources and services based on survey responses by service recipients.[25]

It is clear that the network achieved a great deal in a very short period of time. Clearly, the discontinuation of the HCAP grant program at the federal level, and the subsequent cutting of the network's funding and grant period, required substantial reorganization of the planned programs and activities. Beyond funding issues, the vacuum in leadership that was created when the grant ended appears to have damaged the ability of the network to remain fully intact. When the funding ended in February 2007, the project director position also ended, leaving the impression that there was no longer a formal network administrative structure. Due to a lack of funds, the individual who had served as project director left the agency coordinating the partnership. Generally, the absence of a broker or "network administrative organization" results in informal and weaker networks unless there is a high level of commitment to the goals by the group.[26]

The departure of the project director appears to have affected continued network connections for some of the partners more than others. This is not surprising since one of the community action agencies was able to reallocate funding to permanently hire a project coordinator to specifically maintain the HCAP projects in its service region. This sent an important signal to the partners with whom they had been working and made a significant difference in the ability to sustain the relationships created through the HCAP-funded network. The other community action agency that was primarily in charge of seeking the grant and housed the project director has continued many of the services provided through the HCAP, but through different programs. For example, the lead agency continues to assist individuals in its service region with prescription assistance. Hundreds of individuals in these counties are receiving medications at no charge due to this program.[27] In addition, according to personnel at the lead agency, an important outcome of the HCAP-funded network activities was to strengthen their relationships with county health departments. One potential reason for the different outcomes of the different agencies is their scope of services offered. The lead agency offers many more services and programs in its area and was likely able to absorb and transfer the activities of the HCAP into other programs. While it appears that the secondary agency did "more" to continue the work of the HCAP by, for example, hiring a project coordinator, it is likely that the level of services continuing to be offered that were initiated through the HCAP is quite comparable between the two agencies.

9.8 Lessons Learned

In this section of the case study, we focus on challenges the network faced, how they successfully addressed some of them, and additional "suggested actions" a collaborative group might consider in the future if serving a similar population.[28]

9.8.1 Challenge 1: Lack of Response by Those in Need

Given the dire lack of education, jobs, income, and general assistance available in many poor rural areas, one would expect the response of the population to be overwhelming. In fact, the network initially struggled to develop a base of trust with individuals in the community. The program manager of the network noted that a turning point for her was an interaction with a woman at a county fair where there were very few visitors to the RV for information despite the fact that they were handing out "freebies" to visitors.[29] The program manager asked a lady who did come over to "see what they were doing here" why more people were not coming by. The woman told her that all they saw was a "lady in fancy clothes with a big fancy RV."[30] Following this interaction, network members conducting RV events were instructed to wear jeans and tennis shoes, and a substantial investment was made to decorate the outside of the RV to emphasize they were there to help.

9.8.2 Suggested Action 1: Be Approachable and Build Trust

A simple change in how the RV instructors were dressed at casual events (e.g., county fairs) and being more explicit about their activities garnered a positive response. Building trust in a community may be more challenging. If possible within the guidelines of a group's mission or granting agency, using faith-based organizations to promote the activities of the network may be an efficient and effective way to build trust in a community, as levels of religiosity and church attendance tend to be higher in rural areas compared with their urban counterparts.[31] An additional suggestion is to capitalize on "captive audiences" if appropriate to the network's goals. The network conducted many workshops on nutrition and health at public schools, libraries, and senior citizen centers in an attempt to reach more people.[32]

An exception to the lack of response was to the vouchers. As word spread throughout the communities that the network had vouchers for free dental, medical, and eye care, the response was overwhelming. The granting agency restricted the amount of funds that could be used on direct care to $75,000, which disappeared within only a few months of the start of the program. As individuals in the community sought vouchers for care, caseworkers at the network assessed them for other services such as Medicare, Medicaid, food stamps, heating assistance, and pharmaceutical assistance programs. The network notified individuals seeking voucher assistance that the vouchers were currently gone but asked them to complete some "information sheets" to see if they could help them in some other way. Most people did so since they were there already, and many people were eligible for services they were not receiving.

9.8.3 Challenge 2: Retaining Members of the Network

Interest and enthusiasm were high in the beginning but waned among some members of the network as the HCAP activities unfolded. The project manager noted on several occasions that participation by some members seemed to decline following federal discontinuation of the HCAP grant program and the shortening of the timeline from two years to one year. Ultimately, however, the timeline was reduced by only six months after the network was granted a no-cost extension. Sustaining a network is a topic that has received substantial attention in the scholarly literature. Network managers should consider the need for retaining members of the network and act accordingly. In other words, retention of some members may be critical to the function of the network, but more peripheral members may come and go with little overall impact on the network.

9.8.4 Suggested Action 2a: Identify and Use a Member's Value to the Network

Assuming, however, there is a desire to retain particular members of the network, we suggest network managers carefully assess the value each member or each organization contributes to the network and effectively use it. In some cases, use of a member's value will be obvious, as in the case of medical doctors, dentists, or organizations that assist individuals in very specific ways (e.g., a food bank). Other members, such as faith-based organizations, may play a more nebulous role in the network.

The network we evaluated included a number of faith-based organizations. The original grant specified that individuals from the churches would be trained to conduct nutrition education workshops in the community after the end of the grant. According to the project manager, enthusiasm was high when discussing the role the faith-based groups would have in the network, but participation in the training sessions was so poor that the focus of the Train-the-Trainer program was changed. Instead of individuals from churches being trained to conduct nutrition workshops with adults, high school teens were trained to conduct body-image awareness classes with middle school girls.[33]

We suspect that participation in network activities by the faith-based groups would have been more positive if their strengths in reaching out to the community and building trust among potential recipients of services had been used. In addition, a common problem for the network was transportation of individuals needing medical or dental services. Most churches, particularly in rural areas, have a van they use to transport people to and from church. Use of funds and faith-based groups to assist with transportation in vans that sat unused five or six days of the week would have been a productive use of resources faith-based organizations have to offer in rural communities.

9.8.5 Suggested Action 2b: Develop and Commit to an Agreed Upon Timeline

All network members were involved in the initial planning and development of the two-year timeline for creating a sustainable network. Once this unexpectedly changed, some members concluded that the end goal was no longer attainable and disengaged in the collaboration. When developing a timeline for institutionalizing a collaborative partnership, it is important to ensure that all entities involved are willing to commit even if circumstances (e.g., external funding) change.

9.8.6 Challenge 3: Covering a Large Geographical Area

The five-county service area of the network spans a large geographical area, and thus the members were in contiguous counties, but potentially long distances from one another. Networks may desire to include multiple counties in an effort to reach more people but should consider the time and resources that may be required in traveling as well as the potential obstacles to convene key members of the network. For example, if a network focuses on improved health in a community and doctors and dentists in the region are a key component to the success of the network, it may be unrealistic to expect them to spend several hours away from the office driving to and from network meetings. Without involvement in decision making, however, professionals' commitment to the network may decline. Thus, participating in meetings may be very important, but geographical distance may hinder their ability to do so.

9.8.7 Suggested Action 3: Limit the Service Area or Form Subgroups of the Network

Nonprofit organizations may pursue two avenues in dealing with a large geographical area in need of services. One suggested action is to simply limit the number of recipients served by the network to a smaller geographical area. In some cases, this may not be a feasible suggestion given the expectations of a granting organization, for example. In those cases, an alternative avenue is to form subgroups of the network. This option requires a substantial amount of trust and cooperation, however, among network members and may work best in networks that have an established relationship. The project managers of the network subgroups should meet on a regular basis for information sharing, but convening the entire network would be occasional.

9.8.8 Challenge 4: Lack of Technological Skills and Infrastructure

Some may suggest that a different solution to Challenge 3 would be to use technology to communicate with network members spread over a large geographical area. The network attempted this solution with limited success. All members of the network received new computers, teleconferencing capabilities, and Internet service for the length of the grant to facilitate information sharing. One of the network personnel noted in an interview, however, that the communication strategy did not work as planned. Many of the smaller organizations had very limited knowledge of how to use computers. In addition, most of the rural communities did not have access to cable connections or high-speed Internet connections, so video conferencing was not possible. One of the program coordinators noted that some network members were not able to continue high-speed Internet service once the grant ended due to financial constraints. There were quarterly network meetings, but the intention was to have the capacity for more frequent information sharing and communicating among the members. The lack of communication potentially hindered the ability of the smaller organizations to fully integrate into the network.

9.8.9 Suggested Action 4: Use Traditional Communication Styles

Nonprofit organizations and perhaps some other members of the network serving rural areas may use e-mail and the Internet on a daily basis, but smaller community-based organizations may not be technologically savvy. Network managers partnering with community members may find it more beneficial to rely on traditional means of communication and information sharing such as monthly newsletters with updates from network members. Newsletters, for example, have the added benefit of being easily shared with community members who may not be aware of the programs offered by the network.

One of the two community action agencies that cofounded the network assigned one person the task of spending half her time traveling to each partner in its geographical area for individual face-to-face meetings. Many of these meetings were informal "check-ins" that might last only 10 or 15 minutes, but they provided the agency the opportunity to remind the partner of his or her important contribution to the network as well as an opportunity for the partner to voice any concerns regarding the network. The agency that pursued this regular, direct contact with partners in the network has been more successful in sustaining relationships after the end of the HCAP grant compared with the agency that did not.

9.8.10 Challenge 5: Lack of Providers and Resistance to Buy-In

The lack of health-care providers in rural areas is well documented and noted already. The network reported marked difficulty, however, in getting buy-in from some providers that initially agreed to join the network and others who simply refused to charge a reduced rate for services.

9.8.11 Suggested Action 5: Propose Uniform Reduced Fees for All Health-Care Providers

In small, poor communities where "everyone knows everyone," it is possible that health-care providers fear becoming known as the doctor who will treat you for free. One suggestion for nonprofits seeking to achieve buy-in from health-care providers in the community is to propose the same reduced rate or volunteer service for all providers.[34] Moscovice et al. note that "physician groups in rural locales have limited experience with alternative organizational structures."[35] While some physicians in rural areas likely have experience cooperating with regional rural hospitals, entering into service agreements with nonprofits may be less familiar.[36] Formalizing the agreement may provide assurance that their peers are fulfilling their commitment to assist the network. Nonprofits seeking to include doctors and dentists in network activities may do something as simple as provide a monthly report to each health-care provider detailing the number of individuals and conditions treated and procedures performed by the participating members of the health-care community. A report such as this would also emphasize the continuing and high level of need in the community.

9.9 Conclusion

In this case study, we highlight two issues that are likely to affect numerous nonprofits seeking to build collaborative agreements to serve individuals in rural areas: (1) funding challenges; and (2) challenges presented by the rural landscape. The network met many of these challenges in unique ways and with great flexibility, which is perhaps the most important lesson to be learned from this case study.

Despite waning commitment from some members of the network, the core group continued to provide a wide array of services as originally planned. When parts of the program were not working as expected, such as the Train-the Trainer program, the network adjusted and shifted to training high school students to counsel middle school students on body image awareness and nutrition rather than declaring that objective a failure. When intended recipients of services in the RV were not using services, funds were invested in decorating the RV and changing the appearance of the instructors to blend in better with the intended recipients—a strategy that worked. The creative solutions to problems ensured that much-needed services would be provided to the target population the network served.

Of course, there are often multiple solutions to challenges faced by any organization. We offered a few additional actions that nonprofits might consider when faced with similar challenges the network faced in meeting the objectives of the HCAP grant. Finally, we conclude that providing direct services to needy individuals or working informally with one or two organizations to occasionally coordinate events is quite different from attempting to build a formal network that includes multiple actors from the private, public, and faith-based sectors of several communities. We hope the challenges and suggested actions we provide, based on our experience working with the network, will benefit nonprofit organizations in rural areas seeking to establish networks of service for communities in need.

9.10 Remaining Questions

As with any study, some questions remain unanswered and warrant additional research. Here, we suggest two related areas that we think, based on our case study, deserve additional attention in the future.

1. *Do incentives work to induce participation in networks?* We are specifically thinking about participation by individuals, such as doctors and dentists, as well as participation by faith-based groups. Existing research addresses the benefits of collaborative action for organizations, but little work has been done to examine the motivating factors for sustained participation by individuals in a collaborative effort.

2. *How can a network effectively integrate organizations or individuals with more narrow missions than the network?* In other words, we return to the issue of how a network achieves buy-in and continued commitment from groups or individuals who may have alternative priorities (e.g., profit margin, saving souls). This may be the most pressing challenge many networks face in times of reduced federal government spending on social services coupled with economic hard times.

Endnotes

1. A. Infante and M. Meit, Delivering the U.S. Preventive Services Task Force. Recommendations in a Rural Health Plan. NORC February 2007, No. 8. http://www.norc.org/NR/rdonlyres/CB3E3517-4D9F-4A77-8CB5-231756A27C34/0/WalshCtr2007_NORC_BriefFeb07.pdf; J.P. Jameson and M. Blank, The Role of

Clinical Psychology in Rural Mental Health Services, *Clinical Psychology: Science & Practice, 14* (3): 283–298, 2007; Meit, Public Health in Rural America, *Journal of Public Health Management & Practice, 13* (3): 235–236, 2007; A. Brown, Technical Assistance to Rural Communities: Stopgap or Capacity Building? *Public Administration Review, 40* (1): 18–23, 1980.

2. Brown, Technical Assistance.
3. J. Liu, J. Probst, A. Martin, J. Wang, and C. Salinas, Disparities in Dental Insurance Coverage and Dental Care among U.S. Children: The National Survey of Children's Health, *Pediatrics, 110:* S12–S21, 2007; Meit, Public Health; S. Perry, Foundations Urged to Do More to Aid America's Rural Regions—Philanthropy.com, *Chronicle of Philanthropy, 19* (21): 10, 2007; National Organization of State Offices of Rural Health, *National Rural Health Issues,* September 2006. http://www.nosorh.org/pdf/Rural_Impact_Study_States_IT.pdf; U.S. Department of Agriculture (USDA) Economic Research Service (ERS), Rural Poverty at a Glance, *Rural Development Research Report* No. 100, 2004. http://www.ers.usda.gov/publications/rdrr100/rdrr100.pdf
4. Ratios are 1:3,500 on average, compared with 1:2,000 for an adequately served community. The Health Resources and Services Administration web page: http://bhpr.hrsa.gov/shortage/index.htm.
5. USDA ERS Rural Poverty.
6. Community action agencies (CAAs) are "nonprofit private and public organizations established under the Economic Opportunity Act of 1964 to fight America's War on Poverty. Community Action Agencies help people to help themselves in achieving self-sufficiency." http://www.communityactionpartnership.com. CAA boards are composed of at least one-third low-income individuals, one-third public officials, and one-third members from the private sector. The HCAP project was funded through a grant from the U.S. Department of Health and Human Services (HHS) Health Resources and Services Administration.
7. Bath, Estill, Menifee, Morgan, and Powell counties were the service area covered by the network.
8. University of Kentucky Prevention Research Center. *The Kentucky Obesity Epidemic 2004 Report.* (Frankfort, KY: Kentucky Department of Public Health. The report can be accessed at www.fitky.org.
9. A mail survey was sent in November 2006 to 189 individuals in the five-county target area who received vouchers or assistance from the network signing up for government benefits programs. Of the 189 surveys sent, 20 were returned by the post office. Hence, 169 survey packets were delivered to the addresses provided to the network by service recipients, and ultimately, 67 surveys were completed and returned for a 40% response rate. Given some of the characteristics of the target population (e.g., low education levels, reluctance to reveal personal information, poor literacy skills), the response rate is quite impressive.
10. See information under Table 9.2 for more details about the BMI as an indicator of overweight and obesity.
11. R. Agranoff, Human Services Integration: Past and Present Challenges in Public Administration, *Public Administration Review, 51* (6): 533–42, 1991; Agranoff and M. McGuire, *Collaborative Public Management: New Strategies for Local Governments* (Washington, DC: Georgetown University Press, 2003); L.J. O'Toole Jr., The Implications for Democracy in a Networked Bureaucratic World, *Journal of Public Administration Research and Theory: J-PART, 7* (3): 443–459, 1997; E.L. Baker, R.J.

Melton, P.V. Stange, et al., Health Reform and the Health of the Public: Forging Community Health Partnerships, *Journal of the American Medical Association, 272* (16): 1276–82, 1994; D. Chisholm, *Coordination without Hierarchy: Informal Structures in Multiorganizational Systems* (Berkeley: University of California Press, 1989); K.G. Provan and B. Milward, Do Networks Really Work? A Framework for Evaluating Public-Sector Organizational Networks, *Public Administration Review, 61* (4): 414–423, 2001.

12. Chisholm, *Coordination*; Provan and Milward, A Preliminary Theory of Interorganizational Network Effectiveness: A Comparative Study of Four Community Mental Health Systems, *Administrative Science Quarterly, 40* (1): 1–33, 1995.

13. C. Alter and J. Hage, *Organizations Working Together* (Newbury Park, CA: Sage Publications, 1993).

14. R.J. Chaskin, Building Community Capacity, *Urban Affairs Review, 36* (3): 291–323, 2001; O'Toole, Implications for Democracy; M.A. Veazie, N.I. Teufel-Shone, G.S. Silverman, A.M. Connolly, S. Warne, B.F. King, et al., Building Community Capacity in Public Health: The Role of Action-Oriented Partnerships, *Journal of Public Health Management and Practice, 7* (2): 21–32, 2001.

15. M.W. Kreuter, N.A. Lezin, and L.A. Young, Evaluating Community-Based Collaborative Mechanisms: Implications for Practitioners, *Health Promotion Practice, 1* (1): 49–63, 2000; S.T. Roussos and S.B. Fawcett, A Review of Collaborative Partnerships as a Strategy for Improving Community Health, *Annual Review of Public Health, 21*: 369–402, 2000.

16. A. Wandersman, R. Goodman, and F. Butterfoss, Understanding Coalitions and How They Operate, In *Community Organizing and Community Building for Health,* ed. M. Minkler (New Brunswick, NJ: Rutgers University Press, 1997); Provan and Milward, Do Networks Really Work.

17. O'Toole and Meier, Desperately Seeking Selznick: Cooptation and the Dark Side of Public Management in Networks, *Public Administration Review, 64* (6): 681–693, 2004.

18. Agranoff, Inside Collaborative Networks: Ten Lessons for Public Managers, *Public Administration Review,* (Special Issue): 56–65, December; Provan and Milward, Do Networks Really Work; I. Moscovice, A. Wellever, J. Christianson, M. Casey, B. Yawn, and D. Hartley, Understanding Integrated Rural Health Networks, *Milbank Quarterly, 75* (4): 563–588, 1997; Provan, Veazie, L.K. Staten, and Teufel-Shone, The Use of Network Analysis to Strengthen Community Partnerships, *Public Administration Review, 65* (5): 603–613, 2005.

19. S.B. Fawcett, V.T. Francisco, D. Hyra, A. Paine-Andrews, R.S. Schultz, S. Russo, et al., Building Healthy Communities, In *The Society and Population Health Reader: A State and Community Perspective,* ed. A.R. Tarlov and R.F. St. Peter (New York: New Press, 2000).

20. In this section of the chapter, we focus only on the simple framework presented by Fawcett et al. due to space constraints. Ibid. For more detailed information about the framework and other aspects of public health and communities, see Board on Health Promotion and Disease Prevention, and the Institute of Medicine, *The Future of the Public's Health in the 21st Century* (Washington, DC: National Academies Press, 2002). The interested reader may find additional information on the other three models at the following websites: MAPP (http://www.naccho.org); PATCH (http://www. cdc.org); and CHIP (http://www.nhop.org/documents/iom.pdf).

21. S.B. Fawcett, Some Lessons on Community Organization and Change, In *Reflections on Community Organization: Enduring Themes and Critical Issues*, ed. J. Rothman (Itasca, IL: F. E. Peacock Publishers, 1999).

22. Board on Health Promotion and Disease Prevention, and the Institute of Medicine, *The Future of Public's Health* in the 21st century. Washington, DC: The National Academics Press, 2002, p. 192.

23. The HCAP grant program was discontinued in 2006.

24. The RVs serve multiple purposes. They are currently being used for a Healthy Marriage Initiative Demonstration Program.

25. A formal analysis of this goal was outside the purview of this evaluation and was left to the contractor for the Vertical Integration project.

26. Provan and Milward, Do Networks Really Work.

27. Most of these clients were noncompliant with their medications because they were truly in a position of choosing between buying food or buying medication.

28. A useful exercise for groups embarking on forming a network similar to this one or for the classroom would be to brainstorm more ideas regarding how to address the challenges in addition to the actions taken by the network and our suggested actions.

29. A common strategy to attract people to the information sessions offered on the RV was to give them something at the end of the session. This gift might be a food item or a bottle opener.

30. The program manager noted that their RV likely cost more than the homes of most of the people at the fair.

31. Meit, Public Health.

32. This strategy was very successful. The network conducted 93 events in a 12-month period, with quite a few of the events occurring at schools. The response was very positive from students, teachers, and administrators.

33. A workshop was conducted for high school students in Bath County on body image and nutrition for teens. These students were trained to discuss these issues with middle school students in the county. Although this was not the original intent of the program, it was a creative way to achieve the goal of training individuals in the community to continue the work of the network. Approximately 70 high school students were trained in this program.

34. Networks may propose accepting a certain number of patients per month or particular days of the month when the dentist or doctor will see network-referred patients free of charge or at a reduced rate. One nonprofit participating in the network reports it has one dentist in the community who agrees to accept its clients two days a month and charges a reduced rate. The director of the nonprofit reported in an interview, however, that his organization receives 5 to 10 calls *per day* requesting help with dental problems. Many of the individuals who received vouchers for dental care had never been to a dentist and needed to have many or all of their teeth removed.

35. Moscovice et al., Understanding Integrated.

36. Nonprofits may find it helpful to provide medical personnel with examples of successful partnerships such as the Surgery on Sunday program conducted in Lexington, Kentucky. See http://www.surgeryonsunday.org/.

Chapter 10

Collaboration, Citizen Participation, and Environmental Protection in the Marine Oil Trade of Alaska

George J. Busenberg

Contents

Case Brief

Background and Purpose of the Collaboration: In 1989 the oil
tanker *Exxon Valdez* collided with a reef in the Prince William
Sound region of Alaska and spilled approximately 11 million
gallons of oil into the waters of that region. The oil spilled from
the *Exxon Valdez* subsequently spread over more than 1,000
miles of Alaskan coastline, causing extensive wildlife casualties.
In the aftermath of the *Exxon Valdez* disaster, a new federal law
created a requirement for a citizens' advisory council designed
to represent local communities and interest groups in the region
affected by oil spilled in the *Exxon Valdez* disaster. Before the
Exxon Valdez disaster, the management of the marine oil trade
in Prince William Sound was marked by disagreements among
the oil industry, public administrators, and citizens. The establishment of the citizens' advisory council was intended in part
to promote collaboration between the oil industry and local citizen members affected by the marine oil trade in Prince William
Sound. The Prince William Sound Regional Citizens' Advisory
Council (RCAC) is directed by a board of representatives of
communities in the region affected by oil spilled in the *Exxon
Valdez* disaster as well as representatives of groups representing local interests in the areas of environmental protection, recreation, tourism, commercial fishing, and aquaculture. These
local representatives constitute the voting board of directors
for the RCAC. The RCAC also incorporates nonvoting ex officio
members from state and federal agencies active in this policy
domain, including the Alaska Department of Environmental
Conservation, the U.S. Coast Guard, and the U.S. National
Oceanic and Atmospheric Administration.

Current Status: Collaborative efforts involving the RCAC,
the oil industry, and public administrators have led to a series
of significant policy changes in the marine oil trade of Alaska.
These changes include the deployment of new tug escort vessels, weather reporting equipment, and a marine ice detection
system in Prince William Sound. While the issues of focus in

this case are often highly technical and politically complex, strategic collaboration has repeatedly proven successful in achieving policy reforms that have gained wide acceptance by the many organizations involved in this policy domain.

Lessons for Strategic Collaboration Practice: This case illustrates how a long history of highly adversarial and uncooperative relationships can be overcome with the use of strategic collaboration. The federal law requiring the establishment of a citizens' advisory council acknowledged the presence of conflict in this policy domain, yet also set constructive expectations for the collaborative effort. This case demonstrates the successful application of collaboration methods for developing technical, legal, and political knowledge so that experts and citizens can work together effectively in leadership and research roles to build a common foundation of knowledge. The use of analytical techniques was an important part of processes to build shared understanding and trust to move forward the goals of policy development and implementation. Finally, the case illustrates the practical function of collaboration in achieving progressive policy change over time.

10.1 Introduction

This case examines the use of collaborative strategies designed to improve environmental management practices in the marine oil trade of Alaska. In particular, this chapter examines the role of local citizen participation in the progressive development of collaborative policy efforts involving the oil industry and public administrators. The development of these collaborative efforts resulted from policy reforms enacted in response to the *Exxon Valdez* oil spill disaster in Alaska. In 1989, the oil tanker *Exxon Valdez* collided with a reef in the Prince William Sound region of Alaska and spilled approximately 11 million gallons of oil into the waters of that region. The oil spilled from the *Exxon Valdez* subsequently spread over more than 1,000 miles of Alaskan coastline, causing extensive wildlife casualties.[1] In the aftermath of the *Exxon Valdez* disaster, a new federal law created a requirement for a citizens' advisory council designed to represent local communities and interest groups in the region affected by oil spilled in the *Exxon Valdez* disaster. This advisory council was intended in part to promote collaboration between the oil industry and local citizen members affected by the marine oil trade in Prince William Sound. This goal of promoting collaboration represented a response to a history of uncooperative relations between the oil industry and local citizens in Prince William Sound prior to 1989. The study described in this chapter finds that

In 1989 the oil tanker *Exxon Valdez* hit a reef in the Prince William Sound region of Alaska, spilling oil that spread across more than 1,000 miles of Alaskan coastline. In response to the *Exxon Valdez* disaster, a citizens' advisory council was created to represent local communities and interest groups in the region affected by oil spilled in that disaster. One goal of this advisory council was to promote collaboration between local citizens and the oil industry in Prince William Sound, as a response to a history of uncooperative relations between local citizens and the oil industry in Prince William Sound prior to 1989. This advisory council has developed into an institutional agent for collaborative efforts involving local citizens, oil industry representatives, and public administrators active in the marine oil trade of Prince William Sound. These collaborative efforts have led to significant policy changes designed to reduce the risk of another marine oil spill disaster in Alaska.

the advisory council has developed effective strategies for policy change through multilateral collaborations involving the oil industry and public administrators. Overall, this study finds that a pattern of sustained collaboration has emerged in this policy domain despite a history of prior discord.

The literature on citizen participation has noted the importance of collaboration in allowing citizen participants to contribute to policy change. Citizen participants often lack the resources and authority to implement their policy proposals through unilateral actions. In such cases, citizen participants can attempt to secure the implementation of their policy proposals by collaborating with organizations that can contribute resources and authority not otherwise available to the citizen participants.[2] In such cases, collaboration can become the bridge between citizen participation efforts and the implementation of citizen-supported policy changes.[3] Indeed, collaborative efforts have proven essential in allowing the advisory council examined in this study to contribute to policy change.

Significant practical lessons in strategic collaboration can be drawn by examining the processes and consequences of the collaborative efforts examined in this study. First, this study demonstrates the feasibility of designing institutional arrangements that allow the participants in a policy domain to shift their interactions from discord to collaboration over time. Second, this study demonstrates the viability of involving local citizens in the collaborative management of a complex technological system. Third, this study demonstrates the pivotal role played by public administrators in enabling the implementation of policy proposals emerging from collaborative efforts.

10.2 Research Methods

This study examined the development of strategic collaboration in the marine oil trade of Prince William Sound over the period 1989 through 2007. This study was conducted using case study research methods described by Yin.[4] Field research was conducted in Alaska by the author to gather relevant documents and to interview respondents involved in the management of the marine oil trade of Prince William Sound. Interviews were conducted by the author with 52 respondents representing major organizations active in this policy domain (e.g., government agencies, oil corporations, nonprofit organizations). Numerous reports generated by these organizations were gathered and analyzed in the course of this study. These reports provide a highly detailed documentation of events in this policy domain from 1989 through 2007. References to these reports are provided in this chapter to indicate the extensive document-based evidence that supports this study.

10.3 Situational Context

In March 1989 the oil tanker *Exxon Valdez* grounded on a reef in Prince William Sound due to a navigational error by the crew. The *Exxon Valdez* oil spill spread over more than 1,000 miles of Alaskan coastline, causing extensive wildlife casualties. This environmental catastrophe demonstrated the inadequacy of the safeguards used against marine oil pollution in the sound at that time.[5]

The *Exxon Valdez* disaster was followed by institutional reforms that fundamentally reshaped the environmental management of the marine oil transportation system in Alaska. These reforms included the enactment of the U.S. Oil Pollution Act of 1990 (Public Law 101-380) and changes to Alaska state law found in Alaska Statute Title 46.[6] These new requirements affect state and federal agencies active in the management of the marine oil trade of Alaska, including the Alaska Department of Environmental Conservation (ADEC) and the U.S. Coast Guard. The new requirements also affect oil corporations active in Prince William Sound. These oil corporations include the Alyeska Pipeline Service Company (Alyeska), which manages the marine oil terminal in Prince William Sound, and other corporations that operate oil tankers in Prince William Sound. Furthermore, the Oil Pollution Act of 1990 established a requirement for a citizens' advisory council designed to enhance local citizen participation and collaboration in the environmental management of the marine oil trade in Prince William Sound. This citizens' advisory council would subsequently play an important role in promoting collaborative efforts in the marine oil trade of Alaska. This advisory council is described further in the next section.

10.4 Establishing an Effective Collaborative Structure

Before the *Exxon Valdez* disaster, the management of the marine oil trade in Prince William Sound was marked by disagreements between the oil industry and public administrators. A report on the *Exxon Valdez* disaster noted this discord, stating that "Serious disagreements over oil pollution response in Prince William Sound repeatedly have marred relationships between Alyeska Pipeline Service Company and government agencies."[7] The management of the marine oil trade in Prince William Sound was also marked by a lack of cooperation between the oil industry and local citizens in the sound in the period before the *Exxon Valdez* disaster. A report from the citizens' advisory council in Prince William Sound noted that before 1989 "attempts by Prince William Sound residents to give their input to oil industry representatives were generally met with negative responses."[8] The language of the Oil Pollution Act of 1990 (OPA 90) noted the presence of mistrust and confrontation in the regulation and oversight of crude oil terminals in the United States. OPA 90 further stated that "only when local citizens are involved in the process will the trust develop that is necessary to change the present system from confrontation to consensus."[9] OPA 90 therefore envisioned a pilot program designed to establish a mechanism for the development of partnerships among the oil industry, government, and local communities in the environmental management of crude oil terminals. As part of this demonstration program, OPA 90 established a requirement for a Regional Citizens' Advisory Council for the Prince William Sound region. The Prince William Sound Regional Citizens' Advisory Council (RCAC) was established as a nonprofit organization in 1989, prior to the enactment of OPA 90.[10] This nonprofit RCAC was subsequently certified as meeting the OPA 90 requirement for a citizens' advisory council in Prince William Sound.[11] The processes and procedures of the RCAC are examined in the next section.

10.5 Process and Procedures

The RCAC is directed by a board of representatives of communities in the region affected by oil spilled in the *Exxon Valdez* disaster as well as by representatives of groups representing local interests in the areas of environmental protection, recreation, tourism, commercial fishing, and aquaculture. These local representatives constitute the voting board of directors for the RCAC. The RCAC also incorporates nonvoting ex officio members from state and federal agencies active in this policy domain, including ADEC, the U.S. Coast Guard, and the U.S. National Oceanic and Atmospheric Administration (NOAA).[12] OPA 90 requires that the RCAC receive annual funding from the oil industry active in Prince William Sound. This funding requirement has given the RCAC the resources necessary to support a number of staff and a number of policy projects.[13] The oil industry is not represented on the board of the RCAC, and OPA 90 requires that the RCAC operate as a self-governing organization.[14] Therefore, the RCAC is designed to establish an active partnership in this policy domain (a partnership including local citizens, oil industry representatives, and public administrators) while maintaining the principle of RCAC governance by local citizens.

The RCAC provides advice and assistance to the oil industry and public administrators concerning the environmental management of the marine oil trade in Prince William Sound. That marine oil trade has continued to pose major hazards to the coastal environment of Alaska since the time of the *Exxon Valdez* disaster. Oil shipping has continued to occur in the Prince William Sound region since 1989.[15] Oil shipped in Prince William Sound is produced on the North Slope of Alaska and is transported overland through the Trans Alaska Pipeline System to an oil terminal at the port of Valdez in the Prince William Sound region.[16] The Valdez oil terminal is operated by Alyeska on behalf of the regional oil industry.[17] Tankers are loaded with oil at the Valdez oil terminal and then sail through the waters of Prince William Sound to the Gulf of Alaska.[18] Prince William Sound possesses ecological and scenic values that can be severely damaged by marine oil spills. Furthermore, the sound contains numerous hazards to navigation (e.g., marine ice, severe weather conditions) that can lead to marine oil spills and impede marine oil spill response operations.

In sum, the environmental management of the marine oil transportation system in Prince William Sound poses continuing policy challenges. Over time, the RCAC has developed collaborative strategies that have contributed to significant enhancements in environmental management practices in the marine oil trade of Prince William Sound. These collaborative strategies (and their policy impacts) are examined in the following sections.

10.6 Accountability, Outcomes, and Policy Impacts

The RCAC is accountable to local communities and interest groups in the *Exxon Valdez* oil spill region through the representation of those communities and groups on the RCAC board of directors. The RCAC is also accountable to the U.S. Coast Guard through an annual certification process.[19] The work of the RCAC has led to significant collaborative outcomes and policy impacts over time. The sections that follow examine the development of collaborative strategies involving the RCAC during the period 1989 through 2007 as well as the policy consequences of those collaborative efforts. Collaboration in this policy domain developed over time from a history of discord; indeed, the RCAC initially engaged in a significant adversarial dispute with the regional oil industry. Between 1992 and 1994, the RCAC engaged in a confrontation with the oil industry over the issue of air pollution emitted by the oil terminal in Prince William Sound. The RCAC proposed that the oil industry voluntarily install new air pollution controls at the oil terminal; the oil industry disagreed with this proposal.[20] This policy dispute was characterized by a process of adversarial analysis (often referred to as "dueling scientists") in which the oil industry and the RCAC generated competing technical analyses of the contested issue to support their competing policy positions.[21] This adversarial approach to analysis generated suspicions of mistaken and manipulated analyses (such analyses are referred to here as *distorted communication*). These suspicions of distorted communication prevented the RCAC and oil industry from accepting each other's analyses as valid and therefore prevented the two sides from resolving the policy dispute.[22] The dispute was eventually superseded by the intervention of the U.S. Environmental Protection Agency, which mandated new air pollution controls at the oil terminal in the sound.[23]

Despite this history of confrontation, the RCAC progressively developed collaborative strategies that led to significant enhancements in the safeguards against marine oil pollution in Prince William Sound. These collaborative strategies consist of a series of partnerships involving the RCAC, the oil industry, public administrators, and other participants. This study finds evidence of collaborative strategies being used both for the analysis of policy issues and for the implementation of policy changes in the marine oil trade of Prince William Sound. These examples of collaborative policy analysis and collaborative policy implementation are described in the following sections.

10.7 Collaborative Policy Analysis and Implementation

10.7.1 Collaborative Policy Analysis: The Tug Vessel Dispute

Between 1991 and 1998 the RCAC and the regional oil industry engaged in a series of discussions and debates over the capabilities of the tug vessels used to escort oil tankers in Prince William Sound.[24] Tug escort vessels can assist in the prevention of oil spills by providing additional propulsion and steering for oil tankers that encounter navigational or mechanical problems. Some tug vessels are also equipped with marine firefighting and oil spill response capabilities. State and federal regulations enacted after the *Exxon Valdez* disaster require that two tug vessels escort each tanker laden with oil throughout the passage in Prince William Sound.[25]

Between 1992 and 1998 the RCAC collaborated with the oil industry, U.S. Coast Guard, and ADEC in several studies that informed their discussions concerning tug escort vessels.[26] In 1991 the RCAC raised concerns over the capabilities of the tug escort system in the sound.[27] In 1992 the concerns of the RCAC led to a collaborative study designed to examine the ability of the tug escort system in the sound to prevent a disabled tanker from running aground under extreme conditions. This tug escort study was conducted as a collaborative project involving the RCAC, oil industry, ADEC, and the U.S. Coast Guard.[28]

The results of the tug escort study (released in 1994) demonstrated that there were certain conditions under which a fully laden oil tanker could run aground in the sound, despite the assistance of the existing tug escort system. In response to the results of the tug escort study, the oil industry and U.S. Coast Guard instituted a series of changes in oil tanker navigation and escort procedures intended to counteract this newly revealed risk in the system.[29] However, the tug escort study also set the stage for a major policy dispute between the RCAC and the oil industry. In 1994 the RCAC recommended that the tug escort system in the sound be reinforced by the use of new *tractor tug* escort vessels with enhanced maneuvering and propulsion systems. Tractor tug vessels possessed advanced maneuvering capabilities beyond those of the conventional tug vessels then used to escort laden oil tankers in the sound. The RCAC also recommended the deployment of an *ocean rescue* tug vessel with an enhanced propulsion system in the sound. The RCAC argued that the advanced capabilities of these new tug vessels would reduce the risk of an oil spill in the sound.[30] The oil industry initially opposed the proposal to deploy new tug vessels in the sound as an unnecessary expense, on the grounds that existing studies did not demonstrate that these new tug vessels would enhance the safety of the marine oil trade in the sound.[31]

The eventual resolution of the tug vessel dispute demonstrates an approach to collaboration referred to in the literature as collaborative analysis.[32] Collaborative analysis aims to overcome suspicions of distorted communication in a policy dispute by giving each group in a policy dispute the means to assure that the other groups are not manipulating the analysis. In a collaborative analysis, the groups involved in a policy dispute collaborate to assemble and oversee a joint research team. The goal of the joint research team is to construct a single technical analysis of the disputed issue that will be acceptable to all of the participating groups. Representatives from all of the participating groups work together to select the members of the joint research team, and those representatives also work together to monitor and adjust the joint research project throughout its development. The participating groups pool their resources (e.g., finances, information, equipment) to support the research project.[33]

Collaborative analysis offers several benefits as a means for managing policy disputes involving contested knowledge. First, collaborative analysis can increase the total resources available for the research project (because the participating groups pool their resources). Second, collaborative analysis creates multiple opportunities for the representatives and researchers to learn from each other. Third, collaborative analysis impedes the ability of any of the participants to surreptitiously manipulate the analysis (because each participant has the means to monitor and adjust the research throughout its development). This process also provides a means of counteracting suspicions of manipulated and mistaken analyses among the participants. By allowing the participants to relieve their suspicions of distorted knowledge claims, collaborative analysis increases the likelihood that the project will generate mutually credible results that can be used as the basis for policy negotiations and agreements.[34]

The dynamics of the tug vessel dispute in Prince William Sound provided an example of collaborative analysis in practice. In 1995 the oil industry proposed to resolve the tug vessel dispute through a comprehensive risk assessment of the marine oil trade in the sound. The oil industry agreed to conduct the risk assessment as a jointly managed study with the RCAC, ADEC, and the U.S. Coast Guard. The RCAC and oil industry used the risk assessment as an opportunity to employ collaborative analysis in the resolution of a technically intensive dispute.[35] The interviews revealed that the risk assessment was consciously structured by the participants to avoid the dilemma of adversarial analysis. Suspicions of distorted communication initially pervaded the debate on new tug vessels in the sound. These suspicions made it difficult for any one group in the debate to generate analyses that would be credible to the contesting groups. In describing the likely reaction of the RCAC and local community members to a risk assessment sponsored solely by the oil industry, an oil industry manager remarked that "they would just laugh at us." A member of the RCAC agreed that "nobody would have believed any of it." An ADEC manager added that "we would have been suspicious of it too." A scientist who worked on the risk assessment noted that the participants were concerned about the potential for attempts "to sway the project one way or another."

The collaborative approach to analysis embodied in the risk assessment was therefore structured to allow the participants to relieve their suspicions of manipulated analysis. To accomplish this goal, the project was designed to minimize the possibility of hidden actions by any of the participants in the conduct of the study. The risk assessment was directed throughout by a steering committee consisting of RCAC members, oil industry managers, and public administrators.[36] The initial risk assessment meetings contained the seeds of adversarial analysis. The oil industry representatives hired one team of experts to work on the study; the RCAC representatives responded by hiring their own team of experts. In a conscious attempt to avoid the possibility of adversarial analysis, the steering committee then decided to pursue the study by combining these expert advisors into a single research team. By doing this, an ADEC representative concluded, the steering committee "avoided dueling scientists." The members of the steering committee then agreed to direct the study by a process of unanimous consent and also agreed to share the costs of the project.[37]

Interviews with 10 participants in the risk assessment—seven members of the steering committee, and three members of the research team—were used to identify the effects of collaborative analysis in the tug vessel dispute. As predicted by the collaborative analysis model, the risk assessment promoted mutual learning among the participants. The participants met 15 times throughout the course of the study, which allowed the members of the steering committee and research team to interact and learn from each other as the study evolved. All 10 of the participants who were interviewed agreed that this process allowed the steering committee to gain a better understanding of the technical dimensions of maritime risk assessment. Reflecting on the learning achievements of the steering committee, a member of the research team concluded that "by the end there wasn't much—at a very deep level of the technical processes—that they didn't understand." The research team also learned from the steering committee, which took an active role in assuring that the data used in the risk assessment models were as complete and accurate as possible. A member of the research team commented that this process "increased our understanding of the problem domain and enabled us to get lots of data which we didn't think was available .... The assumptions were brought out in painful detail and explained." The basic data used to inform the initial risk assessment models included historical maritime records, weather data, and vessel traffic data. In the course of the study, the participants concluded that existing maritime records were an insufficient source of data for the risk assessment models. The steering committee therefore decided to draw on the knowledge of the maritime community in the sound as an additional source of data. Steering committee members representing the RCAC and the oil industry then helped the researchers to gather local knowledge on weather, currents, and vessel traffic patterns from mariners in the sound.[38]

The risk assessment closely followed the model of collaborative analysis previously introduced. Suspicions of distorted communication were clearly present at the beginning of the process. The potential for these suspicions to evoke the dilemma of adversarial analysis was recognized by the participants. The participants agreed to counteract this threat by combining their researchers and resources and by monitoring and adjusting the research in a collaborative manner. As a result, material support for the research was enhanced; the participants learned from each other; and the participants were able to counteract the suspicions of distorted communication that had characterized the early stages of the debate. All 10 of the participants who were interviewed agreed that this joint study was more credible to the RCAC than a study of this issue commissioned solely by the oil industry. A member of the steering committee representing the oil industry concluded that this collaborative process "gave the RCAC a feeling that there was no hidden agenda or conspiracy."

The results of the risk assessment were unanimously accepted as valid by the RCAC, oil industry, and government agencies involved in the tug vessel dispute. The participating groups agreed that the study showed the need for an ocean rescue tug vessel in the sound. In 1997 the oil industry responded by deploying an ocean rescue tug vessel in the sound.[39] The policy changes that followed the release of the risk assessment revealed the interaction of politics with analysis in shaping the conclusion of the tug vessel dispute. The interviews revealed that the models used in the risk assessment did not determine if tractor tug vessels would systematically outperform conventional tug vessels in the escort mission. However, the tug vessel debate was further informed by additional collaborative studies that examined (1) different tug vessel technologies and (2) the *best available technology* requirement in Alaska state law (which mandated the use of the best available technology for safeguards against marine oil pollution). These additional studies were conducted as collaborative projects involving the RCAC, ADEC, and the oil industry. Information gathered in these additional studies demonstrated that tractor tug vessels could outmaneuver conventional tug vessels.[40] With support from the governor of Alaska, ADEC held that the advanced maneuvering capabilities of tractor tug vessels constituted the best available technology in the escort mission. Between 1999 and 2001, the regional oil industry responded to the best available technology decision by deploying five new tractor tug escort vessels in the sound. All five of these new tractor tug vessels were equipped with oil spill response equipment and marine firefighting equipment.[41]

Collaborative analysis allowed the participants in the tug vessel dispute to overcome their suspicions of distorted communication. This collaborative approach allowed the risk assessment participants to build a mutually acceptable foundation of knowledge that led to significant policy change. However, the conclusion of the tug vessel dispute was shaped not only by the choice of collaborative analysis as a means of building knowledge but also by decisions made by public administrators working for the state of Alaska (who in turn were supported by provisions in state law and also supported by the Alaska governor). In sum, the issue of tug escort vessels in the sound provides an example of strategic collaboration applied for the purpose of policy analysis. Other examples of collaboration examined in the following sections demonstrate the application of strategic collaboration not only for the analysis of policy issues but also for the implementation of policy changes.

10.7.2 Collaborative Policy Analysis and Implementation: Marine Ice Detection

Marine ice poses significant hazards to oil tankers in Prince William Sound.[42] Before 1989, marine ice monitoring in the sound occurred periodically through vessel reports and satellite imagery. In 1993 the RCAC conducted a survey of oil tanker officers that indicated a need for better marine ice reporting in the sound.[43] In particular, the Columbia Glacier (a tidewater glacier in the sound) was generating numerous icebergs that drifted into the tanker lanes of the sound. The RCAC collaborated with two regional research organizations to support iceberg monitoring research on the Columbia Glacier; this collaborative research found that the flow of marine ice from the Columbia Glacier into the shipping lanes of the sound would probably increase for a period of years to decades. The RCAC also studied a variety of systems for improved marine ice detection in collaboration with NOAA, the Canadian Coast Guard, the oil industry, and an engineering firm.[44]

In 2001 the RCAC embarked on a collaborative project to deploy a new radar system for marine ice detection in Prince William Sound, located on an island near the Columbia Glacier. This marine ice detection radar became operational in 2002 through a multilateral collaboration including contributions from the RCAC, U.S. Coast Guard, U.S. Army, NOAA, ADEC, the regional oil industry, a research organization, and a local community college. In addition to its ice detection function, the radar site would serve as a research and development platform for new technologies designed to enhance marine ice detection.[45] In a 2003 report, a U.S. Coast Guard commander in the region noted that the new marine ice detection system in the sound represented "the best internationally available ice detection technology in existence."[46] In sum, the deployment of a new marine ice detection system in the sound is the result of a multilateral collaboration involving the RCAC, the oil industry, public administrators, and other participants. The issue of marine ice detection in the sound provides an example of strategic collaboration applied for the dual purposes of policy analysis and policy implementation.

10.7.3 Collaborative Policy Implementation: Weather Reporting Systems

Severe weather conditions pose significant hazards to oil tanker navigation in the coastal regions of Alaska, and weather reporting therefore constitutes an important element of navigational safety in Alaska. In 1993 the RCAC conducted a survey of oil tanker officers that indicated a need for better weather reporting in the sound. In the same year, the RCAC proposed the deployment of new weather reporting equipment to fill gaps in the weather monitoring system in the sound, with the goal of reducing the risks posed by severe weather to oil tankers in that region.[47] In an interview, an oil industry manager commented on the value of weather reporting for the marine oil trade in the sound by noting that "the more information you have, the safer you can be." The RCAC proposal was supported by the oil industry, ADEC, and the U.S. Coast Guard. In response, two members of Alaska's congressional delegation sought out federal funding for the new equipment. With the support of federal funding administered through NOAA, new weather reporting equipment was deployed by the U.S. Coast Guard at four sites in the sound in 1995.[48] In 1998, weather reporting equipment was added at a fifth site in the sound. In 2002, networks of additional weather reporting stations were installed in the sound through collaborative projects involving the RCAC, the U.S. Coast Guard, a regional research organization, and local communities.[49] In sum, the deployment of new weather reporting equipment in Prince William Sound has occurred through a series of multilateral collaborations involving the RCAC, public administrators, and other organizations. The issue of weather reporting in the sound serves as an example of strategic collaboration applied for the purpose of policy implementation.

10.7.4 Collaborative Policy Implementation: Marine and Terminal Firefighting

Oil tanker and oil terminal fires can cause massive damages and trigger marine oil spills. Fires therefore present significant hazards in the Alaskan oil trade. In 1992 the RCAC collaborated with the U.S. Coast Guard, the oil industry, and a local community to form a fire protection task force in the sound. The work of the task force led to an oil terminal fire protection exercise in 1993, followed by another terminal fire exercise in 2002.[50] In 1996 the RCAC funded a study of marine fire response in the sound. The study recommended the development of a program to train land-based firefighters in marine firefighting.[51] In an interview, an RCAC staff member summarized the implications of the study for the firefighting teams in the sound: "They had enough resources and equipment to deal with a major fire incident. The problem was that there was no integrated training going on." In particular, shipboard fires posed unusual challenges for land-based firefighters (e.g., confined spaces, hazardous cargo, the possibility of sinking the vessel with the water used to fight the fires). These challenges created the need for training that integrated the skills of land-based firefighting and marine firefighting.[52] The RCAC subsequently collaborated with the oil industry, U.S. Coast Guard, state and local governments, and a local community college to sponsor four marine firefighting training symposia in the sound (in 1997, 1999, 2003, and 2005). These symposia trained land-based firefighters in the strategies needed to effectively combat a major fire aboard oil tankers and other marine vessels.[53] In sum, the development of marine and terminal firefighting exercises and training symposia in the sound is the result of multilateral collaborations involving the RCAC, the oil industry, and public administrators. The issue of marine and terminal firefighting in the sound serves as a further example of strategic collaboration applied for the purpose of policy implementation.

10.8 Conceptual Lessons

The conceptual lessons of this study focus on the successful application of collaboration for policy analysis and policy implementation. In particular, the findings of this study provide empirical support for the concept of collaboration as a viable strategy both for the analysis of policy issues (e.g., the issues of tug escort vessels and marine ice detection in the sound) and for the implementation of policy reforms (e.g., the deployment of a new marine ice detection system and new weather reporting equipment in the sound). For example, collaborative analysis allows the participants to combine their resources and expertise in the joint study of contested policy issues. Collaborative analysis also allows the participants to exercise joint oversight over the research process. Collaborative analysis can therefore allow the participants to enhance their support for the research process, and can also allow the participants to overcome the possibilities (and suspicions) of distorted communication that are inherent in the adversarial approach to analysis. The conceptual advantages of collaborative analysis are demonstrated by the tug vessel debate examined in this study. Some of the benefits of collaborative analysis have parallels in collaborative strategies for policy implementation. Collaborative policy implementation allows the participants to combine their resources and expertise to enhance support for policy implementation projects. The combining of resources through collaborative policy implementation proved particularly important in securing the deployment of a marine ice detection system in the sound (accomplished with support from the RCAC, oil industry, federal agencies, and other organizations). Overall, the findings of this study support the idea of strategic collaboration as an important and consequential concept in the study of environmental management and public administration.[54]

10.9 Lessons for Practice

Several practical lessons in strategic collaboration can be drawn from this study. These lessons include the possibility of creating collaboration from a history of conflict, the feasibility of involving local citizens in complex policy issues, and the vital role played by public administrators in enabling the implementation of collaborative policy reforms. First, this study demonstrates the possibility of designing institutional arrangements that allow the participants in a policy domain to shift their interactions from discord to collaboration over time. The management of the marine oil trade in Prince William Sound was once marked by a lack of cooperation between local citizens and the oil industry, and that lack of cooperation was evident in the dispute over air pollution emissions from the oil terminal in the sound. Yet this study finds that the RCAC, oil industry, and government agencies in this policy domain have adopted a systematic strategy of strategic collaboration over time. This sustained strategy of collaboration has proven effective in promoting enhancements to the safeguards against marine oil pollution in the sound. Second, this study demonstrates the feasibility of involving local citizens in collaborative policy efforts of significant complexity. In essence, the RCAC is an institutional arrangement for citizen participation that has developed over time into an agent for multilateral collaboration. The findings of this study indicate that the RCAC is an effective institutional agent for the constructive involvement of local citizens in the collaborative management of a complex and hazardous marine transportation system. Finally, this study finds that public administrators have played pivotal roles in enabling the implementation of policy proposals emerging from strategic collaborative efforts (reflecting the resources and regulatory authority available to those public administrators).

10.10 Conclusions and Remaining Questions

Overall, this study demonstrates the feasibility of using a citizens' advisory council as an institutional agent for enduring collaborative efforts involving local citizens, industry, and public administrators. Furthermore, this study demonstrates that such strategic collaborative efforts can lead to concrete policy changes. The collaborative efforts examined in this study have produced significant policy changes in the form of new tug escort vessels, marine ice detection equipment, weather reporting equipment, and training for marine and terminal firefighting. In the marine oil trade of Prince William Sound, collaboration has proven to be an effective strategy both for the analysis of policy issues and for the implementation of policy changes.

The findings of this study suggest several questions for further research. The first research question concerns the potential for the success of similar citizen-based collaborative efforts in other environmental policy domains. The policy dynamics examined in this study are marked by sustained collaborative efforts overcoming a history of discord between the participants. An important question for further research is the extent to which disputes in other environmental policy domains might be overcome by similar collaborative efforts. The second research question concerns the role of disasters and crises in triggering the establishment of citizen-based collaborative efforts. The findings of this study indicate that the 1989 *Exxon Valdez* disaster triggered institutional reforms that promoted collaboration in the marine oil trade of Alaska, as noted in the proceedings of a 1999 conference concluding that "the spill forged a partnership that has assessed risks, pioneered innovative technologies, and continues to implement improvements designed to achieve the safest marine transportation system in the world."[55] Therefore, another important question for further research is the extent to which disasters and crises can create windows of opportunity for the establishment of institutional reforms that promote citizen-based collaboration in various environmental policy domains.[56] A third important question for further research is the extent to which the dynamics (and policy consequences) of citizen-based collaborative strategies vary according to the varying characteristics of the environmental policy domains in which those collaborative strategies are attempted. Answering these research questions will require comparative studies that examine the effects of citizen-based collaborative strategies across a broad array of environmental policy domains.

Endnotes

1. Alaska Oil Spill Commission, *Spill: The Wreck of the Exxon Valdez* (Juneau: State of Alaska, 1990).
2. G.J. Busenberg, Citizen Participation and Collaborative Environmental Management in the Marine Oil Trade of Coastal Alaska, *Coastal Management, 35*: 239–253, 2007.

3. T.L. Cooper, T.A. Bryer, and J.W. Meek, Citizen-Centered Collaborative Public Management, *Public Administration Review, 66* (Supplement 1): 76–88, 2006; T.M. Koontz and C.W. Thomas, What Do We Know and Need to Know about the Environmental Outcomes of Collaborative Management? *Public Administration Review, 66* (Supplement 1): 111–121, 2006.

4. R.K. Yin, *Case Study Research: Design and Methods* (3d ed., Thousand Oaks, CA: Sage Publications, 2003).

5. Alaska Oil Spill Commission, *Spill*; Busenberg, Citizen Participation; Busenberg, Managing the Hazard of Marine Oil Pollution in Alaska, *Review of Policy Research, 25* (3): 203–218, 2008; Prince William Sound Regional Citizens' Advisory Council (PWS RCAC), *Then and Now: Changes since the Exxon Valdez Oil Spill* (Anchorage, AK: PWS RCAC, 1993); PWS RCAC, *Then and Now—Changes in Oil Transportation since the Exxon Valdez Spill: 1989–1999* (Anchorage, AK: PWS RCAC, 1999).

6. T.A. Birkland, *After Disaster: Agenda Setting, Public Policy, and Focusing Events* (Washington, DC: Georgetown University Press, 1997); Busenberg, Citizen Participation; Busenberg, Managing the Hazard.

7. Alaska Oil Spill Commission, *Spill*, p. 37.

8. PWS RCAC, *Then and Now—Changes in Oil Transportation*, p. 26.

9. U.S. Oil Pollution Act of 1990, Public Law 101-380, 104 STAT. 545.

10. PWS RCAC, *1991 Annual Report* (Anchorage, AK: PWS RCAC, 1991).

11. PWS RCAC, *1991 Annual Report;* PWS RCAC, *2006–2007 in Review* (Anchorage, AK: PWS RCAC, 2007).

12. PWS RCAC, *2006–2007 in Review.*

13. Busenberg, Citizen Participation.

14. PWS RCAC, *1991 Annual Report*; PWS RCAC, *Then and Now—Changes in Oil Transportation.*

15. Busenberg, Citizen Participation.

16. Busenberg, Managing the Hazard.

17. PWS RCAC, *1991 Annual Report.*

18. Alaska Oil Spill Commission, *Spill*; Busenberg, Managing the Hazard.

19. PWS RCAC, *2006–2007 in Review.*

20. PWS RCAC, *Observer, 3* (1), Anchorage, AK: Prince William Sound RCAC, 1993.

21. Busenberg, Collaborative and Adversarial Analysis in Environmental Policy, *Policy Sciences, 32*: 1–11, 1999; C.P. Ozawa, *Recasting Science: Consensual Procedures in Public Policy Making* (Boulder, CO: Westview Press, 1991); Ozawa and L. Susskind, Mediating Science-Intensive Policy Disputes, *Journal of Policy Analysis and Management, 5* (1): 23–39, 1985.

22. Busenberg, Collaborative and Adversarial Analysis; PWS RCAC, *Observer 3* (1).

23. PWS RCAC, *Observer, 4* (1), Anchorage, AK: PWS RCAC, 1994; PWS RCAC, *Observer, 4* (2), Anchorage, AK: PWS RCAC, 1994; PWS RCAC, *Observer, 5* (3), Anchorage, AK: Prince William Sound RCAC, 1995; PWS RCAC, *Observer, 8* (1), Anchorage, AK: Prince William Sound RCAC, 1998.

24. PWS RCAC, *Observer, 1* (2), Anchorage, AK: PWS RCAC, 1991; PWS RCAC, *Observer, 5* (3).

25. PWS RCAC, *Then and Now: Changes since the Exxon Valdez*; PWS RCAC, *Observer,* 4 (4), Anchorage, AK: PWS RCAC, 1994; PWS RCAC, *Then and Now—Changes in Oil Transportation*; PWS RCAC, *Observer, 15* (1), Anchorage, AK: PWS RCAC, 2005; PWS RCAC, *2004–2005 in Review*, Anchorage, AK: PWS RCAC, 2005; PWS RCAC, *2006–2007 in Review*.

26. Busenberg, Managing the Hazard; PWS RCAC, *1991 Annual Report*; PWS RCAC, *Observer, 1* (2); PWS RCAC, *Observer, 4* (4).

27. PWS RCAC, *1991 Annual Report*; PWS RCAC, *Observer, 1* (2).

28. PWS RCAC, *Observer 1* (2); PWS RCAC, *Oil Spill Prevention: Improvements in Tanker Safety* (Anchorage, AK: PWS RCAC, 1995).

29. PWS RCAC, *Observer, 4* (4); PWS RCAC, *Oil Spill Prevention*.

30. PWS RCAC, Observer, *4* (4).

31. PWS RCAC, Observer, *4* (4); PWS RCAC, *Observer 5* (2); PWS RCAC, *Observer, 5* (4); PWS RCAC, *Oil Spill Prevention*.

32. Busenberg, Collaborative and Adversarial Analysis; Ozawa, *Recasting Science*.

33. Ibid.

34. Ibid.

35. PWS RCAC, *Observer, 5* (2).

36. PWS RCAC, *Observer, 7* (1), Anchorage, AK: PWS RCAC, 1997.

37. PWS RCAC, *Observer, 5* (4).

38. Busenberg, Collaborative and Adversarial Analysis.

39. PWS RCAC, *Observer, 7* (2), Anchorage, AK: PWS RCAC, 1997.

40. Busenberg, Managing the Hazard; PWS RCAC, *Observer, 5* (2); PWS RCAC, *Observer, 5* (4); PWS RCAC, *Observer, 7* (1).

41. Busenberg, Managing the Hazard; PWS RCAC, *Observer, 7* (2); PWS RCAC, *1998–1999 in Review* (Anchorage, AK: PWS RCAC, 1999); PWS RCAC, *Then and Now—Changes in Oil Transportation*; PWS RCAC, *1999–2000 in Review* (Anchorage, AK: PWS RCAC, 2000).

42. Alaska Oil Spill Commission, *Spill*; PWS RCAC, *Oil Spill Prevention*.

43. PWS RCAC, *1993 a Year in Review* (Anchorage, AK: PWS RCAC, 1993); PWS RCAC, *Observer, 4* (1).

44. PWS RCAC, *1996 a Year in Review* (Anchorage, AK: PWS RCAC, 1996); PWS RCAC, *Observer, 6* (3), Anchorage, AK: PWS RCAC, 1996; PWS RCAC, *Observer, 7* (3), Anchorage, AK: PWS RCAC, 1997; PWS RCAC, *1997–1998 in Review* (Anchorage, AK: PWS RCAC, 1998); PWS RCAC, *1998–1999 in Review*; PWS RCAC, *2000–2001 in Review* (Anchorage, AK: PWS RCAC, 2001); PWS RCAC, *2001–2002 in Review* (Anchorage, AK: PWS RCAC, 2002).

45. PWS RCAC, *Observer 9* (2), Anchorage, AK: PWS RCAC, 1999; PWS RCAC, *Observer 10* (1), Anchorage, AK: PWS RCAC, 2000; PWS RCAC, *1999–2000 in Review*; PWS RCAC, *2000–2001 in Review*; PWS RCAC, *Observer, 11* (4), Anchorage, AK: PWS RCAC, 2001; PWS RCAC, *2001–2002 in Review*; PWS RCAC, *Observer, 12* (1), Anchorage, AK: PWS RCAC, 2002; PWS RCAC, *Observer, 13* (1), Anchorage, AK: PWS RCAC, 2003; PWS RCAC, *2002–2003 Year in Review* (Anchorage, AK: PWS RCAC, 2003).

46. PWS RCAC, *Observer 13* (1), Anchorage, AK: PWS RCAC, 2003, p. 3.

47. PWS RCAC, *1993 a Year in Review*; PWS RCAC, *Observer, 4* (1); PWS RCAC, *Observer, 4* (2); PWS RCAC, *Observer 5* (2); PWS RCAC, *Oil Spill Prevention*.

48. PWS RCAC, *Observer, 3* (2); PWS RCAC, *Observer, 4* (2); PWS RCAC, *Observer, 4* (4); PWS RCAC, *Observer, 5* (2).

49. Busenberg, Citizen Participation; PWS RCAC, *Then and Now—Changes in Oil Transportation*; PWS RCAC, *2002–2003 Year in Review*; PWS RCAC, *2003–2004 Year in Review*.

50. PWS RCAC, *Observer 3* (3); PWS RCAC, *2001–2002 in Review*.

51. PWS RCAC, *1996 a Year in Review*; PWS RCAC, *Observer, 7* (1).

52. PWS RCAC, *Observer, 13* (4), Anchorage, AK: PWS RCAC, 2003.

53. PWS RCAC, *Observer, 7* (2); PWS RCAC, *Observer, 7* (3); PWS RCAC, *Observer, 9* (2); PWS RCAC, *1999–2000 in Review*; PWS RCAC, *Observer 13* (4); PWS RCAC, *Observer, 15* (1), Anchorage, AK: PWS RCAC, 2005; PWS RCAC, *Observer 15* (3), Anchorage, AK: PWS RCAC, 2005; PWS RCAC, *2004–2005 in Review*.

54. R.D. Bidwell and C.M. Ryan, Collaborative Partnership Design: The Implications of Organizational Affiliation for Watershed Partnerships, *Society and Natural Resources,* 19: 827–843, 2006; Busenberg, Collaborative and Adversarial Analysis; Busenberg, Citizen Participation; Cooper et al., Citizen-Centered; Koontz, T.A. Steelman, J. Carmin, J.S. Korfmacher, C. Moseley, and C.W. Thomas, *Collaborative Environmental Management: What Roles for Government?* (Washington, DC: Resources for the Future Press, 2004); Koontz and Thomas, What Do We Know.

55. R. Salvador, *Partners in Prevention: A Decade of Progress in Prince William Sound* (Valdez, AK: PWS RCAC, 1999, p. 2).

56. Birkland, *After Disaster*; J.W. Kingdon, *Agendas, Alternatives, and Public Policies* (2d ed., New York: Longman, 1995).

Chapter 11

Paving the Way for Public Transportation in Texas through Public Collaboration

Sarmistha R. Majumdar, Jason Pierce, and Colleen Moynihan

Contents

Case Brief

Background and Purpose of the Collaboration: Denton County is one of the fastest growing counties in northern Texas. Pollution in this region has caused the Environmental Protection Agency (EPA) to designate Denton County as part of the Dallas–Fort Worth eight-hour nonattainment area of ozone. As a result, a group of local residents and local and state elected officials from Denton County petitioned the Texas Legislature for a means to address severe highway congestion caused by the exponential population growth and low state transportation funding. The 78th Texas Legislature in 2001 enacted legislation to create a Coordinated County Transportation Authority in urban "collar" counties adjacent to counties with a population of one million or more, which included Denton County. In 2002, the Denton County Transit Authority (DCTA) was created as a countywide public agency to provide public transportation services (bus and rail) to both residents and nonresidents of Denton County. The collaboration's overall purpose was to ease local traffic congestion, improve air quality, and promote economic development in the region and to meet federal government requirements to comply with the National Environmental Policy Act (NEPA). Since public input is required in development of the final plan, collaboration with the public and other stakeholders was deemed essential. During the period of February 2006 to February 2007, DCTA involved a wide range of stakeholders around issues including route alignment, proposed station locations, engineering design, environmental impacts, and mitigation measures. A similar routine was followed for the Citizens' Advisory Group (CAG), which consisted of concerned neighborhood residents, commuters, educational institutions, and special interest groups.

Current Status: The Technical Advisory Group, composed of bureaucrats from local, state, and federal government offices and the CAG collaborated to exchange information in a timely manner, enabling DCTA to build a stable and trusting relationship with the various local government partners and to decide on a subsequent course of action. Similar success was not experienced in its efforts to collaborate with the public through the use of community roundtables.

Lessons for Strategic Collaboration Practice: This case illustrates the many different types of participants important to strategic collaboration. The collaborative strategies used were successful with the professional audiences to generate useful information and relationships. However, in this case, the required involvement of citizens in the decision processes was not effective, as the collaborators did not sufficiently understand the sociodemographic characteristics of the population and the history of the region in developing collaborative strategies to include community members. Processes must be redesigned when information indicates that they are not working as desired. Public engagement strategies must communicate effectively with target audiences to gather useful information, to bring a diverse set of participants to the table, and to encourage dialogue and feedback if meaningful and inclusionary decision making is to occur.

11.1 Introduction

Collaboration is an action plan for cooperation among organizations, citizens and various stakeholders. It calls for genuine teamwork and negotiation along with sharing of information with citizens and public administrators.[1] Since the 1990s the realization that the success of any government organization depends upon its ability to work with others has made public officials develop a positive attitude toward collaboration. In fact, the 21st century has been proposed as the "era of collaborative state."[2] Currently, we find that more and more organizations are making the strategic choice to collaborate as a means to an effective outcome. For example, in Denton, Texas, a nonprofit transportation agency, the Denton County Transportation Authority (DCTA), has collaborated with the public to ease local traffic congestion and improve air quality in the region. Here, the officials in their collaborative roles have not assumed the role of leaders by virtue of their power or knowledge. Instead, they are the "social players in the theatre of state" and have accepted the responsibility of continuously improving citizens' lives.[3]

"In the meeting they responded with very little information and a lot of rhetoric. They talked a lot and said nothing. Well, one specific question was who makes the decisions or who is going to make the decisions, because the people talking to us weren't the decision makers. They then said the board will. So then I asked, Well who is here from the board? Are there any board members?"

11.2 The Situational Context of Collaboration

Denton County is one of the fastest growing counties in northern Texas. The air pollution in this region has caused the Environmental Protection Agency (EPA) to designate Denton County as part of the Dallas–Fort Worth eight-hour nonattainment area of ozone. To address these problems, a group of local residents and local and state elected officials from Denton County petitioned the Texas Legislature to provide a means whereby the county could address severe highway congestion caused by the exponential population growth and low state transportation funding. The 78th Texas Legislature in 2001 enacted legislation that paved the way for the creation of a Coordinated County Transportation Authority in urban "collar" counties adjacent to counties with a population of one million or more, which included Denton County.

In June 2002, after a series of public meetings, the interim committee adopted a service plan that focused on four goals: (1) improving transportation for the county and the region; (2) improving the quality of life for Denton County residents; (3) improving air quality; and (4) promoting economic development. After the service plan was adopted, a countywide election was held in November in which 73% voted to create the Denton County Transportation Authority, a countywide public agency that was to provide public transportation services to both residents and nonresidents of Denton County.

Once DCTA was established, an election was called in eight municipalities, through which a commuter transit route was proposed with the imposition of a one-half cent city sales tax allocation for its funding. The referendum was approved in three of the eight communities. Today, DCTA collects approximately $1.1 million per month from local sales tax collections to fund its public transportation services. The service plan of DCTA includes multiple rail components—regional rail, three layers of bus service (regional connector bus service, local routes, and demand response service), and a network of park-and-ride/regional rail facilities. Regional rail is the central element of DCTA's service plan. The regional rail system will provide rail service in Denton County by connecting to the Dallas Area Rapid Transit (DART) system's light rail transit facilities in Carrollton, Texas. Thus, strategic collaboration played a key role in DCTA's ability to develop a seamless rail and bus service for its riders as well as riders from DART and to garner public support for the service.

11.3 Partners in Collaboration

Public involvement and collaboration played an intricate and vital role in every step of the creation process, from the development of the service plan and the election creating DCTA to the imposition of its funding source. In development of a regional rail service plan to connect the five largest cities in the county of Denton, DCTA conducted two alternative analyses in 2004 and 2005. By examining the current and future transportation problems in the region along with the demography, land use, and travel demand, public involvement was deemed essential since the proposed route would pass through several residential neighborhoods.

DCTA communicated information to municipalities, community residents, and other stakeholders including local educational institutions and businesses that were likely to be impacted by the regional rail project. Further, because the light rail route plan had to be in conformity with a community's goals and land use practices, approval was required from city council members and residents of neighborhoods. To enable local government officials and citizens to make an informed decision, DCTA collaborated with the affected public and local governments.[4] Additionally, the project required permission from the North Central Texas Council of Governments (NCTCOG) and local regulatory and transportation agencies. Technical assistance had to be sought from existing transit operators such as DART to develop a feasible engineering design. To address the concerns of various stakeholders and to meet regional, local, state, and federal government requirements, DCTA's staff members, in conjunction with the rail project's management team, developed a comprehensive public involvement plan (PIP).

The PIP included strategies to involve various professionals, government administrators, council members, concerned stakeholders, and organized interest groups in the decision-making process. Plans were developed to share information with the public and stakeholders and to provide them with the opportunity to provide inputs. Several events were planned to engage concerned citizens in meaningful discussions and to educate them both on technical issues and economic details of the project. All these planned activities were considered crucial in obtaining consent and support for the project.

Additionally, DCTA had to meet federal government requirements to comply with the National Environmental Policy Act (NEPA), which requires any project with environmental consequences or if deemed environmentally controversial to prepare a draft of environmental impact statement (DEIS). The DEIS is required to include proposals and alternate plans and document that the public is to be provided with the opportunity to voice opinions and pass comments on the draft plan.[5] Since public input is required in development of the final plan, collaboration with the public and other stakeholders was critical (Figure 11.1).

11.4 Process and Procedures Used in Collaboration

To make collaboration effective, DCTA organized its partners into three groups, with each group having distinct characteristics. The expertise and support of each respective group's members were considered as important in the implementation of the proposed project. The Technical Advisory Group (TAG) was composed of

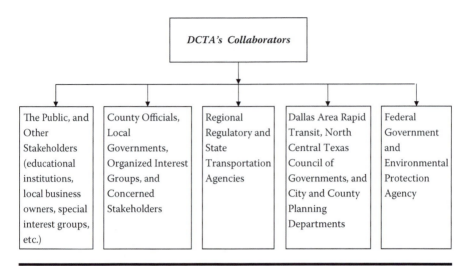

Figure 11.1 DCTA's partners in collaboration.

public administrators from local, state, and federal government offices. The Citizens' Advisory Group (CAG) consisted of concerned neighborhood residents, commuters, educational institutions, and special interest groups. Community roundtables were also organized, and members who either had a known interest in the project or resided in houses or owned businesses adjacent to the proposed rail line were invited to attend. The members in the roundtable were paid $60 each to participate in the focus group discussions. Each group was assigned the responsibility to review technical and nontechnical details of the project, to comment on the DEIS, and to provide inputs for the development of the final plan.[6] During the period of February 2006 to February 2007, four meetings were organized by DCTA. To create awareness about dates and locations of meetings, notices of public meetings were mailed to all persons on the project mailing list including property owners likely to be impacted by the project. Information was posted on the project's website, and the media was extensively encouraged to convey messages about these public hearings and meetings. Local newspapers such as the *Denton Record Chronicle, Lewisville Leader,* and the *Lake City Sun* carried advertisements about the meetings. Public announcements were also made on the local radio and television stations to remind local citizens. Additionally, project newsletters were either mailed or e-mailed to those on the project mailing list. The colorful newsletters not only served as a reminder but also provided information on the project's status, its design, and expected economic and environmental outcomes in neighborhoods and local communities.

At the initial meeting of TAG, the project was introduced to professionals in the field of transportation. This step helped to satisfy the federal government requirements. In subsequent meetings, route alignment, proposed station locations, engineering design, environmental impacts, and mitigation measures were discussed.

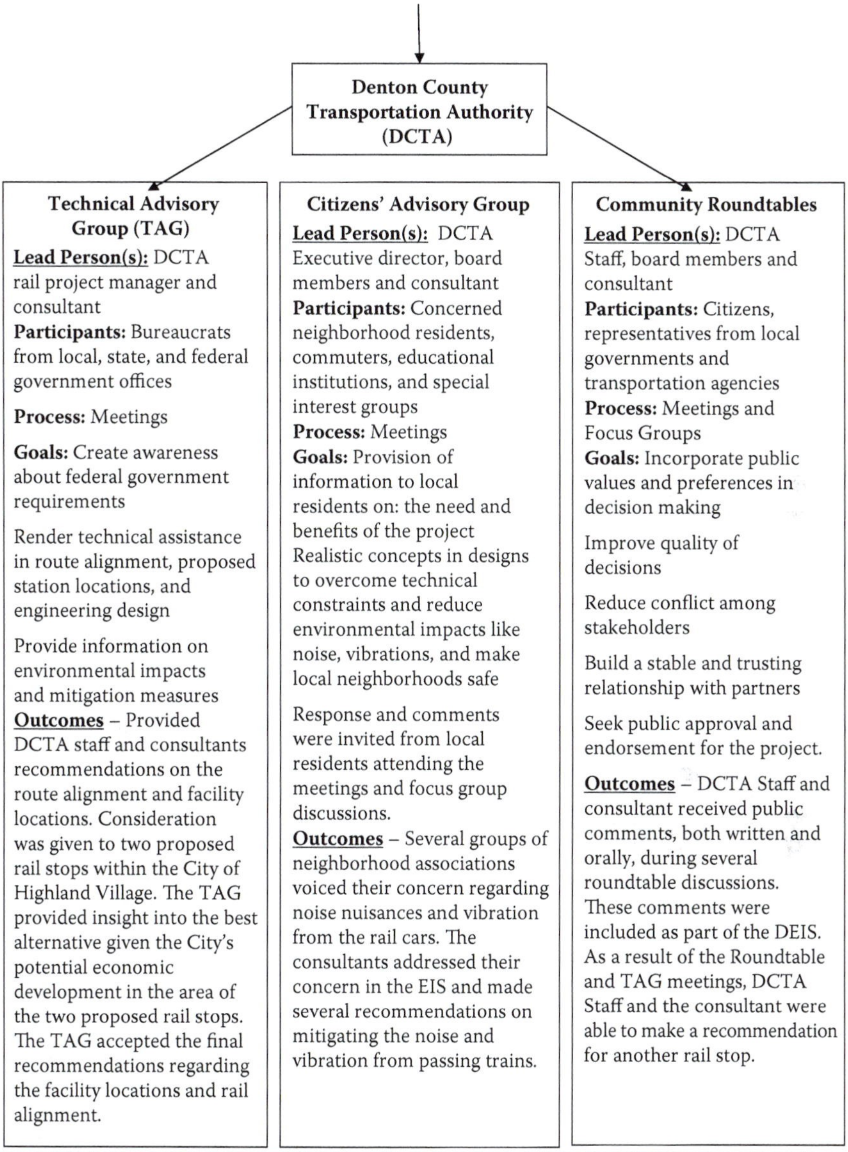

Figure 11.2   DCTA's attempts at collaboration.

A similar routine was followed for the CAG. The community roundtables or focus group discussions were the last to be organized. Here, representatives from local governments and transportation agencies communicated to the laypeople the need for the project along with its realistic concepts in designs that can help to overcome technical constraints and reduce negative environmental impacts such as noise and vibrations (Figure 11.2). There were also discussions on how to make local neighborhoods safe. At each meeting and in focus group discussions, members were additionally encouraged to use comment forms and to communicate with DCTA either through e-mails or letters or by calling the office. All inputs from members were recorded and were later included in a summary report, which is available for public access.

11.5 Measuring Outcomes and Impacts of Collaboration

In review of DCTA's efforts to involve government officials, community groups, and individuals in the decision-making process, it is evident that at times DCTA did deviate from the path of top-down decision making, typical of bureaucratic organizations. Initially, the involvement processes showed commitment toward consensual decision making. The decision to select the eastern rail route was not finalized behind closed doors. Instead, DCTA offered its partners the opportunity to select. Through a study, DCTA identified three alternative rail routes and compared the cost-effectiveness of each route along with other factors such as accessibility to major activity centers, travel time savings, and capital costs. Then DCTA shared the information with the public and various other stakeholders who opted for the eastern route or the Missouri-Kansas-Texas (MKT) route.[7]

From the very beginning, DCTA prioritized dissemination of information along with public education through various means. By granting access to local citizens and their representatives to its office, DCTA expressed the genuine desire to learn about citizens' preferences. It made attempts to collect information from both low-income and minority groups and to incorporate public values in its decision-making process. By adopting a strategic collaborative model, DCTA was able to interact more with local citizens and to assess their needs and immediate concerns. The model helped to obtain and process more information in a systematic manner. It made DCTA realize to a certain extent the weaknesses in its own plans and identify the information gaps that had to be filled prior to seeking public support for its proposed project.

The feedback from various stakeholders helped DCTA to decide on a subsequent course of action and to build a stable and trusting relationship with its community partners. The community roundtables and meetings helped to reduce conflict among stakeholders. Further, the timely inputs from professionals and local government officials helped those involved better improve the substantive quality of decisions while that of the lay members helped to understand the needs and concerns of local citizens in the region.[8]

The entire process of strategic collaboration was time-consuming and expensive, but it helped to make the decision-making process more democratic and worthy of public support. Nevertheless, the public expressed much dissatisfaction with DCTA's collaborative processes. The meetings organized by DCTA were intended to provide the residents of southeast Denton a forum for participation, to communicate their concerns, and to aid the agency's decision-making process. At these public meetings, contrary to the public's expectations, only a small percentage of participants had the opportunity to verbally communicate their concerns due to time constraints.

To obtain insights into DCTA's information-sharing and collection processes, a door-to-door survey of randomly selected residents in a southeastern Denton neighborhood (those who would be directly impacted by the light rail route) was conducted by Moynihan as part of a research study.[9] In this survey, respondents were asked how DCTA responded to their questions at public meetings. Since public meetings are an important component of collaboration, residents' perspectives on the quality of answers provided by DCTA illustrate a breakdown of communication and limited information exchange. The vignette presented at the beginning of this case makes it apparent that the southeast Denton residents were dissatisfied with the quality of answers they received and the manner in which they received them. An individual participating in the survey remarked that meeting organizers "would ignore people with hands up." Some meetings had a high turnout rate, but organizers would stop the meeting after a certain time no matter how many hands were up.

The survey respondents stated that not only were some questions unanswered at public meetings but also that at the next public meeting there would be all new people conducting the meeting with different and more strenuous rules. The overall belief among the surveyed residents was that the transit authority provided them limited information about their greatest concerns. And over 50% of respondents disagreed with the statement, "DCTA has provided accurate information to the community" (Table 11.1). It is evident from the survey results that distrust in DCTA was a prominent problem. Such distrust in the public process can be partly attributed to the past history of the city of Denton. In early 1922, residents of Quakertown (located within the limits of the city), a community of freed slaves, were denied the ability to participate in the decision that relocated their entire

Table 11.1   Has DCTA Provided Accurate Information to the Community?

DCTA Has Provided Accurate Information to the Community?	Number	Percentage
Disagree	21	52
No opinion	15	38
Agree	4	10
Total	40	100
n = 40		

Table 11.2 Participants' Uncertainty about Potential Impacts on Their Community

Why Did You Respond "Unsure" to the Potential Impact on Your Community?	Number	Percentage
Mistrust	2	11
Safety	1	5
Positive and negative	7	39

community next to the MKT rail line.[10] Despite DCTA's attempts to involve the public in the decision-making process, the same fear surfaced again. Also, the lack of information on assessment of impacts of the commuter light rail line on their community intensified their distrust in DCTA (Table 11.2), which interfered with citizens' ability to influence the decision-making process.

The display of skepticism and dissatisfaction by individuals who participated in the survey reflect the shortcomings in the collaborative efforts of DCTA. As stated earlier, the organization made great efforts in dissemination of information and to involve the public in the decision-making process. Inherent weaknesses in DCTA's mode of communication, however, impeded the process of effective collaboration with the public.

11.6 Review of Literature

Collaborative tactics can allow the public the opportunity to deliberate and engage in decision making and collective action. It can reinvigorate the concept of public participation, aid democratic governance, and help to empower citizens for self-governance.[11] The many benefits of collaboration range from reduction in cynicism among people[12] by incorporating their preferences in the decision-making process[13] to ushering in an era of *new civism*.[14] The process of collaboration provides local citizens with greater access to information and education on technical issues. Frequently it is used as a tool to indoctrinate citizens with ideas and decisions that administrators have already made,[15] especially in those issues that are complex in character and require technical expertise. Nonetheless, when used as a tool to gain political support, collaboration can help to make changes in policy directions that could not have been done otherwise.[16] This enables community members to learn how to associate their interests with the interests of others and to petition government organizations using a nonadversarial approach without demonstrations, protests, and litigations.[17] Thus, collaboration can be used to build social capital by developing a trusting and a mutually supporting relationship with members of the society.[18]

In such a partnership, the recognition of the value of citizenship coupled with the realization of the need to develop civic identity helps to engage citizens in the governance process.[19]

In the field of transportation, the principles of collaboration have been applied to address a variety of issues ranging from social equity to sustainability of growth patterns. According to Sperling, transportation services within an existing urban pattern usually generate unequal social benefits and burdens across different groups of people.[20] To promote equity and social stability, the focus should be on the community in the planning process. Involvement of community members can help to better serve the needs of the people and address their immediate concerns. Similarly, Taft points out that public input is essential in reaching a consensus on an efficient plan for transportation.[21] Involvement of the public in the transportation planning process can help to integrate the concepts of land use management, environmental protection, and energy conservation while enhancing the effectiveness of the final plan. Thus, the strategic collaboration framework appears to be especially relevant to transportation planning.

11.7 Practitioners' Perspectives

In reviewing the results of DCTA's PIP, it is clear that the agency scored high marks in making project information available to the public. However, DCTA played a passive role in engaging the local homeowners and other stakeholders who would be directly impacted by the project. Even though information was made available to the public using various means ranging from the media to mailing of newsletters and hosting of a website, those potentially impacted by the proposed light rail were not directly contacted by DCTA. Announcements and reminders about public meetings were not directly mailed to the landowners adjacent to the proposed light rail route. For a project of this magnitude, a greater effort should have been made by DCTA to engage the public in the decision-making process.

In organizing meetings, DCTA simply went through several steps required by the federal process in preparation of the DEIS. The elected officials and local leaders were briefed and made aware of the proposed project; however, that important information never found its way to homeowners and the general public. One explanation for this misstep is that because of the complex and technical character of the project, sharing such information with the public was not deemed essential. Rather, the emphasis was on indoctrinating the public with decisions that had already been made by bureaucrats and other technocrats, an unfortunate but common practice in collaboration.[22]

To disseminate information on construction of the proposed transportation project, DCTA hosted public meetings, offered e-mail updates, and posted information on its website. Despite such efforts, many individuals expressed dissatisfaction with the process used by DCTA. One explanation is that the citizens were not knowledgeable about some of the limitations of a public process—for example, the public meetings often have a time limit—and that complex engineering projects operate in phases involving different experts at each phase. Another reason is the existence of a large percentage of senior citizens in the community. Seniors are less likely to view information posted on the Internet and therefore perceive that the transit authority has provided them with limited information. This led to a breakdown in the communication process and interfered with DCTA's ability to collaborate with its citizen partners.

The TAG and CAG participated in a joint first meeting to discuss the purpose, vision, and goals of the rail project as well as to discuss the PIP process. The joint meeting served to kick off the rail project and to set the stage for discussing alternatives and recommendations at future meetings. Additional meetings were held separately to discuss similar topics, including facility locations, rail alignments, and possible impacts the project would have on neighborhoods adjacent to the rail alignment. However, the results of the respective meetings were not shared with the other groups. A possible reason for meeting separately is that each group has a different focus or perspective of the project. The TAG viewed the discussion topics from a specific technical aspect, while the CAG tried to estimate the possible impacts of the project on local neighborhoods or groups of people. The community roundtables would review and discuss the recommendations of the TAG and CAG; however, the roundtables never met jointly with the TAG and CAG. The consultants presented the TAG and CAG recommendations to the roundtable. While separation of roles may have helped collaboration processes be more efficient, a strategic collaboration framework would suggest more linkages between the two groups.

11.8 Lessons Learned to Build Conceptual Knowledge

The case study offers valuable insights into the process of strategic collaboration. The DCTA in its efforts to collaborate with government officials and group members met with success. Communication and exchange of information in a timely manner enabled DCTA to build a stable and trusting relationship with the various local government partners and to decide on a subsequent course of action. Similar success was not experienced in its efforts to collaborate with the public.

The DCTA staff and the consultant performed very well in presenting information and in educating the citizens. However, public participation was not much encouraged or actively pursued. Thus, in DCTA's model of collaboration, the emphasis was on information exchange rather than on public input. It appeared as if the DCTA staff simply followed the requirements of the federal regulatory process and did nothing more. Notices were published about the various meetings, and information was provided on websites and newsletters, all of which was *available* to the public. For the public to truly participate in this process, the information should have been *taken* to the public, which should have been encouraged to deliberate and participate more in the decision-making process.

In an era of advanced technology, it may seem appropriate to encourage citizens to communicate with an organization through e-mail. The advantages of this mode of communication include savings in time and money, expedites exchange of information, and helps to maintain accurate records for administrative purposes. From such a perspective, DCTA seemed to have made the right choice in its preference for communication with the public using the Internet. But the fallacy of such a decision lies in the fact that DCTA did not realize that a large majority of community members directly impacted by the regional rail plan were senior citizens who preferred a traditional face-to-face communication rather than other options. Hence, DCTA's attempts to publicize the modern mode of communication further limited the scope of public participation and negotiation in the decision-making process, thus weakening the effectiveness of this strategic collaboration.

The formation of three groups with specific objectives is indicative of a well-conceived design for collaboration. However, groups may not perform as expected for various reasons, and in DCTA's case the groups worked in isolation and lacked connectivity. Even though each group had its respective expertise and recommendations, it became difficult for the consultant to fully describe the concerns and comments of each group. One method of overcoming this problem would be to conduct a joint final meeting in which the respective groups interact and openly share their concerns and reasons for their respective recommendations. Unfortunately, after the first joint meeting, participation in the TAG and CAG considerably declined. A possible cause for such a decline was how the meetings were posted and participants were notified. A single e-mail was sent to the participants with notification of the set date and time. If full participation in groups is desired, follow-up notices or other forms of communication should have been used to garner additional participation.

To seek the cooperation and support of community members, it is important to understand the demographic characteristics of the population and the history of the region. Unfortunately, DCTA failed to do this. The organization's lack of understanding of the historical and demographic context served as a major deterrent in building a stable and trustworthy relationship with community members. If DCTA had been more intentional about gaining knowledge of the situational context and the collaborative context, it could have developed a more practical plan and pursued a strategy that might have allayed fears of dislocation and instilled more trust in the organization. Thus, it is imperative for any collaborators to have background knowledge of the community it will be working within to develop an effective action plan for a public project.

In conclusion, the case study, by offering a glimpse into a nonprofit organization's efforts to establish a collaborative relationship with its various partners and stakeholders and citizens, reminds us of the existence of inherent weaknesses even in a well-designed plan for strategic collaboration. Simultaneously, it raises several questions on the process of collaboration itself. Do organizations possess adequate knowledge about collaboration? Is evaluation of outcomes done on a regular basis, and are necessary adjustments made in the process of collaboration? Undoubtedly, the possibilities offered by collaboration cause adoption of this management. To achieve the desired outcomes, managers need to learn from past mistakes when developing an effective plan for strategic collaboration, especially in regards to citizen engagement.

Endnotes

1. E. Vigoda, From Responsiveness to Collaboration: Governance, Citizens and the Next Generation of Public Administration, *Public Administration Review, 62* (5): 527–540, 2002. For problems in collaborating with community members, see Majumdar, S.R., Moynahan, C., and Pierce, J., Public Collaboration in Transportation: A Case Study. *Public Works Mangement and Policy,* 14(1) 55–80, 2009.
2. D.F. Kettl, Managing Boundaries in American Administration: The Collaboration Imperative, *Public Administration Review* (Special Issue): 10–19, 2006, p. 17.
3. T.M. Koontz and C. Thomas, What Do We Know about the Environmental Outcomes of Collaborative Management? *Public Administration Review* (Special Issue): 111–121, 2006, p. 112.
4. DCTA Rail Connection, A Newsletter, RailDCTA Project, Lewisville, Texas, 2006.
5. Environmental Protection Agency (EPA), National Environmental Policy Act (NEPA), 2007. http://www.epa.gov/compliance/basics/nepa.html.
6. DCTA Rail Connection, Newsletter.
7. URS, Denton County Transportation Authority Alternatives Analysis, Denton to Carrollton Corridor, Executive Summary, Prepared by URS Corporation, 2005.
8. S.R. Majumdar and J. Pierce, Public Collaboration in Transportation: A Look at Denton County Transportation Authority's (DCTA) Plan for Public Transportation in North Texas, Paper presented at the 68th National Conference of American Society for Public Administration, Washington, DC, March 23–27, 2007.
9. C.T. Moynihan, An Environmental Justice Assessment of the Light Rail Expansion in Denton County, Texas, Master's thesis, University of North Texas, 2007.
10. Texas State Historical Association, Handbook of Texas Online, Quakertown, TX. http://www.tshaonline.org.
11. A. Fung and E.O. Wright, Deepening Democracy: Innovations in Empowered Participatory Governance, *Politics and Society, 29* (1): 5–41, 2001; T.L. Cooper, T. Bryer, and J.W. Meek, Citizen-Centered Collaborative Public Management, *Public Administration Review* (Special Issue): 76–88, 2006.
12. E.M. Berman, Dealing with Cynical Citizens, *Public Administration Review, 57* (2): 105–112, 1997; J.C. Thomas, *Public Participation in Public Decisions* (San Francisco, CA: Jossey-Bass, 1995); V.H. Vroom and A.G. Jago, *The New Leadership: Managing Participation in Organizations* (Englewood Cliffs, NJ: Prentice Hall, 1988).
13. R.A. Irvin and J. Stansbury, Citizen Participation in Decision Making: Is It Worth the Effort, *Public Administration Review, 64* (1): 55–63, 2004.

14. G.H. Frederickson, The Recovery of Civism in Public Administration, *Public Administration Review, 42* (5): 501–508, 1982.
15. F.E. Rourke, *Bureaucracy, Politics and Public Policy* (Boston: Little Brown, 1984).
16. J.S. Applegate, Beyond the Usual Suspects: The Use of Citizens' Advisory Boards in Environmental Decision-Making, *Indiana Law Journal, 73* (3): 903–957, 1998.
17. Cooper et al., Citizen-Centered Collaborative.
18. G. Loury, Why Should We Care about Group Inequality? *Social Philosophy and Policy, 5* (Spring): 249–271, 1987.
19. C.A. Cooper, A.J. Nownes, and S. Roberts, Perceptions of Power: Interest Groups in Local Politics, *State and Local Government Review, 37* (3): 206–216, 2005.
20. M. DeLuchi, M. MacCracken, D. Sperling, D.G. Burwell, E. Deakin, and R. Forman, Presentations on Transportation Indicators, *Integrating Sustainability into the Transportation Planning Process, Conference Proceedings 37*, Transportation Research Board, pp. 13–16, 2005. http://onlinepubs.trb.org/onlinepubs/conf/CP37.pdf.
21. Heanue, K.E., A. Canby, J. Horsley, H. Kassoff, J. Pucher, and A. Taft, Panel Discussion: Potential Solution to Challenges, In *Integrating Sustainability in the Transportation Planning Process, Conference Proceedings 37*, Transportation Research Board, pp. 24–25, 2005. http://onlinepubs.trb.org/onlinepubs/conf/CP37.pdf.
22. Rourke, *Bureaucracy, Politics*.

Chapter 12

Cape Fear Healthy Carolinians: Taking Risks, Crossing Boundaries

Thomas J. Barth and Elizabeth J. Demski

Contents

Case Brief

Background and Purpose of the Collaboration: Cape Fear Healthy Carolinians of Brunswick and New Hanover counties is a collaborative, community-based network of individuals, businesses, and government and nonprofit organizations whose mission is improving the quality of life by evaluating and addressing community issues, supporting health education and awareness, and promoting resource accessibility. This local organization is supported by Healthy Carolinians staff at the state level in the North Carolina Division for Public Health, established in 1999 by Governor Jim Hunt. The Division of Public Health certifies and provides seed funding to the local grassroots organizations on a competitive basis. The certification process provides guidance for getting started; establishing a steering committee; performing a community assessment; developing an action plan; and monitoring and evaluating progress. The existence of an oversight organization provides guidance and some level of seed money for the local entities, but nonetheless each local unit must be self-initiating and sustaining. Each local entity across the state is very different, but certification requires that a local entity must be addressing at least two of the goals from the Governor's Task Force on Health Objectives for the Year 2010. The six State Healthy Carolinian goals are to (1) increase the span of healthy life of North Carolinians, (2) remove health disparities among the disadvantaged, (3) promote access to preventive care, (4) protect the public's health, (5) foster positive living and working, and (6) develop individual capacities and skills to achieve healthy living.

Current Status: The three original committees—Access to Health Care, Obesity Prevention, and Violence Prevention—continue to work toward accomplishing identified objectives and evolve. The Violence Prevention Committee has morphed into a Technical Advisory Committee under a parallel collaborative called the Blue Ribbon Commission on Youth Violence. This recent development provides a new dynamic and leadership challenge as two entities with similar missions yet distinct identities and histories are attempting to join forces. Most recently a fourth committee, Health Policy, has evolved in response to the need to keep track and take advantage of opportunities from the rapid pace of health-care reform at the federal and state level.

Lessons for Strategic Collaboration Practice: This case emphasizes the important role of a neutral convener in bringing key participants to the table and the importance of a strategic focus, involvement of community leaders, and the ability to bridge cultural and racial gaps to sustain a collaboration over time. The large and complex issues targeted by this collaboration required the creation of substructures so that measurable goals could be developed and addressed. The history of collaboration between various stakeholders facilitated this new effort, but it also compelled participants to think in new ways about old and complex issues. The use of a community champion and attention to processes were essential so that the needs of the highly diverse group were not overrun by professional experts. The use of staged goals—mixing short-term wins with longer-term, loftier goals—was important as elections and community leader priorities naturally cycle. Finally, organizational representatives with a significant stake in the collaborative outcomes appear more committed to the effort; even so, the collaboration leadership must provide sustained strategic focus for success to be reached.

12.1 Introduction

Southeastern North Carolina, otherwise known as the Cape Fear Region due to its location by the Cape Fear River, is an area that has experienced rapid growth and the resulting socioeconomic strains. From 1990 to 2010, the region is expected to grow in population by over 50% (from 200,124 to 313,000). A once quiet, summer beach vacation spot with a southern rural character has transformed into a more urban, bustling atmosphere with an emerging knowledge-based business sector, dramatic influx of professionals and retirees from other parts of the country (particularly the north), and challenges associated with rapid growth including inadequate roads and public transportation, overcrowded schools, environmental degradation, and lack of affordable housing. The region is also characterized by increasing disparities: between higher-income new professionals drawn to coastal living and those struggling to make a living in service industry jobs; between longer-term residents in poorer rural areas and

In spring 2008, a conference was held in Wilmington, North Carolina, at the downtown Hilton to provide a forum for service providers to share their perspective on what needed to be done to address the rising wave of youth violence in the community. Over 50 providers filled the room and spoke with passion about the need for parents, political leaders, and public officials to come together and deal with all of the divisions within the community: black versus white, rich versus poor, small agency versus large agency, educated versus uneducated, police versus student, district attorney's office versus school system, inner city versus gated community, conservatives versus liberals. They also spoke of the need to deal with the multiple dimensions of a problem that involves families, school systems, law enforcement, and more. A principal of one of the largest high schools in the region observed the discussion and afterward stated, "I'm exhausted. This is the third meeting this week with groups with the same goals but different angles on the problem. I simply don't have time to go to all of these meetings. All of the people I feel pressured by are in this room today …. If someone could get these groups to collaborate and coordinate their efforts it would be a huge relief to me."

those living in expensive communities near the "gold coast"; between long-established Southern families and "snow birds" from the North; and among white, black, and Hispanic. Furthermore, these tensions rest within an antitax political culture that is colliding with rising service demands and the need for infrastructure improvements.

The end result of this complex dynamic is a region faced with growing challenges but with a limited ability to respond because of a fragmented civic infrastructure. Regardless of the policy setting, the recurring theme is individuals and organizations working in silos, struggling to cope, fighting for resources, and protecting turf. The social fragmentation, of course, is reinforced by traditional bureaucratic, political, and geographic boundaries that can overwhelm even those otherwise committed to working collaboratively.

This context is important to note because it created both a challenge and an opportunity for the community public health collaboration discussed in this chapter. A fragmented community with a large number of nonprofit agencies chasing limited dollars is very difficult to pull together, yet that same fragmentation creates a sense of urgency and a window of opportunity that can be filled by committed individuals willing to work together to bring about change. The challenge of building and sustaining a collaboration over time is daunting. Fortunately the Cape Fear Healthy Carolinians has had success and overcome the history of fragmentation in the community. The following five key lessons were instrumental in the success of the Cape Fear Healthy Carolinians.

12.1.1 Establish a Neutral Convener

The neutral status of the collaboration (i.e., it is not yet another nonprofit competing for resources) has been a critical factor in building this trust. Since membership in the collaborative is voluntary, individuals and agencies must see the benefit of investing their time; otherwise they will stop participating. The presence of a trusted neutral convener reinforces that there is no agenda for the Cape Fear Healthy Carolinians collaborative other than to see public health objectives achieved by enhancing the capacity of member agencies.

12.1.2 Provide a Sustained Strategic Focus

A collaboration of agencies centered on a particular issue area (rather than multiple, vague concepts) can provide a longer-term, sustained focus on an issue that is more strategic and comprehensive. Furthermore, the collaborative must maintain momentum and enthusiasm by being realistic with stated goals and objectives so that results can be demonstrated, with some "short-term wins" mixed in with longer-term, loftier goals.

12.1.3 Identify Committed Risk Takers with Support of Employers

The leaders of the Cape Fear Healthy Carolinians have exceptional personal commitment to the collaboration but are also supported by their full-time employers that are aligned with and have a stake in the mission of the collaboration. At the same time, this arrangement has allowed committed individuals who are inclined to take risks to use the "cover" of the collaboration without directly involving their employers.

12.1.4 Involve Community Leaders and Institutions

To make unpopular decisions, to counter resistance, and territorialism, to raise awareness, and to establish legitimacy, a collaboration should align the support of key community leaders (both political and civic) as well as institutions early in the process. Although internal process champions are essential and challenging to find and retain, equally important for a community collaborative are champions in the community with visibility and status that provide weight to the effort.

12.1.5 Bridge Culture–Racial Gaps

To keep diverse interests at the table, patience and multicultural competency are necessary attributes of collaboration members. The diverse perspectives and experiences of professional service providers, researchers, community leaders, and targeted populations "on the street" are often essential to completely understand a multilayered issue and to manage the collaborative.

12.2 Community Health Collaboration

Cape Fear Healthy Carolinians of Brunswick and New Hanover counties is a collaborative, community-based network of individuals, businesses, and government and nonprofit organizations whose mission is improving the quality of life for all residents by evaluating and addressing community issues, supporting health education and awareness, and promoting resource accessibility.

This local organization is supported by Healthy Carolinians staff at the state level in the North Carolina Division for Public Health, established in 1999 by Governor Jim Hunt along with a task force that was appointed by executive order. State-level staff members in the Division of Public Health certify and provide seed funding on a competitive basis to the local grassroots organizations. Regional health education consultants are available to provide consultation and technical assistance to local partnerships. The state certification process provides guidance for getting started (e.g., the establishment of a steering committee) and performing a community assessment, developing an action plan, and monitoring and evaluating progress. The existence of such an oversight organization provides guidance and some level of seed money for the local entities, but nonetheless each local unit must be self-initiating and sustaining. Each local entity across the state is very different, but certification requires that a local entity must be addressing at least two of the goals from the Governor's Task Force on Health Objectives for the Year 2010.

The State Healthy Carolinian goals are the following:

1. Increase the span of healthy life of North Carolinians.
2. Remove health disparities among the disadvantaged.
3. Promote access to preventive care.
4. Protect the public's health.
5. Foster positive living and working.
6. Develop individual capacities and skills to achieve healthy living.

Local collaborations are also to be guided by the following specific objectives as they accomplish their goals:

■ Create partnerships to facilitate community health improvement.
■ Seek funding and establish funding priorities.
■ Influence the establishment of health policies.
■ Facilitate community planning processes.

- Guide community health assessments.
- Conduct health education.

The roots of this collaboration began with a small number of health professionals and university faculty focused on the obesity prevention issue, energized by the national publicity generated by alarming obesity statistics. The emergence of this issue provided a great deal of grant money available to local communities. In early 2005, the executive director of Wilmington Health Access for Teens (WHAT) convened a group of health-care organization representatives at the request of the Kate B. Reynolds Charitable Trust health-care division director and the Cape Fear Memorial Foundation executive director. The purpose was to develop a community collaboration to address the serious issue of obesity in Brunswick and New Hanover counties. The purpose of the groups was to establish an effective and efficient inclusive structure to assess community issues and solutions and to plan, acquire resources for, and implement obesity prevention strategies. In the process of meeting around the obesity issue, a group of individuals realized the potential for further collaboration to address other areas of concern that were compatible with the goals and objectives of the Healthy Carolinians initiative. This confluence of community-level interest and commitment supported by a state-level entity set the stage for the birth of the collaboration.

This initial "founding group" of the Cape Fear Healthy Carolinians was essentially self-selected and set the tone for a collaboration that was very open to committed new members who are often invited by existing members. In other words, if you have something to offer and are willing to commit time and energy, you are welcome at the table. However, this initial founding group represented some key institutions, including the regional hospital, the county health departments, and the university. The group's first task was to review a variety of community health assessments that helped guide the selection of three health priorities. The health assessment process was an essential element of the collaboration, for the assessments provided legitimacy for the group's activities but also benchmarks for determining the success of their efforts.

Based on these assessments, the founding partners voted to form committees addressing three areas: access to health care, obesity prevention, and violence prevention. Each committee has cochairs and meets monthly. A steering committee composed of a chair and vice chair and the cochairs of each committee also meets monthly and provided general direction and oversight for the entire collaboration. All members meet on a quarterly basis to discuss progress and identify issues that need a unified response. The coordinated committee structure allowed the collaboration to take on three issues yet remain coordinated overall. Key decisions are decided by vote. Figure 12.1 reflects the structure of the collaboration.

Figure 12.1   Structure of Cape Fear Healthy Carolinians collaboration.

12.3 Collaborative Structure, Strategies, and Accomplishments

This section provides a brief description of the three committees, including key activities and goals. Although each committee operates separately, success is measured by positive outcomes in agreed upon indicators that are tracked through regular assessment reports. Note that each committee lists an extensive set of community partners; all of these agencies are not necessarily at the table at any given time, but their presence as a partner indicates that they receive regular communications and are a resource as needed depending on the particular task or issue.

12.3.1 Obesity Prevention Committee

For the past 15 years, there has been an annual increase in the average body mass index of the citizens of North Carolina. A total of 45% of North Carolina children are overweight or at risk for overweight. These numbers can be attributed to a multitude of causes including lack of access to nutritious foods, sedentary lifestyle factors, and other environmental causes. All of these factors influence individual choices for diet and exercise.

According to the Centers for Disease Control and Prevention, obesity is one of the top causes of preventable diseases, second only to tobacco. New Hanover and Brunswick counties mirror North Carolina in staggering obesity statistics and related chronic diseases including diabetes, heart disease, and other life-threatening illnesses. With 40 community partners, the Cape Fear Healthy Carolinians Obesity Prevention Committee is developing and implementing a variety of strategies to decrease overweight and obesity in both adults and children. Programs and initiatives are aimed at children in schools and after-school settings, at adults in the workplace, and at families in neighborhoods, churches, and other public places.

OBESITY PREVENTION COMMUNITY PARTNERS

- Bethel AME Church
- Northwest, Big and Little Macedonia Church
- Brunswick County Health Department
- Brunswick Community College
- Cape Fear Community College
- Child Advocacy Commission
- City of Wilmington Parks and Recreation
- Coastal AHEC, Coastal Weight Management Center
- Diabetes Coalition
- Food Bank of Central & Eastern NC
- Greater Wilmington Chamber of Commerce
- Island-Time Institute
- Kids in Shape
- Myrtle Grove Evangelical Presbyterian Church
- New Hanover County Administration
- New Hanover County Cooperative Extension
- New Hanover County Department of Aging
- New Hanover County Health Department
- New Hanover County Partnership for Children
- New Hanover County Planning Department
- New Hanover County Schools
- New Hanover Regional Medical Center
- Obesity Prevention Initiative
- Pleasant View Baptist Church
- PPD, Inc.
- UNCW Students
- UNCW Department of Health and Applied Human Sciences
- UNCW Division for Public Service and Continuing Studies
- UNCW Office of Research and Sponsored Programs
- UNCW School of Nursing
- Voices Latinos
- WECT-TV
- Weight Wise Program, UNC–Chapel Hill
- Wilmington Children's Museum
- Wilmington Family YMCA
- Wilmington Health Access for Teens
- Wilmington Housing Authority
- Wilmington Star News
- Wilmington Walks
- YWCA of Lower Cape Fear

Through a fast-moving committee process, the following objectives were identified for the Obesity Prevention Committee:

1. To reduce the percentage of children (ages 2–18) and adolescents who are overweight or obese by 10% by the year 2010.
2. Reduce the percentage of adults (ages 19–64) who are overweight or obese by 10% by the year 2010.
3. Plan and implement a comprehensive marketing promotional campaign to change the behavior of adults, families, and children in the Cape Fear Region regarding the issue of obesity.
4. Plan and implement a community initiative neighborhood by neighborhood, corporation by corporation, and school by school to offer a "wellness template" for each group. The template will offer a menu of best practices in wellness programs and activities for each audience depending on their needs and interests, such as walking programs and incentives (e.g., scales or pedometers), weight-loss programs and incentives, lunch 'n' learns, and nutrition advice.
5. Acquire volunteer and financial resources and support to gradually support a comprehensive community health initiative.

12.3.1.1 Highlights of Accomplishments

In spring 2006, the Obesity Prevention Committee received approximately $511,000 from the Kate B. Reynolds Foundation and the Cape Fear Memorial Foundation to establish obesity prevention initiatives (OPIs). The University of North Carolina–Wilmington (UNCW) Division for Public Service and Continuing Studies vice chancellor organized OPIs to identify ways the university could address the obesity problem. The money allowed OPIs to help coordinate and promote obesity prevention programs and initiatives within the community. In addition, Kate B. Reynolds funded the following partner initiatives:

- The Wilmington Family YMCA received funding to provide a nutrition, exercise, and wellness program for several Wilmington Housing Authority youth and their families. Wilmington Health Access for Teens received funding to provide peer health education and support for overweight adolescents who want to lose weight.
- Wilmington Housing Authority will use funding to plant and maintain a community garden at a public housing development.

- Partnership for Children received funding for a lay health advisor to provide nutrition and physical activity information to Latina women and their children.
- Child Advocacy Commission will provide an interactive nutrition curriculum, "Miss Magic Apron," to child daycare providers in the community.
- New Hanover County Schools will purchase recess packs for 11 elementary schools to help students increase physical activity during recess.

The Obesity Prevention Committee is working with community partners on other important projects designed to improve health outcomes such as the following:

- Winner's Circle: A menu-labeling system that helps consumers identify healthy food choices when they dine away from home. This program has been implemented in all 39 New Hanover County Schools. In addition, this program was implemented on UNCW's campus and some area restaurants starting in 2007.

- Wilmington Walks: A community-based effort to fight obesity in the Cape Fear region through education and programming. Wilmington Walks provides brochures, maps, signs, and trail markers to help establish safe walking paths in neighborhoods throughout the community. The first trail was established in the Forest Hills neighborhood in May 2006. The Downtown Loop was established in November 2006 for people who work, live, and exercise downtown.

12.3.2 Violence Prevention Committee

The Violence Prevention Committee began meeting regularly in 2005 to strategize how to address the violence problem in New Hanover County. Representatives from over 17 agencies have participated in monthly discussions on the topic of violence. The committee met to determine a mission and vision statement: to assist local communities in New Hanover and Brunswick counties to stop violence; to achieve community recognition of the urgency of violence prevention at all levels and funding goals necessary to carry out violence prevention efforts; and to facilitate collaboration in violence prevention efforts by local agencies. Three priorities were also established:

■ **Priority One:** Advisory/collaborative group/facilitation/networking.
  - **Goal:** To facilitate greater collaboration among entities engaged in violence reduction activities to increase effectiveness in programming and resource use.
    • **Objective One:** Increase collaboration among entities involved in violence reduction programming.
    • **Objective Two:** Act as a forum that will enable entities involved in violence reduction programming to meet regularly to increase networking opportunities.
■ **Priority Two:** Funding and information group.
  - **Goal:** To become a sustainable group. To bring in funding for entities engaged in violence reduction programming in the Cape Fear area.
    • **Objective One:** Provide information about the grant writing process and potential funding sources.
    • **Objective Two:** Increase collaboration among entities involved in violence reduction programming in the grant-writing process.
■ **Priority Three:** Data collection/gap analysis.
  - **Goal:** To increase awareness of Cape Fear violence and violence reduction services and to identify and address unmet needs.
    • **Objective One:** Increase community awareness of programs offered by Cape Fear area entities involved in violence reduction programming.
    • **Objective Two:** Survey currently existing services about their needs and opportunities.
    • **Objective Three:** Identify gaps and needs by assessing the data collected.
    • **Objective Four:** Facilitate collaborative effort among entities involved in violence reduction programming to address gaps in services.
    • **Objective Five:** Establish and maintain a clearinghouse of activities, services, and information about evidence-based programming in the violence reduction area.

VIOLENCE PREVENTION COMMUNITY PARTNERS

- New Hanover Partnership for Children
- Child Advocacy Commission
- Coastal Horizons, Community Mediation Center
- Domestic Violence Shelter and Services
- Juvenile Day Treatment Center
- Southeastern Mental Health
- UNCW, Wilmington Police Department, New Hanover County Gang Task Force
- New Hanover County Schools
- Communities in Schools
- Wilmington Health Access for Teens
- New Hanover County Department of Social Services
- Wilmington Housing Authority
- Voces Latinos, New Hanover County Hospital
- New Hanover County District Attorney's Office
- New Hanover County Health Department
- LINC, Inc.
- Burnett-Eaton Museum Foundation

12.3.2.1 Highlights of Accomplishments

As the committee that has experienced the most difficulty getting organized, perhaps the most significant accomplishment of this committee to date is the role it has played in the establishment of a Blue Ribbon Commission (BRC) on Youth Violence in March 2008. Due to a number of political setbacks and resource constraints, past efforts to build a community collaboration to address the violence issue have not been sustainable, with the result being a retreat by individuals and organizations into comfortable silos. Much work is occurring, but there is little coordination and sharing of information and resources. Driven by concern over a rise in drive-by shootings and gang activity, a series of community discussions requested by the mayor and facilitated by a UNCW professor raised the problem of fragmentation. During this process the Violence Prevention Committee became involved and was instrumental in the creation of the BRC. The BRC is a collaborative initiative between several community partners including UNCW, the City of Wilmington, New Hanover County, the 5th Prosecutorial Judicial District, and New Hanover County School Board.

The mission of the BRC is to provide leadership, to foster collaboration, and to develop resources for addressing youth violence in New Hanover County by:

- Providing a cohesive vision and comprehensive strategic plan.
- Overcoming current fragmented programs by consolidating, coordinating, and streamlining communication and eliminating redundancy.
- Securing resources to sustain needed programs.
- Ensuring accountability by monitoring and evaluating progress.
- Advocating for programs.
- Educating the community about the issue of youth violence.

The Blue Ribbon Commission on Youth Violence members include the mayor of Wilmington, New Hanover county commissioner, New Hanover County school superintendent, district attorney of the 5th Prosecutorial Judicial District, superior court judge, district court judge, chief executive officer (CEO) of the Chamber of Commerce, and ministers. The BRC will be supported by a strategic director, who will be a conduit between the commission and a Technical Advisory Committee (TAC) composed of representatives from programs addressing youth violence in the community under the following categories: enforcement, research, prevention, and intervention.

A significant accomplishment to date has been the ability to raise funds to hire a full-time strategic director to oversee the implementation of a comprehensive plan. Significantly, the salary for the position is shared by six different organizations. The overall goal of the BRC is to prepare a statement of youth violence based on current conditions, to make an assessment, to present a gap analysis, and to develop a coordinated strategic plan for addressing youth violence. Importantly, the TAC will be composed primarily of the Violence Prevention Committee of the Healthy Carolinians. Thus, the groundwork for the BRC was laid by the Healthy Carolinians collaborative. A recent indicator of success has been the successful application for a grant to begin a pilot project in a Wilmington neighborhood modeled after the Harlem Children's Zone, a program that has achieved recognition for improving the lives of at-risk children and their families in high-crime neighborhoods in Harlem.

12.4 Access to Healthcare Committee

In the United States today, some 46.6 million people, or almost 16% of the population, do not have insurance. The majority of these people cannot afford health care on their own, so the result is that a large segment of our population has no access to primary health care. In Southeastern North Carolina, about one in five nonelderly people is without insurance. In New Hanover, Brunswick, and Pender Counties, more than 50,000 people are uninsured. Community surveys consistently tell the same story. In 2004–2005, four different community assessment surveys determined access to affordable health care to be a top priority facing the community. Access is as limited, if not more so, for dental and mental health care. The lack of affordable health care not only affects those who cannot visit a doctor when they are sick but also has a broader effect on society, to include employee absenteeism,

ACCESS TO HEALTHCARE COMMUNITY PARTNERS

- Access III of the Lower Cape Fear
- Brunswick County Health Department
- Elderhaus
- First Baptist Church – Wilmington
- Good Shepherd Ministries
- New Hanover Community Health Center
- New Hanover County Department of Social Services
- New Hanover County Health Department
- New Hanover County Partnership for Children
- New Hanover Regional Medical Center
- New Hope Clinic
- Tileston Clinic
- Wilmington Health Access for Teens

stresses within the family, additional burdens on the schools and social service providers, and the impact on overall health-care costs when these patients use emergency care as a substitute for a primary physician.

The Access Subcommittee began meeting in August 2005 and soon added other partners from health and human service agencies in New Hanover and Brunswick Counties. Bolstered by results from four different community assessment surveys in the last two years (Cape Fear Area United Way/UNCW, Coastal Carolinas Health Alliance, New Hanover County Health Department, and Brunswick County Health Department) determining that access to affordable health care was a top priority facing the community, discussion focused on how to help safety-net agencies, or those whose mission includes serving low-income or uninsured people, better deliver care to the poor and uninsured.

This committee adopted two goals:

- Support the New Hanover County Health Department's dental van, which provides children in New Hanover and Brunswick counties primary dental care at their school.
- Collaborate on creating a comprehensive and organized system for creating access to those who are poor and uninsured, not unlike those in at least nine other North Carolina communities.

12.4.1 Highlights of Accomplishments

Several agencies within the Access to Healthcare committee agreed to sign memorandums of understanding, agreeing to work together, and begin to look for funding. The first partner was the Cape Fear Area United Way, which committed $675,000 over a three-year period, beginning in July 2006. The grant will fund an executive director for the new program called Cape Fear HealthNet and an educational product to educate patients, and the area's agencies that serve them, about resources that are available. The grant also funded four of the area's safety-net agencies: Tileston Outreach Medical Clinic, New Hope Clinic, Wilmington Health Access for Teens, and Good Shepherd Ministries. These funds will allow these agencies to either expand services for the poor and uninsured or to continue.

In September 2006, Cape Fear HealthNet's first executive director began work. Funding projects that will help the effort to further take shape are under way. The vision for Cape Fear HealthNet is a centralized system that takes advantage of all the resources available to serve the underserved. The system will act almost like an insurance program, qualifying patients from a central location, referring them to appropriate medical care, helping them meet their medication needs, and educating them on managing their disease. Cost savings and improved health-care access have already been realized by the hiring of patient navigators, case managers, and family nurse practitioners who assess needs, provide guidance, and deliver care to underserved, at-risk populations.

A recent development in spring 2009 related to the work of the Access to Healthcare Committee is the establishment of a Health Policy Council. This group, led by a former federal government executive recently relocated to the area, has been established to track developments in health policy initiatives at the federal and state level to stay abreast of new opportunities such as funding sources that may be relevant to improving health care in the region. Given the rapid pace of health-care reform in the current environment, the council is an important new development that is a direct result of the network created by the Healthy Carolinians collaborative. This development points to the need for a successful collaborative to operate at both the policy and implementation level.

12.5 Linking to the Literature

The collaboration described here is not just an interesting local story but is a nation-wide phenomenon that has spawned the rich array of collaborations described in this book. The nature of contemporary public policy issues such as public health described in this chapter are demanding collective, integrated responses. One sees interconnected problems, fragmented authority, and administrative chaos where there is "too much happening too quickly all at once, and seemingly out of control and incomprehensible."[1] Kirlin suggests that in this dynamic, complex world, traditional single-function–focused policies, programs, organizations, regulations, and funding flows must be supplanted by structures based on region or larger geographic areas that cut across city, county, and state lines that enhance collaborative political leadership, civic infrastructure, and societal learning.[2]

In an earlier study of a collaboration in this region, Barth draws on several theories in the literature that further explain the nature of collective efforts, notably shared power and networks.[3] Using the term *ad hoc alliance* to characterize a group of local politicians coming together to manage growth on a more regional, coordinated basis, he cites the work of Crosby, who explains the dynamics of a new kind of world where power is shared and no one person or organization is formally in charge:

> As most public administrators and officials know all too well, in today's world no single person, group, or organization has the power to resolve any major public problem, yet, at the same time, many people, groups, and organizations have a partial responsibility to act on such problems. Everyone seems to have the ability to say no to proposed solutions, and not enough people have the vision, hope, courage, and will to say yes.[4]

O'Toole notes the emergence of organizational networks, stating that "public administration increasingly takes place in settings of networked actors who necessarily rely on each other and cannot compel compliance on the part of the rest."[5] Networks are becoming necessary to deal with what scholars have called "wicked" problems, or "challenges that cannot be handled by dividing them up into simple pieces in near isolation from each other." However, O'Toole suggests that much work needs to be done to better understand the extent and dynamics of organizational networks, for the prevailing literature and teaching is still focused on traditional concepts of the individual hierarchical agency and its management.

Agranoff reinforces the difficulty of managing collaborations or networks because it requires a different frame of reference.[6] In his analysis of the enduring problem of human services integration in such areas as welfare, homelessness, and AIDS, he argues that the typical or standard attempts to coordinate services over recent history have fallen short because they are rooted in a mindset dominated by the operation of single and separate organizational structures. In other words, as long as the public administrators see and define their world in terms of separate and distinct organizations, attempts to overlay coordination and integration strategies will be superficial and ineffective. He suggests that public administrators must begin to think in terms of a "transorganizational management" perspective that places emphasis on the development and operation of interactive and collective systems.

Focusing more specifically on the challenge of community health planning, Kalos, Kent, and Gates note the common problem faced by communities where "… some people do not value strategic planning or the time it warrants for completion. Within a society that is action-oriented, there is often a desire to move the process to the 'fix' mode before adequate assessment and planning have occurred."[7] We have a society faced with increasingly interconnected, complex problems but lacking familiarity with the tools and models necessary for sustained collaborative planning.

There is thus a clear theoretical case for why collaborations are necessary and the different type of perspective and approach that is needed to operate within them. There remains the very practical question of how to make these entities function effectively in practice and the very real inherent obstacles to sustaining such efforts. We know the pros and cons of traditional bureaucracies after centuries of experience; we need to build a similar knowledge base to better understand formal collaborations. As a contribution toward this challenge, the chapter closes with a discussion of important lessons for practitioners engaged in or considering the establishment of such a collaboration.

12.6 Lessons Learned

This case provides a rich picture of collaboration because there are multilayered lessons to be learned from the experiences of practitioners, at the steering committee level as well as at the three substantive committee levels. Each level has a slightly different story to tell, but common themes across both levels and committees are evident. The following information is based on interviews with key leaders of the Cape Fear Healthy Carolinians.

12.6.1 Establish a Neutral Convener

Given the issues of competition and territorialism that can be obstacles to successful collaborations, trust must be established and cultivated. The neutral status of the umbrella organization has been a critical factor in building this trust. The Healthy Carolinians collaborative is not a formal 501(c)(3), so it cannot receive funding. This status has proven to be an advantage because the organization is not seen as competing for funding but instead as a pathway for new funding. In other words, it is in the self-interest of agencies to be a member of the collaborative. Since membership in the collaborative is voluntary, individuals and agencies must see the benefit of investing their time; otherwise they will stop participating. There is no agenda for the Cape Fear Healthy Carolinians collaborative other than to see public health objectives achieved by enhancing the capacity of member agencies. A similar lesson is evident from the work of the Violence Prevention Committee. Furthermore, faculty and staff are rewarded only if they can demonstrate effective engagement, which means fostering collaborations that show results. A neutral convener is important for building trust among the agencies in a collaborative where there is clear benefit to participation. Related to the theme of a neutral convener is the important role played by the university, an institution that is considered a fairly neutral and objective source of information and expertise.

12.6.2 Provide a Sustained Strategic Focus

The strength of the Cape Fear Healthy Carolinians is also the source of its greatest weakness: It is composed of many individuals with different interests, perspectives, and areas of expertise who are addressing a multilayered community challenge. Such a collaboration can survive only if there is a sustained focus supported by a clear strategy that is apparent to participants, funders, and the community. A good example is the Violence Prevention Committee, which has had the most difficult time becoming organized. This situation may be attributable to the inherent nature of an issue that is highly complex and multidimensional. For example, we know that a stronger family support system is important in reducing the risk of a child becoming interested in gangs, but how does one provide programs that will show measurable improvements in the quality of a family? In comparison, obesity and access to health care are much easier to conceptualize and understand. Not surprisingly, funders are also easier to approach for resources for more focused programs with tangible products, such as nutrition and exercise programs to combat obesity or a dental van to increase access to health care for children at their schools. Despite these challenges, the Violence Prevention Committee has persisted and experienced success bringing diverse groups to the table by organizing strategies around four core domains: family, community, schools, and individuals. Community experts can choose a domain and work with others in that area to develop action steps with concrete goals and objectives.

Focus also is an important factor to remember when selecting priorities and geographic parameters. Cape Fear Healthy Carolinians has been careful to focus on just three priorities that are based on careful assessments and clearly documented need. This approach makes it easier for the community to identify with the effort. In contrast, the Access to Healthcare Committee has been hampered by the decision to cover two counties with very different profiles and needs. It has proven difficult to have discussions and provide integrated solutions when the needs are so varied.

In a similar vein, absent a permanent legislative appropriation, a collaboration lives and dies by revenue streams from foundations, grants, and donations. It can be very difficult to time the receipt of grants to correspond precisely with the capacity of the agencies to use the funds. Most importantly, the collaborative must be realistic with stated goals and objectives so that results can be demonstrated, with some "short-term wins" mixed in with longer-term, loftier goals. Funders want to see results from their investment and will look with disfavor upon agencies with agencies stating lofty, vague goals that are difficult to measure. Experience with the Cape Fear Healthy Carolinians collaborative has demonstrated that although a strong capacity may exist to secure grants, momentum and focus can be lost if partner agencies are not able to effectively implement the grants in a timely manner. A key to success in this arena is for the collaborative to foster a high level of participant activity in the midst of the ebb and flow of grant activity so that the infrastructure is in place and ready to take advantage when funds become available.

A final important element of focus is the development of specific outcome measures that are tracked and reported to the entire collaboration on a regular basis. The bottom line for a community public health collaboration is whether key health indicators are improving significantly. Regular assessments accompanied by discussion and necessary strategic responses by each committee keep participants focused and energized.

12.6.3 Identify Committed Risk Takers with Support of Employers

The leadership and general membership of the Cape Fear Healthy Carolinians are employed by independent agencies or grants; the collaborative has only one part-time central paid staff member who helps administer grants. The chair and vice chair of the steering committee and cochairs of the three substantive committees are employed by the county health departments, independent nonprofit agencies, the local university, and the regional hospital health network. A key to the success of the collaborative is the explicit support of these organizations by allowing their employees to commit considerable time during business hours to the effort. This situation has occurred with this collaborative because the leaders have been strategically selected from agencies with goals and objectives that are aligned; in other words, the agencies benefit from the work of the collaborative. As time has passed, this lesson has become more apparent as the most effective committee (Access to Healthcare) happens to be led by an individual employed by the local health network, an organization that clearly has a great stake in the work of the committee.

However, employer support has been a necessary but not sufficient ingredient for the success of this collaboration. The Cape Fear Healthy Carolinians has relied on the extraordinary commitment of individuals who have invested tremendous personal time and been willing to take risks. A good example is one of the cochairs of the Access to Health Care Committee pointing out that a community health clinic was not reaching people because of a reputation for treating patients poorly. The mantle of the Healthy Carolinians provided some "cover" for this individual (and the hospital that employs him), but it still took courage to take on this situation in a public way.

These "process champions" are often individuals with deep personal commitments to the mission of the collaborative and are often behind the initial building of the entity. However, one pitfall to this situation is that these individuals may leave or reduce their participation for any number of reasons. If care is not taken to continually cultivate new champions within the ranks, the departure of these individuals can have a devastating impact on the ability of the collaborative to sustain momentum over the long term. This lesson has recently been reinforced with the departure of one of the cochairs of the collaborative from the New Hanover

County Health Department. A clear successor was not in place so replacing this key leadership position has been difficult. Based on the experience of this collaborative, about four years is the life expectancy of an effective leader before burnout sets in. Others must be ready to take the baton, or the collaborative will lose steam.

12.6.4 Involve Community Leaders and Institutions

As a community-based collaborative, the support of local leaders and institutions is essential, whether they be formally elected or appointed individuals or just respected civic figures. Their involvement provides symbolic legitimacy for the effort and, of course, access to local and state government funding. Such individuals also have deep relationships with key players in the business and philanthropic sectors. Involving such leaders early in the process is important for establishing awareness and support for a collaboration.

However, the leadership provided by elected leaders can be sporadic, hampering the momentum of the collaboration. Elected officials may be defeated in an election, and perhaps even more crucial is that their interest and commitment may be driven by dynamic political factors. In other words, politicians must focus on visible issues important to their constituencies. For example, a flurry of drive-by shootings on the front pages will stimulate interest in youth violence for a time, but if public concern dies down and shifts elsewhere, so will the focus and attention of the elected official. The public policy problem, nonetheless, remains. For example, an important political supporter of the Healthy Carolinians just lost in the primary election, so a concerted effort must be made to cultivate a new political sponsor. Collaborations must therefore be very strategic in how they use elected officials.

Although internal process champions are essential and challenging to find and retain, equally important for a community collaborative are champions in the community. Unlike formal organizations, collaborations rely on volunteer participation, and visible civic leaders with high levels of respect and legitimacy are needed to rally individuals and agencies to a cause. The Access to Healthcare Committee, for example, has been hampered by the lack of a physician champion to encourage local doctors to join a volunteer doctor network. Such key individuals can be very difficult to find and can hamper an otherwise worthy effort.

12.6.5 Bridge Culture–Racial Gaps

Effective collaborations in policy settings such as public health often require individuals from very different backgrounds to work together. Professional analysts and researchers, for example, may find it very challenging to relate to grassroots community activists and vice versa, yet the diverse perspectives and experiences of both groups are often essential to completely understand a multilayered issue and manage the collaborative. In the youth violence arena, for example, grassroots individuals and organizations have tremendous passion and energy about the issue, but they may lack the organizational skills to bring groups together in an efficient and effective manner. Resentment sets in when more highly trained professionals take over, and this tension can be exacerbated when racial and socioeconomic differences are added to the equation. When power must be shared to achieve success, these gaps can be very difficult to manage. A related theme is evident with the Access to Health Care and Obesity Prevention Committees. Effective strategies to address issues such as barriers to medical facilities or healthy eating habits require a deep understanding of the perspective of populations from different ethnic, socioeconomic, and regional backgrounds. For example, it may be difficult to appreciate health-care access issues if you have never lived without an automobile. Successful collaborations must not just invite people from different backgrounds to the table; they must have the collective ability and patience to listen and fully engage this difference.

The salience of the culture gap issue has become apparent over time with the hiring of a strategic director for the Blue Ribbon Commission on Youth Violence. As an African American, she has had much greater success bringing other minorities to the table than the previous leadership, which was primarily Caucasian. This issue must be recognized in communities with a history of strained race relations. Related to the culture gap issue is the politics of race in a community, particularly when addressing problems like youth violence that have a disproportionate impact on certain racial groups. When selecting individuals to lead a collaborative, it is vitally important to identify individuals who have both the necessary leadership/management skills as well as political capital in the affected communities; one quality without the other can undermine the ability of the collaborative to move forward.

12.7 Conclusion

This chapter has described the background, accomplishments, and lessons from a regional, strategic collaborative focused on improving public health. As the literature suggests, Cape Fear Healthy Carolinians is a response to a series of wicked problems that no one single agency or groups working in silos can effectively or efficiently address. The vignette at the beginning of the chapter paints the picture of a fragmented community attempting to deal with such complex problems from isolated perspectives, and the toll exacted on the leader of a public institution experiencing the negative impacts of these problems without the resources to respond to public demands.

Indeed, funders have recognized this situation and are often refusing to consider applications that cannot demonstrate collaboration across a community. However, despite the well-documented need for collaboration, the public and nonprofit sectors are grappling with how to successfully manage these entities that lack the formal hierarchical structures, mandates, and stable funding to which they are accustomed and often trained and educated to work within. Hopefully the lessons from this case study and others can contribute toward a growing body of knowledge to provide guidance to those in the process of establishing or maintaining strategic collaborations in their communities. Building trust, maintaining a focus, and fostering process and community champions are significant challenges, but it has been shown that it can be done with significant results for our communities. As the former CEO of our regional health network once stated, "The single most important leadership skill for the millennium is the ability to forge coalitions."

Endnotes

1. S.E. Overman, The New Sciences of Administration: Chaos and Quantum Theory, *Public Administration Review, 56* (5): 487–491, 1996.
2. J.J. Kirlin, The Big Questions of Public Administration in a Democracy, *Public Administration Review, 56* (5): 416–423, 1996.
3. T.J. Barth, The Role of *Ad Hoc* Regional Alliances in Managing Growth, *Public Works Management & Policy, 6* (2): 114–125, 2001.
4. Ibid., p. 119.
5. L.J. O'Toole Jr., Treating Networks Seriously: Practical and Research-Based Agendas in Public Administration, *Public Administration Review, 57* (1): 45–53, 1997.
6. R. Agranoff, Human Services Integration: Past and Present Challenges in Public Administration, *Public Administration Review, 51* (6): 533–542, 1991.
7. A. Kalos, L. Kent, and D. Gates, Integrating MAPP, APEXPH, PACE-EH, and Other Planning Initiatives in Northern Kentucky, *Journal of Public Health Management Practice, 11* (5): 401–406, 2005.

Chapter 13

Building a Community–Higher Education Collaboration to Meet the Needs of the Local Nonprofit Sector

Dorothy Norris-Tirrell and Susan Tomlinson Schmidt

Contents

Case Brief

Background and Purpose of the Collaboration: The Memphis Metropolitan Statistical Area evidences social problems common to large urban areas, including crime, infant mortality, bankruptcy, and housing stock decay. Responding to these public issues and needs, the nonprofit sector in the Mid-South is a diverse and vibrant part of the local environment. In 1996, Memphis nonprofit leaders began discussing common staffing needs, identifying the national American Humanics (AH) program as a potential vehicle for improving the pool of entry-level professionals. At the same time, the national AH organization was advocating a collaborative model of program development. (Founded in 1948, the national alliance of American Humanics is made up of 22 national nonprofit partners and 70 higher education institutions around the United States with programs dedicated to educating, preparing, and certifying professionals to strengthen and lead nonprofit organizations.) In 1999, three higher education institutions and 27 local nonprofits began the Mid-South American Humanics Collaborative (MSAHC) with the stated mission *"to recruit and prepare future nonprofit leaders"* and the goal of improving the capacity of local nonprofit organizations to better meet the needs of the Memphis/Mid-South population.

Current Status: Students were admitted to campus programs in fall 2000, and to date 52 students have been certified, 265 MSAHC students have attended the fall professional development workshop, more than 75 students have attended the American Humanics Management Institute sponsored by the AH national organization, and over 100 students have been placed in internships with local nonprofit organizations. Now with 20 local nonprofit partners and two campus partners, the MSAHC hired a part-time executive director in summer 2008 to facilitate the recruitment of new nonprofit partners and to implement the approved strategic plan. The next phase will bring challenges related to the changing collaboration mindset as a new partner funding plan is implemented, new leadership evolves, and the emerging tension around the role of the paid staff member versus volunteer leadership is tackled. Finally, important considerations for this collaboration include consensus on outcome measures and at what point will it or should it evolve to permanent organization status.

Lessons for Strategic Collaboration Practice: This case illustrates the instrumental role of a champion in selling the initial need for the collaborative effort, bringing key players and funding to the table, and allowing quick movement through the early stages of the collaboration life cycle. At the same time, the champion's role had to be tempered with demands for greater levels of involvement from all participants. Developing policies and procedures that spell out tenure of office and responsibilities for key roles enabled the collaboration to move beyond "founder's syndrome." The history of collaboration among many of the participants allowed significant changes in leadership to occur without inhibiting the effort's progress. Finally, the case stresses the benefits of a shared understanding of cost and benefit expectations so that participants can contribute to the important creative processes required for long-term impacts.

13.1 Introduction

Building a strong pool of potential employees for local nonprofit organizations was the purpose for creating the Mid-South American Humanics Collaborative (MSAHC), a Memphis, Tennessee, collaboration that started with 27 nonprofit agencies and three higher education partners. The nonprofit partners represented a varied group of service missions and target populations. The academic partners mirrored this diversity and included a public comprehensive research university, a historically black college, and a private faith-based college. Each campus affiliated with the national American Humanics network, an alliance of 70 colleges and universities with nonprofit studies programs and 22 national nonprofit organizations that work together to prepare, educate, and certify professionals to strengthen and lead nonprofits.

The MSAHC represents a unique collaborative model among the national American Humanics alliance. The typical local American Humanics program is initiated by the academic institution. In contrast, in the MSAHC case the nonprofit community was the key convener. While most campus programs have a community council that serves in an advisory role, the MSAHC is unique in providing financial support and facilitating partnership activity among campus programs. Today, the MSAHC's priorities are financial support, placement opportunities for interns and graduates, and an advisory role for the campus-based programs.

The MSAHC is a useful example of a strategic collaboration. The MSAHC has existed for 10 years, begun through a grassroots effort, and then followed a slow but predictable development process. While the MSAHC has not incorporated as a separate 501(c)(3), it has used written guidelines to maintain formal structures and processes that bring agency executive directors and higher-education administrators together to certify students and place them in local nonprofit agencies. The case

The founding chair of the Mid-South American Humanics Collaborative was a charismatic leader who championed the cause of nonprofit management education and certification. He believed that educational programs specific to nonprofit management would better prepare job candidates for the challenges facing the local nonprofit sector. He was well connected in the community, serving as president of a local federated funder, and was instrumental in the initial phases of building the collaborative. He rallied the "right stakeholders," creating a Founders Circle of 27 nonprofit organization members, two colleges, and one university to build a program to certify nonprofit management graduates for internships and entry-level positions. After six years, this champion decided to shift his focus and minimize his role with the group creating a potential power vacuum. What should happen first? How is the next leader selected? How will new leaders emerge or be recruited? How will the leadership change impact the growth and direction of the collaborative's effort?

offers lessons for understanding the various roles of a collaborative's champion, the primacy of a shared understanding of goals, operations, and measurement, and the importance of partner/stakeholder management to collaboration success.

13.1.1 From the Ground Up: Grassroots Initiative Leads to Collaborative

The Memphis Tennessee Metropolitan Statistical Area (MSA) has a population of 1.3 million that covers five counties in three states. The Memphis Mid-South region is home to 13 higher-education institutions and a number of large medical facilities and serves as a large distribution hub for air and ground transport. As the center of economic activity for a large region, Memphis evidences social problems common to large urban areas. For example, Memphis ranks high on national lists for crime, infant mortality, bankruptcy, and housing stock decay. Responding to these public issues and needs, the nonprofit sector in the Mid-South is a diverse and vibrant part of the local environment. According to the U.S. Census Bureau's 2002 Economic Census, 915 tax-exempt organizations are located in the Memphis MSA, with almost $3.5 billion in total annual receipts and 39,661 employees. These nonprofit organizations cover a wide range of service delivery and advocacy contexts, providing needed services and partnering with public agencies to address the many complex public concerns in the area.

The seeds of what would become the Mid-South American Humanics Collaborative were sown in 1996 when a small group of Memphis nonprofit professionals, connected through the National Society of Fund Raising Executives (now the Association of Fundraising Professionals), began talking about staffing needs in their organizations. A few members of this group knew of American Humanics nonprofit certificate program and suggested it as a potential resource for Memphis. During the same period, the national office of American Humanics, located in Kansas City, Missouri, identified Memphis as a target site for a campus-based program.

Founded in 1948, the national alliance of American Humanics is made up of 22 national nonprofit partners (e.g., United Way of America, Points of Light Foundation, YMCA) and 70 higher education institutions around the United States with programs dedicated to educating, preparing, and certifying professionals to strengthen and lead nonprofit organizations. See Figure 13.1 for a list of American Humanics Alliance members. American Humanics certification is centered on building core competencies for nonprofit management through classroom instruction and experiential learning opportunities. For a list of competencies, see Figure 13.2. Although curriculum and specific certification requirements vary from campus to campus, minimum standards are set by the national office and include membership in a local American Humanics student organization, site visits to local nonprofits, a 300-hour internship with a 501(c)(3) nonprofit organization and attendance at the national conference, American Humanics Management Institute. Campus affiliates pay an $8,000 annual affiliation fee and must provide half-time staffing for the program.

The national American Humanics president came to Memphis in 1997 to meet with nonprofit leaders and academic institutions, suggesting that Memphis test a new community task force model. The goal was for the local agencies to work with national AH representatives to provide support for starting AH campus-based programs and then to transition into advisory groups for the programs.

One of the leaders of the local interest group was the president of the area's federated funder affiliate. He attended these initial meetings and soon became a strong advocate for bringing the American Humanics program to the Mid-South. The proposed collaborative model piqued the interest of the local group because the design maximized resources and met local funder demands for inclusive approaches. The federated funder president agreed to serve as the first chair of the steering committee of the MSAHC and to lead the effort to achieve American Humanics affiliation. In 1998, the new collaborative surveyed local nonprofit executives and found that one of the greatest needs was for well-prepared entry-level staff. The surveyed organizations employed 3,500 people but reported needing to hire approximately 200 new professionals each year.

AH National Alliance	Mid-South AH Collaborative
• American Red Cross	• Aging Commission of the Mid-South
• America's Second Harvest	• Boys & Girls Clubs of Greater Memphis
• Americorps	• Boy Scouts, Chickasaw Council
• The Arc	• Community Foundation of Greater Memphis
• Big Brothers Big Sisters	• Exchange Club Family Center
• Boy Scouts of America	• Junior Achievement of Memphis
• Boys & Girls Clubs	• Leadership Memphis
• Camp Adventure	• Memphis Child Advocacy Center
• Campfire USA	• Memphis & Shelby CSA
• Corp. for National & Community Service	• Memphis Zoo
• Girl Scouts	• Porter-Leath Chil
• Girls Inc.	• Shelby Residential Vocational Services
• GuideStar	• United Way of the Mid-South
• Humane Society of the United States	• Volunteer Memphis
• Junior Achievement	• Youth Villages
• March of Dimes	• YMCA of Greater Memphis
• National Four H Council	
• National Urban League	
• YMCA	
• Points of Light Institute	
• United Way of America	
• Volunteers of America	

Figure 13.1 American Humanics nonprofit partners.

- Board/Committee Development
- Historical & Philosophical Foundations
- Community Outreach/Public Relations
- Nonprofit Management
- Ethics & Values
- Program Planning
- Volunteer Management

- Communications/Marketing
- Fundraising Principles & Practices
- Financial Management & Accounting
- Employability
- Human Development
- Information Management & Technology
- Nonprofit Law & Risk Management

Figure 13.2   Core competencies of American Humanics.

13.2 Establishing the Collaborative Structure

While many Memphis area nonprofits had a history of collaborating, most of these collaborative efforts, even when demanded by funders, struggled to move beyond basic information sharing. In this context, the MSAHC brought a shared and important need to the attention of nonprofit leaders. Aided by the connectedness and clout of the founding steering committee chair, the MSAHC recruited 27 nonprofit agency partners, representing a wide range of missions (some of which were local affiliates of national AH partners; Figure 13.1), which agreed to financial pledges to create the founding circle. The original financial pledges were for four years and ranged from $250 to $2,000 annually based on the size of annual budget of the agency. In addition, three academic partners—University of Memphis (a public comprehensive research university), LeMoyne-Owen College (a historically black college), and Crichton College (a private, faith-based college)—agreed to begin campus-based nonprofit programs. From this group of partners, several nonprofit executives along with representatives from the academic partners volunteered to serve on the initial steering committee to create the structure and processes to support the work of the collaborative. Rather than incorporating as a separate 501(c)(3) organization, the steering committee decided to act as a collaborative using one of the MSAHC partner agencies as fiscal agent. The initial funding came from the pledges from the nonprofit partners ($138,000 over four years), grant funding secured from two local foundations ($360,000 over four years), and matching funds from the campus programs. With the assistance of two consultants hired to staff the planning stages of the collaborative, the structure, responsibilities, and operating procedures of the steering committee were fleshed out through the creation of written guidelines. Steering committee membership included the executive director or salaried president of the nonprofit partners and the academic partners' administrative representatives. Campus program directors would later be added to the steering committee. With the mission "to prepare college students for the nonprofit workforce," the steering committee agreed that the primary responsibilities for the MSAHC would be (1) to ensure the continuous role of the collaborative for four years, (2) to ensure adequate funding and sound fiscal administration, and (3) to implement the three campus programs.

The leadership offices of chair, vice chair, treasurer, and secretary were established. Subcommittees were formed to focus on financial management (finance committee), student support (student focus committee), nonprofit partner involvement (nonprofit focus committee), and steering committee membership development and recruitment (governance/nominating committee). See Figure 13.3 for the MSAHC structure. Additional policies delineated terms of office and the meeting schedule.

With administrative structures and initial funding in place, the work of the collaborative began. Through an initial strategic planning process, the steering committee set goals for student outcomes. At the same time, the three higher education institutions initiated the national American Humanics affiliation process, hired program directors, and started the necessary curriculum and certification development processes. As required by the national American Humanics organization, the formal and informal relationships with the national office are maintained by the campus programs rather than by the MSAHC, and the campus program directors attend an annual student conference in January and an annual campus director conference each June. See Figure 13.4 for an illustration of the student and partner activities used annually.

In the fall of 2000, student recruitment began at the three campus-based programs. For the next several years, the MSAHC continued to do the work it was designed to accomplish. The consultants handled the administrative work of preparing for meetings, renewing grants, and supporting the campus programs between meetings. The steering committee met quarterly to monitor the execution of the strategic plan, to share information, to report on subcommittee work, to attend to policy and program decisions, and to provide financial oversight. Many of the steering committee members knew each other from their similar roles in community agencies, and most were also members of the local Association of Executives of United Way Agencies. These prior relationships proved useful as the MSAHC struggled to create shared expectations and appropriate communication strategies. By design, American Humanics campus programs have a wide range of options for implementing the competency-based programs. Differences in curriculum and activities for certification, however, made comparisons across the three local campus programs difficult. While the initial MSAHC goals focused solely on student outcomes (e.g., certification and job placement), the ongoing dialogue among the MSAHC partners produced a wide range of outcome measures that benefited both the nonprofit partners and academic institutions, including an expanded network for job placements, internships, course guest speakers, and class project sites. However, the importance

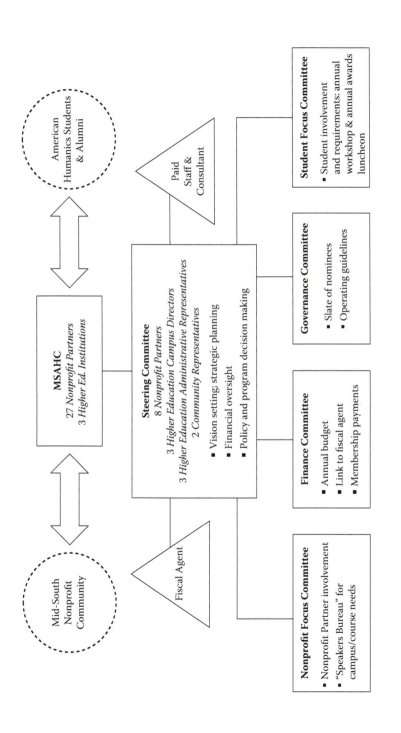

Figure 13.3   Structure of Mid-South American Humanics collaborative.

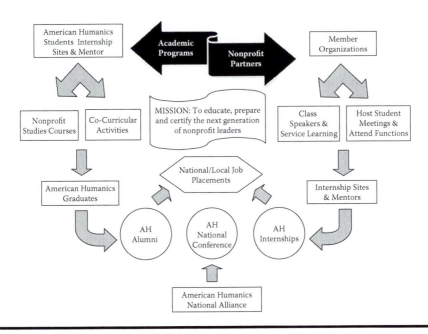

Figure 13.4 Operational overview of Mid-South American Humanics Collaborative.

of equity among partners, appropriateness of cost sharing, and standardized reporting were underlying issues that were not resolved easily.

At the end of the first four years of operation (the timeframe of the original operational pledges from the local nonprofits and the foundation grants), campuses were required to absorb the cost of the program while the MSAHC continued to fund the annual affiliation fees and joint campus student events including a fall workshop, spring awards luncheon, and electronic newsletter. Until this point, the campus partners had received financial support from the MSAHC to fund their programs, including the part-time staff. In 2003, the campuses assumed the costs for operating the programs beyond the annual contributions of the MSAHC. Although all three academic partners agreed to continue with the MSAHC, several nonprofit partners questioned the benefit of membership and did not renew their financial commitments to the MSAHC. Thus, the MSAHC experienced changes in partner agency support.

Four years after the formalization of the MSAHC, 9 of the original 24 founding circle members withdrew, and two new organizations were recruited, leaving 17 nonprofit partners. Staffing changes in campus administrators and campus program directors caused lags in progress. In addition, key nonprofit partner participation changed as executives retired or relocated outside of the Memphis area. However, the founding champion and steering committee chair along with a majority of the steering committee remained in place, carrying the group through its first membership turnover. The founding chair stepped down in 2004 after serving in the role for over six years but continued on the steering committee. The subsequent chair rotated into the position from vice chair. Since the new chair had been closely involved in the group since its inception, he was able to fill the leadership role quickly, assuring a smooth transition. What was less obvious was who would fill other vacant roles, offering the steering committee an opportunity to engage new leaders.

The campus programs evolved during these years as well. Some level of success was evident, even as the private, faith-based college withdrew from the MSAHC in 2005 citing financial constraints. Several annual collaborative activities served as important traditions that brought students and nonprofit executives together to network and learn. The fall workshop grew to be a half-day conference that focused on a contemporary issue in nonprofit management, exposing both students and working professionals to the latest trends. The 2006 fall event served as the local meeting for the inaugural national Nonprofit Congress, drawing a large crowd of nonprofit leaders. The annual spring awards luncheon recognizes collaborative contributions and student accomplishments.

While not intended, the public institution has taken a lead role in the academic program component of the MSAHC. Initially, responsibility for the group activities, such as the fall workshop, was shared by the various campus staffs. For the last few years, the public institution has had full responsibility. At the same time, the public institution has added a graduate-level curriculum track to its American Humanics certificate program. Outcomes for the campus programs mirror this uneven commitment as well, with the public institution's program certifying almost three times the number of students.

13.3 The Mid-South American Humanics Collaborative Today

The MSAHC steering committee and standing subcommittees continue to operate, guiding collaborative activities. The new focus is on communicating results to collaborative members, recruiting new members, and familiarizing the nonprofit community with the MSAHC and its purpose. Technology is becoming an important strategy for outreach, including a MSAHC website that features a posting board for internships and permanent placements as well as student resumes and work interests. The collaborative also instituted an electronic newsletter to disseminate information regarding group activities and to increase awareness.

A second strategic planning process was launched in late spring 2007. The current level of MSAHC activity and the participation in the visioning process suggests that the various partners remain committed to the collaboration's purpose. The 2007–2010 goals focus on (1) student/alumni management, (2) partnership management, (3) brand management and communications, and (4) staffing and sustainability.

At the end of the eighth year of student enrollment in the MSAHC-sponsored academic programs, outcomes are an important part of the steering committee's regular agenda. At the end of the 2008 academic year, the institutions of higher education have collectively certified 52 students and placed 30 in permanent positions with local nonprofits. Other measures of success are now used as steering committee members have come to understand how difficult it is to capture the reach and exposure of the campus-based programs. For example, many students participate at some level but never certify. These additional outcomes include the following:

- Over 265 MSAHC students have attended the fall professional development workshop.
- More than 300 students, AH alumni, and nonprofit partners have attended the annual spring event.
- More than 75 students have attended the American Humanics Management Institute sponsored by the AH national organization.
- Over 100 students have been placed in internships with local nonprofit organizations.

Another area of impact that is difficult to fully capture is alumni outcomes. Alumni may use their certification in significant ways as volunteers but not seek full-time employment in the nonprofit sector. Steering committee members have suggested additional outcomes that focus on a more informal benefit. Anecdotally, steering committee members note that as they take on a higher level of participation with the MSAHC, they have gained important peer networking avenues, a better awareness of the Mid-South nonprofit community including new programs, increased opportunities for funding, and useful management tips.

Sustainability has become the steering committee's primary focus as MSAHC committees have developed effective patterns of activity and are actively seeking new resources. The academic partners are key to the MSAHC's success. The public institution academic partner has institutionalized the American Humanics program with a hard-lined staff position for the part-time American Humanics director, and the program is a key element of several high-visibility initiatives. The other academic partner, while hampered with financial instability, has been able to maintain the needed course work and service-learning emphasis that may lead to greater institutionalization in the future. The number of MSAHC nonprofit partners has stabilized, and there is increased interest from Memphis-area nonprofit agencies about joining. Membership expansion is a key strategy identified in the 2007 strategic plan. To lead this new initiative and facilitate the MSAHC's next stage of development, two local funders agreed to a three-year funding strategy for a MSAHC staff position. The position was filled in July 2009. Initial accomplishments for the MSAHC director include the recruitment of five new nonprofit partners, an enhanced Web page, and a business plan. The infrastructure, personnel, and processes appear to be in place to support the continued growth and success of the MSAHC.

13.4 Collaboration as a Strategy: Connecting to the Research Literature

Practitioners Michael Winer and Karen Ray's definition of collaboration as "a mutually beneficial and well-defined relationship entered into by two or more organizations to achieve results they are more likely to achieve together than alone" provides a useful frame for the MSAHC's operationalization.[1] Other current literature on the increasingly important topic of collaboration offers a descriptive and prescriptive view evidenced in the Mid-South American Humanics case. The related themes of effective collaboration include a commitment of participants to a common mission,[2] establishment of shared vision that builds from a synergy of values,[3] a history of effective relationships among the participants,[4] adequate resources,[5] characteristics of effective collaboration participants,[6] the creation of a governance structure that stresses information exchange and accountability,[7] establishment of formal and informal communication channels,[8] minimization of power disparities,[9] and emphasis on a basic understanding that each participant contributes resources and reputation while sharing the results.[10]

For institutions of higher education—key participants in this case—collaboration seems a natural fit for academic, economic, and community engagement missions. Many factors influence how collaborations are structured and operated when including institutions of higher education such as type of institution (i.e., university, four-year college, community college, private, public), the historical relationship between the community and the higher-education institution, the distribution of power among the participants, and the funding sources.[11]

The leadership function in a collaboration is an important theme in this case. Radin stresses that leadership of a collaboration must be boundary spanning; characterized by flexibility, tolerance for ambiguity, and self-assurance; and capable of articulating the vision for successful collaboration to occur.[12] Huxam and Vangen define leadership in the collaborative initiative as "the mechanisms that are central to shaping and implementing collaborative agendas."[13] The leadership activities include managing power and controlling the agenda, representing and mobilizing member organizations, and enthusing and empowering those who can deliver collaboration aims. They identify change of individuals in the leadership role due to role or job changes as an obstacle to the trust building essential for collaborative success. In addition, Huxam and Vangen found that collaborative success typically comes at the cost of significant personal attention of the leader, suggesting the paradox that "the single-mindedness of leaders appears to be central to collaborative success."[14] John Glaser's work focuses on the collaborative leader's role in creating positive coherence or degree of alignment with the goal of building on each participant's strengths and energy to create a shared unity of purpose and a creative synergy.[15]

Connelly summarizes the existing research to suggest six guiding principles for interorganizational leaders:

1. Establish a common culture.
2. Create a unified vision and strategy.
3. Stress open communications.
4. Maintain trust among all parties.
5. Emphasize flexibility and an "entrepreneurial outlook."
6. Understand that current alliances build new alliances.[16]

The MSAHC case highlights the importance of collaborative structure, processes, and outcomes, including the leadership role. Lessons specific to the practice of collaboration are highlighted in the next section.

13.5 Learning from the Mid-South American Humanics Collaborative

The 10-year time span of the MSAHC case offers a longitudinal perspective to examining key elements of the creation and management of a viable collaboration. These elements include the critical roles of grassroots participation, a champion, and start-up resources in laying a foundation for the collaboration efforts; the need for shared understanding of the collaboration's purpose or mission, operating strategies, and desired outcomes; and the importance of partnership management for continued sustainability.

13.5.1 Lessons from the Founding of the MSAHC

The early stages of development laid a solid foundation for the MSAHC's later success and continued viability. Three factors are key in this case's foundation: (1) the grassroots dimension; (2) the role of the champion; and (3) the importance of a strong financial resource base. First, the MSAHC was the product of the grassroots activity of a group of nonprofit leaders, who identified a need that energized their colleagues, funders, and academic institutions. They created a model for collaborating that motivated agency and campus leaders to invest financially in program implementation. This is in contrast to the traditional American Humanics model that focuses solely on the higher-education institution while the nonprofits play an advisory role. The financial investment by all partners laid the foundation for ongoing, active engagement by most participants. In addition, the grassroots effort was enhanced by prior effective relationships among many of the participants that allowed the collaboration to progress quickly through start-up stages.

A second important factor in the founding of the MSAHC was the role of the champion. The champion who served in the role of the first steering committee chair was instrumental in bringing the founding circle partners to the table and obtaining local foundation support. He clearly and passionately articulated a vision for the MSAHC in meeting what he saw from firsthand experience as an important need in the Memphis nonprofit community. His connections and clout brought nonprofit leaders to the table to build a model to address his vision. His dual role as MSAHC chair and federated funder president, however, may have decreased or muddled partner commitment to the original goal of the MSAHC. As one executive from a nonprofit partner agency answered when encouraged to increase participation, "My agency joined because the chair asked me to. Our annual payment is enough participation." (Note: Yet, when this executive retired, the agency's new executive embraced the American Humanics program and has since committed new funds to the MSAHC for hiring part-time staff.) The potential double-edged sword created by strong founder/champion leadership is difficult to generalize. Without such influential leadership, it is hard to know if the MSAHC would have been successful during the initial stages. However, as the leadership role transitions, some less-engaged but important organizations may choose to discontinue participation. The contribution of the champion was critical in the creation and initial years of the MSAHC, laying the groundwork for the current strategy for continued sustainability of partner/stakeholder management (see following section).

A third important factor in the founding of the MSAHC was a strong financial base. In the first year of operations, the MSAHC obtained financial commitments from 27 nonprofit agencies, three academic institutions, and two local foundations. The nonprofit agency support was a key influence in gaining the foundation dollars. The availability of resources from local foundations leveraged partner support and mitigated risk for starting the new program, making the MSAHC operational before it had to prove itself.

13.5.2 Primacy of Shared Understanding

The need for shared understanding and realistic expectations among collaborative participants developed through ongoing dialogue including attention to processes (e.g., visioning, strategic planning, and reporting) is critical to analyzing the MSAHC case. In particular, successfully navigating the challenges of creating partner equity, realistic expectations, and decision-making ground rules have led to a greater collective understanding and commitment to the mission and goals of the MSAHC.

One factor important for authentic shared understanding in the MSAHC case was participant equity. In this case, there were two types of partners: (1) the nonprofit partners (who paid an annual fee); and (2) the academic partners (who delivered the product: certified students). Initially, a substantial portion of the academic partners' cost for program delivery was covered by the MSAHC. While both partners had defined roles, student outcomes resulting from the academic partner's work were the only measures of success for the MSAHC. The short-term consequence was a two-tiered membership with the nonprofit partners in the "authority" role. This system created tension that hindered open communication, led to unrealistic goals, and subsequently resulted in a sense among the three campuses that they were competing to show progress toward these goals. The MSAHC steering committee meetings in this period, while not openly contentious, were sometimes uncomfortable. Ongoing dialogue during the steering committee and subcommittee meetings and some changes in the individuals serving on the steering committee, including both nonprofit agency and higher-education representatives, allowed the desired outcomes to be redefined and reporting processes to standardize. The subcommittee makeup was also changed to assure that both types of partners were represented. Interestingly, at the point when the external funding ceased and the higher-education institutions took on the significant portion of costs of the program, the role of the partners began to balance as each had a clearer understanding of what others brought to the table.

A second factor important to building shared understanding in the MSAHC was building realistic expectations. Recruiting participants is important for any collaborative effort. In the MSAHC case, one of the benefits touted when recruiting nonprofit partners was the opportunity for internships. Several of the founding nonprofit partners did not renew their membership because they had not received a "free" internship during the initial four-year period. Unfortunately, the agency partner expectation of an intern was introduced without a clear understanding of the academic perspective: (1) agencies would have to meet certain requirements (e.g., the development of a job description that offered more than clerical responsibilities) for the student to earn academic credit; (2) because of their financial situations, most students need a paid internship; and (3) internships are offered in a semester time frame that requires the details of the agency relationship to be established weeks or months before the work will begin. As noted earlier, these expectations were hampered by the unequal status of the academic partners in the early stages of the MSAHC. The steering committee members continue to struggle with the role of internships as an individual nonprofit partner level benefit of participation in the MSAHC. However, ongoing discussion at steering committee meetings and increased interactions with the students and campus personnel have led to a better understanding of what can be promised and delivered.

Finally, decision making was a key factor for the MSAHC's shared understanding. The process of decision making can paralyze the development of a strategic collaboration. Consensus decision making, a hallmark of collaborative success, is often mistakenly defined as 100% agreement on every issue; however, the group may be best served by a process that encourages important input in a transparent manner and leads to decisions on an agreed upon formula (e.g., majority vote, defer to subcommittee decision) and clearly assigns authority and accountability. In the case of the MSAHC, a critical juncture occurred when some members of the steering committee demanded more information from the campuses about staff commitment and student enrollment. The steering committee chair and treasurer met with the president at each academic partner institution asking for a full commitment to the program. At this point, one college determined that it could not commit due to financial constraints. Some steering committee members were hesitant to lose the campus partner, but the hard decision was to move forward without the academic partner. The students who began the program with this partner were allowed to complete the certification process with one of the remaining campuses. Transparency allowed this potentially conflictual decision-making process to occur without negative impacts on the MSAHC.

The bottom line is that strategic collaboration requires ongoing and redundant dialogue to assure a shared understanding of purpose, structure, and outcome. While measures of success in an academic setting are different from the measures of success in a nonprofit setting, information dissemination and feedback opportunities have thus far sustained the MSAHC through the rough spots.

13.5.3 Significance of Partner/Participant Management

Without the commitment of participants to the collaborative effort, there is no collaboration. Therefore, attention to the role and needs of collaborative participants is important. Two areas important to partner management for the MSAHC have been turnover of steering committee members and the important role of staff.

In a long-term collaboration, participant turnover should be expected. Turnover can occur for many reasons including partners who leave due to incompatible or misunderstood expectations, position reassignment or relocation, and unanticipated changes such as new partner leadership or financial constraints. The collaborative's leadership must develop strategies to address shifting membership. In the case of the MSAHC, steering committee members go through an orientation process where mission, goals, operating processes, and outcome measures are discussed. In addition, each steering committee member is asked to serve on a subcommittee. Serving on the steering committee has proved to have a positive impact on partner commitment. Several steering committee members have expressed that they considered not renewing their agency's membership before being asked to serve in a leadership role and learning in a more concrete way the importance of the MSAHC's mission. The task before the steering committee now is to find a way to fully engage all partners, not just those serving on the steering committee.

A second component of partner management for the MSAHC has been the role of paid staff. Executive directors of the nonprofit partner agencies serve on the steering committee in a volunteer capacity. Thus, the time and attention needed to have the MSAHC succeed must be juggled along with the fast-paced and high-pressure demands of managing their own agencies. To keep the operations of the MSAHC under way, paid consultants (three different individuals over the 10-year period) have scheduled meetings, handled communications, taken meeting notes, and written grants. While the consultants have been important in maintaining the momentum of the MSAHC, steering committee members have expressed frustration regarding the consultant's lack of attention to the partner's needs and timeframes. For example, during the recent strategic planning process, partners were often provided materials with only 48 hours to respond. Given the nature of the partner's commitments at their own agencies, this timeframe was unrealistic and left the partners frustrated and the consultant discouraged. The recent planning process concluded that a part-time staff member was required to address needs for growth. The staff member was hired in July 2009 and reports to the MSAHC steering committee chair.

Engaged and committed members are essential to the success of a strategic collaborative effort. Because MSAHC is different from a traditional organization where employees are paid to lead and manage key initiatives, attention must be paid to the needs and constraints of the volunteers serving in these roles. This includes creating strategies for scheduling meetings that are flexible to the time constraints of busy executives who are core to the collaborative's purpose and for information sharing that keeps members informed and connected to their important collaborative responsibilities. Turnover must be anticipated and managed. Finally, the role of paid consultants and staff can be used to support and further the efforts of a volunteer-driven collaboration.

13.6 Conclusion

The MSAHC's smooth transition from the founding steering committee chair to the second chair and integration of new partners in the accompanying clarification of goals and expectations provide evidence that the collaborative had begun a move toward sustainability. Approved written guidelines were in place to facilitate this important transition. The steering committee completed a second strategic planning process in 2007. However, as implementation of this plan was beginning in spring 2008, the second MSAHC chair accepted an executive position in another state. The third individual to serve as chair was also a founding member of the MSAHC, serving as vice chair of the steering committee and chair of the governance committee. While the MSAHC faces challenges in recruiting leadership and new partners, the 10-year history of the effort, the leaders now in place, and the hiring of a staff member suggests that the collaborative will continue to evolve as a key force in strengthening the nonprofit sector in the Mid-South.

13.7 Remaining Questions

■ Building on the Winer and Ray stages of collaboration, the Mid-South American Humanics Collaborative case suggests that strategic collaborations may follow a life cycle of development similar to more traditional organizations.[17] This raises important questions about the knowledge and skills of public and nonprofit managers to effectively guide and facilitate collaborations through this evolutionary process. In particular, how can public and nonprofit administrators assist collaborations through transition periods such as leadership change?

■ This case also raises critical questions about the role of collaboration founder and champion. In the earlier stages of collaboration, the champion's role is clear and integral as participants are recruited, legitimacy of the effort is created, and resources secured. However, if unable to evolve with the collaboration and to allow new processes to emerge, the champion may become an obstacle to progress and goal achievement. Therefore, much remains to be learned about the role of the champion throughout the collaboration life cycle.

Endnotes

1. M.B. Winer and K.L. Ray, *Collaboration Handbook: Creating, Sustaining, and Enjoying the Journey* (St. Paul, MN: Amhurst H. Wilder Foundation, 1994).
2. J.E. Austin, *The Collaboration Challenge: How Nonprofits and Businesses Succeed through Strategic Alliances* (San Francisco, CA: Jossey-Bass Publishers, 2000).
3. R. Freeland, Universities and Cities Need to Rethink Their Relationships, *Chronicle of Higher Education, 20* (51): 36, 2005.
4. C. Guo and M. Acar, Understanding Collaboration among Nonprofit Organizations: Combining Resource Dependency, Institutional, and Network Perspectives, *Nonprofit and Voluntary Sector Quarterly, 34* (3): 340–361, 2005; S.P. Osborne and V. Murray, Collaboration between Nonprofit Organizations in the Provision of Social Services in Canada: Working Together or Falling Apart? *International Journal of Public Sector Management, 13* (1): 9–18, 2000.
5. D. Brinkerhoff and J. Brinkerhoff, Cross-Sectoral Policy Networks: Lessons from Developing and Transitioning Countries, In *Getting Results through Collaboration,* ed. M.P. Mandell (Westport, CT: Quorum Books, 2001), pp. 167–188.
6. S. Goldman and W.M. Kahweiler, A Collaborator Profile for Executives of Nonprofit Organizations, *Nonprofit and Voluntary Sector Quarterly, 10* (4): 435–450, 2000.
7. R. Wells, M. Feinberg, J.A. Alexander, and A.J. Ward, Factors Affecting Member Perceptions of Coalition Impact, *Nonprofit and Voluntary Sector Quarterly, 19* (3): 327–348, 2009. P.G. Foster-Fishman, D.A. Salem, N.A. Alle, and K. Fahrback Facilitating Interorganizational Collaboration: The Contributions of Interorganizational Alliances, *American Journal of Community Psychology, 29* (6): 875–906, 2001.

8. P.W. Mattessich, M. Murray-Close, and B.R. Monsey, *Collaboration: What Makes It Work* (St. Paul, MN: Amherst H. Wilder Foundation, 2001).

9. D. Connelly, Leadership in the Collaborative Interorganizational Domain, *International Journal of Public Administration, 30*: 1231–1262, 2007.

10. K. Sirotnik and J. Goodlad, Eds., *School–University Partnerships in Action: Concepts, Cases, and Concerns* (New York: Teachers College Press, 1988).

11. D. Maurrasse, *Beyond the Campus* (New York: Routledge, 2001).

12. B.A. Radin, Managing across Boundaries, In *The State of Public Management,* ed. D.F. Kettl and H.B. Milward (Baltimore, MD: Johns Hopkins University Press, 1996), pp. 145–167.

13. C. Huxham and S. Vangen, Leadership in Shaping and Implementation of Collaboration Agendas: How Things Happen in a (Not-Quite) Joined Up World, *Academy of Management Journal, 43* (6): 1159–1175, 2000.

14. Ibid.

15. J. Glaser, *Leading through Collaboration: Guiding Groups to Productive Solutions* (Thousand Oaks, CA: Corwin Press, 2005).

16. D. Connelly, Leadership in the Collaborative Interorganizational Domain, *International Journal of Public Administration, 30*: 1231–1262, 2007.

17. Winer and Ray, *Collaboration Handbook.*

Chapter 14

The Mastery of Strategic Collaboration Practice

Joy A. Clay and Dorothy Norris-Tirrell

Contents

14.1 Introduction

> **Strategic collaboration** *is an intentional, collective approach to address public problems or issues through building shared knowledge, designing innovative solutions, and forging consequential change.*

Urgent and lingering complex public problems such as those addressed in preceding cases (Chapters 5 through 13) require a systematic and strategic approach to consultation, coordination, and collaboration, at both a macro- and everyday operational level as boundaries of sectors, organizations, and disciplines are crossed. Whether driven by concerns about the community's vulnerable citizens, threats to public health or safety, or assuring effective use of capital improvement funds, the cases illustrate how the strategic collaboration approach can be used. The key factor leading to the formation of these collaborations was the recognition by key community stakeholders of a need to act and their willingness to step forward and take responsibility. As recognized in the growing research and applied literature, collaboration has become an essential component of governance. Management and leadership competence in collaborative settings has consequently become a job requirement of public and nonprofit managers.[1] To be successful in the context of new governance, public and nonprofit managers must be resolutely strategic in their collaboration-related decisions since collaborative efforts command attention, affect public perceptions of agency and program legitimacy, and place demands on already limited resources.

The reframing of collaboration to strategic collaboration offers an increased likelihood of success and positive outcomes from the collaborative venture as public and nonprofit managers become more purposeful about collaboration design and implementation processes, enable collaboration inclusiveness and effectiveness, decrease collaboration fatigue and frustrations, and proactively steer toward positive outcomes. The framework of strategic collaboration (Figure 14.1) synthesizes what we already know about collaboration with general public administrative practice and adds a concrete approach to understanding the situational and life cycle context of collaboration; the knowledge, skills, and abilities needed for effective strategic collaboration; and the range of impacts that make the effort worthwhile.

Strategic collaborations are nonpermanent arrangements that evolve over time, often serving as an intermediary to a more formal organizational or partnership structure or as the foundation for a new collaborative effort. The collaborative effort may also test the waters sufficiently to demonstrate the lack of support for continued collaborative attention. Thus, the success of strategic collaboration consists not just of the specific outcomes produced but also the impact on future collaborative endeavors, the quality of relationships, and the level of trust built. Consequently, the framework of strategic collaboration incorporates a richer definition of accountability recognizing that participants juggle external pressures and stakeholder rivalry while trying to deliver on promised outcomes.[2]

14.2 Gaining Insights from Collaboration Experiences

The test of any framework's utility for public and nonprofit managers is its ability to reflect everyday operational realities. The nine case narratives included in Chapters 5 through 13 test the framework of strategic collaboration as they illustrate the application of the key concepts and principles but also realistically describe the challenges faced by practitioners. The cases also demonstrate how strategic collaboration can be readily adjusted to fit varying situational and policy arena contexts. Applying the framework to the cases enables the reader to better assess and improve his or her own collaboration practice.

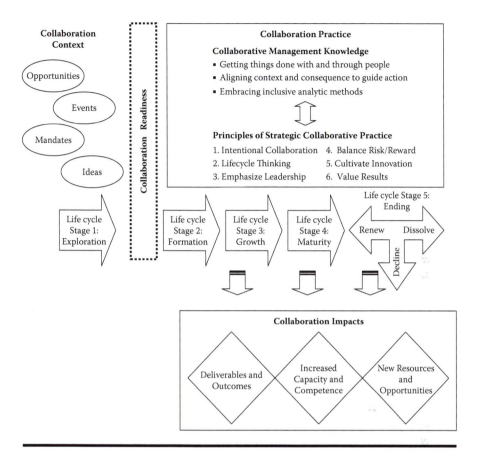

Figure 14.1 Framework of strategic collaboration.

Each of the case chapter collaborations had broad focus, crossed policy arenas, and needed multiorganizational representatives as participants, thus describing the critical elements of strategic collaboration to include the following:

■ Breadth of interests, stakeholders, and participation.
■ High-stakes community collaborative processes that drove a shared sense of purpose, mission, and set of goals and priorities that attracted committed participants.
■ A temporary, although not necessarily short-term, collaborative structure that was intended to address a particular problem rather than become permanent.

For example, the Alaska case crosses not only multiple policy arenas—as the issues touched on various stakeholder interests, including commercial fishing, environmental protection, recreation, tourism, and the oil industry—but also broad intergovernmental participation, as federal, state, and local governments were involved in the collaboration (Chapter 10). The West Nile virus case in Oregon illustrates a collaboration that worked across geopolitical, agency, and disciplinary boundaries (Chapter 7). The Shared Urban Data System case illustrates an evolving collaboration that grew to include both health and public safety policy arenas, crossed local political boundaries, and built relationships between practitioners and university researchers. However, the SUDs case also suggests that expansion to other policy arenas due to funder interest rather than mission alignment may lead to fragmentation and impede sustainability (Chapter 8). Particularly poignant was the principal's comment about the need to form a community-based health collaboration in Wilmington, North Carolina, because he was exhausted from all the meetings with different groups having the same goals but different angles on the problem (Chapter 12).

Most of the cases crossed sectors, generally public and nonprofit, as conveners needed the direct involvement with key stakeholder agencies from across the sectors. The community education case in Memphis, Tennessee, examines a local, nonprofit agency-focused effort that necessarily linked to both public and private universities and a key certifying national nonprofit organization (Chapter 13). In contrast, the transportation case in Denton County, Texas, illustrates the broad intergovernmental participation needed for this collaboration (Chapter 11). Although conventional wisdom suggests that nonprofits may be more likely to seek collaboration on public policy issues, clearly government representatives also perceive nonprofit involvement as necessary and often had a history of positive relationships with community leaders. Quite a few of the cases included participants from the private sector, either from inception (e.g., Chapters 6, 9, 10, and 12) or as they evolved (Chapters 5 and 7).

Six of the cases engaged citizens—some directly, such as in the disaster management case in New Orleans that sought genuine noninstitutional, community input about evacuation needs and procedures (Chapter 5), and others indirectly, such as in the Alaska oil case, in which a citizen's advisory council was created to promote collaboration between citizens and the oil industry (Chapter 10). The transportation case tells a familiar story as the public sector used a very formal process to elicit yet contain public input. The goal of citizen engagement in this particular case was both to assure that public agency officials and transportation experts could understand public needs and concerns but also to gain public support (Chapter 11).

Each of the case collaborations brought together agencies with competing interests and individuals with very different areas of expertise, experiences, and expectations, but all sought to influence the outcome and affect public policy processes. The case chapters describe the complex involvement of government agencies, nonprofit organizations, individuals, interest groups/stakeholders, and disciplinary experts from the relevant policy arenas, from *educators* (Chapters 5, 6, and 13), *environmental management and trade* (Chapters 10 and 11), *transportation* (Chapter 11), and *community health and human services* (Chapters 7, 8, 9, and 12) to *disaster management* (Chapter 5) and *computer specialists* (Chapter 8).

Each case had high-stakes implications, whether assuring the safe evacuation of the elderly during natural disasters (Chapter 5), improving communication between local jurisdictions to protect citizens during times of crisis (Chapter 8), or protecting the community from a new threat to public health (Chapter 7). For each of the cases, the conveners anticipated the collaboration to continue for an indefinite period, given the complexity of the mission of the collaboration, but there was no expectation that the collaboration itself would become an actual formal organization. The transportation planning collaborative lasted slightly more than a year (Chapter 11). In contrast, the collaborative school planning case illustrates the length of time collaborations can take, from inception to fruition, as it took approximately nine years to achieve concurrency in Palm Beach County. Of significance, Palm Beach County was the only county in Florida to be successful in achieving concurrency between development and school planning (Chapter 6). Similarly, the nonprofit education collaboration has been active for 10 years, successfully dealt with leadership turnover, and continued to evolve and build a positive reputation for its work, locally and nationally (Chapter 13). Clearly, to be effective over the long term, strategic collaboration requires patience, perseverance, and commitment to the collaboration's mission.

Each of the case studies articulated a shared mission and set of goals and priorities, with some authors describing the challenges the collaboration participants faced in articulating that mission. Some of the collaborations operated within an established framework, such as those formed according to established state or federal guidelines that were to be used in developing a community collaboration and participation process (Chapters 6, 9, 10, and 12). The elderly evacuation case describes an intentional process for extending the collaboration to include other participants and had clear goals and objectives developed to guide the collaboration's actions. In practice, the goals and objectives of each of the collaborations described in the case narratives strategically attended to mandated requirements or funder expectations as well as other environmental dynamics. The cases clearly illustrate that strategic collaborators must be outcome and process focused as well as relationship oriented to have results.

The cases provide examples for "how to" and "how not to" collaborate in very practical terms. The collective lessons from the nine cases are listed in Table 14.1. Each key guideline is an important element of creating real strategic collaboration and summarizes the deliberate and intentional actions needed to be taken by collaboration conveners/participants. Pragmatically, the 15 guidelines are not always easy to initiate or maintain. However as a set, the keys to collaborating strategically recommend the ideal path to achieve a successful strategic collaboration.

14.3 Fundamentals of Mastery

Fundamental to achieving mastery[3] of strategic collaboration practice is defining collaboration as a problem-solving approach that emerges over time through interdependent and reciprocal relationships. Public and nonprofit managers must learn to skillfully read the collaboration context, including an understanding of key actors motives and

Table 14.1   The Keys to Collaborating Strategically

- Recruit lead champions to serve as neutral convener or trusted broker.

- Err on the side of inclusiveness with participant recruitment, including community leaders and institutions not typically at the table, with greatest resistance to change, and important to implementation success.

- Understand and act on collaboration context, including racial or socioeconomic inequities, history of mistrust, existing partnerships and social networks, geographical or distance challenges, legal requirements and mandates, unique target populations, and high-profile events.

- Carefully consider the role of citizens, thinking through how to bridge knowledge and cultural gaps.

- Consider a wide range of tools for participant recruitment and retention such as incentives, levels of participant involvement, letters of commitment, memorandums of understanding, and participant agreements.

- Invest in ongoing processes to build trust, shared commitment and vision of desired outcomes, and common values and goals.

- Develop explicit structures and operating procedures such as participant requirements, decision-making rules, leadership roles, committees, or other substructures for action.

- Make sure all participants share in the risk and reward (not necessarily equally—but transparently), understand their value to the collaboration's success, and are involved in the collaboration's work.

- Foster a culture that cultivates change and creativity, incorporates ongoing dialogue and feedback, and is flexible to change course as needed based on new information and pooled knowledge.

- Create realistic goals and meaningful measures of success for different points in the strategic collaboration's process including early progress and short- and long-term goals.

- Build systems for communication, information gathering, and outcomes measurement using local knowledge and existing data collection systems where possible.

- Schedule regular orientation and planning sessions to overcome learning curve and commitment with participant changes and additions and to keep all participants up to date on the collaboration's progress.

- Assure that participants grow in their roles developing technical, legal, or political knowledge or the skills of effective collaboration through training, site visits, and expert consultations.

Table 14.1   The Keys to Collaborating Strategically (Continued)

- Sustain strategic focus, by emphasizing short- and long-term agendas, collective capacity building, and outcome assessment.

- Celebrate accomplishments and communicate effectively with participants and external stakeholders, including funders, media, community leaders, and elected officials.

behaviors, and then, most critically, harness collective energy and steer toward results. Mastery of strategic collaboration requires the practitioner to adroitly translate knowledge and experience gained from organizational practice into a more nuanced and fluid situation as well as to continue to learn from collaboration experience.

The six principles of strategic collaboration provide practical guidance for public and nonprofit managers to be more effective in their decision regarding collaboration, as participants in collaborative activities, and as stewards of their agency's mission and resources. Strategic collaboration practice is a blend of both the art and science of public administration practice as adept strategic collaboration practitioners must be grounded in the social science of evidence-based action, problem and policy analytic methods, and smart practice related to group processes and interorganizational dynamics. As public and nonprofit managers successfully navigate collaborative whitewater and reflexively learn from successes and failures, mastery will grow and develop.

14.4 Overcoming Common Roadblocks

Roadblocks to collaboration can be anticipated and, if not overcome, will impede the successful evolution of the strategic collaboration. Given the emergent and politically charged nature of strategic collaboration, public and nonprofit managers need to effectively use their people, analytic, leadership, and conflict resolution skills to overcome these roadblocks. For example, while moving the effort forward, strategic collaborators must continue to review their assumptions and reassess the contextual factors that drove the collaboration's formation. This process reinforces shared

SIX PRINCIPLES OF STRATEGIC COLLABORATION PRACTICE

Principle 1: Choose strategic collaboration wisely.
Principle 2: Understand the strategic collaboration life cycle.
Principle 3: Strengthen leadership capacity.
Principle 4: Balance risk and reward transparently.
Principle 5: Cultivate innovation for meaningful change.
Principle 6: Emphasize outcomes and impacts.

understanding of collaboration goals and important context issues. To avoid participant impatience with this review process, however, it should be undertaken only at
strategic moments in time (e.g., at a retreat where participants have agreed to focus
on strategic planning or on improving collaboration processes). In addition, collaboration participants need to realistically adjust expectations to existing resources.
Conveners will likely underestimate resource needs or overestimate availability.
Without direct action and transparent reallocation of priorities among participants,
this misalignment could seriously damage the ability of the collaboration to develop
and achieve the identified goals. The ability to meet initial goals that sparked participant commitment is important for continued investment and progress.

Other common roadblocks include incorrectly interpreting the life cycle stage
and thus not having the best fit with collaborative processes (e.g., proceeding with
setting goals before reaching clarity of purpose); underestimating challenges to
established turf, status, and systems; misreading collaborative readiness signals;
failing to get up-front agreement on who "owns" the collaboration by not securing
consensus on how decisions will be made; and not building into collaborative processes the understanding that successful collaboration requires reciprocity so that
all participants share reward and risk. A past history of failed collaborative efforts or
community distrust may negatively affect the collaboration's effectiveness. Again,
effective leadership and facilitation skills are called for in these situations as is the
ability of the conveners to get or sustain buy-in and keep the collaboration moving forward. If conveners notice a sense of cynicism on the part of participants, it
may also be helpful to understand that this may be a self-defense on the part of
participants because they have become disillusioned or frustrated due to unmet
expectations.[4] Realistic and pragmatic attention both to participant self-interest
and collective interest (e.g., issues of status and power), assuring transparency of
collaborative processes, and setting reasonable expectations will help the collaboration avoid this potentially dysfunctional dynamic.

While not having critical players involved can be an insurmountable roadblock,
just as problematic are the "difficult" people at the table. Given the wide range of
personality characteristics, the individual variance in commitment levels, and the
diversity in leadership and followership styles and skills among the participants,
strategic collaboration conveners must anticipate the human relations issues that
will confound collaborative processes. Of course, some people just have a propensity
for provocative behavior and comments.[5] At the same time, there are "toxic" people
and agencies that consciously or subconsciously do not readily fit well in group
situations or agree to participate with the intended goal of impeding success. The
tendency of experts to try to "power over" other participants may also negatively
affect collaboration dynamics. While dealing with these difficult situations may
be uncomfortable, conveners and collaboration leaders must be skillful in proactively and deliberately facilitating group processes so that the participants can share
needed expertise and knowledge in a meaningful way. Each of these roadblocks can
severely impede the work of the collaboration. While technology can be a tool for

Table 14.2 Avoiding Strategic Collaboration Failure

Pitfall 1	Critical players not at the table.
Pitfall 2	No shared vision of collaboration vision and impacts.
Pitfall 3	Bad participant behavior (e.g., bullying, naysaying, absent without leave [AWOL]) ignored.
Pitfall 4	Hidden agendas (e.g., competitive goals, turf protection) impede progress.
Pitfall 5	Wrong participants at the table (no people skills and unwilling to learn).
Pitfall 6	Insufficient knowledge of context and policy area (and unwilling to seek).
Pitfall 7	Inadequate attention to power and status.
Pitfall 8	Early markers for success not achieved.
Pitfall 9	Overestimate technology as the answer for communication.
Pitfall 10	Inertia and status quo win.

efficiently sharing information, it can also be an impediment if used inappropriately. Table 14.2 summarizes the pitfalls to avoid strategic collaboration failure.

14.5 Looking Ahead to New Technologies

When the problem being addressed by a collaborative endeavor is controversial or calls for significant change, the ideal medium for collaboration is face-to-face meetings. Face-to-face meetings are especially important to furthering relationships when participants are relatively unknown to each other. At the same time, public and nonprofit managers need to keep abreast of advances in technology that can assist and enrich collaboration. This is especially true for collaborations challenged by distance, such as in rural areas or in regions having geographic barriers that impede straightforward logistics. Video and teleconferencing techniques may prove useful in concert with face-to-face meetings. The prospect of electronic collaboration strategies continues to advance through various Web-based technologies that include a range of interactive and user-generated options such as "wikis" and various free Google applications (e.g., Google Groups or GoogleDocs) as well as vendor-supported options. In addition, Web-based methods are available for disseminating findings and successes of the collaborative activities and for archiving and storing digital and electronic materials at a reasonable cost. For example, Healthy People 2010, mentioned in Chapter 3, has an extensive website (http://

www.healthypeople.gov) that serves as a useful vehicle to electronically provide resources and data for those involved in this broad-based national health promotion effort as well as to recruit new collaborators.

Clearly there are advantages to using technology to facilitate collaboration, especially to decrease meeting overhead as the size of the group increases (e.g., dealing with conflicting schedules, finding centrally located and neutral meeting space, copying costs of extensive handouts). At the same time, using technology can be a mixed blessing as conveners will need to address training needs and software compatibility and be sensitive to the quality of communication exchange (e.g., clarity, avoiding jargon, potential for misunderstanding meaning). Although electronic exchange of information offers a reasonable alternative for personal meetings, availability of computers is not yet universal, and the skill level of participants in using the software varies suggesting that adoption of electronic strategies should be made cautiously.

14.6 Supplemental Resources

Successful strategic collaboration practitioners must effectively perform tasks that many may consider mundane but with a "big picture" perspective, such as scheduling and managing meetings, clarifying roles and responsibilities, and developing procedures. These tasks must be accomplished with an overarching judgment that recognizes the policy environment, competition and sensitivities among stakeholders, deep knowledge of the community, how to elicit both individual and agency commitment, the challenge of presenting data and expert knowledge, and attention to the need for continued legitimacy of the effort and problem. To assist the reader in implementing strategic collaboration, the appendices provides a variety of resources to supplement the materials provided in the earlier book chapters. These resources were developed with practitioners in mind and provide concrete assistance on the various operating tasks associated with guiding collaborative activities:

- Appendix A. Recommended Collaboration Practice Reading List: This resource provides a list of 10 recommended publications that provide a solid foundation for understanding the increased role of collaboration in governance, dimensions of collaboration practice, and collaboration competencies.
- Appendix B. Collaboration Operating Guidelines: This resource provides a sample set of operating guidelines. Similar to bylaws for a more traditional nonprofit organization, operating guidelines set forth the rules for structuring and operating the collaboration. While the rules can and will change over time, the important point is that the rules are established and maintained in an inclusive and transparent manner.
- Appendix C. Participant Agreement: Just as employees and volunteers benefit from having position descriptions that outline their roles and responsibilities, drafting an agreement regarding expectations of the collaborative participants

can also further having participants more informed about the collaboration's expectations and reduce the potential for misunderstanding.

- Appendix D. Matrix of Collaboration Participant Roles: This resource was developed to clarify roles and responsibilities among a diverse set of collaborative participants who represent various agencies and interests. To avoid unnecessary duplication and further communication among the participants, this tool was developed to clarify who had what responsibilities and to further discussion to make sure there was shared agreement about the roles. This resource is also useful in thinking through whether the conveners have everyone needed at the collaborative table.

- Appendix E. Checklist for Strategic Collaboration Meetings: This checklist offers suggestions for planning and managing meetings. Strategically thinking through what needs to be accomplished over what period of time and who needs to be involved at what points is critical to assuring inclusion and attention to results. To be effective, meeting conveners need to attend to both the task and socioemotional elements of meetings and also to proactively think about how to organize the collaboration's agenda for the future.

- Appendix F. Parliamentary Procedure Highlights for Effective Meetings: This resource provides an overview of methods for conducting meetings to help assure that group consensus is reached and that discussions remain focused and on schedule. The degree of formality of the meetings should align with participant expectations and convener skills. *Robert's Rules of Order*, or some variation of them, are commonly used for effective meetings.

- Appendix G. Collaborative Analysis of a Contested Policy Issue Checklist: This resource provides a checklist to help collaborations involved in a policy area where the stakeholders have a great deal of disagreement. The Marine Oil Trade of Alaska case (Chapter 11) illustrated how this was used to help the collaborators work through very complex issues.

- Appendix H. Review of Collaboration Literature: This resource provides a summary review of the collaboration literature appearing in American Society for Public Administration (ASPA)-sponsored journals in the last five years, addressing collaborative context, collaboration capacity, and citizen engagement.

In addition, the Internet offers a wealth of resources as professional associations increasingly help their members be collaboratively successful. Readers can use search engines to seek information or rely on their professional associations for materials or professional development workshops. A wide assortment of printed materials is also available to help practitioners on useful topics including meeting management, community and stakeholder involvement, and professional writing.[6] Use caution when using any resource to ensure that the tool fits the collaborative situation, furthers the collaboration's purpose, and can readily adjust to changing circumstances as the collaboration evolves.

14.7 Promise of Strategic Collaboration—Revisited

Although engaged in collaborative practice for years, public and nonprofit managers all too often stumble into the practice of collaboration without a strategic orientation, leaving them:

- Overwhelmed by the process, as the phrase "herding cats" becomes all too true.
- Frustrated because they underestimate the time and resources needed to build and sustain the collaboration.
- Impatient as participants' energy and commitment levels naturally fluctuate over time.
- Disheartened when participants lose interest, are distracted by their other priorities, or become impatient with group process.
- Exasperated when leadership struggles occur as key stakeholders vie for power.
- Panicked when there is turnover in agency representatives' leadership positions.

This book argues that the underlying problem is with how collaboration has been framed and practiced. Moving from an *ad hoc* and silo-based approach to strategic collaboration offers a public problem-solving framework to make positive changes in our communities and advance public service practice.

The collaboration life cycle model presents a developmental perspective that brings attention to the changing needs and demands at each stage so that public and nonprofit managers can adjust their roles accordingly and better facilitate collaborative structures and processes through transitions. More systematic attention to collaboration readiness enables collaboration conveners to make a more informed decision about whether to proceed with formation and clarifies potential vulnerabilities. Understanding why and how managers in public and nonprofit organizations engage in strategic collaborative structures and processes; how they strategically administer, lead, or facilitate collaboration; and how they can enable the collaboration to be effective and accountable is essential knowledge for advancing collaborative practice.

Of course, there is much more to learn. Collaboration is an active research focus area for public and nonprofit administration scholars, and this book is indebted to the researchers who have enriched our knowledge about collaboration. As illustrated in the literature review in Appendix H, the quantity and quality of research on collaboration continues to grow. As researchers and practitioners become even more sophisticated in their knowledge and understanding of collaboration governance and practice, more synthesis across disciplines will be developed and frameworks empirically tested. The cases in Chapters 5 through 13 suggest next steps for learning more about the uses of and processes important to strategic collaboration practice including the following:

- The differences in successful and unsuccessful collaborative efforts. Can specific indicators be pinpointed such as a culture of competition versus collaboration, the diversity of professional cultures involved, or changing priorities of funders or participating agencies?

■ Characteristics of the effective conveners, convening agencies or champions, and how these roles evolve over the collaboration life cycle.

■ When and how to involve citizens meaningfully in strategic collaboration.

■ When and how can incentives (or disincentives) be used to increase participant retention and performance.

■ How to efficiently and effectively develop a cadre of public and nonprofit managers, community leaders, and other interested parties that possess the needed knowledge, skills, abilities, and values for collaboration success.

Additional areas of focus for research include a fuller understanding of collaboration impacts, particularly beyond the outcomes of a specific collaborative effort; processes by which collaborations evolve and learn; and institutional structures and designs that assure sufficient attention to equity and fairness, outcomes, and improvements.

Although effective collaboration may be used for ends that are not legal or moral,[7] the emphasis here is on the important role that strategic collaboration can play in advancing the common good. Consequently, strategic collaboration practice invests heavily in the transparency of processes, openness of methods, broad inclusiveness of participants, and accountability of outcomes and impacts. The promise of strategic collaboration is to envision a better future and to serve as a catalyst for action.

Endnotes

1. Collaboration governance requires that public and nonprofit managers must be skilled at managing vertically, horizontally, and inclusively, within their particular collaborative context, skillfully interacting and negotiating with environmental pressures. For example, see R. Agranoff and M. McGuire, *Collaborative Public Management: New Strategies for Local Government* (Washington, DC: Georgetown University Press, 2003); L. O'Toole, K. Meier, and S. Nicholson-Croty, Managing Upward, Downward and Outward, *Public Management Review, 7* (1): 45–68, 2005; L. Bingham and R. O'Leary, Conclusion: Parallel Play, Not Collaboration: Missing Questions, Missing Connections. *Public Administration Review, 66* (Supplement): 161–67, 2006; D.F. Kettl, Managing Boundaries in American Administration: The Collaboration Imperative, *Public Administration Review, 66* (Supplement): 10–19, 2006; J. Bryson, B.C. Crosby, and M. Stone, The Design and Implementation of Cross-Sector Collaborations: Propositions from the Literature, *Public Administration Review, 66* (Supplement): 44–55, 2006. As noted in the summary literature review, researchers are increasingly recognizing that there is no one best way to collaborate just as there is no one reason that drives individuals and organizations to choose to collaborate and that practitioners must have a comprehensive set of collaboration skills to be effective (see Appendix H).

2. Page convincingly argues that collaboration requires consideration of four platforms of accountability, external authorization, internal inclusion, results measurement, and managing for results. S. Page, Measuring Accountability for Results in Interagency Collaboration, *Public Administration Review, 64* (5): 591–606, 2004.

3. Goodsell describes mastery as an essential element of public administration craftsmanship, suggesting that achieving master status occurs only after a period of hard work and progressive development as the practitioner demonstrates "that rare ability of being able to do something to its fullest potential." C. Goodsell, The Public Administrator as Artisan, *Public Administration Review, 52* (3): 248, 1992.

4. Insights from organizational research provide help in assessing collaboration dynamics. In trying to understand a diminished sense of engagement on the part of employees, Naus found that employees engaged in cynicism as a self-defense. Naus, van Iterson, and Roe found that employees became cynical when they perceived the organization not living up to moral principles such as truth, honesty, and fair dealing. These researchers argue that cynicism should be added to exit, voice, neglect, and loyalty as employee responses to adverse organization dynamics. See F. Naus, A. van Iterson, and R. Roe, Organizational Cynicism: Extending the Exit, Voice, Loyalty, and Neglect Model of Employees' Responses to Adverse Conditions in the Workplace, *Human Relations, 60* (5): 683–718, 2007.

5. While "flaming comments" may be provocative, Decker argues that they can actually help further discussion if handled well. See his 10 tips for surviving public meetings. L. Decker, *Over My Dead Body! A Workbook for Community Involvement* (Phoenix, AZ: Lindworth Press, 2005), pp. 158–160. These pages provide a helpful strategy for dealing with contentious meetings and emotionally charged topics.

6. For example, Kaner et al. is a helpful resource on facilitation of groups, including team facilitation and participatory decision making. S. Kaner, L. Lind, C. Toldi, S. Fisk, and D. Berger, *Facilitator's Guide to Participatory Decision-Making* (2d ed., San Francisco: Jossey-Bass, 2007). From a business analyst perspective on facilitation and effective meetings, see A. Zavala and K. Hass, *The Art and Power of Facilitation: Running Powerful Meetings* (Vienna, VA: Management Concepts, 2008). Also, for practical advice on managing and mediating community participation, see Decker, *Over My Dead Body!* Also consider the target audience of your information and reports. N. Macris, *Planning in Plain English: Writing Tips for Urban and Environmental Planners* (Chicago, IL: American Planning Association, 1999) provides helpful advice in making complex information, often filled with jargon, more accessible to lay audiences. Also see M. Mintrom, *People Skills for Policy Analysts* (Washington, DC: Georgetown University Press, 2003) for advice on how to present policy issues, to work with diverse audiences, to facilitate meetings, and to handle conflict.

7. Researchers have found that networks and collaborative structures are used for illegal and immoral ends. These types of activities, however, tend to invest a great deal of attention to secrecy and lack of transparency to stay out of sight of authorities. For interesting research on illegal networks see J. Raab and H. Milward, Dark Networks as Problems, *Journal of Public Administration Research and Theory, 13* (4): 433–439, 2003; W. Baker and R. Faulkner, The Social Organization of Conspiracy: Illegal Networks in the Heavy Electrical Equipment Industry, *American Sociological Review, 58* (6): 837–860, 1993.

Appendix A: Recommended Reading List for Collaborative Practice

Agranoff, R. 2006. Inside Collaborative Networks: Ten Lessons for Public Managers. *Public Administration Review, 66* (Supplement): 56–65.

Bardach, E. 1998. *Getting Agencies to Work Together: The Practice and Theory of Managerial Craftsmanship*. Washington, DC: Brookings Institution Press.

Decker, L. 2005. *Over My Dead Body! A Workbook for Community Involvement*. Phoenix, AZ: Lindworth Press.

Getha-Taylor, H. 2008. Learning Indicators and Collaborative Capacity: Applying Action Learning Principles to the U.S. Department of Homeland Security. *Public Administration Quarterly, 32* (2): 125–146.

Goldsmith, S. and W. Eggers. 2004. *Governing by Network: The New Shape of the Public Sector*. Washington, DC: Brookings Institution Press.

Gray, B. 1989. *Collaborating: Finding Common Ground for Multiparty Problems*. San Francisco: Jossey-Bass.

Huxham, C. and S. Vangen. 2005. *Managing to Collaborate: The Theory and Practice of Collaborative Advantage*. London: Routledge.

Kretzman, J. and J. McKnight. 1993. *Building Communities from Inside Out: A Path toward Finding and Mobilizing a Community's Assets*. Evanston, IL: Asset-Based Community Development Institute (ACTA Publications).

Lukensmeyer, C. and L. Torres. 2006. *Public Deliberation: A Manager's Guide to Public Deliberation*. Washington, DC: IBM Center for the Business of Government.

Mandell, M., Ed. 2001. *Getting Results through Collaboration: Networks and Network Structures for Public Policy and Management*. Westport, CT: Quorum Books.

Mattessich, P., M. Murray-Close, and B. Monsey. 2001. *Collaboration: What Makes It Work*, 2nd edition. St. Paul, MN: Wilder Foundation.

McGuire, M. 2006. Collaborative Public Management: Assessing What We Know and How We Know It. *Public Administration Review, 66* (Supplement): 33–43.

Milward, H. B. and K. Provan (2006). *A Manager's Guide to Choosing and Using Collaborative Networks*. Washington, D.C: IBM Center for the Business of Government.

O'Toole, L., K. Meier, and S. Nicholson-Crotty. 2005. Managing Upward, Downward and Outward. *Public Management Review, 7* (1): 45–68.

Appendix B: Collaboration Operating Guidelines Sample

Similar to the bylaws of a nonprofit organization, operating guidelines provide the basic rules or operation for collaboration. This sample suggests basic information that may be useful in the collaboration's formation stage. Collaboration leaders are encouraged to revisit the operating guidelines as needed.

Mission

State the mission of the collaboration.

Membership

Describe how members are selected, nominated, appointed, or recruited. Include any categories of membership and any requirements such as annual payments.

Governance

1. *Describe the roles and responsibilities of the governing body.* For example, the Steering Committee is the principal oversight and management entity for the XXXX Collaboration. As such, the committee is responsible for strategic planning, fundraising, policymaking, and operational and financial oversight. This includes, but is not limited to, development, implementation, and evaluation of the strategic and business plans, including goal setting and evaluation for all programs; hiring, managing, and evaluating lead

staff and consultants; providing oversight for the development; and ensuring that the XXXX Collaboration operates within the context of its values and principles.

2. *Describe the composition and selection of the governing body.* For example, the Steering Committee will have no more than 17 members nominated by the Committee on Governance and elected by the collaboration membership. Steering Committee members may serve up to two consecutive three-year terms. After one year off the steering committee, she or he may be elected to return to the Steering Committee for up to an additional two consecutive three-year terms. Any vacancy occurring in the interim between elections must be filled by nominations from the Committee on Governance with approval of the Steering Committee.

3. *Describe any special requirements for members of the governing body.* For example, each Steering Committee member may be required to participate in at least one committee.

4. *Describe the collaboration's officers and duties.* For example:
   - The chair will be responsible for conducting the regular meetings and business of the XXXX Steering Committee, appointing all committee chairs, providing primary oversight of the director, and representing the collaboration in the media. The term for the chair is two years.
   - The chair-elect acts as the chair in the chair's absence, oversees all evaluation efforts, and performs other duties as assigned. The chair-elect shadows the work of the chair to make a smooth transition into the office of the chair. The term for the chair-elect is two years.
   - The treasurer coordinates with the fiscal agent of the collaborative, receives and disburses revenues, prepares and maintains required fiscal reports, monitors spending, and makes at least quarterly financial reports to the Steering Committee. The term for the treasurer is two years.

5. *Describe the collaboration subgroups such as committees and task forces and their governance rules.* For example, all committees will be chaired by a member of the Steering Committee and have at least one member of the committee from a partner organization that is not represented on the Steering Committee. The standing committees of the XXXX Steering Committee and their responsibilities are as follows:
   a. Committee on Governance
      (1) Recommends policies and procedures.
      (2) Serves as the nominating committee.
      (3) Ensures the involvement of partners, funders, and students.
   b. Finance Committee (treasurer is chair)
      (1) Responsible for developing and implementing the business model.
      (2) Responsible for budget development and allocation.
      (3) Provides fiscal and administrative oversight.

        (4) Prepares reports for funders and recommends fiscal policies including any investments.

        (5) A representative of the fiscal agent serves as a member of this committee.

  c. Fundraising/Resource Development Committee

        (1) Raises funds.

        (2) Seeks new members.

        (3) Seeks opportunities for funding through grant writing.

  d. Evaluation Committee

        (1) Researches benchmarks and comparison data.

        (2) Develops and coordinates data collection and analysis.

        (3) Coordinates reports and presentations for sharing data.

Decision-Making Rules

Describe the required quorum and any voting rules. For example, setting and revision of goals (e.g., strategic plans and business plans) and approving budgets requires a two-thirds majority vote of collaboration members.

Revision of Operating Guidelines

Describe how the operating guidelines will be revised. For example, revising the operating guidelines requires a two-thirds majority vote of collaboration members.

Dissolving the Collaboration

Describe the procedures for dissolution. Dissolving the collaboration requires a two-thirds majority vote of the collaboration membership. If the choice is made to dissolve, the fiscal agent will be responsible for assuring that assets are disbursed appropriately.

Appendix C: Participant Agreement

We welcome you as a member of the XXX Collaboration. It is a policy of XXXX that all members read and sign the following agreement. The purpose of this agreement is to ensure that members have mutual expectations as to their respective roles and responsibilities.

As a member of the XXXX, I agree to the following:

1. I am responsible for overseeing and supporting the vitality and growth of this collaboration.
2. I will work to carry out the mission of the XXXX and to help the collaboration achieve its strategic goals in an ethical manner.
3. I am responsible for the oversight of the fiscal health of the XXXX.
4. I am responsible for understanding and approving, as needed, all policies and programs and for overseeing reports on their implementation.
5. I will support XXXX through annual contributions of $ _____.
6. I will actively engage in fund raising for the XXXX, in whatever ways I can best participate.
7. I will attend at least 75% of the quarterly meetings and be available as needed for phone consultations.
8. I will serve on one standing committee, as appointed by the chair.
9. I will treat all XXXX business and information deemed confidential by the XXXX Collaboration as confidential and proprietary.
10. I will avoid actual or perceived conflicts of interest with other activities or organizations with which I may be involved.

_____   _____
Signature, XXXX Collaboration Member   Date

Appendix D: Matrix of Collaboration Participant Roles

Matrix of Collaboration Participant Roles[1]

	Neighborhood Development Corporation	Neighborhood Association Umbrella Agency	Neighborhood Business Association	Neighborhood-Focused Social Services Organization	Neighborhood University/College or Other "Anchor"	Neighborhood Congregation Association
Real Estate Planning/Development	Leads	Participates	Supports	Supports	Participates	Supports
Neighborhood Organizing/Communication Advocacy	Participates	Leads	Supports	Supports	Supports	Supports
Business Services	Participates	Supports	Leads	Supports	Supports	Supports
Social Services Coordination/Delivery	Supports	Supports	Supports	Leads	Supports	Supports
Neighborhood/Anchor Partnerships	Participates	Participates	Participates	Participates	Leads	Supports
Faith Based Outreach	Supports	Supports	Supports	Supports	Supports	Leads

Definitions:

Leads: Coordinates and provides oversight for plans/programs/activities.
Participates: Takes an active role in the planning and implementation of programs/activities.
Supports: Fully aware of and supportive of efforts of lead entity.

[1] Developed by Steve Barlow (2009), Executive Director, University District Development Corporation.

Appendix E: Checklist for Strategic Collaboration Meetings

The following checklist is offered to help avoid some common missteps when thinking through how to guide and facilitate strategic collaboration meetings:

1. Respect participants' time:
   a. Meet only when justified.
   b. Start and end the meeting as scheduled.
   c. Consider the type of meeting necessary to accomplish the agenda: regular business meeting, retreat or planning meeting, working meeting focused on one topic, site visit.
2. Arrange for a suitable meeting location and space that contributes to discussion and open exchange. (Often nonprofit agencies or community libraries make their space available for community collaborations.)
3. Provide materials at least two days prior to the meeting, including the agenda, even if it is only an outline.
   a. Design the agenda.
      (1) Ensure that needed information is shared. Request brief status reports on assignments/tasks to confirm progress or identify obstacles but to avoid allowing lengthy expositions that do not relate specifically to the rest of the meeting's agenda. Written summaries should be distributed in advance of the meeting to maximize time for productive exchange.
      (2) Allow sufficient time for discussion and feedback. Be prepared to ask probing questions, and refocus the discussion as needed.
      (3) Build in opportunity for brainstorming or learning something new (e.g., guest speakers, site visits) to encourage shared experiences

and understanding or to develop participant collaboration skills proactively (e.g., managing conflict).

(4) Recognize the contributions of the collaboration's participants and
celebrate milestones and successes.

(5) As appropriate, allocate time to assess the collaboration's processes.
   i. What needed expertise is missing?
   ii. What has changed since the collaboration began?
   iii. Do participants understand assigned roles and responsibilities?
   iv. Are we making progress?
   v. How should our processes (e.g., meetings, agendas, reporting) be
   revised to be more useful or transparent?

b. If materials are sent electronically, confirm receipt.

c. Date materials to avoid miscommunication, in case various versions begin
to be floated.

4. Know in advance who will be attending.

a. Watch for patterns on absences to troubleshoot disengagement.

b. Consider using committee or group coleaders to avoid breakdown in
communication due to absences.

5. Arrive early and be prepared for the agenda topics.

6. Assign or elicit a volunteer to document key actions (write minutes, either
formal or informal style) or decisions made during the meeting.

7. Assure an open and inclusive meeting environment.

a. The meeting leaders should actively facilitate, maintaining the meeting's
focus and attending to time constraints.

b. All of the participants should take responsibility for addressing conflict in a
productive and empowering manner.

Selected References

Bens, I. 2000. *Facilitating with Ease! A Step-by-Step Guidebook with Customizable Worksheets on CD-ROM.* San Francisco: Jossey-Bass.

Decker, L. 2005. *Over My Dead Body! A Workbook for Community Involvement.* Phoenix, AZ: Lindworth Press.

Justice, T. and D. Jamieson. 1999. *The Facilitator's Fieldbook: Step-by Step Procedures, Checklists and Guidelines, Samples and Templates.* New York: American Management Association.

Kaner, S., L. Lind, C. Toldi, S. Fisk, and D. Berger. 2007. *Facilitator's Guide to Participatory Decision-Making,* 2nd edition. San Francisco: Jossey-Bass.

Mintrom, M. 2003. *People Skills for Policy Analysts.* Washington, DC: Georgetown University Press.

Schwarz, R. 2002. *The Skilled Facilitator: A Comprehensive Resource for Consultants, Facilitators, Managers, Trainers, and Coaches.* San Francisco: Jossey-Bass.

Zavala, A. and K. Hass. 2008. *The Art and Power of Facilitation: Running Powerful Meetings.* Vienna, VA: Management Concepts.

Appendix F: Parliamentary Procedure Highlights for Effective Meetings

Parliamentary procedure provides a set of rules for constructive and democratic meetings. *Robert's Rules of Order* is the traditional source of rules and procedures for deliberation and debate in all kinds of meetings. While some consider the rules too formal, the intent of the rules is to ensure that meetings stay focused, that all issues will be fairly judged, and that all members have the opportunity to participate.

Highlights of Use

- Quorum: The minimum number of members required to be present at an assembly before business can be conducted.
- Motions: Brings new business before the assembly: "Mr. President, I move that we…."
- Amendments: Insertions or deletions of words or paragraphs; must be adopted by the full body: "I move to amend the motion by…."
- Division of the question: Dividing a motion into two or more separate motions, both of which must be able to stand on their own. This is a slight verification of a voice vote. It does not require a count unless the chair so desires. Members raise their hands or stand.
- Lay on the table: To stop discussion on a motion: "I move to table the motion…."

- Take from the table: Resuming of an issue previously tabled: "I move to take from the table...."
- Orders of the day: Refers to the agenda, calls for adherence to that particular agenda.
- Points of order: Violation of the rules or improper conversation; must be stated immediately after. The member will rise and say, "I rise to a point of order," or simply, "Point of order." The chair should recognize the member, who will then state the point of order.
- Majority rule: More than half of the votes; 51% is applicable only when the quorum is exactly 100, and "50%+1" can be used only for even numbers of membership.

Resources

Evans, W. J., D. H. Honemann, H. M. Robert III, and T. J. Balch. 2004. *Robert's Rules of Order, Newly Revised in Brief.* Cambridge, MA: Da Capo Press.

Lewis, A. T. and H. M. Robert III. 2006. *Robert's Rules Simplified.* Mineola, NY: Dover Publications.

Zimmerman, D. P. (2005). *Robert's Rules in Plain English: A Readable, Authoritative, Easy-to-Use Guide to Running Meetings.* 2nd edition. New York: Collins.

Appendix G: Collaborative Analysis of a Contested Policy Issue Checklist

George J. Busenberg

The goal of a collaborative analysis is to generate an analysis of a contested policy issue that will be acceptable to all the involved stakeholders as a valid basis for policy negotiations and decisions. The following checklist describes the principles for a collaborative analysis:

1. The analysis of the contested issue is overseen by a Steering Committee.
2. All stakeholders involved in the contested issue are represented on the Steering Committee.
3. The analysis of the contested issue is conducted by one research team.
4. The members of the research team are selected by the Steering Committee.
5. The Steering Committee establishes decision rules for the oversight of the analysis.
6. The Steering Committee and research team communicate periodically about the analysis throughout its development.
7. All Steering Committee members can monitor the analysis throughout its development.
8. The Steering Committee can adjust the approach of the analysis throughout its development.

Appendix H: Recent Collaboration Practice Literature

Joy A. Clay

This summary highlights recent (2004 to early 2009) collaborative practice literature published by the American Society of Public Administration (ASPA)-sponsored journals.[3] The current period was selected since sufficient time has passed for the integration of earlier work. ABI/Inform was used to identify literature including *collaboration* and *public* as keywords and supplemented by a further scan of the tables of contents of the 16 journals. After a review of the abstracts, 76 (including 12 case studies of exemplary collaborative managers included in the 2006 PAR special supplement on collaborative public management) were found relevant; full copies of these materials were collected and read. Part of the challenge of building a cohesive understanding of this topic is that *collaboration* has different meanings used to describe both the structure and processes of collective action. We included as many articles as possible to represent the broad range of research and theory building efforts on collaboration but focused on those that used quantitative or qualitative research or advanced theory or described specific ways that collaboration is being used in the public or nonprofit sector. Three themes emerged from the review of the literature and organize this summary: collaborative context, collaborative capacity, and citizen engagement.

Collaborative Context: Environmental Factors Key to Understanding Collaboration

Researchers continue to examine how public and nonprofit administrators manage collaboration vertically, horizontally, and inclusively, within their particular policy, organization, and community context, to wrestle with difficult public problems (Bingham and O'Leary, 2006; Brecher and Wise, 2008; Bryson, Crosby, and

Stone, 2006; Kettl, 2006; Koontz and Thomas, 2006). Consequently, the collaborative context literature addresses the mix of both informal and formal dynamics as well as the inherently cyclical and iterative collaborative processes as collaborators interact and negotiate with environmental pressures and develop commitments and agreements (Bryson et al.; Feiock, Steinacker, and Park, 2009; Gazley, 2008; Keast et al., 2004; Thomson and Perry, 2006; Wise, 2006). Collaboration is described as driven by a shared sense of a problem (Bryson et al.; O'Leary and Bingham, 2007; Weber and Khademian, 2008; Weber, 2009), brokered by champions/ entrepreneurs or mediating agents (Agranoff, 2005; Alexander, 2006; Alford and Hughes, 2008; Bushouse, 2006; Bryson et al.; Eagle and Cowherd, 2006; Emison, 2006; Getha-Taylor, 2006; Kathi, Cooper, and Meek, 2007; Keast et al., 2004; Rhodes and Murray, 2007; Sears and Lovan, 2006; Tschirhart, Christensen, and Perry, 2005), or mandated by funders or authorities (Agranoff, 2008; Berry, Krutz, Langner, and Budetti, 2008; Heck and Roussell, 2007; Page, 2004; Selden, Sowa, and Sandfort, 2006) for a variety of reasons, including opportunity to enhance resources, increase innovation and efficiency, reduce unnecessary duplication of services, overcome inadequacies of existing structures to respond to service needs, increase the breadth and quality of service, exchange information, and enhance legitimacy and increase stability (Berner and Bronson, 2005; Berry et al., 2008; Brecher and Wise; Clay and Mirvis, 2006; Collard, 2006; Payne, 2007; Robinson, Berrett, and Stone, 2006; Selden et al.; Simo and Bies, 2007; Thurmaier, 2006; Weber and Khademian, 2008). There is also wide variation in collaborative structures, including interorganizational service integration or service contracting (Berry et al.; Gazley, 2008; Hall and Kennedy, 2008; Keast, Brown, and Mandell, 2007); collaboration around technology dissemination (Pirog and Johnson, 2008); inter-local and regional cooperation (Feiock et al; Leroux and Carr, 2007; Macmanus and Carson, 2008; Mason, 2008; Thurmaier, 2006); network types, informational, developmental, outreach, and action (Agranoff, 2006, 2008); and citizen participation in governance (Cooper, Bryer, and Meek, 2006; Fung, 2006).

Importantly, there is an increased call for a more nuanced understanding of collaboration. Clearly, there is no "one best way," and public and nonprofit managers need to carefully analyze their particular situation to determine the best collaborative design, tools, skills, and implementation methodology to fit the circumstances (Agranoff, 2006; Alford and Hughes, 2008; Belefski, 2006; Bryson et al., 2006; Dawes, Cresswell, and Pardo, 2009; Fung, 2006; Heck and Roussell, 2007; Keast et al., 2007; Leavitt and Morris, 2007; Thomson and Perry, 2006; Weber and Khademian, 2008), especially the policy issue area (Feldman et al., 2006).

The literature includes insightful cases about collaboration in specific policy/ program areas, including the following:

- Health, education, and social services (Berry et al., 2008; Bushouse, 2006; Chen, 2008; Collard, 2006; Friedrichsen, 2006; Keast et al., 2004, 2007; Page, 2004; Selden et al., 2006; Vogel, Ransom, Wal, and Luisi, 2007).

- Emergency and crisis management (Brudney and Gazley, 2009; Donahue, 2006; Getha-Taylor, 2006, 2008b; Kiefer and Montjoy, 2006; Krutz, Langner, and Budetti, 2008; MacManus and Caruson, 2008; Menifield and Joachim, 2006; Norris-Tirrell and Clay, 2006; Pynes and Tracy, 2007; Robinson, Berrett, and Stone, 2006; Simo and Bies, 2007; Waugh and Streib, 2006; Wise, 2006).
- Environment (Alexander, 2006; Belefski, 2006; Emison, 2006; Leach, 2006; Welsh, 2004; Weber, 2009; Yandle, 2006).
- Economic development and land use (Agranoff, 2005; Berner and Bronson, 2009; Feiock et al., 2009; English and Peretz, 2004; Mason, 2008; Rhodes and Murray, 2007; Sears and Lovan, 2006).
- Public safety and criminal justice (Heck and Roussell, 2007; Payne, 2007; Schneider, 2009; Thurmaier, 2006).
- Information technology (Pirog and Johnson, 2008; Dawes et al., 2009).
- Infrastructure and public works, including parks (Brecher and Wise, 2008; Bryer, 2009; Bryer and Cooper, 2007; Eagle and Cowherd, 2006; Leavitt and Morris, 2007; Leroux and Carr, 2007; Van Buuren, 2009).

This policy/program area literature describes various approaches to collaboration, including the following:

- Formal partnering, cost-sharing or service delivery arrangements, informal coordination among service agencies, such as linking public housing and public health to improve services to the elderly (Vogel et al., 2007).
- Local-to-local agreements to overcome funding shortfalls for emergency management (Macmanus and Carson, 2008) and consolidation of public safety dispatch centers (Thurmaier, 2006).
- Emergency preparedness, including joint planning with voluntary and non-profit organizations (Norris-Tirrell and Clay, 2006; Simo and Bies, 2007; Brudney and Gazley, 2009) or behavioral and mental health service agencies (Pynes and Tracey, 2007).
- Collaborative program evaluation of a nonprofit agency responsible for promoting revitalization efforts, funded by a special local tax (Berner and Bronson, 2005).
- A community-based collaboration formed to resolve environmental and developmental tensions in a large watershed in Montana (Weber, 2009).

Although the policy-area literature often is based on qualitative research using case analysis, the level of sophistication in methodology is increasing as research-ers compare multiple cases to identify patterns or test frameworks (e.g., Agranoff 2008; Chen, 2008; Simo and Bies, 2007; Vogel et al., 2007; Welsh, 2004).

Attending to Collaborative Capacity: A Key to Effectiveness and Success

To overcome bureaucratic barriers to collaboration and expected resistance to change, researchers have generally found that attention must be paid to collaboration capacity building, individual, organizational, and relational, which necessarily means that adequate care, time, and attention are given to emergent problem definition, visioning and planning, securing resources, assessing status of existing relationships, and setting agreed upon goals as well as considering the resource demands that success might have on the collaborators and the effect on participants' distinct and collaborative identity (Alford and Hughes, 2008; Berry et al., 2008; Bryson et al., 2006; Dawes et al., 2009; Donahue, 2006; McGuire, 2006; Norris-Tirrell and Clay, 2006; Pirog and Johnson, 2008; Simo and Bies, 2007; Tschirhart et al., 2005; Vogel et al., 2007). How organizations seek, add, or hinder knowledge transfer and learning further affects collaborative capacity and is integral to collaborative performance and effectiveness (Agranoff, 2005, 2006, 2008; Belefski, 2006; Bryson et al.; Bushouse, 2006; Feldman et al., 2006; Friedrichsen, 2006; Getha-Taylor, 2008b; Leach, 2006; Mischen and Jackson, 2008; Weber, 2009; Weber and Khademian, 2008; Dawes et al.; Schneider, 2009; Van Buuren, 2009). Van Buuren offers useful criteria for assessing available knowledge in collaborations, inclusive fact-finding; perspicuity (coherent and not contradictory), robustness (proven quality as perceived by multiple actors), impartiality (perceived as established, not manipulated), and convincingness (established credibility by experts and the public). Understanding how collaborations gain knowledge, learn, and evolve thus becomes an important dimension of effective collaborative engagement (Feldman et al., 2006; Weber; Weber and Khademian; Van Buuren).

Collaborative functions add to management complexity and uncertainty as these activities may conflict with existing priorities, threaten power bases, introduce more politics into administrative processes, and fragment organizational resources (Kettl, 2006; McGuire, 2006; Thomson and Perry, 2006). Getting people and organizations with different or competing values and priorities to collaborate effectively requires that public and nonprofit administrators be skillful facilitators, mediators, negotiators, team builders, and communicators as well as being politically astute (Bryer and Cooper, 2007; Dawes et al., 2009; Getha-Taylor, 2008a; O'Leary and Bingham, 2007; Thomson and Perry). McGuire argues that traditional managerial skills—such as managing human and financial resources, managing the structure and rules that guide operations, and designing and implementing effective communication, information management, strategic management, and conflict management practices—are common in either hierarchical organizations or collaborative contexts. In addition, however, he categorizes the distinctive collaborative skills needed as those related to activation, framing, mobilizing, and synthesizing.

Organizational skills of negotiation, facilitation, convening, and collaborative problem solving (O'Leary, Gerard, and Bingham, 2006), conflict resolution (O'Leary and Bingham), brokering (Keast et al., 2004), and the ability to build trust and social capital (Alford and Hughes, 2008; Bryson et al., 2006; Kathi et al., 2007; Keast and Mandell, 2007; McGuire; Thomson and Perry; Waugh and Streib, 2006) are consistently recognized as necessary collaborative skills.

Getha-Taylor (2008a) empirically examined the linkage between federal government human resource managers and the actual demonstrated behaviors on the part of exemplary collaborators to distinguish the superior collaborative practice from average. Contrary to the human resource managers' emphasis on organizational awareness and relationship building, Getha-Taylor found that these "are trumped by interpersonal understanding and teamwork/cooperation as keys to collaborative effectiveness" (p. 115). She argues that this disconnect has implications for recruiting and reward systems if the federal government is to improve collaborative capacity. Her list of superior collaborative competencies include interpersonal understanding (demonstrates empathy, understands motivation), teamwork and cooperation (inclusive perspective on achievements, altruistic perspective on resource sharing, and collaborative conflict resolution), and team leadership (bridges diversity and creates line of sight). Indicating a future research agenda, she developed an impressive list of concrete behaviors as indicators of competency (p. 116).

The complexity of collaboration requires that public and nonprofit managers understand how various collaborative processes may each impact tangible and intangible, social capital, and organizational outcomes (Agranoff, 2005, 2008; Chen, 2008; Koontz and Thomas, 2006; Schneider, 2009) and use multiple lenses to assess collaborative performance, such as external authorization, internal inclusion, results measurement, and managing for results (Page, 2004), agency-focused outcomes such as the resulting sense of shared authority and resources (Gazley, 2008), type and intensity of relationships (Selden et al., 2006), transparency of decision processes (Bushouse, 2006; Leach, 2006; Yandle, 2006), and more tangible and objective outcomes, such as service agreements, joint projects, memorandums of understanding, or realized (and measured) improvements (Agranoff, 2005, 2008; Kathi and Cooper, 2008; Koontz and Thomas). As the literature is expanding, researchers are also more nuanced in the variance of collaborative outcomes and impacts examined, including the effect on time taken to establish, goals/perspective, structural linkages and interdependence, degree of formality, and risks/rewards (Keast and Mandell, 2007; Keast et al., 2007). Unpacking coordination, cooperation, and collaboration as forms of horizontal integration furthers the "understanding of how different options and strategies will accommodate different purposes, require different types of relationships and resource commitments, and produce different outcomes" (Keast et al., 2007, p. 28).

Citizen Engagement: A Key to Legitimacy and Improved Policy

There is growing attention on improving the ability of public sector managers to inclusively and authentically engage citizens, neighborhoods, and communities (Bryer, 2009; Bryer and Cooper, 2007; Callahan, 2007; Cooper et al., 2006; Feldman et al., 2006; Kathi and Cooper, 2007; Leach, 2006; Weber, 2009; Welsh, 2004; Yang and Callahan, 2007). The underlying value of citizen participation is to build relationships and trust with and among individuals and organizations and, consequently, legitimacy for policy decisions (Cooper et al.; Lukensmeyer and Torres, 2006; Norris-Tirrell and Clay, 2006; Yang and Callahan) as well as to add local knowledge to make better policy choices (Fung, 2006; Kiefer and Montjoy, 2006; Welsh; Weber). Based on their extensive review of the literature, Cooper et al. suggest that public and nonprofit managers be very open to citizen engagements as "deliberative approaches to engagement are most likely to lead to citizen-centered collaborative public management ... and are most likely to build citizen efficacy, citizen trust in government, and citizen competence" (pp. 79–80). From their study of neighborhood councils and local government departments in Los Angeles, Cooper and Bryer (2007) conclude that the ability to be responsive to citizen involvement in governance "requires sustained commitment, leadership support, clear motivation, a supportive culture, political awareness" (p. 211).

Importantly, government managers are advised not to take on the role of "expert" or attempt to "manage" the process if the collaboration is to be successful (Bryer, 2009; Welsh, 2007) and to create processes that adopt more inclusive interactions and an emergent posture (Feldman et al., 2006; Getha-Taylor, 2008b; Kiefer and Montjoy, 2006; Van Buuren, 2009). Working with three sets of neighborhood councils and city agencies in Los Angeles, using a community-based action-research framework, university conveners proactively set about building trust and relationships, using facilitated workshop presentations, group discussions, informal networking, and participant reflection to yield interchange and interaction (Kathi and Cooper, 2008, p. 623). Representing a counterpressure to citizen participation, public managers may view citizen involvement in decision making as too risky as it threatens "administrative order and power" (Yang and Callahan, 2007, p. 259) or may be fearful about going out of their comfort zone (Bryer; Keast et al., 2007). The challenge for public service managers is finding the right balance between access and reasonableness; thus, collaborative processes should include "mediation, negotiation, consensus building, and deliberation" (Callahan, 2007, p. 64).

Importantly, researchers caution against a naïve view of citizen participation. Fung (2006) argues that no single participatory design will serve all three key values—legitimacy, justice, and effectiveness. Also, citizens are not duped by "hollow exercises" of expert-driven participation activities "as they hold on to and control the outcome" (Yang and Callahan, 2007, p. 259). Advising caution about the type of organizational collaboration envisioned, public managers have a duty to engage with their political environment, alerting political overseers and stakeholders since determining what the collective citizenry values is problematic, and to carefully think through their participatory strategies (Alford and Hughes, 2008; Fung). Further, funding from advocacy organizations also has political implications as public managers must balance particularistic versus public interests (Brecher and Wise, 2008).

Conclusion

Successful collaboration practice requires public and nonprofit managers to have the following:

■ Organizational awareness, understanding their agency's organizational culture and procedures (Bryer and Cooper, 2007; Dawes et al., 2009; Feldman et al., 2006; Tschirhart et al., 2005; Vogel et al., 2007).
■ Self-awareness of the manager's perceived roles and responsibilities (Bryer, 2009).
■ Policy awareness, including relevant legal, political, democratic, regulatory, and procedural knowledge (Agranoff, 2008; Bryer and Cooper, 2007; Bryson et al., 2006; Dawes et al., 2009; Page, 2004).
■ Process and performance awareness (English and Peretz, 2004; Fung, 2006; Getha-Taylor, 2008b; Kathi and Cooper, 2007; Mandell and Keast, 2007; Mischen and Jackson, 2008; Rhodes and Murray, 2007).
■ Place and social awareness (Callahan, 2007; Feldman et al., 2006; Kiefer and Montjoy, 2006; Weber, 2009).
■ Technology awareness (Pirog and Johnson, 2008).

Recognizing the challenge that new governance places on public service managers, an explosion of scholarly and applied research has been published over the last two decades. This literature has significantly furthered our understanding of collaboration dynamics, competencies, structures, and performance. The articles and exemplary cases included in the special issue of *Public Administration Review* (December 2006) were a major contribution to the collaboration literature, as well as the other current literature highlighted here. There remains the need for more synthesis of the research across disciplines and empirical testing of models and frameworks (Bingham and O'Leary, 2006; Bryson et al., 2006; Cooper et al., 2006; Mischen and Jackson, 2008; O'Leary et al., 2006). Moreover, questions persist as government and nonprofit leaders seek to improve the collaborative capacity of managers and to create and support agency methodologies that promote collaborative success, including addressing the following:

- How collaborations evolve and learn (Bryer and Cooper, 2007; McGuire, 2006; Weber and Khademian, 2008).
- How decisions are made about the degree of collaboration, coordination, or cooperation; participant selection; goal setting; desired outcomes; and collaborative design (Bingham and O'Leary, 2006; Keast et al., 2007; Mandell and Keast, 2007).
- How to manage this fluid process in a systematic manner (Bryson et al., 2006; Thomson and Perry, 2006).
- How to assure sufficient attention to equity and fairness, outcomes and improvements (Brecher and Wise, 2008; Callahan, 2007; Clay and Mirvis, 2006; Feldman et al., 2006; Koontz and Thomas, 2006; Weber, 2009).
- How public managers and sectors interpret their context (Bingham and O'Leary, 2006; Bryson et al., 2006; Clay, 2006; Gazely, 2008; Norris-Tirrell and Leach, 2006; Simo and Bies, 2007; Waugh and Streib, 2006).
- A deeper understanding of public participation and civic engagement in collaborations (Fung, 2006; O'Leary et al., 2006; Welsh, 2004).

Endnotes

1. Developed by Steve Barlow, executive director, University District Development Corporation, in 2009.
2. Developed by George J. Busenberg, associate professor, Soska University, in 2009.
3. The 16 ASPA-sponsored journals (http://www.aspanet.org) are *Public Administration Review, American Review of Public Administration, Chinese Public Administration Review, Criminal Justice Policy Review, International Public Management Journal, Journal of Health and Human Services Administration, Journal of Public Affairs Education, Journal of Public Management and Social Policy, Public Administration Quarterly, Public Budgeting and Finance, Public Integrity, Public Performance and Management Review, Public Voices, Public Works Management and Policy, Review of Public Personnel Administration,* and *State and Local Government Review.*

References

Agranoff, R. 2005. Managing Collaborative Performance. *Public Performance & Management Review, 29* (1): 18-45.

Agranoff, R. 2006. Inside Collaborative Networks: Ten Lessons for Public Managers. *Public Administration Review, 66* (Supplement): 56-65.

Agranoff, R. 2008. Enhancing Performance through Public Sector Networks: Mobilizing Human Capital in Communities of Practice. *Public Performance & Management Review, 31* (1): 320-347.

Alexander, R. 2006. Kirk Emerson and the U.S. Institute for Environmental Conflict Resolution. *Public Administration Review, 66* (Supplement): 156-157.

Alford, J. and O. Hughes. 2008. Public Value Pragmatism as the Next Phase of Public Management. *American Review of Public Administration, 38* (2): 130-148.

Belefski, M. 2006. Collaboration at the U.S. Environmental Protection Agency: An Interview with Two Senior Managers. *Public Administration Review, 66* (Supplement): 143-144.

Berner, M. and M. Bronson. 2005. A Case Study of Program Evaluation in Local Government: Building Consensus Through Collaboration. *Public Performance & Management Review, 28* (3): 309-325.

Berry, C., G. Krutz, B. Langner, and P. Budetti. 2008. Jump-Starting Collaboration: The ABCD Initiative and the Provision of Child Development Services through Medicaid and Collaborators. *Public Administration Review, 68* (3): 480-490.

Bingham, L., and R. O'Leary. 2006. Conclusion: Parellel Play, Not Collaboration: Missing Questions, Missing Connections. *Public Administration Review, 66* (Supplement): 111-121.

Brecher, C. and O. Wise. 2008. Looking a Gift Horse in the Mouth: Challenges in Managing Philanthropic Support for Public Services. *Public Administration Review, 68* (Special Issue): S146-S161.

Brudney, J. and B. Gazley. 2009. Planing to be Prepared: An Empirical Examination of the Role of Voluntary Organizations in County Government Emergency Planning. *Public Performance & Management Review, 32* (3): 372-399.

Bryer, T. 2009. Explaining Responsiveness in Collaboration: Administrator and Citizen Role Perceptions. *Public Administration Review, 69* (2): 271-83.

Bryer, T., and T. Cooper. 2007. Challenges in Enhancing Responsiveness in Neighborhood Governance. *Public Performance & Management Review, 31* (2): 191-214.

Bryson, J., B. Crosby, and M. Stone. 2006. The Design and Implementation of Cross-Sector Collaborations: Propositions from the Literature. *Public Administration Review, 66* (Supplement): 44-55

Bushouse, B. 2006. West Virginia Collaboration for Creating Universal Prekindergarten. *Public Administration Review, 66* (Supplement): 154-155.

Callahan, K. 2007. Citizen Participation: Questions of Diversity, Equity and Fairness. *Journal of Public Management and Social Policy, 13* (1): 53-68.

Chen, B. 2008. Assesing Interorganizational Networks for Public Service Delivery: A Process-Perceived Effectiveness Framework. *Public Performance & Management Review. 31* (3): 348-363.

Clay, J., and D. Mirvis. 2008. Health and Economic Development: Introduction to the Symposium. *Journal of Health and Human Services Administration, 31* (1): 4-9.

Collard, E. 2006. Collaboration to Address the Asthma Problem among Native Americans. *Public Administration Review, 66* (Supplement): 157-158.

Cooper, T., T. Bryer, and J. Meek. 2006. Citizen-centered collaborative public management. *Public Administration Review, 66* (Supplement 1): 76-88.

Dawes, S., S., A. Cresswell, and T. Pardo. 2009. From "Need to Know" to "Need to Share": Tangled Problems, Information Boundaries, and the Building of Public Sector Knowledge Networks. *Public Administration Review, 69* (3): 392-402.

Donahue, A. K. 2006. The space shuttle Columbia recovery operation: How collaboration enabled disaster response. *Public Administration Review, 66* (Supplement): 141-142.

Eagle, K., and P. Cowherd. 2006. Collaborative Capital Planning in Charlotte-Mecklenburg County, North Carolina. *Public Administration Review, 66* (Supplement): 146-147.

Emison, G. 2006. The EPA Bureaucrat Who Could. *Public Administration Review, 66* (Supplement): 152-153.

English, M., J. Peretz, and M. Manderschied. Building Communities while Building Plans: A Review of Techniques for Participatory Planning Processes. 2004. *Public Administration Quarterly, 28* (1/2): 182-221.

Feiock, R., C., A. Steinacker, and H. Park. 2009. Institutional Collective Action and Economic Development Joint Ventures. *Public Administration Review, 69* (2): 256-70.

Feldman, M. S., A. M. Khademian, H. Ingram, and A. S. Schneider. 2006. Ways of Knowing and Inclusive Management Practices. *Public Administration Review, 66* (Supplement): 89-99.

Friedrichsen, S. 2006. Collaborative Public Management in San Francisco. *Public Administration Review, 66* (Supplement): 150-151.

Fung, A. 2006. Varieties of Participation in Complex Governance. *Public Administration Review, 66* (Supplement): 66-75.

Gazley, B. 2008. Beyond the Contract: The Scope and Nature of Informal Government—Nonprofit Partnerships. *Public Administration Review, 68* (1): 141-154.

Getha-Taylor, H. 2006. Preparing Leaders for High Stakes Collaborative Action: Darrell Darnell and the Department of Homeland Security. *Public Administration Review, 66* (Supplement): 159-160.

Getha-Taylor, H. 2008a. Identifying Collaborative Competencies. *Review of Public Personnel Administration, 28* (2): 103-119.

Getha-Taylor, H. 2008b. Learning Indicators and Collaborative Capacity: Applying Action Learning Principles to the U.S. Department of Homeland Security. *Public Administration Quarterly, 32* (2): 125-146.

Hall, L., and S. Kennedy. 2008. Public and Nonprofit Management and the "New Governance." *American Review of Public Administration, 38* (3): 307-321.

Heck, C., and A. Roussell. 2007. State Administration of Drug Courts. *Criminal Justice Policy Review, 18* (4): 418-433.

Kathi, P., and T. Cooper. 2008. Connecting Neighborhood Councils and City Agencies: Trust Building through the Learning and Design Forum Process. *Journal of Public Affairs Education, 13* (3/4): 617-630.

Kathi, P., Cooper, T., and Meek, J. 2007. The Role of the University as a Mediating Institution in Neighborhood Council-City Agency Collaboration. *Journal of Public Affairs Education, 13* (2): 365-382.

Keast, R., K. Brown, and M. Mandell. 2007. Getting the Right Mix: Unpacking Integration Meanings and Strategies. *International Public Management Journal, 10* (1): 9-33.

Keast, R., M. Mandell, K. Brown, and G. Woolcock. 2004. Network Structures: Working Differently and Changing Expectations. *Public Administration Review, 64* (3): 363-371.

Kettl, D. 2006. Managing boundaries in American administration: the collaboration imperative. *Public Administration Review, 66* (Supplement): 10-19.

Kiefer, J., and R. Montjoy. 2006. Incrementalism before the Storm: Network Performance for the Evacuation of New Orleans. *Public Administration Review, 66*: 122-130.

Koontz, T., and C. Thomas. 2006. What do we know and need to know about the environmental outcomes of collaborative management? *Public Administration Review, 66* (Supplement 1): 111-121.

Leach, W. D. 2006. Collaborative Public Management and Democracy: Evidence from Western Watershed Partnerships. *Public Administration Review, 66* (Supplement): 100-110.

Leavitt, W., and J. Morris. 2007. Public Works Service Arrangements in the 21st Century. *Public Works Management & Policy, 12* (1): 325-330.

Leroux, K., & J. Carr. 2007. Explaining Local Government Cooperation on Public Works. *Public Works Management & Policy, 12* (1): 344-358.

MacManus, S., and K. Caruson. 2008. Financing Homeland Security and Emergency Preparedness: Use of Interlocal Cost-Sharing. *Public Budgeting & Finance, 28* (2): 48-86.

McGuire, M. 2006. Collaborative Public Management: Assessing What We Know and How We Know It. *Public Administration Review, 66* (Supplement): 33-43.

Mandell, M., and R. Keast. 2007. Evaluating Network Arrangements: Toward Revised Performance Measures. *Public Performance & Management Review, 30* (4): 574-597.

Mason, S. 2008. Policy Design and Regional Cooperation under the Workforce Investment Act. *State and Local Government Review, 40* (2): 101-114.

Menifield, C. and H. Joachim. 2006. Natural Disasters: Impact, Policy, Assessment, and Collaboration. *Journal of Public Management & Social Policy, 12* (1), 63-76.

Mischen, P., and S. Jackson. 2008. Connecting the Dots: Applying Complexity Theory, Knowledge Management and Social Network Analysis to Policy Implementation. *Public Administration Quarterly, 32* (3): 314-338.

Norris-Tirrell, D., and J. Clay. 2006. Collaborative Planning as a Tool for Strengthening Local Emergency Management, *Journal of Public Management & Social Policy, 12* (1), 25-36.

O'Leary, R., C. Gerard, and L. Bingham. 2006. Introduction to the Symposium on Collaborative Public Management. *Public Administration Review, 66* (Supplement): 6-9.

O'Leary, R. and L. Bingham. 2007. Conclusion: Conflict and Collaboration in Networks. *International Public Management Journal, 10* (1): 103-109.

Page, S. 2004. Measuring Accountability for Results in Interagency Collaboratives. *Public Administration Review 64*, (5): 591-606.

Payne, B. 2007. Victim Advocates' Perceptions of the Role of Health Care Workers in Sexual Assault Cases. *Criminal Justice Policy Review, 18* (1): 81-94.

Pirog, M., and C Johnson. 2008. Electronic Funds and Benefits Transfers, E-Government, and the Winter Commission. *Public Administration Review*, (Special Issue): S103-S114.

Pynes, J.. and P. Tracy. 2007. Flirting with Disaster: A Case Study. *Public Performance & Management Review, 31* (1): 101-117.

Rhodes, M., and J. Murray. 2007. Collaborative Decision Making in Urban Regeneration: A Complex Adaptive Systems Perspective. *International Public Management Journal, 10* (1): 79-101.

Robinson, S., B. Berrett, and K. Stone. 2006. The Development of Collaboration of Response to Hurricane Katrina in the Dallas Area. *Public Works Management & Policy, 10* (4): 315-327.

Schneider, A. 2009. Why do Some Boundary Organizations Result in New Ideas and Practices and Others only Meet Resistance?: Examples From Juvenile Justice. *American Review of Public Administration, 39* (1): 60-79.

Sears, D., and W. Lovan. 2006. Encouraging Collaboration in Rural America. *Public Administration Review, 66* (Supplement): 153-154.

Selden, S., J. Sowa, and J. Sandfort. 2006. The Impact of Nonprofit Collaboration in Early Child Care and Education on Management and Program Outcomes. *Public Administration Review, 66* (3): 412-425.

Simo, G. and A. Bies. 2007. The Role of Nonprofits in Disaster Response: An Expanded Model of Cross-Sector Collaboration. *Public Administration Review, 67* (Supplement): 125-142.

Thomson, A., and J. Perry. 2006. Collaborative Processes: Inside the Black Box. *Public Administration Review, 66* (Supplement): 20-32.

Thurmaier, K. 2006. High-Intensity Interlocal Collaboration in Three Iowa Cities. *Public Administration Review, 66* (Supplement): 144-146.

Tschirhart, M., R. K Christensen, and J. L Perry. 2005. The Paradox of Branding and Collaboration. *Public Performance & Management Review, 29* (1): 67-84.

Van Buuren, A. 2009. Knowledge for Governance, Governance of Knowledge: Inclusive Knowledge Management in Collaborative Governance Processes. *International Public Management Journal, 12* (2): 208-235.

Vogel, A., P. Ransom, Sidique Wai, Daria Luisi. 2007. Integrating Health and Social Services for Older Adults: A Case Study of Interagency Collaboration. *Journal of Health and Human Services Administration, 30* (2): 199-228.

Waugh, W. L., and G. Streib. 2006. Collaboration and Leadership for Effective Emergency Management," *Public Administration Review, 66* (Supplement): 131-140.

Weber, E. 2009. Explaining Institutional Change in Tough Cases of Collaboration: "Ideas" in the Blackfoot Watershed. *Public Administration Review, 69* (2): 314-327.

Weber, E. and A. Khademian. 2008. Wicked Problems, Knowledge Challenges, and Collaborative Capacity Builders in Network Settings. *Public Administration Review, 68* (2): 334-349.

Welsh, M. 2004. Fast-Forward to a Participatory Norm: Agency Response to Public Mobilization over Oil and Gas Leasing in Pennsylvania. *State and Local Government Review, 36* (3): 186-197.

Wise, C. 2006. Organizing for Homeland Security after Katrina: Is Adaptive Management What's Missing. *Public Administration Review, 66* (3): 302-318.

Yandle, T. 2006. The Challenger Scallop Enhancement Company: Collaborative Management of a Natural Resource Based in the Private Sector. *Public Administration Review, 66* (Supplement): 148-150.

Yang, K. and K. Callahan. 2007. Citizen Involvement Efforts and Bureaucratic Responsiveness: Participatory Values, Stakeholder Pressures, and Administrative Practicality. *Public Administration Review, 67* (2): 249-264.

References

Adizes, I. 1988. *Corporate Life cycles: How and Why Corporations Grow, Die and What to Do about It.* Englewood Cliffs, NJ: Prentice Hall.

Agranoff, R. 1991. Human Services Integration: Past and Present Challenges in Public Administration. *Public Administration Review, 51* (6): 533–542.

Agranoff, R. 2005. Managing Collaborative Performance. *Public Performance & Management Review, 29* (1): 18–45.

Agranoff, R. 2006. Inside Collaborative Networks: Ten Lessons for Public Managers. *Public Administration Review, 66* (Supplement): 56–65.

Agranoff, R. 2008. Enhancing Performance through Public Sector Networks: Mobilizing Human Capital in Communities of Practice. *Public Performance & Management Review, 31* (1): 320–347.

Agranoff, R. and M. McGuire. 2003. *Collaborative Public Management: New Strategies for Local Government.* Washington, DC: Georgetown University Press.

Alaska Oil Spill Commission. 1990. *Spill: The Wreck of the Exxon Valdez.* Juneau: State of Alaska.

Alexander, J. and R. Nank. 2009. Public - Nonprofit Partnership: Realizing the New Public Service. *Administration & Society, 41* (3): 364–386.

Alford, J. and O. Hughes. 2008. Public Value Pragmatism as the Next Phase of Public Management. *American Review of Public Administration, 38* (2): 130–148.

Ansell, C. and A. Gash. 2008. Collaborative Governance in Theory and Practice. *Journal of Public Administration Research and Theory, 18* (4): 543–571.

Alter, C. and J. Hage. 1993. *Organizations Working Together.* Newbury Park, CA: Sage.

Ambite, J., Y. Arens, W. Bourne, S. Feiner, L. Gravano, V. Hatzivassiloglou, et al. 2002. Data Integration and Access. In *Advances in Digital Government: Technology, Human Factors, and Policy*, ed. W. J. McIver and A. K. Elmagarmid, pp. 85–106. Boston: Kluwer Academic Publishers.

Andersen, D. F. and S. S. Dawes. 1991. *Government Information Management: A Primer and Casebook.* Englewood Cliffs, NJ: Prentice Hall.

Applegate, J. 1998. Beyond the Usual Suspects: The Use of Citizens' Advisory Boards in Environmental Decision-making. *Indiana Law Journal, 73* (3): 903–957.

Archibald, M. 2007. An Organizational Ecology of National Self-Help/Mutual-Aid Organizations. *Nonprofit Voluntary Sector Quarterly, 36* (4): 598–621.

Austin, J. 2000. *The Collaboration Challenge: How Nonprofits and Businesses Succeed through Strategic Alliances.* San Francisco, CA: Jossey–Bass.

Babiak, K. and L. Thibault. 2008. Challenges in Multiple Cross-Sector Partnerships. *Nonprofit and Voluntary Sector Quarterly, 38*: 117–143.

Baker, E., R. Melton, P. Stange, M. Fields, J. Koplan, F. Guerra, et al. 1994. Health Reform and the Health of the Public: Forging Community Health Partnerships. *Journal of the American Medical Association, 272* (16):1276–1282.

Baker, W. and R. Faulkner. 1993. The Social Organization of Conspiracy: Illegal Networks in the Heavy Electrical Equipment Industry. *American Sociological Review, 58* (6): 837–860.

Bajaj, A. and S. Ram. 2007. A Comprehensive Framework towards Information Sharing between Government Agencies. *International Journal of Electronic Government Research, 3* (2): 29–44.

Bardach, E. 1998. *Getting Agencies to Work Together: The Practice and Theory of Managerial Craftsmanship.* Washington, DC: Brookings Institution Press.

Barret, K. and R. Greene. 2001. *Powering Up: How Public Managers Can Take Control of Information Technology.* Washington DC: CQ Press.

Barth, T. 2001. The Role of Ad Hoc Regional Alliances in Managing Growth. *Public Works Management & Policy, 6* (2): 114–125.

Beaglehole, R., R. Bonita, R. Horton, O. Adams, and M. McKee. 2004. Public Health in the New Era: Improving Health through Collective Action. *Lancet, 363*: 2084–2086.

Bens, I. 2000. *Facilitating with Ease! A Step-by-Step Guidebook with Customizable Worksheets on CD-ROM.* San Francisco: Jossey-Bass.

Benson, L. and I. Harkavy. 2002. The Role of Community-Higher Education-School Partnerships in Educational and Societal Development and Democratization. *Universities and Community Schools, 7* (1–2): 5–27.

Berke, P., D. Godschalk, and E. Kaiser with D. Rodriguez. 2006. *Urban Land Use Planning,* 5th edition. Urbana: University of Illinois Press.

Berman, E. 1997. Dealing with Cynical Citizens. *Public Administration Review, 57* (2): 105–112.

Berman, E. 2006. *Performance and Productivity in Public and Nonprofit Organizations.* 2nd edition. Armonk, NY: M. E. Sharpe.

Berner, M. and M. Bronson. 2005. A Case Study of Program Evaluation in Local Government: Building Consensus through Collaboration. *Public Performance & Management Review, 28* (5): 309–325.

Bhandar, M., S. Pan, and B. Tan. 2006. Towards Understanding the Roles of Social Capital in Knowledge Integration: A Case Study of a Collaborative Information Systems Project. *Journal of the American Society for Information Science and Technology, 58* (2): 263–274.

Bidwell, R. and C. Ryan. 2006. Collaborative Partnership Design: The Implications of Organizational Affiliation for Watershed Partnerships. *Society and Natural Resources, 19*: 827–843.

Bingham, L. and R. O'Leary. 2006. Conclusion: Parallel Play, Not Collaboration: Missing Questions, Missing Connections. *Public Administration Review, 66* (Supplement): 111–121.

Birkland, T. 1997. *After Disaster: Agenda Setting, Public Policy, and Focusing Events.* Washington, DC: Georgetown University Press.

Board on Health Promotion and Disease Prevention, and the Institute of Medicine. 2002. *The Future of the Public's Health in the 21st Century.* Washington, DC: The National Academies Press.

Boris, E. and C. Steuerle, Eds. 2006. *Nonprofits & Government: Collaboration and Conflict,* 2nd edition. Washington, DC: Urban Institute Press.

Boyer, E. 1990. *Scholarship Reconsidered: Priorities of the Professoriate.* San Francisco, CA: Jossey-Bass.

Brecher, C. and O. Wise. 2008. Looking a Gift Horse in the Mouth: Challenges in Managing Philanthropic Support for Public Services. *Public Administration Review, 68* (Special Issue): S146–S161.

Brinkerhoff, D. and J. Brinkerhoff. 2001. Cross-Sectoral Policy Networks: Lessons from Developing and Transitioning Countries. In *Getting Results through Collaboration,* ed. M. Mandell, pp. 167–188. Westport, CT: Quorum Books.

Brown, A. 1980. Technical Assistance to Rural Communities: Stopgap or Capacity Building? *Public Administration Review, 40* (1):18–23.

Brukardt, M., B. Holland, S. Percy, and N. Zimpher. 2004. Calling the Question: Is Higher Education Ready to Commit to Community Engagement. Report published by the Milwaukee Idea Office, University of Wisconsin–Milwaukee.

Bryer, T. 2009. Explaining Responsiveness in Collaboration: Administrator and Citizen Role Perceptions. *Public Administration Review, 69* (2): 271–283.

Bryson, J. 2004. *Strategic Planning for Public and Nonprofit Organizations: A Guide to Strengthening and Sustaining Organizational Achievement,* 3rd edition. San Francisco: Jossey-Bass.

Bryson, J. 2005. *Creating and Implementing Your Strategic Plan: A Workbook for Public and Nonprofit Organizations,* 2nd edition. San Francisco: Jossey-Bass.

Bryson, J., B. Crosby, and M. Stone. 2006. The Design and Implementation of Cross-Sector Collaborations: Propositions from the Literature. *Public Administration Review, 66* (Supplement): 44–55.

Busenberg, G. 1999. Collaborative and Adversarial Analysis in Environmental Policy. *Policy Sciences 32*: 1–11.

Busenberg, G. 2007. Citizen Participation and Collaborative Environmental Management in the Marine Oil Trade of Coastal Alaska. *Coastal Management 35*: 239–253.

Busenberg, G. 2008. Managing the Hazard of Marine Oil Pollution in Alaska. *Review of Policy Research, 25* (3): 203–218.

Caffrey, L. 1998. *Information Sharing between & within Governments: A Study Group Report of the Commonwealth Secretariat.* London: The International Council for Technology in Government Administration.

Callahan, K. 2007. Citizen Participation: Questions of Diversity, Equity and Fairness. *Journal of Public Management and Social Policy, 13* (1): 53–68.

Callahan, K. and K. Kloby. 2007. Collaboration Meets the Performance Measurement Challenge. *Public Manager, 36* (2): 11–24.

Cape Fear Healthy Carolinians. 2008. Cape Fear Healthy Carolinians. http://www.capefearhealthycarolinians.org.

Centers for Disease Control and Prevention (CDC). 1998. *Preventing Emerging Infectious Diseases: A Strategy for the 21st Century. Overview of the Updated CDC Plan.* Atlanta, GA: U.S. Department of Health and Human Services.

Centers for Disease Control and Prevention (CDC). 2003a. *Epidemic/epizootic West Nile Virus in the United States: Guidelines for Surveillance, Prevention, and Control.* Fort Collins, CO: Centers for Disease Prevention and Control.

Centers for Disease Control and Prevention (CDC). 2003b. National Center for Infectious Disease—Emerging Infections Programs, September 11. http://www.cdc.gov/ncidod/osr/site/eip/index.htm (accessed April 15, 2008).

Centers for Disease Control and Prevention (CDC). 2005. Compendium of Measures to Prevent Disease Associated with Animals in Public Settings. *Morbidity and Mortality Weekly Report* 54 (RR-4). http://www.cdc.gov/mmwr/PDF/rr/rr5404.pdf (accessed May 2, 2008).

Centers for Disease Control and Prevention (CDC). 2007a. West Nile Virus—Final 2001 West Nile Virus Activity in the United States, May 29. http://www.cdc.gov/ncidod/dvbid/westnile/Mapsactivity/surv&control01Maps.htm (accessed April 15, 2008).

Centers for Disease Control and Prevention (CDC). 2007b. West Nile Virus—Statistics, Surveillance, and Control, May 31. http://www.cdc.gov/ncidod/dvbid/westnile/surv&control.htm (accessed April 15, 2008).

Chang, S., G. Gable, E. Smythe, and G. Timbrell. 2000. A Delphi Examination of Public Sector ERP Implementation Issues. In *Proceedings of the Twenty First International Conference on Information Systems*, pp. 494–500. Atlanta, GA: Association for Information Systems.

Chaskin, R. 2001. Building Community Capacity. *Urban Affairs Review, 36* (3):291–323.

Chisholm, D. 1989. *Coordination without Hierarchy: Informal Structures in Multiorganizational Systems*. Berkeley: University of California Press.

Clinton, J., B. Hagebak, J. Sirmons, and J. Brennan. 1995. Lessons from the Georgia Floods. *Public Health Reports, 110* (6): 684–688.

Comfort, L. 1985. Integrating Organizational Action in Emergency Management: Strategies for Change. *Public Administration Review, 45* (Special Issue): 155–164.

Comfort, L. 2005. Risk, Security, and Disaster Management. *Annual Review of Political Science, 8:* 335–356.

Comfort, L., B. Wisner, S. Cutter, R. Pulwarty, K. Hewitt, A. Oliver-Smith, et al. 1999. Reframing Disaster Policy: The Global Evolution of Vulnerable Communities. *Environmental Hazards, 1* (1): 39–44.

Connelly, D. 2007. Leadership in the Collaborative Interorganizational Domain. *International Journal of Public Administration, 30:* 1231–1262.

Cooper, C., A. Nownes, and S. Roberts. 2005. Perceptions of Power: Interest Groups in Local Politics. *State and Local Government Review, 37* (3): 206–216.

Cooper, T., T. Bryer, and J. Meek. 2006. Citizen-centered Collaborative Public Management. *Public Administration Review, 66* (Supplement): 76–88.

Crosby, B. 1996. Leading in a Shared Power World. In *Handbook of Public Administration,* ed. J. L. Perry, pp. 613–631. San Francisco: Jossey-Bass.

Dawes, S. 1996. Interagency Information Sharing: Expected Benefits, Manageable Risks. *Journal of Policy Analysis and Management, 15* (3): 377–394.

Dawes, S., T. Birkland, G. Tayi, and C. Schneider. 2004. Information, Technology, and Coordination: Lessons from the World Trade Center Response, June. Albany: Center for Technology in Government, University at Albany, State University of New York. http://demo.ctg.albany.edu/publications/reports/wtc_lessons (accessed April 15, 2008).

Dawes, S., A. Cresswell, and B. Cahan. 2004. Learning from Crisis: Lessons in Human and Information Infrastructure from the World Trade Center Response. *Social Science Computer Review, 22:* 52–56.

Dawes, S., A. Cresswell, and T. Pardo. 2009. From "Need to Know" to "Need to Share": Tangled Problems, Information Boundaries, and the Building of Public Sector Knowledge Networks. *Public Administration Review, 69* (3): 392–402.

Dawes, S. and T. Pardo. 2002. Building Collaborative Digital Government Systems. In *Advances in Digital Government: Technology, Human Factors, and Policy,* ed. W. J. McIver and A. K. Elmagarmid, pp. 259–274. Boston: Kluwer Academic Publishers.

Dawes, S., T. Pardo, and A. Cresswell. 2004. Designing Electronic Government Information Access Programs: A Holistic Approach. *Government Information Quarterly, 21* (1): 3–23.

DCTA Rail Connection. 2006. A Newsletter, RailDCTA Project, Lewisville, Texas.

Decker, L. 2005. *Over My Dead Body! A Workbook for Community Involvement.* Phoenix, AZ: Lindworth Press.

Delfin, F. and S. Tang. 2006. Philanthropic Strategies in Place-Based, Collaborative Land Conservation: The Packard Foundation's Conserving California Landscape Initiative. *Nonprofit and Voluntary Sector Quarterly, 35* (3): 405–429.

DeLuchi, M., M. MacCracken, D. Sperling, D. G. Burwell, E. Deakin, and R. Forman. 2005. Presentations on Transportation Indicators, *Integrating Sustainability into the Transportation Planning Process, Conference Proceedings 37,* Transportation Research Board, pp. 13–16. http://onlinepubs.trb.org/onlinepubs/conf/CP37.pdf.

Donahue, A. K. 2006. The Space Shuttle Columbia Recovery Operation: How Collaboration Enabled Disaster Response. *Public Administration Review, 66* (Supplement): 141–142.

Downs, A. 1957. *An Economic Theory of Democracy.* New York: Harper & Row, Publishers.

Dubb, S. 2007. *Linking Colleges to Communities: Engaging the University for Community Development.* College Park: Democracy Collaborative, University of Maryland.

Emergency Management Accreditation Program (EMAP). 2006. *EMAP Standard.* Lexington, KY: Emergency Management Accreditation Program.

English, M., J. Peretz, and M. Manderschied. 2004. Building Communities while Building Plans: A Review of Techniques for Participatory Planning Processes. *Public Administration Quarterly, 28* (1–2): 182–221.

Environmental Protection Agency (EPA). 2007. National Environmental Policy Act (NEPA). http://www.epa.gov/compliance/basics/nepa.html.

Evans, D. and D.Yen. 2005. E-government: An Analysis for Implementation: Framework for Understanding Cultural and Social Impact. *Government Information Quarterly, 22*: 54–373.

Fawcett, S. 1999. Some Lessons on Community Organization and Change. In *Reflections on Community Organization: Enduring Themes and Critical Issues,* ed. J. Rothman. Itasca, IL: F. E. Peacock Publishers.

Fawcett, S., V. Francisco, D. Hyra, A. Paine-Andrews, S. Schultz, S. Roussos, et al. 2000. Building Healthy Communities. In *The Society and Population Health Reader: A State and Community Perspective,* ed. A. R. Tarlov and R. F. St. Peter. New York: New Press.

Feldman, M., A. Khademian, H. Ingram, and A. Schneider. 2006. Ways of Knowing and Inclusive Management Practices. *Public Administration Review, 66* (Supplement): 89–99.

Fernandez, L., D. Byard, C. Lin, S. Benson, and J. Barbera. 2002. Frail Elderly as Disaster Victims: Emergency Management Strategies. *Prehospital and Disaster Medicine, 17* (2): 67–74.

Foster-Fishman, P., S. Berkowitz, D. Lounsbury, S. Jacobson, and N. Allen. 2001. Building Collaborative Capacity in Community Coalitions: A Review and Integrative Framework. *American Journal of Community Psychology, 29* (2): 241–261.

Foster-Fishman, P. G., D. A. Salem, N. A. Alle, and K. Fahrback. 2001. Facilitating Interorganizational Collaboration: The Contributions of Interorganizational Alliances. *American Journal of Community Psychology, 29* (6): 875–906.

Frederickson, G. H. 1982. The Recovery of Civism in Public Administration. *Public Administration Review, 42* (5): 501–508.

Fountain, J. 2001. *Building the Virtual State: Information Technology and Institutional Change.* Washington, DC: Brookings Institution.

Freeland, R. 2005. Universities and Cities Need to Rethink Their Relationships. *Chronicle of Higher Education, 51* (36): B20.

Fung, A. 2006. Varieties of Participation in Complex Governance. *Public Administration Review, 66* (Supplement): 66–75.

Fung, A. and E. Wright. 2001. Deepening Democracy: Innovations in Empowered Participatory Governance. *Politics and Society, 29* (1): 5–41.

Gardner, S. 1999. *Beyond Collaboration to Results: Hard Choices in the Future of Services to Children and Families.* Phoenix: Arizona Prevention Resource Center, Center for Collaboration for Children.

Getha-Taylor, H. 2008a. Identifying Collaborative Competencies. *Review of Public Personnel Administration, 28* (2): 103–119.

Getha-Taylor, H. 2008b. Learning Indicators and Collaborative Capacity: Applying Action Learning Principles to the U.S. Department of Homeland Security. *Public Administration Quarterly, 32* (2): 125–146.

Gil-Garcia, J., I. Chengalur-Smith, and P. Duchessi. 2007. Collaborative E-government: Impediments and Benefits of Information Sharing Projects in the Public Sector. *European Journal of Information Systems, 16* (2): 121–133.

Gil-Garcia, J. and T. Pardo. 2005. E-government Success Factors: Mapping Practical Tools to Theoretical Foundations. *Government Information Quarterly, 22*:187–216.

Gil-Garcia, J., C. Schneider, T. Pardo, and A. Cresswell. 2005. Inter-organizational Information Integration in the Criminal Justice Enterprise: Preliminary Lessons from State and County Initiatives. In *Proceedings of the 38th Hawaiian International Conference on System Sciences (HICSS'05).* Los Alamitos, CA: IEEE Computer Society Press.

Glaser, J. 2005. *Leading through Collaboration: Guiding Groups to Productive Solutions.* Thousand Oaks, CA: Corwin Press.

Goldman, E. 2007. Strategic Thinking at the Top. *MIT Sloan Management Review, 48* (4): 75–81.

Goldman, S. and W. Kahweiler. 2000. A Collaborator Profile for Executives of Nonprofit Organizations. *Nonprofit and Voluntary Sector Quarterly, 10* (4): 435–450.

Goldsmith, S. and W. Eggers. 2004. *Governing by Network: The New Shape of the Public Sector.* Washington, DC: Brookings Institution Press.

Golembiewski, R. T. 2000. *Handbook of Organizational Consultation,* 2nd edition, revised and expanded. New York: Marcel Dekker.

Goodsell, C. 1992. The Public Administrator as Artisan. *Public Administration Review, 52* (3): 246–253.

Gray, B. 1989. *Collaborating: Finding Common Ground for Multiparty Problems.* San Francisco, CA: Jossey-Bass.

Griffin, M., A. Rafferty, and C. Mason. 2004. Who Started This? Investigating Different Sources of Organizational Change. *Journal of Business and Psychology, 18* (4): 555–570.

Gullette, M. 2006. Katrina and the Politics of Later Life. In *There Is No Such Thing as a Natural Disaster,* ed. C. Hartman and G. D. Squires. New York: Routledge.

Guo, C. and M. Acar. 2005. Understanding Collaboration among Nonprofit Organizations: Combining Resource Dependency, Institutional, and Network Perspectives. *Nonprofit and Voluntary Sector Quarterly, 34* (3): 340–361.

Hatry, H. 2007. *Performance Measurement: Getting Results,* 2nd edition. Washington, DC: Urban Institute.

Heanue, K. E., A. Canby, J. Horsley, H. Kassoff, J. Pucher, and A. Taft. 2005. Panel Discussion: Potential Solution to Challenges. In *Integrating Sustainability in the Transportation Planning Process, Conference Proceedings 37,* Transportation Research Board, pp. 24–25. http://onlinepubs.trb.org/onlinepubs/conf/CP37.pdf.

Hickman, G. 1998. *Leading Organizations: Perspectives for a New Era.* Thousand Oaks, CA: Sage.

Hirschman, B. 2001. Bush Ties Schools to Development—Governor Looks to Link New Homes to Construction of Classroom Space. *Sun Sentinel,* January 19, 1A.

Holtzblatt, K. and S. Jones. 1993. Contextual Inquiry: A Participatory Technique for System Design. In *Participatory Design: Principles and Practices,* ed. D. Schuler and A. Namioka, pp. 177–210. Hillsdale, NJ: Lawrence Erlbaum.

Huxam, C. and D. Macdonald. 1992. Introducing Collaborative Advantage: Achieving Interorganizational Effectiveness through Meta-strategy. *Management Decision, 30* (3): 50–56.

Huxham, C. and S. Vangen. 2000. Leadership in Shaping and Implementation of Collaboration Agendas: How Things Happen in a (Not-quite) Joined Up World. *Academy of Management Journal, 43* (6): 1159–1175.

Huxham, C. and S. Vangen. 2005. *Managing to Collaborate: The Theory and Practice of Collaborative Advantage.* London: Routledge.

Imperial, M. 2005. Using Collaboration as a Governance Strategy: Lessons from Six Watershed Management Programs. *Administration & Society, 37* (3): 281–320.

Infante, A. and M. Meit. 2007, Delivering the U.S. Preventive Services Task Force Recommendations in a Rural Health Plan. NORC Feb. 2007, No. 8. http://www.norc.org/NR/rdonlyres/CB3E3517-4D9F-4A77-8CB5-231756A27C34/0/WalshCtr2007_NORC_BriefFeb07.pdf

Institute of Medicine (IOM). 2003. *The Future of the Public's Health in the 21st Century.* Washington, DC: National Academy Press.

Irani, Z., P. Love, T. Elliman, S. Jones, and M. Themistocleous. 2005. Evaluating E-government: Learning from the Experiences of Two UK Local Authorities. *Information Systems Journal, 15*: 61–82.

Ireland, R. and M. Hitt. 1999. Achieving and Maintaining Strategic Competitiveness in the 21st Century: The Role of Strategic Leadership. *Academy of Management Executive, 13* (1): 43–57.

Irvin, R. and J. Stansbury. 2004. Citizen Participation in Decision Making: Is It Worth the Effort? *Public Administration Review, 64* (1): 55–63.

Jameson, J. and M. Blank. 2007. The Role of Clinical Psychology in Rural Mental Health Services. *Clinical Psychology: Science & Practice, 14* (3): 283–298.

Jenkins, P., S. Laska, and G. Williamson. 2008. Connecting Future Evacuation to Current Recovery: Saving the Lives of Older Adults. *Generations, 31* (4): 49–52.

Justice, T. and D. Jamieson. 1999. *The Facilitator's Fieldbook: Step-by Step Procedures, Checklists and Guidelines, Samples and Templates.* New York: American Management Association.

Kalos, A., L. Kent, and D. Gates. 2005. Integrating MAPP, APEXPH, PACE-EH, and Other Planning Initiatives in Northern Kentucky. *Journal of Public Health Management Practice, 11* (5): 401–406.

Kaner, S., L. Lind, C. Toldi, S. Fisk, and D. Berger. 2007. *Facilitator's Guide to Participatory Decision-Making,* 2nd edition. San Francisco: Jossey-Bass.

Kathi, P. and T. Cooper. 2008. Connecting Neighborhood Councils and City Agencies: Trust Building through the Learning and Design Forum Process. *Journal of Public Affairs Education, 13* (3–4): 617–630.

Kathi, P., T. Cooper, and J. Meek. 2007. The Role of the University as a Mediating Institution in Neighborhood Council-City Agency Collaboration. *Journal of Public Affairs Education, 13* (2): 365–382.

Kearney, R. and E. Berman, Eds. 1999. *Public Sector Performance: Management, Motivation, and Measurement.* Boulder, CO: Westview.

Keast, R., K. Brown, and M. Mandell. 2007. Getting the Right Mix: Unpacking Integration Meanings and Strategies. *International Public Management Journal, 10* (1): 9–33.

Keast, R., M. Mandell, K. Brown, and G. Woolcock. 2004. Network Structures: Working Differently and Changing Expectations. *Public Administration Review, 64* (3): 363–371.

Kettl, D. 2002. The Transformation of Governance: Public Administration for the 21st Century. Baltimore: Johns Hopkins University Press.

Kettl, D. F. 2006. Managing Boundaries in American Administration: The Collaboration Imperative. *Public Administration Review* (Supplement): 10–19.

Kiefer, J. and R. Montjoy. 2006. Incrementalism before the Storm: Network Performance for the Evacuation of New Orleans. *Public Administration Review, 66* (Supplement): 122–130.

Kimberly, J. and R. Miles. 1980. *The Organizational Life Cycle.* San Francisco: Jossey-Bass.

Kingdon, J. 1995. *Agendas, Alternatives, and Public Policies,* 2nd edition. New York: Longman.

Kirlin, J. 1996. The Big Questions of Public Administration in a Democracy. *Public Administration Review, 56* (5): 416–423.

Knowles, R. and B. Garrison. 2006. Planning for Elderly in Natural Disasters. *Disaster Recovery Journal, 19* (4): 1–3.

Koontz, T, T. Steelman, J. Carmin, K. Korfmacher, C. Moseley, and C. Thomas. 2004. *Collaborative Environmental Management: What Roles for Government?* Washington, DC: Resources for the Future Press.

Koontz, T. and C. Thomas. 2006. What Do We Know and Need to Know about the Environmental Outcomes of Collaborative Management? *Public Administration Review,* 66 (Supplement): 111–121.

Kotter, J. 1995. Leading Change: Why Transformation Efforts Fail. *Harvard Business Review, 73* (2): 59–67.

Kretzman, J. and J. McKnight. 1993. *Building Communities from Inside Out: A Path toward Finding and Mobilizing a Community's Assets.* Evanston, IL: Asset-Based Community Development Institute (ACTA Publications).

Kreuter, M., N. Lezin, and L. Young. 2000. Evaluating Community–Based Collaborative Mechanisms: Implications for Practitioners. *Health Promotion Practice, 1* (1): 49–63.

Lasker, R. D. 2004. *Redefining Readiness: Terrorism Planning through the Eyes of the Public.* New York, NY: The New York Academy of Medicine.

Leach, W. D. 2006. Collaborative Public Management and Democracy: Evidence from Western Watershed Partnerships. *Public Administration Review, 66* (Supplement): 100–110.

Liu, J., J. Probst, A. Martin, J. Wang, and C. Salinas. 2007. Disparities in Dental Insurance Coverage and Dental Care among US Children: The National Survey of Children's Health. *Pediatrics, 110:* S12–S21.

Loury, G. 1987. Why Should We Care about Group Inequality? *Social Philosophy and Policy, 5* (Spring): 249–271.

Lowe, S. and A. Fothergill. 2003. A Need to Help: Emergent Volunteer Behavior after September 11th. In *Beyond September 11th: An Account of Post-disaster Research,* ed. J. L. Monday, pp. 293–314. Boulder: University of Colorado.

Lowndes, V. and C. Skelcher. 1998. The Dynamics of Multi-organizational Partnerships: An Analysis of Changing Modes of Governance. *Public Administration, 76* (2): 313–333.

Lukensmeyer, C. and L. Torres. 2006. *Public Deliberation: A Manager's Guide to Public Deliberation.* Washington, DC: IBM Center for the Business of Government.

Macris, N. 1999. *Planning in Plain English: Writing Tips for Urban and Environmental Planners.* Chicago, IL: American Planning Association.

Majumdar, S. R., Moynihan, C., and Pierce, J., Public Collaboration in Transportation: A Case Study. *Public Works Management and Policy, 14* (1), 55–80.

Majumdar, S. and J. Pierce. 2007. Public Collaboration in Transportation: A Look at Denton County Transportation Authority's (DCTA) Plan for Public Transportation in North Texas. Paper presented at the 68th National Conference of American Society for Public Administration, March 23–27, Washington DC.

Mandell, M. 2001. *Getting Results through Collaboration: Networks and Network Structures for Public Policy and Management.* Westport, CT: Quorum Books.

Mandell, M. and R. Keast. 2007. Evaluating Network Arrangements: Toward Revised Performance Measures. *Public Performance & Management Review, 30* (4): 574–597.

Mattessich, P, M. Murray-Close, and B. Monsey. 2001. *Collaboration: What Makes It Work.* Saint Paul, MN: Amherst H. Wilder Foundation.

Maurrasse, D. 2001. *Beyond the Campus.* New York: Routledge.

McCampbell, A. 2003. Best Practices Model: Including the Needs of People with Disabilities, Seniors, and Individuals with Chronic Mental Illness in Emergency Preparedness and Planning. Report to the New Mexico Department of Health.

McGuire, M. 2006. Collaborative Public Management: Assessing What We Know and How We Know It. *Public Administration Review, 66* (Supplement): 33–43.

McKnight, J. 1995. *The Careless Society: Community and Its Counterfeit.* New York: Basic Books.

Meit, M. 2007. Public Health in Rural America. *Journal of Public Health Management & Practice, 13* (3): 235–236.

Milward, H. B. and K. Provan. 2006. A Manager's Guide to Choosing and Using Collaborative Networks. IBM Center for the Business of Government.
http://www.businessofgovernment.org/pdfs/ProvanReport.pdf.

Minkler, M. 2000. Using Participatory Action Research to Build Healthy Communities. *Public Health Reports, 115* (2–3): 191–197.

Minkler, M. and N. Wallerstein. 2003. *Community Based Participatory Research for Health.* San Francisco, CA: Jossey-Bass.

Mintrom, M. 2003. *People Skills for Policy Analysts.* Washington, DC: Georgetown University Press.

Mintzberg, H. 1984. Power and Organization Life Cycles. *Academy of Management Review, 9:* 207–225.

Moore, M. 1995. *Creating Public Value: Strategic Management in Government.* Cambridge, MA: Harvard University Press.

Morrow, B. 1999. Identifying and Mapping Community Vulnerability. *Disasters, 23* (1): 1–18.

Moscovice, I., A. Wellever, J. Christianson, M. Casey, B. Yawn, and D. Hartley. 1997. Understanding Integrated Rural Health Networks. *Milbank Quarterly, 75* (4): 563–588.

Moynihan, C. 2007. An Environmental Justice Assessment of the Light Rail Expansion in Denton County, Texas. Master's thesis, University of North Texas, Denton.

National Association of State Information Resource Executives (NASIRE). 2000. Toward National Sharing of Governmental Information, February. Lexington, KY, National Association of State Information Resource Executives. http://www.nascio.org/publications/documents/NASCIO-JusticeReport_Feb2000.pdf (accessed April 15, 2008).

National Association of State Public Health Veterinarians (NASPHV). n.d. About Us. http://www.nasphv.org/aboutUs.html. (accessed May 2, 2008).

National Commission on Terrorist Attacks upon the United States (NCTAUUS). 2004. *The 9/11 Commission Report: Final Report of the National Commission on Terrorist Attacks upon the United States.* Washington, DC: National Commission on Terrorist Attacks upon the United States.

National Organization of State Offices of Rural Health. 2006. National Rural Health Issues, September. http://www.nosorh.org/pdf/Rural_Impact_Study_States_IT.pdf.

Naus, F., A. van Iterson, and R. Roe. 2007. Organizational Cynicism: Extending the Exit, Voice, Loyalty, and Neglect Model of Employees' Responses to Adverse Conditions in the Workplace. *Human Relations, 60* (5): 683–718.

Nelson, C., A. Kurtz, E. Gulitz, G. Hacker, M. Lee, and P. Craiger. 1988. Post-Hurricane Survey of Evacuees Sheltered in the Tampa Bay Region during Hurricane Elena in 1985. Tampa, FL: Department of Community Affairs, Division of Emergency Management, with Support of the Tampa Bay Regional Planning Council, University of South Florida.

Norris-Tirrell, D. and J. Clay. 2000. The Production of Useable Knowledge. In *Handbook of Organization Consultation,* ed. R. T. Golembiewski, pp. 829–834. New York: Marcel Dekker.

Norris-Tirrell, D. and J. Clay. 2006. Collaborative Planning as a Tool for Strengthening Local Emergency Management. *Journal of Public Management & Social Policy, 12* (1): 25–36.

Norton, R. 2005. More and Better Local Planning. *Journal of the American Planning Association, 71* (1): 55–71.

Nunn, S. and M. Rosentraub. 1997. Dimensions of Interjurisdictional Cooperation. *Journal of the American Planning Association, 63* (2):205–219.

O'Leary, R. and L. Bingham. 2007. Conclusion: Conflict and Collaboration in Networks. *International Public Management Journal, 10* (1): 103–109.

O'Leary, R., C. Gerard, and L. B. Bingham. 2006. Introduction to the Symposium on Collaborative Public Management. *Public Administration Review, 66* (Supplement): 6–9.

Oregon Department of Human Services (DHS). 2002. *State of Oregon Mosquito-Borne Disease Response Plan.* Portland: Oregon Department of Human Services.

Oregon Department of Human Services (DHS). 2007a. Acute and Communicable Disease Prevention, November 29. http://oregon.gov/DHS/ph/acd/about_us.shtml (accessed April 15, 2008).

Oregon Department of Human Services (DHS). 2007b. *Public Health West Nile Virus Emergency Response Plan.* Portland: Oregon Department of Human Services.

Osborne, S. and V. Murray. 2000. Collaboration between Nonprofit Organizations in the Provision of Social Services in Canada: Working Together or Falling Apart? *International Journal of Public Sector Management, 13* (1): 9–18.

O'Toole, L., Jr. 1997. Treating Networks Seriously: Practical and Research-Based Agendas in Public Administration. *Public Administration Review, 57* (1): 45–53.

O'Toole, L. Jr., and K. Meier. 2004. Desperately Seeking Selznick: Cooptation and the Dark Side of Public Management in Networks. *Public Administration Review, 64* (6): 681–693.

O'Toole, L., K. Meier, and S. Nicholson-Crotty. 2005. Managing Upward, Downward and Outward. *Public Management Review, 7* (1): 45–68.

Overman, S. 1996. The New Sciences of Administration: Chaos and Quantum Theory. *Public Administration Review, 56* (5): 487–491.

Ozawa, C. 1991. *Recasting Science: Consensual Procedures in Public Policy Making.* Boulder, CO: Westview.

Ozawa, C. and L. Susskind. 1985. Mediating Science-Intensive Policy Disputes. *Journal of Policy Analysis and Management, 5* (1): 23–39.

Page, S. 2004. Measuring Accountability for Results in Interagency Collaboration. *Public Administration Review, 64* (5): 591–606.

Pardo, T. A., J. R. Gil-Garcia, and G. B. Burke. 2007a. Informal Leadership and Networks: Lessons from the Response to the West Nile Virus Outbreak in North America. Paper presented at the eChallenges 2007 Conference, October 24–26, The Hague, The Netherlands.

Pardo, T. A., J. R. Gil-Garcia, and G. B. Burke. 2007b. Sustainable Cross-boundary Information Sharing. In *Digital Government: E-government Research, Case Studies, and Implementation,* ed. C. Hsinchun, L. Brandt, S. S. Dawes, V. Gregg, E. Hovy, A. Macintosh, et al., pp. 421–438. New York: Springer-Verlag.

Patel, K. and M. Rushefsky. 2005. *The Politics of Public Health in the United States.* Armonk, NY: M. E. Sharpe.

Parr, A. 1987. Disasters and Disabled Persons: An Examination of the Safety Needs of a Neglected Minority. *Disasters, 11*: 148–159.

Palm Beach County (PBC). 2000. Transcript of the Palm Beach County Board of County Commissioners' June 6 Meeting.

Palm Beach County (PBC). 2001. Palm Beach County Interlocal Agreement with Municipalities of Palm Beach County and the School District of Palm Beach County to Establish Public School Concurrency. http://www.pbcgov/PZB/planning/school currency/agreement.pdf.

Percy, S. L., N. Zimpher, and M. Brukardt. 2006. *Creating a New Kind of University: Institutionalizing Community-University Engagement.* Bolton, MA: Anker Publishing.

Perry, D. and W. Wiewel. 2005. *The University as Urban Developer: Case Studies and Analysis.* New York: M. E. Sharpe.

Perry, S. 2007. Foundations Urged to Do More to Aid America's Rural Regions—Philantrophy. com. *Chronicle of Philanthropy, 19* (21):10.

Peters, B. 1998. "With a Little Help from Our Friends": Public–Private Partnerships as Institutions and Instruments. In *Partnerships in Urban governance,* ed. J. Pierre, pp. 11–33. New York: St. Marten's.

Pirog, M. and C. Johnson. 2008. Electronic Funds and Benefits Transfers, E-Government, and the Winter Commission. *Public Administration Review,* (Special Issue on the Winter Commission Report): S103–S114.

Poister, T. 2003. *Measuring Performance in Public and Nonprofit Organizations.* San Francisco: Jossey-Bass.

Powell, D. and M. Gazica. 2005. And Now ... School Concurrency. *Florida Bar Journal, 79* (10): 44–47.

Prokopiadou, G., C. Papatheodorou, and D. Moschopoulos. 2004. Integrating Knowledge Management Tools for Government Information. *Government Information Quarterly, 21*: 170–198.

Provan, K. and H. Milward. 1995. A Preliminary Theory of Interorganizational Network Effectiveness: A Comparative Study of Four Community Mental Health Systems. *Administrative Science Quarterly, 40* (1): 1–33.

Provan, K. and B. Milward. 2001. Do Networks Really Work? A Framework for Evaluating Public-Sector Organizational Networks. *Public Administration Review, 61* (4): 414–423.

Provan, K., M. Veazie, L. Staten, and N. Teufel-Shone. 2005. The Use of Network Analysis to Strengthen Community Partnerships. *Public Administration Review, 65* (5):603–613.

Prince William Sound Regional Citizens' Advisory Council (PWS RCAC). 1991a. *1991 Annual Report*. Anchorage, AK: PWS RCAC.

Prince William Sound Regional Citizens' Advisory Council (PWS RCAC). 1991b. *The Observer* 1(2). Anchorage, AK: PWS RCAC.

Prince William Sound Regional Citizens' Advisory Council (PWS RCAC). 1993a. *1993 A Year in Review*. Anchorage, AK: PWS RCAC.

Prince William Sound Regional Citizens' Advisory Council (PWS RCAC). 1993b. *The Observer* 3(1). Anchorage, AK: Prince William Sound RCAC.

Prince William Sound Regional Citizens' Advisory Council (PWS RCAC). 1993c. *The Observer* 3(2). Anchorage, AK: PWS RCAC.

Prince William Sound Regional Citizens' Advisory Council (PWS RCAC). 1993d. *The Observer* 3(3). Anchorage, AK: PWS RCAC.

Prince William Sound Regional Citizens' Advisory Council (PWS RCAC). 1993e. *Then and Now: Changes since the Exxon Valdez Oil Spill*. Anchorage, AK: PWS RCAC.

Prince William Sound Regional Citizens' Advisory Council (PWS RCAC). 1994a. *The Observer* 4(1). Anchorage, AK: PWS RCAC.

Prince William Sound Regional Citizens' Advisory Council (PWS RCAC). 1994b. *The Observer* 4(2). Anchorage, AK: PWS RCAC.

Prince William Sound Regional Citizens' Advisory Council (PWS RCAC). 1994c. *The Observer* 4(4). Anchorage, AK: PWS RCAC.

Prince William Sound Regional Citizens' Advisory Council (PWS RCAC). 1995a. *The Observer* 5(2). Anchorage, AK: PWS RCAC.

Prince William Sound Regional Citizens' Advisory Council (PWS RCAC). 1995b. *The Observer* 5(3). Anchorage, AK: Prince William Sound RCAC.

Prince William Sound Regional Citizens' Advisory Council (PWS RCAC). 1995c. *The Observer* 5(4). Anchorage, AK: PWS RCAC.

Prince William Sound Regional Citizens' Advisory Council (PWS RCAC). 1995d. *Oil Spill Prevention: Improvements in Tanker Safety*. Anchorage, AK: PWS RCAC.

Prince William Sound Regional Citizens' Advisory Council (PWS RCAC). 1996a. *1996 A Year in Review*. Anchorage, AK: PWS RCAC.

Prince William Sound Regional Citizens' Advisory Council (PWS RCAC). 1996b. *The Observer* 6(3). Anchorage, AK: PWS RCAC.

Prince William Sound Regional Citizens' Advisory Council (PWS RCAC). 1997a. *The Observer* 7(1). Anchorage, AK: PWS RCAC.

Prince William Sound Regional Citizens' Advisory Council (PWS RCAC). 1997b. *The Observer* 7(2). Anchorage, AK: PWS RCAC.

Prince William Sound Regional Citizens' Advisory Council (PWS RCAC). 1997c. *The Observer* 7(3). Anchorage, AK: PWS RCAC.

Prince William Sound Regional Citizens' Advisory Council (PWS RCAC). 1998a. *1997–1998 in Review*. Anchorage, AK: PWS RCAC.

Prince William Sound Regional Citizens' Advisory Council (PWS RCAC). 1998b. *The Observer* 8(1). Anchorage, AK: Prince William Sound RCAC.

Prince William Sound Regional Citizens' Advisory Council (PWS RCAC). 1999a. *The Observer* 9(2). Anchorage, AK: PWS RCAC.

Prince William Sound Regional Citizens' Advisory Council (PWS RCAC). 1999b. *1998–1999 in Review*. Anchorage, AK: PWS RCAC.

Prince William Sound Regional Citizens' Advisory Council (PWS RCAC). 1999c. *Then and Now—Changes in Oil Transportation since the Exxon Valdez Spill: 1989–1999*. Anchorage, AK: PWS RCAC.

Prince William Sound Regional Citizens' Advisory Council (PWS RCAC). 2000a. *The Observer* 10(1). Anchorage, AK: PWS RCAC.

Prince William Sound Regional Citizens' Advisory Council (PWS RCAC). 2000b. *1999–2000 in Review*. Anchorage, AK: PWS RCAC.

Prince William Sound Regional Citizens' Advisory Council (PWS RCAC). 2001a. *2000–2001 in Review*. Anchorage, AK: PWS RCAC.

Prince William Sound Regional Citizens' Advisory Council (PWS RCAC). 2001b. *The Observer* 11(4). Anchorage, AK: PWS RCAC.

Prince William Sound Regional Citizens' Advisory Council (PWS RCAC). 2002a. *2001–2002 in Review*. Anchorage, AK: PWS RCAC.

Prince William Sound Regional Citizens' Advisory Council (PWS RCAC). 2002b. *The Observer* 12(1). Anchorage, AK: PWS RCAC.

Prince William Sound Regional Citizens' Advisory Council (PWS RCAC). 2003a. *The Observer* 13(1). Anchorage, AK: PWS RCAC.

Prince William Sound Regional Citizens' Advisory Council (PWS RCAC). 2003b. *2002–2003 Year in Review*. Anchorage, AK: PWS RCAC.

Prince William Sound Regional Citizens' Advisory Council (PWS RCAC). 2003c. *The Observer* 13(4). Anchorage, AK: PWS RCAC.

Prince William Sound Regional Citizens' Advisory Council (PWS RCAC). 2004. *2003–2004 Year in Review*. Anchorage, AK: PWS RCAC.

Prince William Sound Regional Citizens' Advisory Council (PWS RCAC). 2005a. *The Observer* 15(1). Anchorage, AK: PWS RCAC.

Prince William Sound Regional Citizens' Advisory Council (PWS RCAC). 2005b. *The Observer* 15(3). Anchorage, AK: PWS RCAC.

Prince William Sound Regional Citizens' Advisory Council (PWS RCAC). 2005c. *2004–2005 in Review*. Anchorage, AK: PWS RCAC.

Prince William Sound Regional Citizens' Advisory Council (PWS RCAC). 2007. *2006–2007 in Review*. Anchorage, AK: PWS RCAC.

Quinn, R. and K. Cameron. 1983. Organization Life Cycles and Shifting Criteria of Effectiveness: Some Preliminary Evidence, *Management Science, 29*: 33–51

Raab, J. and H. Milward. 2003. Dark Networks as Problems. *Journal of Public Administration Research and Theory, 13* (4): 433–439.

Radin, B. 1996. Managing across Boundaries. In *The State of Public Management*, ed. D. Kettl and H. Milward, pp. 145–167. Baltimore, MD: Johns Hopkins University Press.

Rainey, H. 2003. *Understanding & Managing Public Organizations,* 3rd edition. San Francisco: Jossey-Bass.

Redman, T. 1998. The Impact of Poor Data Quality on the Typical Enterprise. *Communications of the ACM, 41* (2): 72–77.

Rhodes, M. and J. Murray. 2007. Collaborative Decision Making in Urban Regeneration: A Complex Adaptive Systems Perspective. *International Public Management Journal, 10* (1): 79–101.

Riad, J. and F. Norris. 1997. Hurricane Threat and Evacuation Intentions: An Analysis of Risk Perception, Preparedness, Social Influence, and Resources. http://dspace.udel.edu:8080/dspace/handle/19716/107.

Ring, P. and A. Van deVen. 1994. Developmental Process of Cooperative Interorganizational Relationships. *Academy of Management Review, 19*: 10–18.

Rocheleau, B. 2006. *Public Management Information Systems.* Hershey, PA: Idea Group.

Rodin, J. 2007. *The University and Urban Revival: Out of the Ivory Tower and into the Streets.* Philadelphia: University of Pennsylvania Press.

Rourke, F. 1984. *Bureaucracy, Politics and Public Policy.* Boston: Little Brown.

Roussos, S. and S. Fawcett. 2000. A Review of Collaborative Partnerships as a Strategy for Improving Community Health. *Annual Review of Public Health, 21*: 369–402.

Rowitz, L. 2006. *Public Health for the 21st Century: The Prepared Leader.* Sudbury, MA: Jones and Bartlett.

Salamon, L. 2002. *The Tools of Government: A Guide to the New Governance.* New York: Oxford University Press.

Salvador, R. 1999. *Partners in Prevention: A Decade of Progress in Prince William Sound.* Valdez, AK: PWS RCAC.

Schaap, L. and M. vanTwist. 1997. The Dynamics of Closedness in Networks. In *Managing Complex Networks,* edited by W. J. M. Kickert, E.-H. Klijn, and J. F. M. Koppenjan, pp. 62–78. London: Sage.

Schulz, A., B. Israel, and P. Lantz. 2004. Assessing and Strengthening Characteristics of Effective Groups in Community-Based Participatory Research Partnerships. In *Handbook of Social Work with Groups,* ed. M. Galinsky and L. M. Gutierrez, pp. 557–587. New York: Guilford Publications.

Schwarz, R. 2002. *The Skilled Facilitator: A Comprehensive Resource for Consultants, Facilitators, Managers, Trainers, and Coaches.* San Francisco: Jossey-Bass.

Selden, S., J. Sowa, and J. Sandfort. 2006. The Impact of Nonprofit Collaboration in Early Child Care and Education on Management and Program Outcomes. *Public Administration Review, 66* (3): 412–425.

Seppanen, R., K. Blomqvist, and S. Sundqvist. 2007. Measuring Inter-organizational Trust—A Critical Review of the Empirical Research in 1990–2003. *Industrial Marketing Management, 36* (2): 249–265.

Sharkey, P., 2007. Survival and Death in New Orleans: An Empirical Look at the Human Impact of Katrina. *Journal of Black Studies, 37* (4): 482–501.

Silver, I. 2004. Negotiating the Antipoverty Agenda: Foundations, Community Organizations, and Comprehensive Community Initiatives. *Nonprofit and Voluntary Sector Quarterly, 33* (4):606–628.

Simo, G. and A. Bies. 2007. The Role of Nonprofits in Disaster Response: An Expanded Model of Cross-Sector Collaboration. *Public Administration Review: Administrative Failure in the Wake of Katrina, 67* (December): 125–142.

Sirotnik, K. and J. Goodlad, Eds. 1988. *School–University Partnerships in Action: Concepts, Cases, and Concerns.* New York: Teachers College Press.

Solli, G., and E. Dalehite. 2006. Interlocal Cooperation to Achieve School Concurrency. Unpublished paper presented at the South Eastern Conference of Public Administration, September 28, Athens, GA.

Sowa, J. 2008. Implementing Interagency Collaborations. *Administration & Society, 40* (3): 298–323.

Soska, T. and A. Butterfield. 2004. *University-Community Partnerships: Universities in Civic Engagement.* Binghamton, NY: Haworth Social Work Practice Press.

Stallings, R. and E. Quarentelli. 1985. Emergent Citizen Groups and Emergency Management. *Public Administration Review, 45* (Special Issue): 93–100.

Stevens, S. 2003. *Nonprofit Life cycles: Stage-based Wisdom for Nonprofit Capacity.* Long Lake, MN: Stagewise Enterprises, Inc.

Takahashi, L. and G. Smutny. (2002). Collaborative Windows and Organizational Governance: Exploring the Formation and Demise of Social Service Partnerships. *Nonprofit and Voluntary Sector Quarterly, 31* (2): 165–185.

Tan, C. and S. Pan. 2003. Managing E-transformation in the Public Sector: An E-government Study of the Inland Revenue Authority of Singapore (IRAS). *European Journal of Information Systems, 12*: 269–281.

Texas State Historical Association. n.d. Handbook of Texas Online, Quakertown, TX. http://www.tshaonline.org.

Thomas, J. 1995. *Public Participation in Public Decisions.* San Francisco, CA: Jossey-Bass.

Thomson, A. and J. Perry. 2006. Collaborative Processes: Inside the Black Box. *Public Administration Review, 66* (Supplement): 20–32.

Thomson, A., J. Perry, and T. Miller. 2009. Conceptualizing and Measuring Collaboration. *Journal of Public Administration Research and Theory, 19* (1): 23–56.

Turnock, B. 1997. *Public Health: What It Is and How It Works.* Gaithersburg, MD: Aspen.

Thurmaier, K. 2006. High-Intensity Interlocal Collaboration in Three Iowa Cities. *Public Administration Review, 66* (Supplement): 144–146.

Travis, S. 2000. County, Towns, Cities to Tie Development to School Space—The Last of 28 Governments Signed Off on Plan That Will Limit Housing Development if Nearby Schools Are Overcrowded. *Stuart News*, December 23, C2.

Turning Point Leadership Development National Excellence Collaborative. 2001. Collaborative Leadership and Health: A Review of the Literature. 2001. http://www.turningpointprogram.org/toolkit/content/cllitreview.htm (accessed July 12, 2009).

URS Corporation. 2005. Denton County Transportation Authority Alternatives Analysis, Denton to Carrollton Corridor, executive summary, prepared by URS Corporation.

U.S. Department of Agriculture Economic Research Service. 2004. Rural Poverty at a Glance. *Rural Development Research Report* No. 100. http://www.ers.usda.gov/publications/rdrr100/rdrr100.pdf.

U.S. Department of Health and Human Services. 2000. *Healthy People 2010*, 2nd ed. *With Understanding and Improving Health and Objectives for Improving Health.* 2 vols. Washington, DC: U.S. Government Printing Office.

Van Buuren, A. 2009. Knowledge for Governance, Governance of Knowledge: Inclusive Knowledge Management in Collaborative Governance Processes. *International Public Management Journal, 12* (2): 208–235.

Vangen, S. and C. Huxham. 2003. Nurturing Collaborative Relations: Building Trust in Interorganizational Collaboration. *Journal of Applied Behavioral Science, 39* (1): 5–31.

Van Wart, M. 2005. *Dynamics of Leadership in Public Service: Theory and Practice.* Armonk, NY: M. E. Sharpe.

Veazie M., N. Teufel-Shone, G. Silverman, A. Connolly, S. Warne, B. King, et al. 2001. Building Community Capacity in Public Health: the Role of Action-Oriented Partnerships. *Journal of Public Health Management and Practice, 7* (2):21–32.

Vigoda, E. 2002. From Responsiveness to Collaboration: Governance, Citizens and the Next Generation of Public Administration. *Public Administration Review, 62* (5): 527–540.

Vogel, A, P. Ransom, S. Wai, and D. Luisi. 2007. Integrating Health and Social Services for Older Adults: A Case Study Interagency Collaboration. *Journal of Health and Human Services Administration, 30* (2): 199–228.

Vroom, V. and A. Jago. 1988. *The New Leadership: Managing Participation in Organizations.* Englewood Cliffs, NJ: Prentice Hall.

Waitzkin, H., T. Britt, and C. Williams. 1994. Narratives of Aging and Social Problems in Medical Encounters with Older Persons. *Journal of Health and Social Behavior, 35* (4): 322–348.

Walter, L. and E. Quarantelli. 1996. Global Change and Natural Hazards. Aspen Global Change Institute. AGCI Summer Session I.

Wandersman, A., R. Goodman, and F. Butterfoss. 1997. Understanding Coalitions and How They Operate. In *Community Organizing and Community Building for Health,* ed. M. Minkler. New Brunswick, NJ: Rutgers University Press, p. 292–313.

Waugh, W. and G. Streib. 2006. Collaboration and Leadership for Effective Emergency Management. *Public Administration Review, 66* (Supplement): 131–140.

Weber, E. 2009. Explaining Institutional Change in Tough Cases of Collaboration: "Ideas" in the Blackfoot Watershed. *Public Administration Review, 69* (2): 314–327.

Weber, E. and A. Khademian. 2008. Wicked Problems, Knowledge Challenges, and Collaborative Capacity Builders in Network Settings. *Public Administration Review, 68* (2): 334–349.

Weiss, C. 1998. *Evaluation: Methods for Studying Programs and Policies,* 2nd edition. Upper Saddle River, NJ: Prentice Hall.

Wells, R., M. Feinberg, J. Alexander, and A. Ward. 2009. Factors Affecting Member Perceptions of Coalition Impact. *Nonprofit and Voluntary Sector Quarterly, 19* (3): 327–348.

West, J. and E. Berman. 2001. The Impact of Revitalized Management Practices on the Adoption of Information Technology: A National Survey of Local Governments. *Public Performance and Management Review, 24* (3): 233–253.

Whetten, D. 1988. Issues in Organization Decline. In *Readings in Organizational Decline: Frameworks, Research and Prescriptions,* ed. K. S. Cameron, T. I. Sutton, and D. Whetten, pp. 3–19. Cambridge, MA: Ballinger Publishing.

Wholey, J., H. Hatry, and K. Newcomer, Eds. 2004. *Handbook of Practical Program Evaluation,* 2nd edition. San Francisco: Jossey-Bass.

Wiewel, W. and Perry, D. 2008. *Global Universities and Urban Development: Case Studies and Analysis.* New York: M. E. Sharpe.

Wikin, B. and J. Altschuld. 1995. *Planning and Conducting Needs Assessments: A Practical Guide.* Thousand Oaks, CA: Sage.

Winer, M. and K. Ray. 1994. *Collaboration Handbook: Creating, Sustaining and Enjoying the Journey.* Saint Paul, MN: Amhurst H. Wilder Foundation.

Winkler-Schmit, D. 2006. No Place to Go. *Gambit Weekly.* March 7. http://www.bestofneworleans.com/dispatch/2006-03-07/healthfeat.php.

Wise, T. 2006. "Eracing" Katrina: Historical Revisionism and the Denial of the Obvious. http://www.lipmagazine.org/~timwise/eracingkatrina.html.

Yang, K. and K. Callahan. 2007. Citizen Involvement Efforts and Bureaucratic Responsiveness: Participatory Values, Stakeholder Pressures, and Administrative Practicality. *Public Administration Review, 67* (2): 249–264.

Yin, P. 1982. Fear of Crime as a Problem for the Elderly. *Social Problems, 30* (2): 240–245.

Yin, R. 2003. *Case Study Research: Design and Methods,* 3rd ed. Thousand Oaks, CA: Sage.

Zavala, A. and K. Hass. 2008. *The Art and Power of Facilitation: Running Powerful Meetings.* Vienna, VA: Management Concepts.

Zhang J., A. Cresswell, and F. Thompson. 2002. Participants' Expectations and the Success of Knowledge Networking in the Public Sector. Paper presented at the annual Americas Conference on Information Systems, Dallas, TX, August 9–12, 2002.

Index